U.S. Fish & Wildlife Service

Morris
Wetland Management District

Comprehensive
Conservation Plan and
Environmental Assessment

Comprehensive Conservation Plans provide long-term guidance for management decisions; set forth goals, objectives and strategies needed to accomplish refuge purposes; and, identify the Fish and Wildlife Service's best estimate of future needs. These plans detail program planning levels that are sometimes substantially above current budget allocations and, as such, are primarily for Service strategic planning and program prioritization purposes. The plans do not constitute a commitment for staffing increases, operational and maintenance increases, or funding for future land acquisition.

Morris

Wetland Mangement District

Comprehensive Conservation Plan Approval
U.S. Fish and Wildlife Service, Region 3

Submitted by:

_____ 4-3-03

Steven Delehanty   Date
WMD Manager

Concur:

_____ 4-17-03

James T. Leach   Date
Refuge Supervisor (RFS 3)

_____ 4.17.2003

Nita M. Fuller   Date
Regional Chief
National Wildlife Refuge System

Approve:

_____ 4/17/03

Marvin E. Moriarty   Date
Acting Regional Director

Acknowledgments

Many organizations, agencies and individuals provided invaluable assistance with the preparation of this Comprehensive Conservation Plan. We gratefully acknowledge the input and support of Tom Larson, Mike Marxen, John Schomaker, Mary Mitchell, Sean Killen, and Jane Hodgins, Planners with the Division of Ascertainment and Planning and all of the dedicated employees of the Wetland Management Districts of the U.S. Fish and Wildlife Service.

Region 3 of the U.S. Fish and Wildlife Service is grateful to the many conservation organizations active in western Minnesota for their dedication to the Wetland Management Districts in making them outstanding examples of cooperation and partnership with the many local communities. The Region is equally grateful to every volunteer who contributes time to the programs offered on the Wetland Management Districts. You are truly the backbone of conservation efforts.

Contents

Executive Summary

Morris Wetland Management District is part of a unique natural ecosystem and an equally unique legacy of human partnership.

The ecosystem is known as the tallgrass prairie ecosystem, and its combination of prairie grasslands and small wetlands made it among the most biologically diverse and intricate landscapes in the world. When European settlers arrived and discovered the land's tremendous productivity, the tallgrass prairie ecosystem became one of the most altered ecosystems on earth. The landscape changed rapidly, and little of the original prairie was saved. Today only fragments exist in small, isolated blocks.

Partnerships have been inherent in efforts to preserve the remaining prairie. From the Duck Stamp Act of 1934 to the Wetland Loan Act of 1961 to the Small Wetland Acquisition Program of 1962, the U.S. Fish and Wildlife Service (Service) and hunters, environmentalists, and communities have worked together to preserve land and wildlife. Funding for acquisition of Waterfowl Production Areas (WPA) comes in large part from funds generated through the Duck Stamp Act, making duck hunters a key partner in preserving critical habitat within the prairie pothole region. Waterfowl Production Areas are upland grasslands and wetlands purchased by the Service to provide nesting habitat for waterfowl. Wetland Management Districts (WMD) are the federal administrative units charged with acquiring, overseeing and managing WPAs and easements within a specified group of counties.

The Morris Wetland Management District, originally established in 1964 as the Benson Wetland Management District, includes the following Federal property: 246 WPAs totaling 51,208 acres in fee title ownership and 595 wetland easements encompassing 20,074 wetland acres, 27 habitat (grassland) easements covering 1,787 acres, 22 conservation easements covering 1,211 acres on property formerly controlled by the Farmers Home Administration, and two easement units of the Northern Tallgrass Prairie National Wildlife Refuge covering 110 acres. Both fee and easement areas are scattered throughout Big Stone, Chippewa, Lac Que Parle, Pope, Stevens, Swift, Traverse, and Yellow Medicine counties. The total surface area of the eight-county district is 3,334,580 acres. The total Fish and Wildlife Service property interest of 74,390 acres (excluding Big Stone NWR) represents 2.2 percent of the total area of the District.

Managing the District demands long range planning that reflects vision, science and people. This Draft Comprehensive Conservation Plan describes how we intend to improve wildlife habitat, foster waterfowl production, and expand opportunities for compatible recreation, including hunting, wildlife observation, and environmental education.

The management direction identified in this Draft Comprehensive Conservation Plan charts a course for the next 15 years. This course is summarized in three broad categories – Wildlife and Habitat, People, and Operations.

Comprehensive Conservation Planning

The Comprehensive Conservation Plan, or CCP, is a guide for management on the Morris WMD over the next 15 years. The document provides an outline for how we will accomplish our mission and make our vision become a reality. Several legislative mandates within the National Wildlife Refuge System Improvement Act of 1997 have guided the development of the Plan. These mandates include:

- The focus of management on the District is to benefit wildlife conservation.

- Wildlife-dependent recreation activities, (hunting, fishing, wildlife observation, wildlife photography, environmental education and interpretation) are encouraged when they are compatible with wildlife conservation.

The CCP will benefit management of Morris WMD by:

- Providing a clear statement of direction for future management of the District.

- Giving District neighbors, visitors and the general public an understanding of the Service's management actions on and around the Districts.

- Ensuring that the District's management actions and programs are consistent with the mandates of the National Wildlife Refuge System.

- Ensuring that District management is consistent with other federal, state, and local plans when practicable.

- Establishing that wildlife-dependent recreation uses (compatible uses including hunting, fishing, wildlife observation and photography, or environmental education and interpretation) are the priority public uses within the Refuge System.

- Providing a basis for the development of budget requests on operation, maintenance, and capital improvement needs.

The Planning Process

The planning process for this Comprehensive Conservation Plan began October 1, 1997, when a Notice Of Intent to prepare a comprehensive management plan was published in the Federal Register (Vol 62: 51482). Because the six Districts face similar issues, Managers and planners decided to follow a shared CCP process that would result in separate documents for each District. This chapter describes the planning process that was employed.

Initially, members of the planning team identified a list of issues and concerns that were likely to be associated with the management of the District. These preliminary issues and concerns were based on the team members' knowledge of the area, contacts with citizens in the community, and ideas already expressed to the District staff. District staff and Service planners then began asking District neighbors, organizations, local government units, schools, and interested citizens to share their thoughts in a series of open house events.

> *Vision Statement for the Minnesota Wetland Management Districts*
>
> *The Districts will emphasize waterfowl production and ensure the preservation of habitat for migratory birds, threatened and endangered native species, and resident wildlife. The Districts will provide opportunities for the public to hunt, fish, observe and photograph wildlife and increase public understanding and appreciation of the Northern Tallgrass Prairie Ecosystem.*

Open houses were conducted at each District as well as the Regional Office at Ft. Snelling, Minnesota.

People were invited to send in written comments describing their support or concerns about the Districts. Fifty-one written comments were received.

A survey of public use was conducted and focus group meetings were conducted to develop the issues, goals, and objectives for the Plan. These meetings included the District Managers and invited participants from the University of Minnesota, The Nature Conservancy, and the U.S. Geological Survey, Northern Prairie Wildlife Research Center. Concurrent with the focus group meetings, planning staff met with individual District staff members numerous times to review issues and discuss District management.

A wide range of issues, concerns and opportunities were expressed during the planning process. Numerous discussions among District and planning staff, focus groups and resource specialists brought to light several recurring themes. Issues fall into broad categories of wildlife, habitat and people. Dealing with these issues is at the core of the development of goals and objectives for the management of the Wetland Management Districts in Minnesota.

Management Alternatives

An environmental assessment (EA) encompassing all six of the Minnesota Wetland Management Districts was prepared as part of the planning process. Three management alternatives were evaluated in the EA, including: maintaining management of current wetland management district acres but not acquiring more land; increasing land holdings to meet the goal acres and maintain current management practices; and improving WMDs for waterfowl and other trust species. The Service has selected the third alternative, improving the Districts for waterfowl and other trust species, as the preferred alternative. Each alternative is briefly described in the following paragraphs.

Alternatives Development

Project Leaders on WMDs within the major waterfowl breeding habitats of the United States have been charged with the responsibility to identify tracts of land that meet the goals of the Small Wetland Acquisition Program (SWAP) for inclusion in the National Wildlife Refuge System (NWRS). Of all the responsibilities Project Leaders carry, identifying lands to include in the NWRS has the longest lasting implications and is by far the most important. The land, once acquired, needs to be managed intensively with a variety of tools available to the managers. The intensity of management is limited by the number of staff available and the scattered distribution of the land holdings across a wide landscape in 28 counties of western Minnesota. The following alternatives identify three approaches meeting the goals and responsibilities of land ownership and management.

The main goal of the SWAP has been, and still is, to purchase a complex of wetlands and uplands that provide habitat in which waterfowl can successfully reproduce. The basic concept has been to purchase, in fee title, key brood marshes that include adequate nesting cover on adjacent uplands while protecting under easement surrounding temporary and seasonal wetland basins as

breeding pair habitat. Once this is accomplished the land must be managed through seeding with native grasses and forbs, burning, and spraying or otherwise controlling exotic and/or invasive species. Additionally, abandoned human infrastructure (wells, barns, etc.) must be removed. The areas are signed and sometimes fenced to provide safe public access.

The SWAP began in 1958 and accelerated rapidly in the early 1960s with passage of the Wetlands Loan Act. The original 1960s delineations were prepared for each fee title parcel based on their suitability to provide brood rearing habitat for waterfowl. These delineations designated wetlands as priority A, B, and C for fee title purchase. These tracts had few upland acres and only existing wetlands with no drainage facilities were considered for fee or easement purchase. In some locations, these original delineations have been reevaluated and revised. In Minnesota, a 1974 exercise produced maps showing proposed boundaries of each fee title delineation, as well as wetlands within a 2-mile radius that were eligible for easement purchase. A 1984 effort produced maps of "significant wetland areas" for fee title purchase. Although dated, these efforts were biologically sound and provide valuable information in deciding which properties to purchase today.

Over the years our understanding of breeding waterfowl biology has increased and the landscape of the Upper Midwest has changed dramatically. The SWAP itself has evolved to include purchase of drained wetlands, increased upland acreage, and grassland easements along with new counties that include lands within intensely agricultural and urbanized landscapes.

Three possible alternatives to acquisition and management were considered as we thought about the future of the programs for the wetland management districts. The three alternatives were (1) manage what lands we currently own; (2) acquire additional lands and manage them as we currently manage the lands that we own; and (3) acquire additional lands and expand management beyond the present level of intensity.

In the following sections we summarize what we would do under each alternative. More detail is provided in Chapter 2 of the EA (Appendix N of this document). The third alternative is our preferred alternative, which is developed in more detail as the Comprehensive Conservation Plan.

Alternative 1 – Maintain Management on Current Acres With No Additional Land Acquisition

Under this alternative we would manage fee title land already in the system and would not increase the holdings to the agreed goal acres for each county within

the District. We would restore native grasslands using local ecotypes of mixed native grasses and forbs and improve wetlands by increasing water control and improving watersheds. We would regularly evaluate our approach to waterfowl production. We would maintain the recruitment rate of waterfowl and the current level of inspection of our lands and easements. We would continue to conduct the 4-square-mile monitoring program and the monitoring of nesting structures under this alternative. We would continue routine surveys such as the scent post survey and bird counts and non-routine surveys when requested, such as the deformed frog survey. We would continue to avoid any actions that would harm endangered or threatened species, and we would note the presence of any species that is federally listed as endangered or threatened.

We would maintain the public access to WPAs that currently exists. We would complete and document development plans for every WPA on the District as time and staffing permit. The development plans would be recorded in a geographic information system (GIS) and document boundaries, habitat, facilities and history of management.

Each District would continue with the current level of staffing. We would identify and replace facilities and equipment that do not meet Service standards. We would expect that the maintenance backlog would be reduced, but not eliminated, over the life of the CCP.

Alternative 2 – Increase Land Holdings to Goal Acres and Maintain Current Management Practices (No Action)

Under this alternative we would continue acquiring land up to the negotiated goal acres within each county in the District (See Table A). We would expand the size of WPAs in areas of prime waterfowl use through easements and working with partners.

We would restore native grasslands using local ecotypes of mixed native grasses and forbs and improve wetlands by increasing water control and improving watersheds. We would regularly evaluate our approach to waterfowl production. We would maintain the recruitment rate of waterfowl and the current level of inspection of our lands and easements. We would continue to conduct the 4-square-mile monitoring program and the monitoring of nesting structures under this alternative. We would continue routine surveys such as the scent post survey and bird counts and non-routine surveys when requested, such as the deformed frog survey. We would continue to avoid any actions that would harm

Table A: Fee Title Acres Approved and Goal Acres Per District in Accordance with the Land Exchange Board

Wetland Management Districts	Fee Title Acres Approved for Purchase by the Land Exchange Board	Goal Acres	Remainder
Detroit Lakes	41,615	89,280	47,665
Fergus Falls	43,417	74,675	31,258
Litchfield	33,213	76,220	46,007
Big Stone	2,343	0	0
Morris	51,208	74,830	23,622
Windom	12,669	24,476	11,807

endangered or threatened species. We would note the presence of any species that is federally listed as endangered or threatened.

We would continue current public access on existing areas and add access to new acquisitions over several years. We would complete and document development plans for every WPA on the District as time and staffing permit. The development plans would be recorded in a GIS and document boundaries, habitat, facilities, and history of management.

Each District would continue with the current level of staffing. We would identify and replace facilities and equipment that do not meet Service standards. We would expect that the maintenance backlog would be reduced, but not eliminated, over the life of the CCP.

Alternative 3 – Increase Land Holdings to Goal Acres and Expand Management for Waterfowl, Other Trust Species and the Public. (Preferred Alternative)

Photo by Bernie Angus

Under this alternative we would continue acquiring land up to the negotiated goal acres for each county within the District (See Table A). We would expand the size of WPAs in areas of prime waterfowl use through easements and working with partners. We would focus whenever possible on prime habitat as outlined in the Habitat and Population Evaluation Team (HAPET) "thunderstorm" maps. These maps reveal high density waterfowl populations and, because the results are color coded, look somewhat like weather maps.

We would follow the Strategic Growth of the SWAP Guidelines for Fee and Easement Purchase (See Appendix K). These Guidelines specify that:

1) The program will focus on providing the mission components for the WMD landscape: wetland complexes, surrounding grasslands and a predator component that approaches a naturally occurring complement (i.e., coyotes vs. red fox).

2) The program will focus on established delineation criteria (size, location, ratio of upland to wetlands, soil composition, etc.) for all fee title, habitat and wetland easements (Appendix K).

3) The program will prioritize acquisition based on thunderstorm maps, land cover (grassland acres), landscape characteristics, and data on predator populations. Prioritization will be given to tracts that benefit waterfowl, but other wildlife benefits will be considered in the priorities such as native prairie, endangered or threatened species and colonial nesting birds. Additional considerations may include expanding and protecting large tracts of grassland as Grassland Bird Core Conservation Areas as proposed by Fitzgerald et al. (1998).

We would restore native grasslands using local ecotypes of mixed native grasses and forbs and improve wetlands by increasing water control and improving watersheds. We would, where practicable, follow HAPET recommendations for nesting platforms and predator management (electric fencing, predator control, islands, etc.). Cooperating landowners within the District's watershed would be offered incentives and/or compensated through cost-sharing agreements for applying conservation and environmental farming practices on their lands and for creating, maintaining, or enhancing habitat for wildlife.

We would regularly evaluate our approach to waterfowl production and improve waterfowl monitoring. We would strive to increase the recruitment rate of waterfowl and increase inspection of our lands and easements. We would work to prohibit the introduction of wildlife species that are not native to the Northern Tallgrass Prairie Ecosystem.

We would employ a scientifically defensible means to monitor and evaluate habitats and populations under this alternative. We would increasingly use GIS in our monitoring. We would inventory the hydrological systems within the District, invertebrate communities, and monitor contaminant levels in water flowing to and from District wetlands. We would increase our surveys and monitoring of threatened and endangered species, invertebrates, and unique

communities under this alternative. We would seek opportunities to enhance and reintroduce native species in the District.

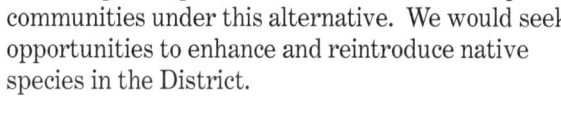
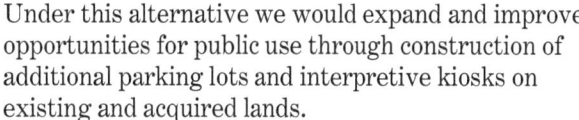

Under this alternative we would expand and improve opportunities for public use through construction of additional parking lots and interpretive kiosks on existing and acquired lands.

We would complete and document development plans for every WPA on the District within three years under this alternative. The development plans would be recorded in a GIS and document boundaries, habitat, facilities, and history of management.

Staff would be added to the Districts under this alternative. Implementation of the CCP would rely on partnerships formed with landowners in the watershed, volunteers and interested citizens, farm and conservation organizations, and with appropriate government agencies. We would identify and replace facilities and equipment that do not meet Service standards. Our goal would be to meet the standards by 2010.

Management of the Districts would be more consistent among the Minnesota Districts and with the Districts in Iowa, Wisconsin and the Dakotas.

Planning Issues and Management Direction

A wide range of issues, concerns and opportunities were expressed during the planning process. Numerous discussions among District and planning staff, focus groups and resource specialists brought to light several recurring themes. Issues fall into broad categories of wildlife, habitat and people. In the following paragraphs, we list the issues that were identified in this planning process and our objectives for addressing that issue.

Wildlife and Habitat

Can we improve waterfowl productivity?
We will work to increase waterfowl production through effective monitoring of populations, evaluating current management actions and increasing recruitment. We will strive to increase recruitment through cropland conversion to grassland and artificial structures where appropriate, and protecting existing National Wildlife Refuge System lands as well as other waterfowl habitats in cooperation with District partners.

Strategic Acquisition: Can we buy the highest priority land in the most efficient and cost-effective manner possible?

We will ensure strategic land acquisition by evaluating current acquisition guidelines, identifying priority acquisition areas, and evaluating acreage goals while securing rapid responses to sellers through close coordination with the acquisition office.

Managing Uplands: Can we improve prairie restoration by planting the right seeds and using the right management tools?

We will seek to reestablish and manage native plant communities by seeding a diverse mixture of local grasses and forbs each year as determined through the WPA development plans. We will actively manage to maintain quality grassland habitats using fire, grazing and/or haying, and haying as viable management tools.

Managing and Restoring Wetlands: How do we manage wetlands to maintain or increase productivity?

We will strive to restore and manage wetlands primarily within identified priority areas, increasing the amount and quality of water level management, monitoring hydrological systems, and encouraging and cooperating in research of these systems.

Can we improve biological inventories and monitoring on WPAs?

We will improve biological inventories and monitoring through planning, training, expanded species data gathering, research, and use of GIS.

Can we stem the loss of migratory birds in the Northern Tallgrass Prairie Ecosystem?

We will try to stem the loss of all migratory birds by expanding restoration of upland wetland and riparian habitats on private lands.

Can we manage District land to preserve, restore and enhance threatened and endangered species, rare and declining species, and address regional priority species?

We will preserve, restore and enhance threatened and endangered species and rare and declining species through the collection of baseline population and habitat data, tailored management activities, enforcement of regulations, and cooperation with partners.

Under what circumstances should we reintroduce rare native species to District land?

We will seek to reintroduce rare native species where feasible by identifying, evaluating and prioritizing opportunities. All reintroduction programs will be conducted in close cooperation with the Minnesota Department of Natural Resources.

How do we mitigate negative external influences such as contaminants on WPAs and reduce its impact on long-term health and productivity of District land?

We will work to mitigate negative external influences on Service lands by identifying, monitoring and developing action plans to address threats such as pesticide use, contaminants, soil erosion, and poor water quality.

How do we balance management for Federal trust species with the needs of resident species?

We will balance management of Federal trust species with the needs of resident species by communicating with state wildlife agencies and local conservation organizations to provide compatible food and cover sources where there are documented needs.

How do we reduce crop loss caused by Canada geese foraging on private land adjacent to WPAs?

We will work to reduce crop loss caused by Canada Geese foraging on private lands adjacent to Waterfowl Production Areas by developing a Memorandum of Understanding with the Minnesota Department of Natural Resources which defines agency responsibilities to provide alternate feeding areas and long-term solutions.

Invasive species, both exotic and native, are negatively impacting the natural ecological balance of grasslands and wetlands on WPAs.

We will seek to control the negative impacts of invasive species by taking aggressive control measures against exotic plants, documenting and eradicating invasive plant populations, and increasing long-term resolution of these problems through biological controls.

What is the Long Range Goal of the Partners for Fish and Wildlife Program (Private Lands) on Wetland Management Districts?

We will identify the long-range goals of the District's Partners for Fish and Wildlife Program (private lands) by developing priority action items that could include identification of partners in key project areas, and developing a brochure for the public to better define the Partners program and its benefits.

People

There are conflicting views concerning the costs and benefits of federally owned land in a community. Who benefits? Who pays?

We will identify the benefits and costs of Federally owned land to a community by investigating the economic value of wetlands and federal land ownership as well as revenue sharing in relation to local taxes. We will seek to determine the social values of wildlife and natural habitats to people.

How do we provide adequate facilities and programs for the public to fully enjoy wildlife-related recreation in a way that is compatible with our mission?

We will provide adequate facilities and programs for public enjoyment of compatible wildlife-dependent recreation by enhancing public use experiences with accessible facilities that meet National Visitor Service Standards as well as providing current maps and District information. We will increase environmental education opportunities through additional "hands-on" exhibits, specific on-site interpretative opportunities, and building volunteer programs.

Operations

Districts need sufficient staff in critical areas to fully meet resource challenges and opportunities.

We will meet staffing needs for resource challenges and opportunities by hiring additional administrative, biological, technical, and maintenance personnel.

Districts need office, maintenance, and equipment storage facilities to carry out their mission.

We will provide adequate maintenance and storage facilities by selecting and developing a secure maintenance and equipment storage area within the boundaries of the Wetland District.

Vehicles and other necessary equipment need to be replaced on a regular basis according to Service standards.

We will schedule vehicle and equipment replacements to achieve industry standards when normal life expectancy is reached and acquire all necessary equipment to achieve Wetland Management District Goals.

Funding is needed to develop and manage newly acquired WPA land and facilities.

We will develop newly acquired Waterfowl Production Areas by identifying these needs, securing funding, and carrying out projects immediately after lands are purchased. We will identify the costs of new lands to the District's annual operation and maintenance budget.

We will maintain existing waterfowl production areas at Service standards including delineated boundaries, nature trails, parking lots, access trails, water control structures and fences by maintaining a current inventory of maintenance needs on the Maintenance Management System database, and updating these costs and priorities annually.

Individual WPA development plans and record keeping need to be updated.

We will ensure that Waterfowl Production Area Development Plans are current by performing complete resource inventories and utilizing the most current GIS technology and complete unit planning to meet trust responsibilities.

The Districts need to be consistent in their application of policy and resource protection efforts.

We will seek consistency in policy and practices on all Service Wetland Management Districts by attending coordination meetings and following Service policy when implementing programs.

Essential Staffing, Mission-Critical Projects and Major Maintenance Needs

The Service relies on two systems to track the needs of the Wetland Management Districts and other units of the National Wildlife Refuge System. These systems are the Refuge Operating Needs System and the Maintenance Management System. Each station has scores of projects in each system, representing a need which is often beyond the realities of funding. However, each station has identified its most critical needs which form a realistic assessment of funding needed to meet many of the goals, objectives, and strategies identified in the CCP. These needs also form the basis for the President's budget request to Congress. These critical needs are listed below in the categories of essential staff, mission-critical projects, and major maintenance projects. A complete listing of projects in the Operating Needs System is found in Appendix G of this document and it represents the long-term needs of the Morris Wetland Management District to operate at optimum levels.

Essential Staffing Needs
Wildlife Biologist
Visitor Services Specialist

Mission-Critical Projects
Prairie Chicken Reintroductions
Native Prairie Restoration
Water Level Management
Visitor Services

Major Maintenance Projects
Replace Storage Building at Benson Site
Replace Roof on Maintenance Building
Replace Boundary Fences
Replace Tractor
12 Additional Projects

Total Funding Needs: $1,435,000

Chapter 1: Introduction and Background

Overview: History of Refuge Establishment, Acquisition, and Management

The Wetland Management Districts of Minnesota are set in a landscape that was once a mosaic of prairie and wetlands. From north to south the land varied between woodland, sandy ridges and hills covered with prairie flowers, dotted with small, blue wetlands and oak savannah. It was beautiful, rolling country teaming with waterfowl and other wildlife. Early explorers from Europe described its park-like quality with wonder. The combination of prairie grasslands and small wetlands made it among the most biologically productive landscapes in the world; supporting many people and an abundance of wildlife.

U.S. Fish & Wildlife Service Photo

The prairie harbored bison herds estimated at 50 to 60 million. From Alexander Henry's January 14, 1801, journal reporting from the Red River Valley, "...At daybreak I was awakened by the bellowing of buffaloes...I dressed and climbed my oak for a better view. I had seen almost incredible numbers of buffalo in the fall, but nothing in comparison to what I now beheld. The ground was covered at every point of the compass, as far as the eye could reach, and every animal was in motion."

Only 100 years after this entry, the myth of the prairies' unlimited abundance was severely tested. Many important game species were driven to near extinction by intensive and uncontrolled killing and commercial over-harvest encouraged by East Coast and European markets. Free-roaming bison, the Great Plains wolf, swift fox, pronghorn antelope and grizzly bear were eliminated from Minnesota. Black bear and elk were removed from their prairie niche. Many Native American tribes that depended on these resources were decimated by disease and conflict.

When European settlers arrived on the prairies, they recognized the land's productivity and rapidly turned it to agriculture. In a few decades it ranked among the richest agricultural land in the world. The landscape changed so rapidly, little of the original prairie was saved. Today, only fragments remain in isolated, small blocks. With fragmentation and the loss of large predators, smaller predators such as raccoon, striped skunks, and fox increased, much to the detriment of ground-nesting birds and other native grassland species.

Perhaps no other ecosystem on earth as been so dramatically altered, in such a short time, as the tallgrass prairie ecosystem of the Midwest.

The early mission of the Fish and Wildlife Service was to protect species from over-harvest and manage wildlife for a quality hunt. Waterfowl have been a central focus from the very beginning. Many species of prairie waterfowl and shorebirds were saved by legislation formed to protect them from market hunting.

Early surveys of the Prairie Pothole Region revealed a strong correlation between prairie wetlands and waterfowl breeding habitat. Biologists learned that waterfowl success is directly linked to the number of wetlands. When winter snows fill the small wetlands, waterfowl populations soar. Since the wetlands are shallow by nature, their value to waterfowl varies from year to year depending on the amount of snow and rain. In years of drought, wetlands dry and waterfowl populations plummet. The crucial link between wetlands and waterfowl was made during a time when wetlands throughout the prairies were being drained at an unprecedented rate for agriculture.

In 1934 the Duck Stamp Act was passed, setting the stage for the most aggressive land acquisition campaign for conservation of wildlife habitat in American history. Although the original Act did not allow purchase of small wetlands, it created a way for hunters to actively participate in maintaining waterfowl populations. In 1958 the Act was amended, making it possible for the Service to buy small wetlands and uplands for breeding waterfowl and for hunting. The acquired wetlands became Waterfowl Production Areas (WPAs) and formed the core of the Wetland Management Districts.

Photo Copyright Jan Eldridge

The Act was passed in the nick of time. Between 1780 and 1980 approximately 78.7 percent of wetlands in the Prairie Pothole and Parkland Transition areas were drained (Dahl 1990). In intensive agricultural areas of the Prairie Pothole Region, wetland losses often exceed 90 percent. Today over 70,000 miles of ditches drain wetlands in Minnesota with a continuing annual wetland loss of 2.4 percent per year.

At the time the Small Wetland Acquisition Program (SWAP) began in 1962, the U.S. Fish and Wildlife Service entered into a Procedural Agreement with the State of Minnesota. This document laid out the rules for the purchase of wetlands as required by the Wetland Loan Act of 1961. The agreement was amended in 1976 when the number of counties authorized for acquisition increased from 19 to 28, and the goal acreage was increased. In 1991, the Minnesota Land Exchange Board gave the Service approval to expand its land acquisition program to all 87 counties of the state. The state goal of 231,000 acres in fee title and 365,170 acres in easements, as established in 1976, remains unchanged (See Appendix A for a complete listing of the District legal mandates).

In western Minnesota, as of March 31 1999, the Service owned 171,863 acres, of which 56,693 acres were wetlands (Figure 1). In addition, the Service administers perpetual easement agreements on 266,171 acres, of which 62,098 acres are wetlands. Wetlands that were once drained have been restored; on Waterfowl Production Areas, more than 4,000 wetland restorations have impounded 15,900 wetland acres.

The program has been remarkably successful in the face of great odds. The Wetland Management Districts combine to form a greater land mass than the largest national wildlife refuge in the lower 48 states. Each District has, on average, 23,400 to 73,400 breeding ducks each year; all Districts combined average 240,600 breeding ducks each year (Figure 2).

Figure 1: Minnesota Wetland Management Districts

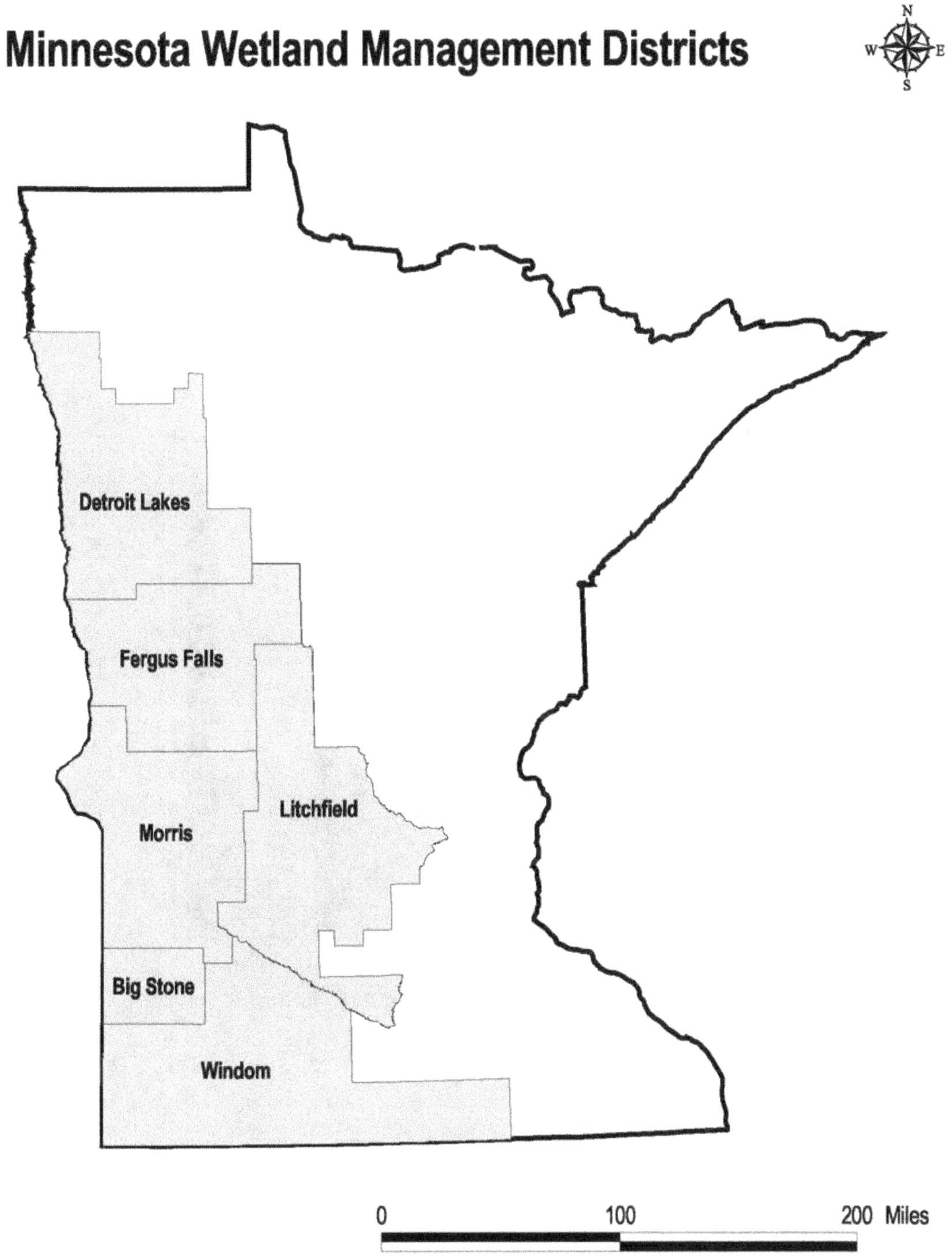
Minnesota Wetland Management Districts
N
W
E
S
Detroit Lakes
Fergus Falls
Morris
Litchfield
Big Stone
Windom
0
100
200 Miles

Figure 2: Breeding Pair Population (averaged) for Major Duck Species in Minnesota Wetland Management Districts 1987-2000

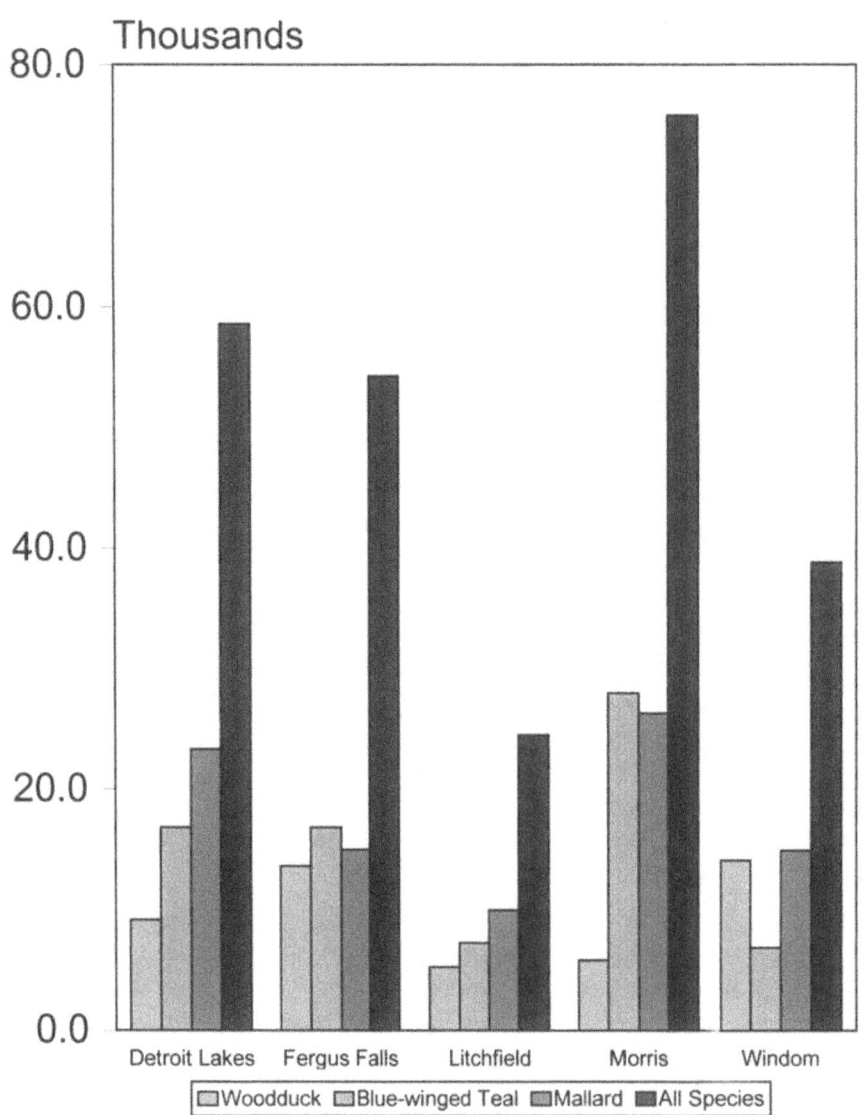

Data values are for 13 species (mallard, gadwall, blue-winged teal, northern shoveler, northern pintail, wigeon, green-winged teal, wood duck, redhead, canvasback, scaup, ringneck and ruddy duck).

Litchfield, Roseau and Windom wetland management districts data are for the years 1989-2000.

Source: Waterfowl Breeding Populations and Production Estimates, for the Prairie Pothole Region of Minnesota (4 square mile survey). Habitat and Population Evaluation Team, U.S. Fish and Wildlife Service, Fergus Falls, Minnesota

Background

Purpose and Need for the Comprehensive Conservation Plan

This Comprehensive Conservation Plan, or CCP, is a guide for management on the Wetland Management Districts over the next 15 years. The document provides an outline for how we will accomplish our mission and make our vision become a reality. Several legislative mandates within the National Wildlife Refuge System Improvement Act of 1997 have guided the development of the Plan. These mandates include:

- The focus of management on the Districts is to benefit wildlife conservation.

- Wildlife-dependent recreation activities, (hunting, fishing, wildlife observation, wildlife photography, environmental education and interpretation) will be emphasized when compatible.

This CCP will benefit management of Wetland Management Districts by:

- Providing a clear statement of direction for future management of the Districts.

- Giving District neighbors, visitors and the general public an understanding of the Service's management actions on and around the Districts.

- Ensuring that the Districts' management actions and programs are consistent with the mandates of the National Wildlife Refuge System.

- Ensuring that District management is consistent with federal, state and county plans.

- Establishing that wildlife-dependent recreation uses (compatible uses including hunting, fishing, wildlife observation and photography, or environmental education and interpretation) are the priority public uses within the Refuge System.

- Communicating that other uses have lower priority on the Refuge System and are only allowed if they are compatible with the mission of the Refuge System, and with the purposes of the individual refuge.

- Providing a basis for the development of budget requests on the District's operation, maintenance, and capital improvement needs.

The U.S. Fish and Wildlife Service

The U.S. Fish and Wildlife Service as we know it today has evolved and changed with the country's use of natural resources and the growing respect for the environment. Today the Service is the primary Federal agency responsible for conserving, protecting, and enhancing fish and wildlife and their habitats for the continuing benefit of the American people.

Specific responsibilities include enforcing Federal wildlife laws, managing migratory bird populations, restoring nationally significant fisheries, administering the Endangered Species Act, and restoring wildlife habitat such as wetlands. The Service also manages the National Wildlife Refuge System.

The National Wildlife Refuge System

The National Wildlife Refuge System is a significant focus of the Service. Founded in 1903 by President Theodore Roosevelt with the designation of Pelican Island as a refuge for brown pelicans, the National Wildlife Refuge System is the world's largest collection of lands specifically managed for fish and wildlife. The System is a diverse network of more than 500 national wildlife refuges encompassing more than 92 million acres of public land and water. Most of the land – 86 percent – is in Alaska, with approximately 15 million acres spread across the lower 48 states and several island territories. Refuges provide habitat for more than 5,000 species of birds, mammals, fish, and insects.

Like Pelican Island, many early national wildlife refuges were created for herons, egrets, and other water birds. Others were set aside for large mammals like elk and bison. By far the most refuges have been created to protect migratory waterfowl. This is a result of the United States' responsibilities under international treaties for migratory bird conservation as well as other legislation, such as the Migratory Bird Conservation Act of 1929. A map of the National Wildlife Refuge System shows refuges dotting the four major flyways that waterfowl follow from their northern nesting grounds to southern wintering areas.

National wildlife refuges also play a vital role in preserving endangered and threatened species. Among the refuges that are well known for providing habitat for endangered species are Aransas National Wildlife Refuge in Texas, the winter home of the whooping crane; the Florida Panther Refuge, which protects one of the nation's most endangered mammals; and the Hawaiian Islands Refuge, home of the Laysan duck, Hawaiian monk seal and many other unique species.

Refuges also provide unique opportunities for people. When it is compatible with wildlife and habitat needs, refuges can be used for wildlife-dependent activities such as hunting, fishing, hiking, wildlife observation, photography, environmental education, and environmental interpretation. Many refuges have visitor centers, wildlife trails, automobile tours, and environmental education programs. Nationwide, more than 33 million people visited national wildlife refuges in 1999.

The National Wildlife Refuge System Improvement Act of 1997 established many mandates aimed at making the management of national wildlife refuges more cohesive. The preparation of Comprehensive Conservation Plans is one of those mandates. The legislation requires the Secretary of the Interior to ensure that the mission of the National Wildlife Refuge System and purposes of the individual refuges are carried out. It also requires the Secretary to maintain the biological integrity, diversity, and environmental health of the Refuge System.

Minnesota Wetland Management Districts Vision Statement

The Districts will emphasize waterfowl production and ensure the preservation of habitat for migratory birds, threatened and endangered native species, and resident wildlife. The Districts will provide opportunities for the public to hunt, fish, observe and photograph wildlife, and increase public understanding and appreciation of the Northern Tallgrass Prairie Ecosystem.

Legal and Policy Guidance

Waterfowl Production Areas within the Morris Wetland Management District are acquired under the establishing authority of the Migratory Bird Hunting Stamp Act (Duck Stamp Act) as amended (16 U.S.C. 718-718h).

"The Secretary of the Interior is authorized to utilize funds made available under subsection (b) of this section for the purposes of such subsection, and such other funds as may be appropriated for the purposes of such subsection, or of this subsection, to acquire, or defray the expense incident to the acquisition by gift, devise, lease, purchase or exchange of, small wetland and pothole areas, interests therein, and rights of way to provide access thereto. Such small areas, to be designated as " Waterfowl Production Areas" may be acquired without regard to the limitations and requirements of the Migratory Bird Conservation Act, but all the provisions of such Act which govern the administration and protection of lands acquired thereunder, except the inviolate sanctuary provisions of such Act, shall be applicable to areas acquired pursuant to this subsection."

In addition to the Morris Wetland Management District's establishing authority legislation and the National Wildlife Refuge System Improvement Act of 1997, several Federal laws, executive orders, and regulations govern its administration. See Appendix A for a list of the guiding laws and orders.

Existing Partnerships: The Ecosystem Approach

The Service initiated its Ecosystem Approach in March of 1994. The primary goal of the Ecosystem Approach is conserving natural biological diversity and ecosystem integrity while supporting a sustainable level of human use. Nationally, the Service divided the country into 53 ecosystems based upon watersheds. Ecosystem teams, which include project leaders within each of the ecosystem boundaries, are the primary forum through which the Service implements the Ecosystem Approach.

The Service has set new standards for teamwork, creativity, flexibility, and communication between and among our operational units and with all partners within the ecosystem. The Service participates in public and private partnerships at many levels. Since many of the species under our care do not respect state and national borders, we also have a role within the larger ecosystem of the Western Hemisphere via such treaties as the Migratory Bird Treaty with our neighbors in Mexico and Canada.

In Minnesota, Wetland Management Districts fall within three organized ecosystem efforts, namely the Northern Tallgrass Prairie Habitat Protection Area, the Mississippi Headwaters/Tallgrass Prairie Ecosystem, and the Prairie Pothole Joint Venture of the North American Waterfowl Management Plan. The District programs are consistent with the goals and objectives of these major projects as well as the plan objectives for the Partners in Flight, and the U.S. Shorebird Conservation Plan.

Migratory Bird Conservation Initiatives

Over the last decade, bird conservation planning has become increasingly exciting as it has evolved from a largely local, site-based focus to a more regional, landscape-oriented perspective. Significant challenges include locating areas of high-quality habitat for the conservation of particular guilds and priority bird species, making sure no species are inadvertently left out of the regional planning process, avoiding unnecessary duplication of effort, and identifying unique landscape and habitat elements of particular tracts targeted for protection, management and restoration. Several migratory bird conservation initiatives have emerged to help guide the planning and implementation process. Collectively, they comprise a tremendous resource as refuges engage in comprehensive conservation planning and its translation into effective on-the-ground management.

Signed in 1986, the North American Waterfowl Management Plan (NAWMP) outlines a broad framework for waterfowl management strategies and conservation efforts in the United States, Canada, and Mexico. The goal of the NAWMP is to restore waterfowl populations to historic levels. The NAWMP is designed to reach its objectives through key joint venture areas, species joint ventures, and state implementation plans within these joint ventures.

The Districts are in the Upper Prairie Pothole Joint Venture. One of 12 habitat-based joint ventures, this Joint Venture encompasses the states of Montana, North Dakota, South Dakota, portions of Minnesota and Iowa, and three Canadian provinces. The goal of this Joint Venture is to increase populations of waterfowl through habitat conservation projects that improve natural diversity across the U.S. Prairie Pothole landscape.

The objectives of this Joint Venture are:

Objective 1: By the year 2001, conserve habitat capable of supporting 6.8 million breeding ducks that achieve a recruitment rate of 0.6 under average environmental conditions, with all managed areas achieving a recruitment rate of 0.49 at a minimum.

Objective 2: Stabilize or increase populations of declining wetland/grassland-associated wildlife species in the Prairie Pothole Region, with special emphasis on non-waterfowl migratory birds.

Formed in 1990, Partners in Flight (PIF) is concerned with most landbirds and other species requiring terrestrial habitats. Partners in Flight has developed Bird Conservation Plans for numerous Physiographic Areas across the U. S. (see http://www.partnersinflight.org). These plans include priority species lists, associated habitats, and management strategies.

The U. S. Shorebird Conservation Plan and the North American Waterbird Conservation Plan are plans that address the concerns for shorebird and waterbirds. These larger scale plans identify priority species and conservation strategies.

In a continental effort, the Partners in Flight, North American Waterfowl Management, U. S. Shorebird Conservation, and the North American Waterbird Conservation plans are being integrated under the umbrella of the North American Bird Conservation Initiative (NABCI). The goal of NABCI is to facilitate the delivery of the full spectrum of bird conservation through regionally-based, biologically-driven, landscape-oriented partnerships (see http://www.dodpif.org/nabci/index.htm). The NABCI strives to integrate the conservation objectives for all birds in order to optimize the effectiveness of management strategies. NABCI uses Bird Conservation Regions (BCRs) as its planning units. Bird Conservation Areas are becoming increasingly common as the unit of choice for regional bird conservation efforts; The Districts lie within Prairie Potholes (BCR 11) and the Boreal Hardwood Transition (BCR 23).

Each of the four bird conservation initiatives has a process for designating conservation priority species, modeled to a large extent on the PIF method of calculating scores based on independent assessments of global relative abundance, breeding and wintering distribution, vulnerability to threats, area importance (at a particular scale, e.g. PA or BCR), and population trend. These scores are often used by agencies in developing lists of bird species of concern; e.g., the U. S. Fish and Wildlife Service based its assessments for its 2002 list of nongame Birds of Conservation Concern primarily on the PIF, shorebird, and waterbird status assessment scores.

Region 3 Fish and Wildlife Resource Conservation Priorities

The Resource Conservation Priorities list is a subset of all species that occur in the Region and was derived from an objective synthesis of information on their status. The list includes all federally listed threatened and endangered species and proposed and candidate species that occur in the Region; migratory bird species derived from Service-wide and international conservation planning efforts; and rare and declining terrestrial and aquatic plants and animals that represent an abbreviation of the Endangered Species program's preliminary draft "Species of Concern" list for the Region.

Although many species are not included in the priority list, this does not mean that we consider them unimportant.

The list includes species from the Service's Mississippi Headwaters/Tallgrass Prairie Ecosystem. The list can be accessed at http://midwest.fws.gov/pdf/priority.pdf.

Biological Needs Assessment

The National Wildlife Refuge System Biological Needs Assessment (U.S. Fish & Wildlife Service, 1998) resulted from a self-analysis of biology within the System. The Assessment addressed issues related to the biological aspect of Refuge management and proposed six goals for their resolution along with actions and strategies for achieving those goals.

The goals are:

Goal 1: Address inadequate and inconsistent biological program staffing.

Goal 2: Focus biological program activities through goals and objectives.

Goal 3: Integrate evaluation and oversight into the biological program.

Goal 4: Increase the amount and accountability of funding for the biological program.

Goal 5: Provide for career and professional needs of biological program staff.

Goal 6: Meet information needs of the biological program.

The Biological Needs Assessment provides a benchmark in measuring progress toward meeting the biological mandates of the National Wildlife Refuge System Improvement Act of 1997.

Working With Partners

The Wetland Management Districts are composed of small parcels of land throughout western Minnesota. The effectiveness of this habitat for wildlife is enhanced when located near other protected areas. Land in programs such as The Nature Conservancy, Minnesota Department of Natural Resources, and set-asides such as the Conservation Reserve Program (CRP), and Reinvest in Minnesota (RIM) can add to "effective habitat size."

The Districts can not solve the problems posed by habitat fragmentation and contamination on its own and will work to increase "effective habitat size" by combining efforts with many partners, such as The Nature Conservancy, Ducks Unlimited, Minnesota Department of Natural Resources, as well as in programs such as CRP and RIM.

Chapter 2: Planning Process, Issues and Goals

Description of Planning Process

The planning process for this Comprehensive Conservation Plan began October 1, 1997, when a Notice Of Intent to prepare a comprehensive management plan was published in the Federal Register (Vol 62: 51482). Because the six Districts face similar issues, Managers and planners decided to follow a shared CCP process that would result in separate documents for each District. This chapter describes the planning process that was employed.

Initially, members of the planning team identified a list of issues and concerns that were likely to be associated with the management of the District. These preliminary issues and concerns were based on the team members' knowledge of the area, contacts with citizens in the community, and ideas already expressed to the District staff. District staff and Service planners then began asking District neighbors, organizations, local government units, schools, and interested citizens to share their thoughts in a series of open house events.

Open houses were conducted on the following schedule:

November 17, 1997 – Detroit Lakes Wetland Management District, 7 attended
November 18, 1997 – Fergus Falls Wetland Management District, 9 attended
November 19, 1997 – Morris Wetland Management District, 9 attended
November 20, 1997 – Litchfield Wetland Management District, 1 attended
November 25, 1997 – Windom Wetland Management District, 15 attended
February 4, 1998 – Regional Office, Twin Cities, 62 attended

People were also invited to send in written comments describing their support or concerns about the Districts. Fifty-one written comments were received.

A survey of public use on the Wetland Management Districts was conducted through contract with Dr. Dorothy Anderson, University of Minnesota. Forty individuals, all regular users of the Wetland Management Districts, were invited to participated in this survey. Participants had extensive experience with the Fish and Wildlife Service managers (i.e., they contacted WMD managers an average of almost 11 times/ year) and had good working relationships with managers. Almost all participants had visited waterfowl production areas, and many were members of conservation organizations (e.g. Ducks Unlimited, Pheasants Forever, and other organizations). Of the 40 people interviewed, 37 were men, averaging 51 years of age and averaging 39 years living in the area.

The participants were able to list benefits of the Wetland Management District activities provide to rural communities and citizens. The following list of benefits is ordered from benefits frequently mentioned, to benefits not as frequently discussed but still mentioned often.

- Provides areas for hunting waterfowl and upland bird species,
- Protects wetland areas for ecological reasons,
- Retains water and helps with flood control,
- Improves water quality
- Improves communities economically through purchasing of hunting equipment
- Provides opportunities to introduce children to hunting, and
- Adds to the overall quality of life for rural residents

Many participants believed that the Wetland Management District managers were good at acquiring and managing land. They appreciated the habitat provided in the Waterfowl Production Areas and the work that District managers do with farmers to increase wildlife habitat by taking drained wetlands out of agricultural production. Participants also praised the cooperative role managers have with local citizens and conservation organizations.

In addition to public meetings and survey, the following focus group meetings were conducted to develop the issues, goals, and objectives for the Plan. These meetings included the District Managers and invited participants from the University of Minnesota, The Nature Conservancy, and the U.S. Geological Survey, Northern Prairie Wildlife Research Center.

The following focus groups meetings were held:

- Fergus Falls, Minnesota March 2-4, 1999
- Alexandria, Minnesota July 27-29, 1999
- Twin Cities, Minnesota August 26, 1999

Concurrent with the focus group meetings, planning staff met with individual Districts numerous times to review issues and discuss District management.

A wide range of issues, concerns, and opportunities were expressed during the planning process. Numerous discussions among Refuge and planning staff, focus groups, and resource specialists brought to light several recurring themes. Issues fall into broad categories of wildlife, habitat, and people. Dealing with these issues is at the core of the development of goals and objectives for the management of the Minnesota Wetland Management Districts.

Planning Issues

Wildlife and Habitat

1. Can we improve waterfowl productivity?

2. Strategic Acquisition: Can we buy the highest priority land in the most efficient and cost-effective manner possible?

3. Managing Uplands: Can we improve prairie restoration by planting the right seeds and using the right management tools?

4. Managing and Restoring Wetlands: How do we manage wetlands to maintain or increase productivity?

5. Can we improve biological inventories and monitoring on WPAs?

6. Can we stem the loss of migratory birds in the Northern Tallgrass Prairie Ecosystem?

7. Can we manage District land to preserve, restore, and enhance threatened and endangered species, rare and declining species, and address Regional priority species?

8. Under what circumstances should we reintroduce rare native species to District land?

9. How do we mitigate negative external influences such as contaminants on WPAs and reduce its impact on long-term health and productivity of District land?

10. How do we balance management for Federal trust species with the needs of resident species?

11. How do we reduce crop loss caused by Canada geese foraging on private land adjacent to WPAs?

12. Invasive species, both exotic and native, are negatively impacting the natural ecological balance of grasslands and wetlands on WPAs.

13. What is the Long Range Goal of the Partners for Fish and Wildlife Program (Private Lands) on Wetland Management Districts?

Public Use

14. There are conflicting views concerning the costs and benefits of federally owned land in a community. Who benefits? Who pays?

15. How do we provide adequate facilities and programs for the public to fully enjoy wildlife-related recreation in a way that is compatible with our main mission?

Operations

16. Districts need sufficient staff in critical areas to fully meet resource challenges and opportunities.

17. Districts need office, maintenance, and equipment storage facilities to carry out their mission.

18. Vehicles and other necessary equipment need to be replaced on a regular basis according to Service standards.

19. Funding is needed to develop and manage newly acquired WPA land and facilities.

20. Discretionary money is needed for managing newly acquired land. Historic preservation responsibilities and other cultural resource concerns add cost and delays.

21. Individual WPA development plans and record keeping need to be updated.

22. The Districts need to be consistent in their application of policy and resource protection efforts.

Comprehensive Conservation Plan Goals

The following Goals were identified through a variety of meetings to address the issues raised during the planning process:

Wildlife and Habitat

Wildlife: Strive to preserve and maintain diversity and increase the abundance of waterfowl and other key wildlife species in the Northern Tallgrass Prairie Ecosystem. Preserve, restore, and enhance resident wildlife populations where compatible with waterfowl and the preservation of other trust species. Seek sustainable solutions to the impact of Canada geese on adjacent private croplands.

Habitat: Restore native prairie plant communities of the Northern Tallgrass Prairie Ecosystem using local ecotypes of seed and maintain the vigor of these stands through various processes. Restore functioning wetland complexes and maintain the cyclic productivity of wetlands. Continue efforts for long-term solutions to the problem of invasive species with increased emphasis on biological control to minimize damage to aquatic and terrestrial communities. Continue efforts to better define the role of each District in assisting private landowners with wetland, upland, and riparian restorations

Acquisition: Within current acquisition acreage goals, identify the highest priority acres for acquisition taking into account block size and waterfowl productivity data. These priority areas should drive acquisition efforts whenever possible. Service land acquisition should have no negative impact on net revenues to local government. Understand and communicate the economic effects of federal land ownership on local communities

Monitoring: Collect baseline information on plants, fish, and wildlife and monitor critical parameters and trends of key species and/or species groups on and around District units. Promote the use of coordinated, standardized, cost effective, and defensible methods for gathering and analyzing habitat and population data. Management decisions will be based on the resulting data.

Endangered Species/Unique Communities: Preserve, enhance, and restore rare native northern tallgrass prairie, flora, and fauna that are or may become endangered. Where feasible in both ecological and social/economic terms, reintroduce native species on WPAs in cooperation with the Minnesota DNR

People

Public Use/ Environmental Education: Provide opportunities for the public to use the WPAs in a way that promotes understanding and appreciation of the Prairie Pothole Region. Promote greater understanding and awareness of the Wetland Management District's programs, goals, and objectives. Advance stewardship and understanding of the Prairie Pothole Region through environmental education.

Operations

Preparation of WPA Development Plans: Complete Geographic Information System (GIS) based WPA Development Plans for each unit in each District. Provide Districts with GIS to assist with acquisition, restoration, management and protection of public and private lands.

Provide necessary levels of maintenance, technician, and administrative support staff to achieve other Wetland Management District goals: Provide all Districts with adequate and safe office, maintenance, and equipment storage facilities Acquire adequate equipment and vehicles to achieve other District goals. Maintain District equipment and vehicles at or above Service standards.

Ensure that annual capital development funds are large enough to meet necessary development of new WPA land: Have adequate funds available each year to permit completion of maintenance needs for each Wetland District's current land base of Waterfowl Production Areas.

Develop and apply consistent policies for habitat, public use, and resource protection and ensure frequent coordination among Districts, both in Minnesota and in neighboring states with WPAs (North and South Dakota, Iowa, and Wisconsin).

Chapter 3: The Environment

Geographic/Ecosystem Setting

Three landscapes come together in Minnesota: prairies, deciduous woods, and coniferous forests of the north. This variation in landscape is caused by changes in climate and precipitation from north to south and is reflected in the wide diversity of plants and animals inhabiting the state (Wendt and Coffin 1988; Hargrave 1993; Aaseng, et al. 1993). The Districts own land within all three habitat types and all have changed dramatically since settlement, none more than the prairie landscape (Figure 3).

Photo Copyright by Jan Eldridge

Prairie Grasslands

At one time, the western edge of Minnesota was continuous prairie and scattered woodlands dotted with small wetlands, known as potholes. Snow melt and spring rains were contained in these small wetlands and released slowly into surrounding streams. The wetlands acted like a natural flood control system. All of this has changed since settlement. Now, only 150,000 acres of native prairie remain out of an original 18 million (Noss, et al. 1995). In some areas, virtually all of the potholes have been drained. Remnants of prairie and their associated wetlands are scattered and rare. They form the last refuge for many species of prairie plants and wildlife.

Deciduous Woods

The deciduous forest of Minnesota extends from the northern aspen parkland to maple basswood forests of the southeast. The term "deciduous" refers to trees that lose their leaves in the fall. There are many forest communities within this landscape. The northern aspen parkland is typical of a more Canadian landscape, with open understory, wet meadows, aspen, willow, and alder thickets. The communities include wild flowers like the northern gentian and prairie-fringed orchid, wildlife such as the moose, sandhill crane, sharp-tailed grouse, black-billed magpie and yellow rail. Further south, the deciduous forest changes to one dominated by maple and basswood and scattered oak savannahs. Birds of these hardwood forests include the tufted titmouse, scarlet tanager, eastern screech owl, broad-winged hawk, barred owl, red-eyed vireo, and wood thrush to name just a few. Wild flowers in the spring are a special feature of these woods including trillium, hepatica, blood root, trout lily, Dutchman's breeches and spring beauty (Moyle and Moyle 1977; Henderson and Lambrecht 1997).

Figure 3: Minnesota Wetland Management Districts Ecosystems

Minnesota Wetland Management Districts Ecosystems

Lake Agassiz, Aspen Parklands

MINNESOTA

Red River Valley

Detroit Lakes

Northern Minnesota Drift and Lake Plains

Fergus Falls

West Superior Uplands

Minnesota & NE Iowa Morainal Oak Savannah

Morris

Litchfield

North Central Glaciated Plains

Big Stone

Windom

0   100   200 Miles

Coniferous Forest

The coniferous forests dominate the northeastern portion of Minnesota. They are characterized by red and white pines, balsam-fir, spruce, and white cedar mixed with other deciduous species. While the coniferous forests dominate Minnesota landscapes, the Districts own very little in this landscape because it is not particularly productive for waterfowl.

Climate

The climate of Minnesota is seasonal and highly variable. Average annual precipitation ranges from 20 inches in the northern aspen parklands to 32 inches in the southwestern prairie coteau. Within the eastern Great Plains, precipitation falls during two peak periods, one in early summer and a less pronounced peak in September. Average maximum annual temperature ranges from 50 degrees Fahrenheit in the northern aspen parklands to 58 degrees Fahrenheit in the prairie coteau. Average minimum annual temperature ranges from 23 degrees F in the aspen parklands to 36 degrees F in the prairie coteau. The growing season ranges from 125 days in the aspen parklands to 180 days in the prairie coteau (Hargrave 1993; Ostlie et al. 1996).

Hydrology

Conversion of the prairie to agriculture and the general development of the area over the past 130 years has greatly changed the region's hydrology.

The Districts contain five major watersheds: the Red, the Upper Mississippi, the Minnesota, the Missouri, the Cedar and Des Moines Rivers (Figure 4). Of these, the Red, Minnesota, and Des Moines are clearly the most important hydrologically and culturally in terms of water flow, impacts to land use, and associated water resources. The Minnesota River is considered the state's most polluted river. The Red River watershed has been degraded by dam construction, agricultural practices, channelization, and loss of riparian vegetation.

The Red River is the only major American river that drains northward into Hudson Bay. Total drainage area in the U.S. is 39,200 square miles, of which 17,806 are in Minnesota. Due to regional patterns in precipitation, evapotranspiration, soils, and topography, the Red receives most of its flow from its eastern tributaries. Ten of these tributaries traverse the Districts.

Many rivers in the Districts have been channelized in the downstream reaches to improve agricultural drainage. Most of the small wetlands that once held spring melts have been drained for agriculture through ditches or subsurface tile systems. As a result of this facilitated drainage, damaging summer floods are becoming more common.

River hydrology has been further altered through the construction of approximately 270 flood control structures within the Minnesota basin of the Red River. Despite these flood control projects, the Red remains a flood-prone system due to heavy spring snow melt, the flatness of the area, and snow/ice melting in the upstream area of the basin before that in the downstream areas.

Photo Copyright by Jan Eldridge

Figure 4: Minnesota Wetland Management Districts Hydrology and Key Rivers

The Roseau, Red Lake, Wild Rice, and Buffalo rivers account for three-fourths of the flood damage on the Minnesota tributaries.

The Minnesota River drains an area of 15,500 square miles within the District area. The Minnesota River begins in Browns Valley, where it is separated from the watershed of the Red River (Lake Traverse) by the Big Stone Moraine. As it flows toward its meeting with the Mississippi, the Minnesota River is impeded by four flood control reservoirs located at Big Stone, Big Stone/Whetstone, Marsh Lake, and Lac Qui Parle. Two smaller dams near Granite Falls slow the flow, but do not impound any water within the floodplain. One small hydroelectric dam operates near Mankato on the Blue Earth River. Flooding along the Minnesota is common within the floodplain, but does not have the same cultural or ecological impacts as on the Red River because the steep slopes of the Minnesota contain the river.

Southwestern Minnesota differs dramatically from the flat topography to the north and east. The Coteau des Prairies region grades from gently undulating to steeply rolling and hilly. These glacial moraines and ridges are well drained and have few depressions. This area flows mostly southwest into the Missouri River. The outer edges of the Coteau are less well drained and contain numerous wetlands and lakes. The Big and Little Sioux rivers are the two largest rivers in this area. Both flow to the southwest and into Iowa.

Geology

The area has a varied geological history but throughout the region, the departure of the last glacier, The Wisconsin, is still evident upon the land. The retreating glacier left behind gently rolling hills of gravel deposits with many scattered potholes, remnants left by melting glacial ice. In relative geologic time, the rivers that drain this land are new and inefficient (Ojakangas and Matsch 1982).

The southwest corner of Minnesota escaped the Wisconsin glaciation and features more bedrock exposures because that area escaped a blanket of glacial till or drift. Big Stone District is named after some of the rocky features of the bedrock exposure. Rivers and streams in this area are better developed, resulting in more efficient drainage systems.

Thousands of natural basins were left in the wake of thawing ice. Glacial lakes, the largest of these being Lake Agassiz, left behind a series of beaches and as they overflowed, they cut huge river channels. Lake Agassiz created a moraine at Browns Valley that spilled over to become the glacial River Warren, later to become the Minnesota River. The water volume of the Minnesota is a fraction of the River Warren, which flowed through its broad river valley with high stream terraces, dwarfing today's river. The Minnesota has eroded deeply into the glacial sediment and has exposed some of the world's oldest rocks along its narrow valley.

Wind-blown loess was also a major influence in the soils of Minnesota, especially in southwest Minnesota. The disintegration of the Wisconsin Glacier left a distinctive, fine-textured till containing a high volume of Paleozoic limestone and Cretaceous shale fragments. Combined with the loess swept by surface winds, it is the parent material for most of today's prairie soils of western and southern Minnesota.

District Resources

Wildlife

Waterfowl

The prairie pothole region has historically been recognized as the most important waterfowl production area in North America. Surveys have shown that although this area represents only 10 percent of the breeding habitat, it averages 50 to 75 percent of the duck recruitment each year in North America.

Waterfowl species that use the prairie wetlands of Minnesota include: Ruddy, Wigeon, Redhead, Northern Shoveler, Blue-winged Teal, Mallard, Gadwall, Wood Duck, Canvasback, and Canada Goose. Other waterfowl use the prairie wetlands to a lesser degree: Pintail, Lesser Scaup, and Ring-necked Duck. These species rely on grains for food most of the year but during the spring and summer, they shift to aquatic plants and insects. They depend on the wetlands for food during the breeding season.

File Photograph

The Habitat and Population Evaluation Team (HAPET) Office census waterfowl populations within the Wetland Management Districts of western Minnesota. Summary statistics generated by HAPET provide a necessary overview of waterfowl production and land use in the Districts. Their results show the variability between districts in breeding pair density. The average duck pair density ranges from 23.5 in the Fergus Falls WMD to 3.7 in the Windom WMD (Figure 5).

Rich soils and prairie wetlands make the region ideal for waterfowl, but also highly productive for agriculture. The corn and soybean belt overlaps extensively with the southern prairie pothole region. Massive conversion of wetlands and prairie to agricultural fields has dramatically altered the landscape, the hydrology, and the region's carrying capacity for waterfowl

Some waterfowl species are more susceptible than others to the transformation of prairie into agriculture. Mallards and Blue-winged Teal have been fairly successful in agricultural landscapes such as western Minnesota. Northern Pintails, on the other hand, have declined more dramatically than any other waterfowl species in North America (Ducks Unlimited 1990). At the turn of the century, Pintails were probably as common in the prairies as Mallards (Roberts 1932). Pintails favor ephemeral ponds, which were the first and easiest to drain. They often nest far from water and ducklings have to move overland to get to ponds shortly after they hatch. In the current landscape, newly hatched ducklings cross plowed agricultural fields in the spring and they are vulnerable to predation. Like Pintails, Gadwalls were once very common in this region. In 1879, Gadwalls were reported to be as abundant as Mallards if not more so (Roberts 1932, in Galatowitsch and van der Valk 1994). Now, Gadwalls comprise less than 1 percent of the breeding population in western Minnesota (Green and Janssen 1975). Roberts (1930) reported, the gadwall "...suffered most severely from the settling of the country, probably as much from breaking-up of the prairie, where it commonly nested, as from the hunters." (Galatowitsch and van der

Figure 5: Estimated Average Duck Pair Density, 1987-1999

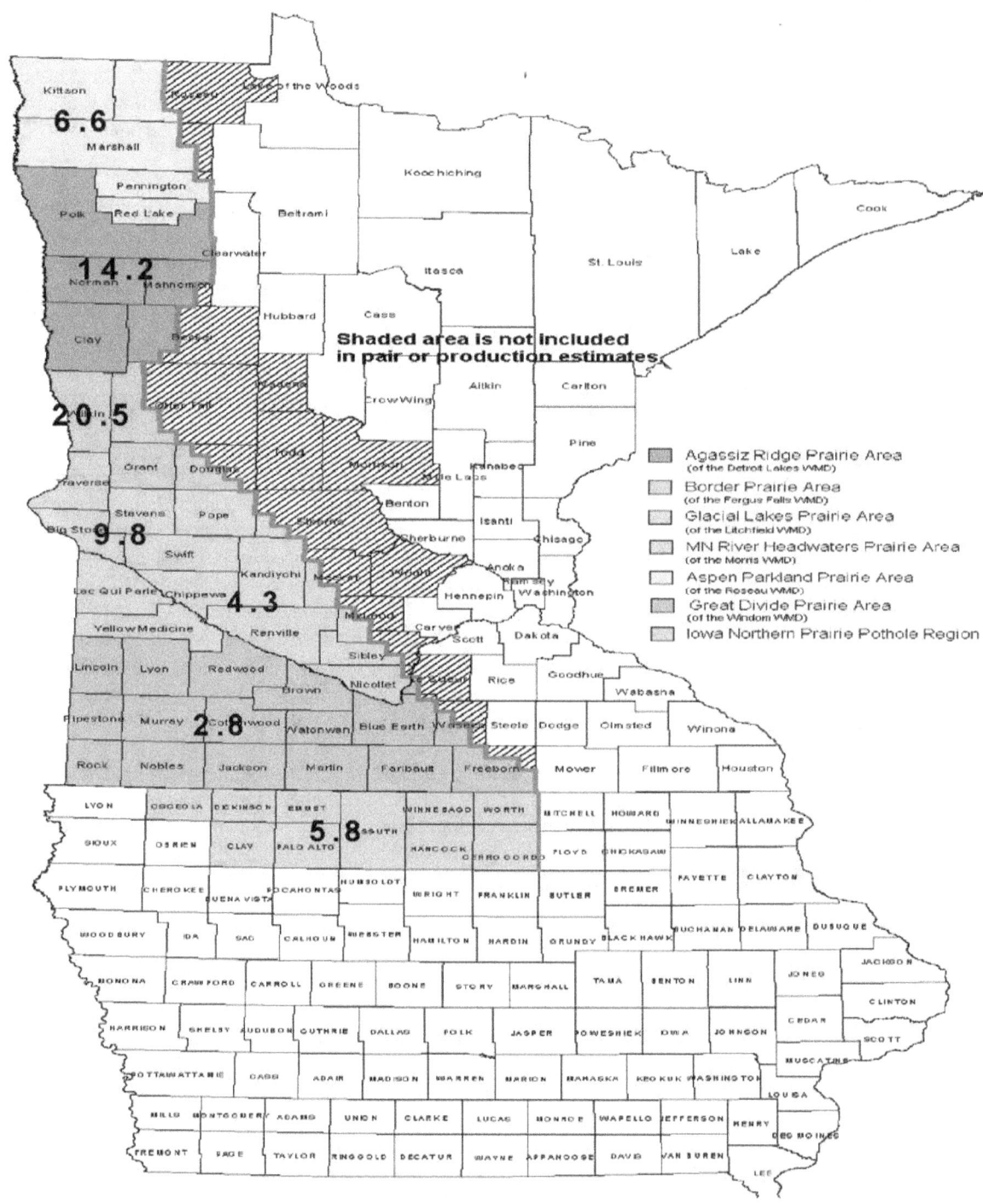

ESTIMATED DUCK PAIRS / SQ. MILE*

Shaded area is not included in pair or production estimates.

Agassiz Ridge Prairie Area
(of the Detroit Lakes WMD)

Border Prairie Area
(of the Fergus Falls WMD)

Glacial Lakes Prairie Area
(of the Litchfield WMD)

MN River Headwaters Prairie Area
(of the Morris WMD)

Aspen Parkland Prairie Area
(of the Roseau WMD)

Great Divide Prairie Area
(of the Windom WMD)

Iowa Northern Prairie Pothole Region

*ESTIMATES ARE FOR 13 SPECIES

Valk, 1994). At the turn of the century, Canvasback and Redheads were common on the largest lakes and marshes. Initially, over-hunting depleted Canvasback populations but the decline of wetland habitat, especially the wild celery beds, made it difficult for them to recover (Galatowitsch and van der Valk 1994). Another diving duck, the Scaup, was also common but is now primarily a migrant through the region.

Research has shown that ducks nesting in large blocks of grassland habitat (1,000 to 10,000 acres) reproduce more successfully than ducks nesting in smaller blocks (200 to 500 acres) (Burger et al. 1994; Ball et al. 1995). Ron Reynolds of the HAPET Office in North Dakota found waterfowl production increased on WPAs near large blocks of CRP land (personal communication). His results show the importance of working with partners to increase effective habitat block size and offset habitat fragmentation.

A major factor depressing duck numbers is low nest success due to nest destruction by predators on small units of habitat. Predators are quick to find these remnant areas and concentrate their hunting activities on the vulnerable ground nests of waterfowl. In some habitats, predators such as red fox, raccoon, mink, and skunk are able to take virtually every duck nest and many of the attendant hens.

Although agriculture has been an important feature in this area for over 100 years, it has been particularly intensive during the last several decades. Conversion from small, diverse family farms to large agricultural operations specializing in monocultures of small grain and row crops has eliminated habitat on private lands such as pasture, hayland, and wetlands. Grassland birds are forced to nest in ever-dwindling fragments of remaining cover. Often the only nesting sites available are small isolated areas such as roadside ditches, abandoned farmsteads, rock piles or isolated patches of habitat such as our Waterfowl Production Areas (WPAs).

The average block size for Waterfowl Production Areas in western Minnesota is only 210 acres. In part, the small size of most acquisitions is due to the nature of the Small Wetlands Acquisition Program (SWAP). The original SWAP approach was simple — purchase only a minimum of acres in fee-title and surround them with permanent easements.

In truth, it is difficult to purchase large tracts of land in prime agricultural areas. What research identifies as an optimal size for wildlife is not always possible given the competing needs for the land. Local county land boards often will not support taking large blocks of land out of agricultural production and off the tax role. Areas that are important for waterfowl may not be available or for sale. To purchase land strategically, managers are faced with the difficult task of finding willing sellers in the most productive areas for waterfowl.

The landscape level monitoring by the HAPET Office shows that waterfowl success varies depending on location within the state. There is even great variance between WPAs within a single District. The HAPET Office has produced a map for each district that ranks locations for waterfowl production. The maps are known as "thunderstorm maps" because they resemble doppler radar weather maps (Figure 6).

Existing GIS mapping data can be used to evaluate land acquisitions. Available information can be compiled to pick land parcels that have high potential for waterfowl and that are located near other conservation lands, such as state, county, or CRP set-aside land to increase the "effective size" of each unit. This approach can aid in setting priorities of acquisition. Ideally, managers could use these maps to identify "hot spots" within their district for purchase as WPAs.

Figure 6: Predicted Settling Density of Dabbling Duck Pairs

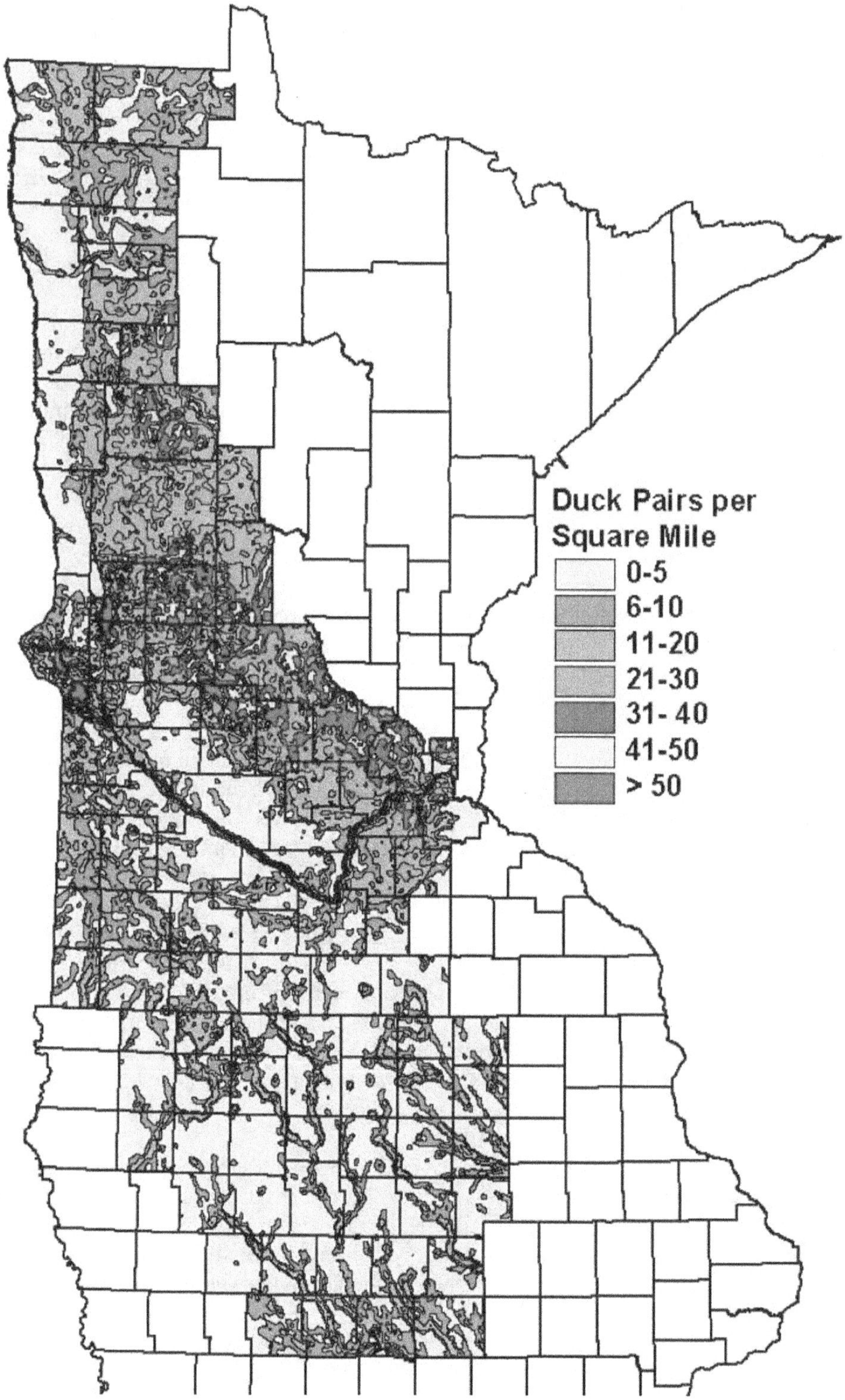

Duck Pairs per
Square Mile

	0-5
	6-10
	11-20
	21-30
	31- 40
	41-50
	> 50

The Districts are trying to combat the unnatural impact of predators in small pieces of habitat by removing abandoned buildings and brush. Abandoned farmsteads are prime denning sites for major nest predators such as skunks (Lariviere and Messier 1998a, 1998b; Lariviere et al. 1999). In addition, the Districts place nesting platforms in many wetlands, and predator control is practiced on a limited scale in conjunction with electric fence exclosures on 350 acres in Fergus Falls and 10 acres in the Morris Wetland Management Districts.

Another threat to waterfowl reproduction is the increasing application of agricultural chemicals such as fertilizers, insecticides, and herbicides on cropland adjacent to WPAs. Research has identified agricultural chemicals as important factors in decreasing bird populations directly as well as affecting their food resources in wetlands (see Chapter 3, External Threats).

Not all species of waterfowl are in decline. In recent years, the population of Giant Canada Geese has exploded across many of the Districts. Many WPAs contain the large wetlands favored by geese. These wetlands are often adjacent to private agricultural land. Canada Geese are upland grazers and, like most wildlife, will take advantage of the bounty planted nearby, whether it be succulent sprouts of soybeans, corn, or the grass of lawns and golf courses. On certain areas, geese can cause considerable financial hardship for farmers by wiping out relatively large areas of crops.

Although the more common species of ducks and geese in Minnesota have increased over the last decade, many are still below the goals of the North American Plan.

Migratory Birds

Minnesota Wetland Management Districts contain habitat important to bird species other than waterfowl, including songbirds, marsh and wading birds, shorebirds, raptors, and upland game birds. Approximately 243 species of birds regularly use the Districts at some time during the year, with 152 nesting species (Appendix B).

Photo Copyright by Jan Eldridge

The U.S. Fish and Wildlife Service and the Minnesota Department of Natural Resources, Partners in Flight, an international bird conservation initiative, and others have evaluated the status of migratory birds, identifying "species of concern" at the state, regional, and national levels. Partners in Flight have developed a bird conservation plan that focuses on declining grassland and wetland birds in the Northern Tallgrass Prairie Bird Conservation Region. This plan provides information on the habitat needs of these species and proposes a model of landscape-level habitat conservation for grassland birds (Fitzgerald et al. 1998). In the Districts, 48 birds identified as "species of concern" are rare, declining, or dependent on vulnerable habitats, including 43 that breed there. This list does not include hunted waterfowl or federally-listed threatened or endangered species, which are dealt with in another section of this document (Appendix B).

About 44 percent of the species of concern depend on some type of grassland habitat. Important habitats in the District include native and restored prairies, seeded grasslands (cool- or warm-season grasses), light- to moderately-grazed pastures, Conservation Reserve Program lands (CRP), sedge meadows, old fields, and hayfields (if not mowed before July 15). In North America, grassland birds have exhibited steeper declines than any other avian group. Their decline has a number of causes: loss of breeding and wintering habitat from agriculture, urbanization, habitat degradation from fire suppression, inappropriate grazing regimes, woody plantings, pesticides, and nest predation and Cowbird parasitism.

Within the category of "grassland birds," individual species show a variety of habitat preferences based on vegetation height, cover density, grass/forb ratio, soil moisture, litter depth, degree of woody vegetation, and plant species composition. It is important to maintain a mosaic of grassland habitats to meet the varying needs of grassland birds.

Some of the species of concern found in the Districts are area-sensitive, which means they require large, contiguous blocks of habitat to reproduce successfully. Area-sensitive species include the greater prairie-chicken, northern harrier, upland sandpiper, bobolink, Henslow's sparrow, and savannah sparrow.

Vertebrate and Invertebrate Species of Concern

"Species of concern" refers to those species for which the Service has incomplete and inconclusive information, but which might be declining in range, numbers, or security. Service and state agency biologists and other experts confer on and use natural heritage data bases and other published and unpublished information to follow the welfare of these species. They have no protection under the Endangered Species Act (Act) and are not candidates for listing.

Species of concern are a diverse group of animals united by two factors: (1) the Service is watching them, and (2) they occur within the general area and thus could appear in or near tracts within the Districts. Some of these animals occur only in prairie habitats. Some of the arthropods can live only in good tallgrass prairie habitat and thus are good indicators of high quality prairies. It is not possible to predict which, if any, of the species may occur on tracts within the Districts, nor predict how their occurrence would be a factor in decisions regarding individual tracts. They are necessary components of a healthy, functioning tallgrass prairie ecosystem and are indicators of prairie tract quality.

Region 3 of the U.S. Fish and Wildlife Service has developed a Resource Conservation Priorities (RCP) document that includes all species of concern within the Region (U.S. Fish and Wildlife Service 2002). The Minnesota Department of Natural Resources maintains an official state list of animals being watched for changes in abundance and distribution, and of animals that are endangered or threatened and protected by state law. The Service will consider species listed by the State of Minnesota along with Service species of concern in evaluating prairie sites and developing site protection measures.

Reptiles, Amphibians, and Insects, Vertebrates and Invertebrates

Reptiles, amphibians, and insects may have limited popular appeal, but each species plays an important role in the prairie ecosystem. The degree of interconnectedness in the tallgrass prairie ecosystem is high. Landmark species such as the eagle, badger and coyote find their food sources in these groups. Prairie plant diversity depends upon pollination and seed dispersal, as well as soil aeration by the great variety of insects. Grasshoppers (family Orthoptera) are major herbivores in the prairie ecosystem, and many native prairie flowers rely on bees, butterflies, and others for pollination. Numerous prairie birds, amphibians, reptiles and small mammals feed exclusively or partly on insects. The web of successes and failures within tallgrass prairie communities is anchored to every point of diversity within the system, and the protection of this entire spectrum is necessary for the persistence of its varied parts.

Listed Endangered and Threatened Vertebrates and Invertebrates
This section describes animals that are Federally listed under the Endangered Species Act of 1973, as amended, and are listed as either endangered or threatened.

Threatened Mammals
Gray wolf, ***Canis lupus***: Experts estimate approximately 2,000 gray wolves presently occur in Minnesota. Wolf numbers and range appear to be increasing in Minnesota. Wolves are no longer exclusive residents of Minnesota's forested wilderness areas, and adult wolves from Minnesota have dispersed through central and western Minnesota to North and South Dakota. The Service recognizes the improving range and security of the species and reclassified the wolf from "endangered" to "threatened."

Threatened/Endangered Birds
Bald Eagle, ***Haliaeetus leucocephalus***: Bald Eagles have increased in abundance and distribution across the United States, including Minnesota, and have been reclassified from endangered to threatened. In the 1990s, nesting territories increased in Minnesota every year from 437 in 1990 to 618 in 1995. Increasing numbers of migrating and wintering eagles also occur across Minnesota where they find sheltered night roosts and feed on waterfowl, smaller wild mammals, and fish in open water areas. Bald Eagles became endangered because of habitat loss, but especially because of DDT use following World War II. Today, the DDT threat is largely gone. Now the challenge is to prevent contamination and loss of sites that eagles depend on for nesting, feeding, migration, and wintering.

Piping Plover, ***Chadarius melodus***: Piping Plovers are tenuously present in Minnesota. They nest in Lake of the Woods, east of the Districts. Piping Plovers nest in coastal areas, but they are also prairie birds, nesting across the Great Plains of the United States and Canada, but in perilously low numbers. The Great Plains populations is listed as threatened. The loss of prairie wetland areas contributes to their decline. Like many shorebirds, Piping Plovers feed on immature and adult insects and other invertebrates at the water's edge. They winter primarily along beaches, sandflats, and algal flats on the Gulf of Mexico.

Least Tern (eastern population), ***Sterna antillarum***: Listed as endangered, the Least Tern nests along large rivers of the Colorado, Red, Mississippi, and Missouri River systems. This species is a potential nester in the Missouri River area. It nests on sand and gravel bars and protected beach areas of large rivers and winters in coastal Central and South America. The species is endangered because human disturbance and alteration of river systems has rendered much of its nesting habitat unusable. Pesticides may reduce food available to the tern by reducing the numbers of small fish in their feeding areas.

Reintroductions
The public has an interest in seeing presettlement native wildlife species returned to the landscape. Examples include greater prairie chickens, trumpeter swans, bison, and wolves. Giant Canada Geese, once thought extinct, have returned to the prairies of Minnesota in numbers as a result of captive breeding and reintroduction programs. However, at times restoration efforts, and the ensuing adaptability of the species like the Canada Goose, can create its own set of management problems (see next issue).

Due to the relatively small size of WPAs and the concerns for impacts off of WPAs, reintroductions of species like bison and wolves are not practical. However, Trumpeter Swan reintroductions have been successful and well-received by the public, while prairie chicken reintroduction is showing some sign of success depending on the area. There is also the potential for reintroducing species of prairie plants and native small mammals, reptiles, and amphibians and even insects like the Dakota Skipper butterfly on certain units.

<u>Management of Resident Species</u>

Federal trust species are generally those that cross state and international boundaries or are afforded national protection through various laws and treaties, such as the Migratory Bird Treaty Act and the Endangered Species Act. The well-being of waterfowl populations is a classic Federal trust responsibility and the main purpose for the creation of the Small Wetland Acquisition Program in the 1960s. This does not mean that resident species such as white-tailed deer and pheasants found on WPAs should not receive management attention. Rather it is the degree of management focus, based on the knowledge that management for trust resources like waterfowl will usually benefit the myriad of resident wildlife that share the prairie-wetland landscape.

Local and regional residents, however, may often favor the management for those species like white-tailed deer and pheasant that provide consumptive recreation opportunities. Thus, managers are often faced with requests for food plots, tree and shrub plantings, or direct stockings of game species that may have a negative effect on the primary purpose of waterfowl production and the broader goals of restoring native plant communities. The key is to seek the proper balance between practices focused on trust species and those that can accommodate the public's desire for resident wildlife management.

Habitat

<u>Wetlands and Riparian Habitat</u>

Prairie wetlands and prairie streams are an important part of the prairie ecosystem. Minnesota is naturally rich in wetland and riverine habitats (Appendix D). Western Minnesota is part of the prairie pothole

region, characterized by numerous, shallow wetlands known as potholes. These wetlands provide essential fish and wildlife habitat, permit ground water recharge, and act as filters of sediment and pollutants. They reduce floods by storing water and delaying runoff. The region once included about 20 million acres of these small wetlands. They were unconnected and poorly drained and in the spring they retained water, acting like a great landscape sponge. Over the course of the season, water drained slowly.

Settlers found the shallow wetlands difficult to farm. In addition, the wetlands kept the water table high so much of the land was saturated in a wet year. When the land was converted to farms, the new owners built drainage ditches, straightened streams and drained shallow wetlands off their land. Today, only about 5.3 million acres remain in 2.7 million basins within five states. Now, in the spring, water rushes off the land and floods the streams and rivers. Drainage has been so extensive that in

Figure 7: Wetland Distribution by Type, Morris WMD

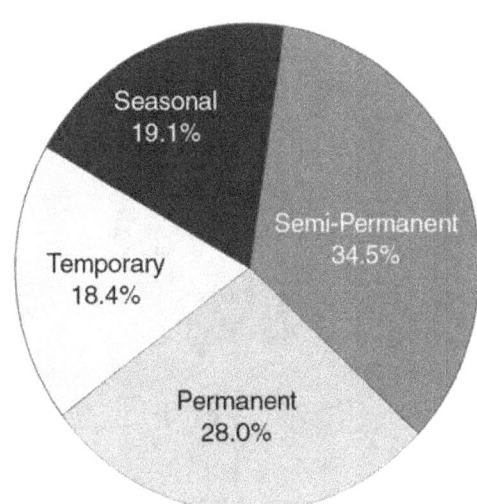

many areas the water table has been lowered and the hydrology of the entire region has been transformed.

More than 78 percent of the remaining wetland basins are smaller than 1 acre in size. Nearly two out of three of the remaining wetlands in Minnesota are privately owned; consequently, they are vulnerable to continued drainage, development, and pollution.

The Wetland Management Districts have focused on saving and restoring the small wetlands of Western Minnesota. They have been remarkably successful in saving a variety of wetland types (Figure 7). Wetland diversity is important because wetlands change continuously; a single wetland can not be maximally productive all the time. Waterfowl use specific types of wetlands at different times during the breeding season. Laying hens may forage in ephemeral, temporary and seasonal wetlands early in the season and shift to semipermanent and permanent wetlands after the brood is hatched. Marsh birds need a variety of wetlands in close proximity so they can shift from one wetland to another as the wetlands cycle through different phases. It is very important that natural wetland complexes be preserved. Wetland complexes include a variety of basins, some shallow and some deep, in close proximity. Diverse wetland complexes are rare today because most shallow ephemeral, temporary, and seasonal basins have been drained.

Saving single, isolated wetlands is much less valuable than saving several wetlands in a wetland complex. The Wetland Management Districts focus on acquiring wetland complexes with a variety of wetland types.

The fluctuating water levels in the shallow wetlands are natural to the dynamic pattern of precipitation in the prairie. The changing water level results in circular bands of vegetation around each basin because different plant species have different tolerances for saturated soils. The depth of the basin also affects the kind of vegetation that grows. The drying pattern is one of the features used to classify wetland

Figure 8: Marsh Vegetation Cycles

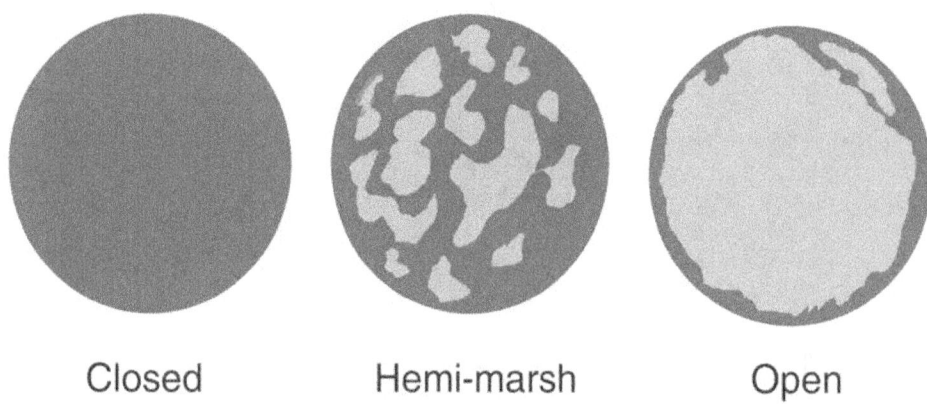

Closed   Hemi-marsh   Open

basins (Cowardin et al.). Deeper basins have perennial emergent vegetation such as cattail and dry every 5 to 10 years. Wetlands that dry every other year or on a several year cycle are called semi-permanent or permanent wetlands. Basins that dry every year are temporary and seasonal wetlands. Some very shallow basins dry early in the spring after the frost leaves the ground and as a result are called ephemeral wetlands.

Freshwater wetlands like those in the prairie pothole region are among the most productive in the world (Weller 1982). The dynamic water cycle creates a rich environment for many waterfowl and other marsh birds. Cycling water accelerates decomposition of marsh vegetation, resulting in a natural fertilizer. When the basins recharge in the spring, the water becomes a soup of nutrients and supports a diverse and healthy population of aquatic invertebrates, which feed reproducing waterfowl and marsh birds throughout the spring and summer. In the larger basins, the vegetation changes from densely closed cattail or bullrush cover to completely open over a period of years (Figure 8). In the process of transition, the cover vegetation moves through a phase, known as hemi-marsh, when clumps of emergent vegetation are interspersed with open water (Weller 1982). In this phase, the structure of the vegetation itself creates habitat and stimulates the production of aquatic invertebrates. The marsh, in this phase, hosts the maximum number of marsh birds. Unfortunately, the phase is only temporary and most wetlands cycle out of it in 1 to 3 years.

The prairie potholes are too shallow to be fish habitat but they have been used in the past as hatcheries for minnows and walleye fingerlings. Leeches are also harvested from these shallow ponds. Unfortunately, many of these artificially introduced native species consume the same aquatic invertebrates as waterfowl. Fathead minnows occur naturally in some wetlands in the region and have a significant negative effect on the invertebrate populations of the wetlands (Hanson and Zimmer 1999).

Wetland restoration and management are high priorities in the Districts. In many areas, the entire hydrology of the area has been altered and restoration is not always a straightforward matter of plugging drains and filling in ditches (Galatowitsch and van der Valk 1994). Restored wetlands employ water control structures for water level management to mitigate the disruptive impact of wide scale drainage that has altered natural water cycles. Many wetlands on WPAs are flooded because surrounding wetlands on private land have been drained and the excess water moves into the WPA. Water control structures are often necessary, but these structures require funding to install and staff to maintain. Neither are in adequate supply to do what is needed.

<u>Partners for Fish and Wildlife Program</u>
Wetland Districts in Minnesota have led the nation in the sheer number of wetlands restored through the cooperation of private landowners in the Partners for Fish and Wildlife Program (Private Lands). The program assists private landowners with the improvement or restoration of wildlife habitat on their land. Technical assistance, contracting, cost-sharing assistance and actual earth work is provided to private landowners throughout the Districts. Since the program's inception in 1987, 12,000 wetlands totaling more than 40,000 acres have been restored. However, some Districts are now finding it more difficult to find landowners willing to restore wetlands. More staff effort is required with longer trips and greater expense to seek out landowners willing to restore wetlands. Managers have also begun to explore assisting landowners with efforts to restore native prairie and riparian areas.

Districts have also restored more than 10,000 acres of native grasslands on private property through the Partners for Fish and Wildlife Program during the same period. In the past 2 years, new funding sources within the Partners for Fish and Wildlife Program have placed added emphasis on riparian and instream habitat restoration, and this has the potential to create additional opportunities for the Districts to accomplish habitat restoration on private lands.

U.S. Department of Agriculture (USDA) programs have created many new opportunities for Districts to assist in the restoration of a variety of trust resource habitats on private lands. The USDA's Conservation Reserve Program (CRP) has placed an emphasis on wetland and native prairie restoration as a condition of enrollment, and many new participants are making their lands available for wildlife habitat restoration. This presents an important role for the Districts to lend their restoration experience and expertise to make these CRP restorations as high-quality as possible. The USDA's Wetlands Reserve Program (WRP) likewise presents opportunities for Districts to accomplish migratory bird objectives on private lands utilizing other agency programs and dollars by making experience and expertise available to implement habitat restoration projects.

The Districts' perpetual easement program, which encompasses both wetland and conservation easements (both wetlands and uplands on a property), has greatly benefited from the success of the Partners for Fish and Wildlife Program over the past 10 years. Many of the private landowners who have restored wetlands on their lands through the Partners Program have since come back to the District seeking establishment of a permanent easement on their property to offer protection to their project in future years. In some Districts it is fair to say that the vast majority of new easements recorded in the past few years first started as Partners projects. This continues to meet the needs of landowners who wish to improve their land for wildlife, for themselves and for future generations.

By providing habitat restoration funds to complete restoration projects initiated by the Districts as well as technical assistance funds to provide restoration experience and expertise to other agencies' programs, the Partners for Fish and Wildlife Program puts the Wetland Management Districts in a wonderful position to accomplish a multitude of, and a variety of, trust species habitat restoration projects over the next 10 years.

Prairie Restoration

Prairie landscapes are much more diverse than they seem at first glance. They contain hundreds of species of plants, invertebrates, and wildlife. Some prairies contain as many as 200 plant species. The landscape is dominated by a relatively small number of widespread, sod-forming bunch grasses such as big bluestem, northern dropseed, and porcupine needlegrass, but flowering plants constitute the greatest number of species (80 percent in some areas). Most abundant members are from the pea and sunflower families such as wild indigos, prairie clovers and scurf peas (pea family); and asters, gay-feathers, goldenrods, coneflowers, and sunflowers (aster family) (Henderson and Lambrecht, 1997).

Over the past decade, virtually all plantings of upland cover on Waterfowl Production Areas have been with native grasses. In recent years, a more diverse mixture of native forbs and warm and cool season native grasses have been used. Plants within a single species vary with latitude (called ecotypes) and an effort is being made to plant local ecotypes in restorations. Harvesting techniques of existing tallgrass prairie and refinement of the cleaning and seeding process has made seed gathering easier. However, many native prairie forbs remain in short supply and are extremely costly for large areas.

Prescribed fire remains a critical tool for maintaining the diversity and vigor of existing and restored prairie plants. Prescribed burns can only be done during a small window of time in the spring, so the number of acres that can be burned each spring is limited. As a result, most WPAs can not be burned on a rotation frequent enough to suppress invading shrubs and trees. Some of the Districts use haying and grazing as additional means of maintaining grassland integrity.

The Districts also manage grasslands through the selective application of herbicides during restoration. In 1990, 15,825 pounds of active ingredients representing 20 herbicides were applied to 15,533 acres of Service-managed lands in Minnesota (USFWS 1990). The most heavily and most frequently used chemical was 2,4-D. In 1987, approximately $100,000 was spent on noxious weed control on approximately 16,000 acres of District lands (USFWS 1992). Because of concern that chemical use could impact water quality (See Issue 9), the Twin Cites Ecological Services Field Office conducted a 2-year study beginning in 1992 to determine the impact of the herbicide application on wetlands in the Districts. Results indicated that concentrations of 2,4-D were consistently low and at concentrations that have not been shown to have an adverse affect on aquatic life (Ensor and Smith 1994).

Rare Communities

Waterfowl Production Areas provide one of the last bastions of grassland and wetland habitat in the prairie area of Minnesota. These areas provide some of the last remaining habitat for threatened, endangered, rare or unique wildlife and plants. Examples include the threatened western prairie fringed orchid and prairie bush clover, and numerous species of grassland and wetland-dependent species that are declining in numbers. There is a need to have better baseline information on what species are present on each WPA, and to monitor the effects of wetland and prairie restoration efforts on these species of special concern.

Minnesota County Biological Survey (Survey) conducted systematic surveys of rare biological features from 1987-1995. The goal of the Survey was to identify significant natural areas and to collect and interpret data on the distribution and ecology of rare plants, rare animals, and natural communities. The Nature Conservancy, through a cooperative agreement with the Service, consolidated these data and the data of the Natural Heritage Information Systems of the Minnesota Natural Heritage, and Nongame Research Program. From this data, the existing protected areas within Minnesota were mapped and community types were identified.

Within the northern tallgrass prairie ecoregion (Iowa, Manitoba, Minnesota, North Dakota, and South Dakota), 97 terrestrial natural communities have been documented.

Rare communities most at risk are the mesic, wet, and dry prairie types. Three grassland communities (mesic tallgrass prairie, sedge meadow, and lake plain wet prairie) are critically endangered in the United States (Noss et al., 1995). The tallgrass prairie ecosystem includes the following community types:

Dry Prairie	Mixed Emergent Marsh
Mesic Prairie	Shrub Swamp
Wet Prairie	Aspen Woodland
Mesic Brush Prairie	Aspen Openings
Wet Brush Prairie	Dry Oak Savanna
Calcareous Seepage Fen	Mesic Oak Savanna
Rich Fen	Oak Woodland/Brushland

Some community types are broken down into subtypes, for example: Sand-Gravel Subtype of the Dry Prairie Type. Others include hill and barrens (dry prairie type), saline (wet prairie type), and prairie (calcareous seepage fen type). The prairie type of Calcareous Seepage Fen is one of the most valued of the rare plant communities in the Districts. These fens typically are surrounded by wet-mesic prairie species. The seepage area itself commonly contains patches of emergent aquatic species such as cattail, hard-stemmed bulrush, and common reed. Such areas occur throughout the Districts but are more common in the Lake Agassiz Beach Ridges.

Prairie community types are diverse, some are rarer than others; but with less than 1 percent of all northern tallgrass prairie remaining, special consideration is warranted for all types and subtypes. It can be argued that all intact prairie plant communities are rare. Tallgrass prairies have the highest percentage (65 percent) of rare community types of any group. The importance and uniqueness of individual tracts become apparent when ecotype variation is considered. For instance, warm season grasses generally vary one day in flowering time with each 9-14 miles in a north-south gradient. No doubt many more subtle ecotype variations occur.

Due to the disproportionate loss of community types, individual plant species of the prairie are becoming rare. For example, the western prairie fringed orchid was historically widespread and common in calcareous mesic to wet mesic prairies and sedge meadows. Wholesale conversion of its habitat to agriculture has resulted in the plant being placed on the Federal endangered species list.

Plant Species of Concern
"Species of concern" is an informal term in this document for species which the Service has incomplete and inconclusive information, but which might be declining in

range, numbers, or security. Service biologists confer with state agency botanists and other experts, and use state natural heritage program data bases and other published and unpublished information to follow the welfare of these species. Species of concern have no standing or protection of any kind under the Endangered Species Act (Act) and they are not candidates for listing under the Act. Nevertheless, the Service is interested in them and is alert for need to provide early assistance to these species to avoid the need to list them under the Act.

These species are a diverse group of plants united by two factors: (1) the Service is watching them, and (2) they occur within the general area and thus could appear in or near District tracts. It is impossible to predict which, if any, of the species may occur on tracts managed by the Districts. It is also impossible to predict how the occurrence of one of these species on or near a tract would factor in decisions regarding individual tracts beyond the Service's intent to recognize these species as valid and necessary components of a healthy, functioning tallgrass prairie ecosystem and as indicators of prairie tract quality.

The Minnesota Department of Natural Resources maintains an official state list of plants being watched for changes in abundance and distribution, and of plants that are endangered or threatened and protected by state law. There are approximately 80 such species in the counties of Minnesota. Biologists of the state natural resource agency and the Service maintain ongoing communication regarding these species, some of which are excellent indicators of prairie quality.

Listed Plants
This section describes plants that are federally listed under the Endangered Species Act of 1973, as amended, and are listed as either endangered or threatened.

Prairie bush clover, *Lespedeza leptostachya*: Occurs in dry, gravelly hill prairies and in thin soil prairies over granite bedrock. Common on prairies with big bluestem (*Andropogon gerardi*) and Indian grass (*Sorghastrum nutans*). More sites are known for this species than were known when it was listed and it appears able to grow in disturbed areas. The species may be stable or, if declining, declining slowly. The need for protection remains.

Western prairie fringed orchid, *Platanthera praeclara:* Occurs in moist, calcareous subsaline prairies and prairie sedge meadows and swales (Coffin and Pfannmuller 1988). The species may be stable, but loss of tallgrass prairie habitat has markedly reduced its original range. Present sites are threatened by human activities and land use changes and by invasion by leafy spurge (*Euphorbia esula*).

External Threats

Drainage and Pesticides
Waterfowl Production Areas are often islands in a sea of intensive agriculture. Natural drainage patterns have been altered throughout the landscape, increasing the frequency, intensity, and duration of water flowing into many units. Siltation, nutrient loading, and contamination from point and non-point sources of pollution are a serious problem on many WPAs. Waterfowl Production Areas are also threatened by farming trespass, dumping, wildfires, and pesticide applications on adjacent agricultural land. A recent study in Ontario examined the effects of habitat and agricultural practices on birds breeding on farmland and determined that the most important variable decreasing total bird species abundance was pesticide use (Freemark and Csizy 1993).

Recent changes in agriculture have accelerated the impact of pesticides on surrounding land. Genetically altered Round-up ready corn, soybeans, and sugar beets have expanded the window of opportunity for pesticide applications and promises to kill everything green on fields except the genetically altered crops. Another altered crop, Bt. Corn, contains a genetically engineered insecticide. Even the pollen from this plant can kill certain insects, such as monarch butterflies.

Research has shown that insecticides commonly used for sunflowers, soybeans and corn can kill wildlife directly and indirectly by decreasing the amount of food available. For example, ducks feed on grain much of the year but in the spring they shift to aquatic invertebrates (insect larvae, amphipods, snails) and they depend on this food source for reproduction and survival. Even when aerial pesticide applications are done carefully and wetlands are avoided, the chemicals drift into wetlands in measurable amounts and kill aquatic invertebrates (Tome et al. 1991 and Grue et al. 1986).

Insecticides have a direct effect by killing aquatic invertebrates, but herbicides also have an indirect effect on food available to waterfowl. The Service conducted a study of the impact of agricultural chemicals on selected wetlands in four of the Wetland Management Districts (Ensor and Smith, 1994). Herbicides from surrounding agricultural land enter wetlands and disrupt the functional interaction between vegetation structure and aquatic invertebrate life. The changing dynamic reduces food available to breeding waterfowl.

Seasonal and semipermanent wetlands (the majority of WPA wetlands) are the most exposed to agricultural chemicals. These wetlands are small and interspersed with croplands, which increases the probability of pesticides from over-spray and aerial drift. Most herbicides and insecticides are applied to crops in the spring and early summer, coincident with maximum runoff and waterfowl breeding. Ensor and Smith (1994) write:

> "A result of our survey... indicates that prairie pothole wetlands may involve interactions of multiple herbicides (and potentially insecticides) comprising chemical "soups" unique to individual wetlands."

This study showed that "typical agricultural use" of pesticides on surrounding land had a significant impact in reducing the biological quality of WPA wetlands. Currently, the Minnesota Pollution Control Agency (MPCA) exempts "normal farming practices" from the State's wetland protection (See: Specific Standards of Quality and Purity for Class 2 Waters of the State; Aquatic Life and Recreation, Minnesota Chapter 7050, 1994).

Invasive Species

Noxious weeds are a continuing problem both ecologically and socially/politically. Invasive species present a daunting challenge to land managers. Canada thistle, leafy spurge and spotted knapweed can displace native vegetation over large areas and are a serious concern to neighboring farmers and county officials. Purple loosestrife can effectively displace cattails and other native wetland vegetation and turn productive marshes into a sea of purple flowers. Carp can destroy native submergent vegetation, which provides the base for invertebrates. Minnows, often from past stockings by bait dealers, can cause serious damage to wetland food chains by reducing invertebrate populations needed by breeding waterfowl and ducklings.

Control of these problem species is often costly, both in terms of chemicals, equipment, and staff time. Managers strive to use a balanced approach in controlling these species. Direct control, such as chemical application or mowing, is often needed on serious problem areas. Once healthy native plant communities are reestablished, they can often compete successfully against invasive weeds. Water level control, including complete drawdowns, can eliminate carp and minnow populations on wetlands where this capability is present. Virtually all Districts are experimenting with biological controls by introducing insects that control the invading plant in its native country.

Rural Development
Rural development also threatens District lands in counties with growing populations, such as Wright County. Lands adjoining WPAs are often seen as highly desirable rural building lots that are purchased as small hobby farms or rural homesites. This can result in the WPA being "ringed" by homes, with a series of negative impacts on the WPA. Such development can limit future management such as prescribed fire; increase trespass on District lands by neighbors using ATVs, horses, or vehicles; increases threats to wildlife from stray pets (cats and dogs); increases use of District land by neighbors for illegal uses such as dumping, gardening, equipment storage, etc.; and can place hunters and neighbors at odds over concerns about safety during the hunting seasons. Large-scale rural development would also bring threats from noise and storm water runoff.

Cultural Resources

Archeological and Cultural Values

Responding to the requirement in the law that comprehensive conservation plans will include "the archaeological and cultural values of the planning unit," the Service contracted for a cultural resources overview study of Minnesota Wetland Management District. This section of the CCP derives mostly from the report, *"Cultural Resources Overview Study,"* by Teresa Halloran and others, Loucks & Associates Inc., dated August 1998. Several other sources have been used.

Context
Archeological evidence for human occupation in western Minnesota extends back 10,000 years when the last glaciers retreated to the north. Small bands of hunters moved into the tundra and boreal forest and left behind their distinctive Clovis and Folsom fluted lanceolate spear points and other tools. Now identified as PaleoIndian, these people lived in diverse settings and often on the margins of lakes and wetlands.

The long Archaic period began with a warmer and drier climate that peaked with the altithermal around 4700-3000 B.C. Surface waters evaporated and rivers shriveled; bison herds dwindled, and so did the human population. In the harsh conditions, the people developed an array of stone, bone, and copper tools. The human population expanded after the altithermal.

The subsequent Woodland period commenced around 500 B.C. and extended to the arrival of Europeans. The climate and vegetation were similar to 20th century conditions. The people of this period constructed pottery and burial mounds, used the bow and arrow, and adopted agriculture. Some people lived in larger, even fortified, summer villages. The seasonal round included bison hunting, maple sugar collecting, and wild rice harvesting. Exotic trade items came from more complex societies to the south and from other sources.

Natural and human events disrupted the traditional patterns and tribal locations. The Little Ice Age began about A.D. 1550 and caused many prairie tribes to relocate. Arrival of Europeans with Western culture goods and material and practices also caused tribes to change traditional cultural patterns and territory. Thus connecting modern Indian tribes with prehistoric antecedent cultures found in the archeological record is problematic.

Seventeenth century French and English fur traders built posts at the confluence of rivers or on the shores of larger lakes, usually near Indian villages. Western Minnesota became part of the United States as part of the Louisiana Territory, and in the second half of the 19th century immigrants settled the land as railroads expanded accessibility and markets. Settlers soon replaced dugouts and sod houses with frame houses and larger farms and farmsteads. Indian wars and treaties led to concentration of Indian tribes on reservations within and beyond the state. Highway construction, farm consolidation, urbanization, and recreational pursuits characterized the second half of the 20th century.

Existing Conditions and Cultural Resources Potential

A review of the National Register of Historic Places showed, as of October 16, 2000, the 40 Minnesota counties having WPAs and easements contained 426 properties listed on the National Register of Historic Places. The vast majority of these properties are buildings in towns and cities. A number of the properties are located in rural areas and are indicative of the kinds of historic properties that can be found on the Districts: farmsteads and farm buildings, especially barns; bridges; segments of the Red River Oxcart trail; mill sites; battle sites; prehistoric archeological sites such as mounds, villages, camps, and rock art. Historic archeological sites can also be found.

Many more cultural resources sites are reported on and around the waterfowl production areas, including:

- Big Stone WMD has eight sites on WPAs, none eligible for the National Register, and 188 additional sites in the two counties.

- Detroit Lakes WMD has 114 sites on WPAs, of which 33 are not eligible for the National Register, and 531 additional sites in the five counties.

- Fergus Falls WMD has 130 sites on WPAs, of which 51 are not eligible for the National Register, and 616 additional sites in the four counties.

- Litchfield WMD has 95 sites on WPAs, of which 30 are not eligible for the National Register, and 1,128 additional sites in the nine counties.

- Morris WMD has 91 sites on WPAs, of which 17 are not eligible for the National Register, and 555 additional sites in the eight counties.

- Windom WMD has 44 sites on WPAs, of which 12 are not eligible for the National Register, and 980 additional sites in the twelve counties.

Archeological surveys have been completed on 7,400 acres of District lands.

Although cultural resources can be found almost anyplace on the landscape, prehistoric archeological sites are often found on the shores (especially the east shore) of lakes larger than 40 acres, on islands and peninsulas, where streams enter and exit lakes, and near permanent streams. Early historic period sites are often associated with water. Thus, WPAs are often in the same setting as archeological sites.

Museum collections include art, ethnography, history, documents, botany, zoology, paleontology, geology, environmental samples, and artifacts. A museum collection at a District office or visitor center must adhere to the requirements in 411 DM. At this time only Morris WMD has identified a museum collection that consists of five historic objects. Archeological collections from WPAs are stored at the Minnesota Historical Society under terms of a cooperative agreement. Big Stone WMD has none; Detroit Lakes WMD has one collection of 29 items; Fergus Falls WMD has one collection of 40 items; Morris WMD has four collections of 698 items, and Windom WMD has seven collections of approximately 1,010 items. All District museum collections are covered under the Region-wide Scope of Collections Statement.

Indian Tribes and Other Interested Parties

Several Federal laws and executive orders respond to the part of the American public for whom cultural resources are an important part of the human environment and of understanding the American past and present.

For the intent of these laws to be met, persons and organizations need to be informed of Federal activities that could affect cultural resources. Contacts with Indian tribes are government-to-government unless the tribe has a Tribal Historic Preservation Officer. Seventeen tribes have been identified as having potential interest in one or more of the Districts. Other contacts include the county historical societies, local governments, state government agencies such as the Department of Natural Resources, and other Federal agencies such as the Natural Resources Conservation Service. In addition, the District Manager issues a news release in the project area.

Management of Cultural Resources

Cultural Resources are "those parts of the physical environment - natural and built - that have cultural value to some kind of sociocultural group ... [and] those non-material human social institutions...." Cultural resources include historic sites, archeological sites and associated artifacts, sacred sites, traditional cultural properties, cultural items (human remains, funerary objects, sacred objects, and objects of cultural patrimony), and buildings and structures.

An undertaking is any Federal or federally-funded, -licensed, -permitted, or -assisted activity or project that could affect a significant (i.e., historic) property. Ground disturbance, buildings and structures modification or neglect, and landscape changes must be analyzed for impacts on archeological sites, farmsteads, objects, traditional cultural properties, sacred sites, and cultural items.

The District Managers inform the Regional Historic Preservation Officer early in the planning stage of all undertakings to allow qualified analysis, evaluation, consultation, and mitigation as necessary.

Archeological investigations and collecting are performed only in the public interest by qualified archeologists working under an Archaeological Resources Protection Act permit issued by the Regional Director. District Managers take steps to prevent unauthorized collecting by the public, contractors, and FWS personnel. Violations are reported to the Regional Historic Preservation Officer (RHPO).

If the public turns over to District personnel "found" artifacts, the District Manager will try to determine provenance, will attempt to replace the artifact where found if it can be secure from further public collections, or will hold it until the RHPO is notified and can move it to the historical society.

Cultural Resources Management Objective: Establish a plan to fulfill requirements of Section 14 of the Archaeological Resources Protection Act for surveying lands to identify archeological resources; and Section 110(a)(2) of the National Historic Preservation Act for a preservation program.

People

Public Use of Waterfowl Production Areas

The Refuge Improvement Act established six priority uses of the Refuge System, which includes the more than 800 WPAs in Minnesota. These priority uses all depend on the presence of, or expectation of the presence, of wildlife, and are thus called wildlife-dependent uses. These uses are hunting, fishing, wildlife observation, photography, environmental education, and interpretation. Waterfowl Production Areas have been open to these uses for decades. Although Congress clearly expects managers to facilitate these priority uses, they must be compatible with the purpose for which the unit or WPA was established and the mission of the Refuge System. Compatibility Determinations for these priority uses and numerous other uses in compliance with the Refuge Improvement Act and national compatibility policy and regulations are included (Appendix E).

Most recent estimates show that 250,000 people visit WPAs each year for hunting, wildlife observation, photography, interpretive and environmental education, fishing, trapping, and other uses. Waterfowl Production Areas differ from national wildlife refuges in that they are open to hunting, fishing, and trapping by specific regulation, and open to the other wildlife-dependent activities by notification in general brochures available at each District office. New and existing WPAs are thus "open until closed" versus national wildlife refuges, which are "closed until opened."

Hunters and hunting have a long and linked history with WPAs. When Congress amended the Migratory Bird Hunting and Conservation Stamp Tax Act (Duck Stamp Act) in 1958, it authorized the acquisition of wetlands and uplands as WPAs and waived the usual "inviolate sanctuary" provisions for new migratory bird units. Thus, WPAs were intended to be open to waterfowl hunting, in part because waterfowl hunters, through the purchase of Duck Stamps and support for price increases of the stamp, played a major role in acquisition of these areas. Hunting, for both waterfowl and resident game species, accounts for more than half of the visits to WPAs.

Wildlife observation, interpretation, and environmental education are encouraged on WPAs and increasing in popularity with the public. Districts are taking a more active role in fostering these uses by developing wildlife trails, interpretive signs and kiosks, outdoor classrooms, and even auto tour routes on select WPAs. At the Fergus Falls Wetland Management District, the Prairie Wetlands Learning Center provides residential environmental education programs to schools throughout Minnesota.

In addition to these wildlife-dependent public uses, each District receives on a regular basis requests for various non-wildlife-dependent uses such as dog trials, horseback riding, plant collecting, berry picking, and special events. Also, various economic uses such as haying, grazing, and timber harvest are used as habitat management tools and involve the issuance of special use permits. There are numerous other "uses" which managers must make regular decisions on including rights-of-way requests for new or expanded roads, utilities, pipelines, and communications equipment.

USFWS Photo

To promote an understanding of what uses are and are not allowed, or allowed only on a case-by-case evaluation, the operations section describes the policies that will guide uses on WPAs.

Two major issues surfaced during plan development related to overall public use on WPAs. First, there is debate on the value of WPAs to the general public and local units of government due to changes in land use and taxation when WPAs are purchased from willing sellers. Second, funding and staff for adequate programs and facilities to better serve the public have never been on par with the generally larger and better known national wildlife refuges.

When land is purchased for a WPA, it becomes the property of the United States government and is exempt from taxation. To offset this loss in tax revenue for local governments, the Service pays three-fourths of 1 percent of the appraised value of the land to the counties in which the WPA is located. In most years, Congress has not appropriated sufficient funds to cover this level of entitlement. The result is resentful local governments and a serious issue when new tracts are brought before county commissioners and the Minnesota Land Exchange Board for approval.

The Refuge Improvement Act mandates that compatible, wildlife-dependent recreational uses involving hunting, fishing, wildlife observation, wildlife photography, environmental education and interpretation are the priority public uses of the Refuge System. In accordance with law and regulation, waterfowl production areas are open to hunting, fishing, wildlife observation, photography, trapping and environmental education.

Many WPAs lack the basic facilities, such as parking and trails, that help the public enjoy these wildlife-dependent uses. Also, Districts do not have the funds to provide quality maps that show the public how to find WPAs. Interpretive and environmental education opportunities are limited by the lack of trained public use specialists.

Disabled User Access

Each of the wetland management districts will provide compatible and accessible wildlife-dependent recreation on Waterfowl Production Areas. Each WMD will eventually develop at least one WPA per county or cluster of counties with enhanced opportunities for disabled users. These features might include accessible hunting blinds, accessible trails or scenic vistas, or other opportunities for accessible wildlife-dependent recreation. Disabled users will be directed to these units with improved accessibility. We do not plan to provide exclusive use for disabled users on these units. These WPAs will be open to all users but will provide a place for disabled visitors to enjoy wildlife-dependent recreation without having to seek special privileges. Disabled visitors who prefer not to use these enhanced facilities may be given special privileges at other WPAs. These privileges would be granted at the manager's discretion and would be limited to driving on existing trails. No user, disabled or otherwise, will be given permission to drive off of existing trails. Disabled users who receive special access privileges will be granted special use permits restricting their travel to designated routes on designated WPAs. The permit will include a map identifying allowable routes of travel.

For the purposes of this section, we intend to follow state standards on disabilities for special hunting privileges. The State of Minnesota is reviewing these standards. We expect the revised standards to roughly include people dependent on wheelchairs or supplemental oxygen as a reasonable standard of a disability requiring enhanced opportunities for access. If state standards do not meet our needs, we may develop our own standards in the future.

Operations

Individual WPA Development Plans

At the heart of on-the-ground restoration and management of WPAs is the writing of individual WPA development plans. These plans inventory existing resources and describe plans for wetland and grassland restoration, structure and debris removal, and planned facilities such as parking, fencing, and wildlife observation sites. They are also means for recording management activities to provide a history for future management decisions. As miniature comprehensive conservation plans, they are critical step-down plans to carry out the goals, objectives, and strategies outlined in this comprehensive conservation plan.

However, many WPAs lack development plans. With new technology employing Geographic Information Systems, this planning and recording of management actions has become simpler and faster, as illustrated in Figure 9. Each District is currently setting up a GIS planning system, but the entering of data is hampered by lack of staffing devoted to the effort. In addition, once all plans are done, they will need to be updated on a rotational basis to be useful in the future.

Consistent Use

The visiting public, WPA neighbors, local units of government, and the Minnesota Department of Natural Resources benefit when management and permitted uses on WPAs are consistent from one end of the State to the other. This comprehensive conservation plan provides the opportunity to articulate policies that have been in place for many years but have not always been consistently applied or communicated. New national policies and regulations governing management and use of the Refuge System also prompted a review and fine tuning of what uses will and will not be allowed, and the stipulations all Districts will follow when allowing certain uses.

Figure 9: GIS for WPA Development Planning

GIS used for initial planning:

- Identification and delineation of existing and potential habitats and structures (parking lots, fences, etc.)
- Area/length measurements
- Cost and material calculations
- Generate development schedule

Dovray WPA Development Schedule

5/3/01

FEATURE	UNIT NAME	DESCRIPTION	PRIORITY	STATUS	DATE	ACRES
Grass_Seeded_Warm						
Grass_Seeded_Warm	Dovray	seed local natives	1	Development Needed	5/1/02	1.1
Grass_Seeded_Warm	Dovray	seed local natives	1	Development Needed	5/1/02	55.9
	2					57.0
Wetland_Type_1						
Wetland_Type_1	Dovray	tile/ditch plug	1	Development Needed	8/15/01	0.4
Wetland_Type_1	Dovray	tile/ditch plug	1	Development Needed	8/15/01	0.3
Wetland_Type_1	Dovray	tile/ditch plug	1	Development Needed	8/15/01	0.2
Wetland_Type_1	Dovray	tile/ditch plug	1	Development Needed	8/15/01	0.1
Wetland_Type_1	Dovray	remove tile	1	Development Needed	8/15/01	0.1
	5					1.1
Building_Site						
Building_Site	Dovray	Remove/bury	1	Development Needed	9/30/01	0.5
	1					0.5
Other						
Other	Dovray	Parking Lot	2	Development Needed	9/15/02	0.1
	1					0.1

GIS Maps Assist Habitat Restoration and Other Development Activities

- On-site coordination with contractors and field staff.

- GIS used to document restoration and other development accomplishments.

-Development maps become the base map to record future

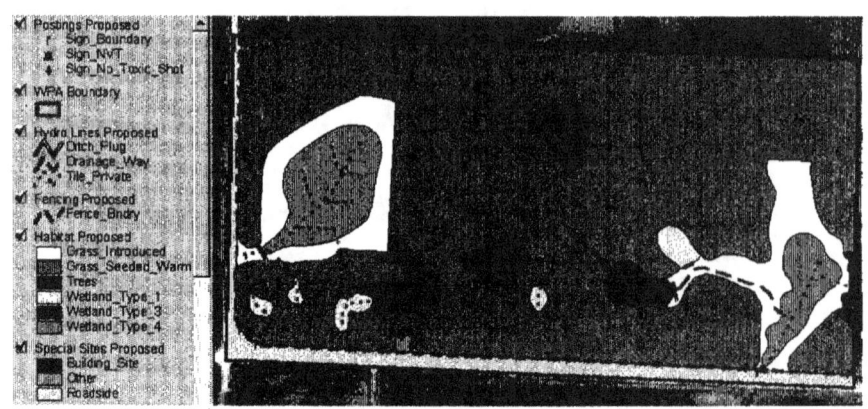

management accomplishments (ie. burning, weed control, etc.)

The following is a summary of generally prohibited and permitted uses and activities on WPAs in Minnesota. For each of the permitted activities, the reader is encouraged to review the compatibility determination for each found in Appendix E. Stipulations or operating guidelines in each compatibility determination will be followed by each District when administering the uses.

In addition to these policies, there will be a continuing need to ensure consistency of operations on a variety of management issues such as law enforcement, native seed types and seeding methods, signing, and land acquisition. Goal 10 speaks to this ongoing need.

Public Uses **Generally Prohibited**
- Off-road vehicle use, including snowmobiles and ATVs
- Camping
- Open fires
- Discharge of firearms except during State hunting seasons
- Use of motorized water craft
- Dog trials
- Horseback riding
- Commercial bait collecting
- Beekeeping

Public Uses Permitted (See Compatibility Determinations in Appendix E)
- Hunting in accordance with State seasons and regulations
- Wildlife observation
- Photography
- Fishing in accordance with State seasons and regulations
- Environmental education
- Interpretation for individuals or groups
- Trapping in accordance with State seasons and regulations
- Berry and nut collecting for personal use
- Limited plant and seed collection for decorative purposes

(Note: these uses include the use of non-motorized means of access including hiking, snowshoeing, cross-country skiing, or where appropriate, bicycling on existing trails)

Generally Permitted **Management** Activities Done by Others, **and** Miscellaneous Activities/Programs
(See Compatibility Determinations in Appendix E)
- Haying for grassland management
- Farming for grassland management
- Grazing for grassland management
- Timber or firewood harvest
- Food plots and feeders for resident wildlife
- Wildlife nesting structures
- Archaeological surveys
- Special access for disabled users
- Irrigation travelways across easement wetlands
- Temporary road improvement outside of existing right-of-way
- Special dedications/ceremonies
- Wetland access facilities
- WPA parking facilities
- Local Fire Department Training – Prescribed Burning

- Local Fire Department Training – Burning of Surplus Buildings on New Acquisitions

Other Reoccurring Uses Handled on Case-by-Case Basis
- New or expanded rights-of-way requests
- Major new facilities associated with public uses
- Commercial filming
- Special events
- Animal collecting requests
- Other requests for uses not listed above

Drainage

We often receive requests to maintain, improve, or construct drainage systems onto or across WPAs. The Morris Wetland Management District's drainage policy is included in this document as Appendix N. Briefly, legitimate drainage maintenance will be allowed to the original scope and effect of the drainage system. No new drainage will be allowed.

Chapter 4: Management Direction

Morris Wetland Management District

This chapter of the Comprehensive Conservation Plan steps down overall guidance to the Morris Wetland Management District through station-specific objectives and strategies. The objectives and strategies are unique to the Morris Wetland Management District and identify activities that achieve the Plan's goals, the District's purpose and the National Wildlife Refuge System mission (Chapters 1 and 2).

The Morris Wetland Management District, originally established in 1964 as the Benson Wetland Management District, includes the following Federal property: 246 WPAs totaling 51,208 acres in fee title ownership and 595 wetland easements encompassing 20,074 wetland acres, 27 habitat (grassland) easements covering 1,787 acres, 22 conservation easements covering 1,211 acres on property formerly controlled by the Farmers Home Administration, and two easement units of the Northern Tallgrass Prairie National Wildlife Refuge covering 110 acres. Both fee and easement areas are scattered throughout Big Stone, Chippewa, Lac Que Parle, Pope, Stevens, Swift, Traverse, and Yellow Medicine counties. The total surface area of the eight-county district is 3,334,580 acres. The total Fish and Wildlife Service property interest of 74,390 acres (excluding Big Stone NWR) represents 2.2 percent of the total area of the District.

The topography of west-central Minnesota is extremely diversified, ranging from the granite outcrops of the Minnesota River bottoms to the rolling hills of Pope County. The flat agricultural land of the Red River Valley of the north blends into the transition zone between the tall grass prairie and the eastern deciduous forest. Soils of the region are generally productive, which contributed to the historically high concentrations of breeding waterfowl.

Major Habitat Types of Waterfowl Production Areas
in the Morris Wetland Management District (in acres)

Native Prairie (virgin)	7,035
Other Grasslands/Farmland	23,969
Forested/Brushland	2,268
Wetland/Riverine	17,936

Figure 10: Morris Wetland Management District

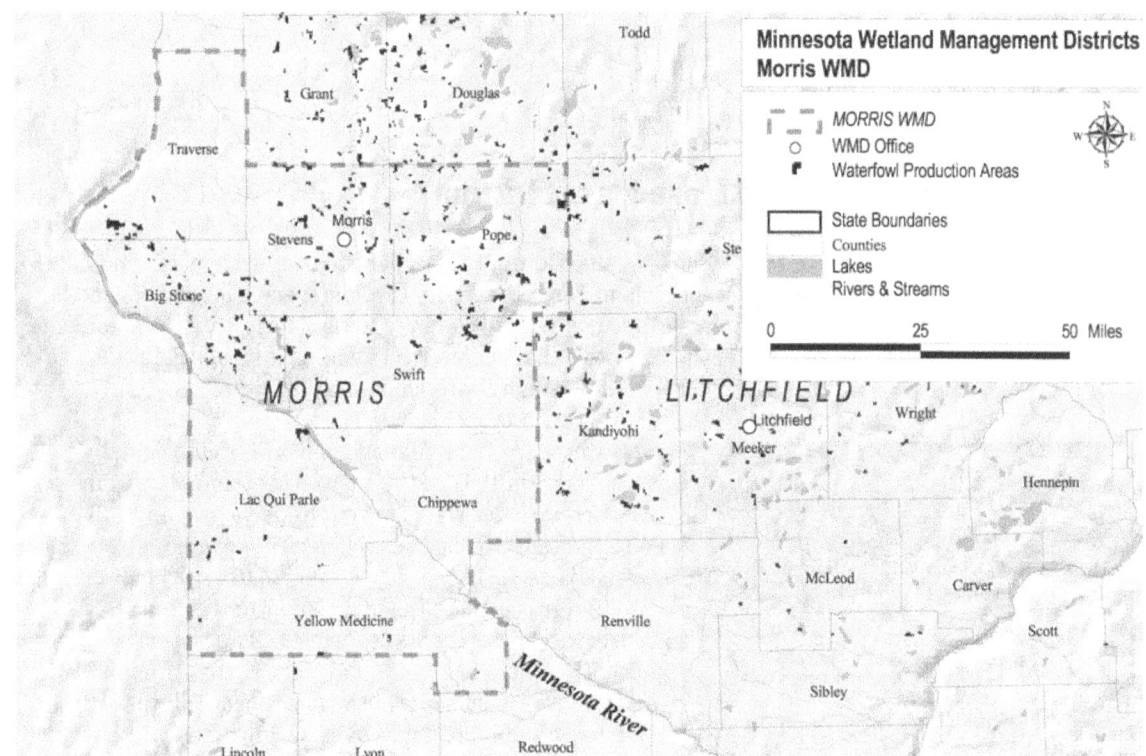

Goals, Objectives and Strategies

Wildlife and Habitat

Goal 1: Wildlife

Strive to preserve and maintain diversity and increase the abundance of waterfowl and other key wildlife species in the Northern Tallgrass Prairie Ecosystem. Seek sustainable solutions to the impact of Canada Geese on adjacent private croplands. Preserve, restore, and enhance resident wildlife populations where compatible with waterfowl and the preservation of other trust species.

Objective 1.1:   Update MAAPE Process. The District will request the Fergus Falls Habitat and Population Evaluation Team (HAPET) to review the "Multi-Agency Approach to Planning and Evaluation" (MAAPE) process every 5 years to incorporate monitoring results and reevaluate strategies for increasing waterfowl production within the Districts.

　　　　　　　　Strategy 1.1.1:　Update MAAPE in 2004: Contact HAPET office in 2003 to schedule a review of MAAPE waterfowl production issues and opportunities for 2004. RONS Project No. 99001

Objective 1.2:   Alternative Waterfowl Monitoring. The District will develop alternative monitoring techniques by the year 2007 for waterfowl abundance and productivity estimates in areas of Districts that are not well-covered by the four-square-mile monitoring program. These estimates should be developed in cooperation with the HAPET office since the current 4-square-mile data is used in the mallard model and forms the basis of the MAAPE process.

Strategy 1.2.1: Improve Population Monitoring Techniques: Work with HAPET office to identify information gaps inhibiting waterfowl abundance and productivity estimates. RONS Project No. 99004

Strategy 1.2.2: Improve Population Monitoring: Obtain information to allow monitoring of waterfowl abundance and productivity for species not covered by 4-square-mile survey. RONS Project No. 99004

Objective 1.3: Recruitment Rate. The District will strive to increase potential recruitment rate of mallards in an average year from the current level of 0.52 to 0.60 by 2015.

Strategy 1.3.1: Nest Structures on WPAs: Annually maintain 300 hen-house nesting structures and 100 wood duck boxes on WPAs. RONS Project No. 97001

Strategy 1.3.2: Nest Structures on Private Land: Annually provide 300 hen-house nesting structures and 100 wood duck boxes for use on private land until 7,750 hen houses are maintained and used on private and public land. RONS Project No. 97001

Strategy 1.3.3: Intensive Nesting Site Management: Conduct comprehensive analysis of district for islands, peninsulas, and other sites with high potential for intensive management, including predator control. Strive for 100 acres of peninsula cutoffs, 1,218 acres of predator exclosures, and four managed natural islands. RONS Project No. 97024

Strategy 1.3.4: Construct Nesting Islands: Create 13 nesting islands on existing WPAs on previously identified sites. RONS Project No. 99002

Strategy 1.3.5: Remove Hostile Habitat: On WPAs, remove rock piles, junk piles, and woody cover identified as hostile habitat for waterfowl and not essential for resident wildlife. RONS Project No. 98030

Strategy 1.3.6: Promote Coyote Populations: Work with sporting and agricultural communities to promote stable, viable coyote populations in suitable parts of the District. RONS Project No. 99003

Objective 1.4: Violations. Each year, the District will inspect all WPA, FmHA Conservation Easement and Habitat Easement for compliance to insure protection of migratory waterfowl and other habitats. Any illegal activity will be responded to immediately and restored as soon as possible.

Strategy 1.4.1: WPA and Easement Enforcement: Obtain adequate staff to monitor WPAs and easements. RONS Project No. 97012

Objective 1.5: Working With Partners. The District will cooperate with all USDA, Minnesota DNR and any other local agency programs as well as participate as a partner with local conservation groups which would increase waterfowl habitat and production.

Strategy 1.5.1: Fully Participate in Partnership opportunities. Increase staff ability to participate financially and technically in partnerships leading to improved waterfowl habitat and production. RONS Project No. 99020

Objective 1.6: Identify, evaluate, and prioritize opportunities to reintroduce native species documenting the needs in a plan by 2007.

Strategy 1.6.1: Organize coordination meeting with partners for 2006. RONS Project No. 97005

Objective 1.7: By 2010 begin a reintroduction program to reintroduce one species per year until all goal species identified under Objective 1.6 are reintroduced.

Strategy 1.7.1: Develop reintroduction plan for species and implement. RONS Project Nos. 99023, 99035

Objective 1.8: Develop a Memorandum of Understanding with the Minnesota DNR which clearly articulates the responsibilities of Wetland Districts for the handling of landowner complaints originating from geese on WPA wetlands.

Strategy 1.8.1: Participate in actions as outlined in MOU. RONS Project No. 99024

Objective 1.9: Cooperation. The Districts will cooperate with state wildlife offices and local organizations to provide winter food sources on documented wintering areas to benefit resident species of wildlife.

Strategy 1.9.1: Identify Needs: By 2004, identify with DNR crucial resident wildlife winter food needs on WPAs. RONS Project No. 99022

Strategy 1.9.2: Identify Options: By 2004, identify with DNR viable winter food options for resident wildlife on WPAs. RONS Project No. 99022

Strategy 1.9.3: Identify Unit Management Actions: By 2005, identify management actions on units with critical resident wildlife winter food needs. Eliminate food plots on non-critical areas.

Goal 2: Habitat

Restore native prairie plant communities of the Northern Tallgrass Prairie Ecosystem using local ecotypes of seed and maintain the vigor of these stands through natural processes. Restore functioning wetland complexes and maintain the cyclic productivity of wetlands. Continue efforts for long-term solutions to the problem of invasive species with increased emphasis on biological control to minimize damage to aquatic and terrestrial communities. Continue efforts to better define the role of each District in assisting private landowners with wetland, upland and riparian restorations.

USFWS Photo

Objective 2.1: Prairie Restoration. Restore an average of 500 acres in fee title to native seeded grassland species each year. Begin the process on all new acquisitions within 5 years of purchase. Seed a diverse mix of predominantly native grasses and forbes using the ecotype recommendations of the Mississippi Headwater Tallgrass Prairie Ecosystem Team. Replicate, to the extent possible, the structure, species composition, and processes of native ecological communities in the Tallgrass Prairie to improve migratory bird habitat and improve existing soil and water quality within respective watersheds. Judiciously use non-native plantings when desirable to meet waterfowl and migratory bird population objectives.

Strategy 2.1.1: Plant Native Grasslands: Convert an average of 500 acres per year of cropland to native vegetation. RONS Project Nos. 97011, 97017, and 97019

Strategy 2.1.2: New Seeding Technique: Experiment with new seeding techniques including fall seeding and broadcast seeding and broadcast seeding minimally cleaned seed. RONS Project No. 99006

Strategy 2.1.3: Local Ecotype Seed: Working with others, by 2008 produce or have access to eight grass and 30 forb species that are all local genotype tallgrass prairie natives in sufficient quantity to seed 1,000 acres per year. RONS Project No. 99006

Objective 2.2: Grassland Management. Renovate and seed or interseed 500 acres of existing grasslands to improve diversity and vigor.

Strategy 2.2.1: Replace Poor Cover on WPAs: Reseed or interseed 500 acres per year of existing inferior cover on WPAs to a diverse mix of native species. RONS Project Nos. 97015, 97016

Objective 2.3:   Prescribed Burn. Plan and conduct prescribed burns on 3,000-5,000 acres annually to maintain and restore native prairie plant species to improve waterfowl and wildlife utilization, and to prepare selected sites for native seed harvest.

Strategy 2.3.1:   Expand Burning Season: Expand burning season beyond current spring season to include summer and fall. Maintain program if monitoring confirms that alternate seasons produce desired effects. RONS Project No. 99007

Strategy 2.3.2:   Employ Two Prescribed Fire Crews: Employ and equip two trained prescribed fire crews to allow two simultaneous prescribed fires. RONS Project No. 98010

Strategy 2.3.3:   Hire Contract Prescribed Fire Crews: Identify and implement opportunities for accomplishing prescribed fires through contractors. RONS Project No. 99008

Objective 2.4:   Manage existing WPA and easement grasslands so that each acre is treated at least once every 7 years by burning, mowing, haying, grazing, or other management.

Strategy 2.4.1:   Increase acres managed by mowing. RONS Project No. 99009

Strategy 2.4.2:   Increase acres managed by grazing. RONS Project No. 97015

Strategy 2.4.3:   Increase acres managed by haying. RONS Project No. 97015

Strategy 2.4.4:   Identify and eliminate woody cover that is hostile to grassland species and which is not critical for resident wildlife. Woody cover will include old farm groves, field windbreaks, and woody species invading grasslands. RONS Project Nos. 97008, 99021

Objective 2.5:   Restoration. Restore an average of 100 wetlands per year both on and off refuge system land to serve migratory birds as migration, breeding and nesting habitat.

Strategy 2.5.1:   Increase outreach effort to identify and restore wetlands. RONS Project No. 97021

Objective 2.6:   Management. Manage water levels on 100 percent of the wetlands that have built-in water control structures to increase vegetation and nutrient recycling for the benefit of waterfowl.

Strategy 2.6.1:   New Water Control Structures: Install water control structures on 10 appropriate wetlands that now have fixed spillways. RONS Project No. 99010

Strategy 2.6.2   Remove existing water control structures from sites where they are not functional.

Objective 2.7:   Monitoring. Inventory hydrological systems in the Districts as identified in the monitoring plan, including chemical water analysis, water level, water flow and the interaction of Federal lands and private lands within the watershed.

Strategy 2.7.1:   Inspect all water control structures and determine management needs on an annual basis to improve marsh productivity as brood rearing and breeding habitat for migratory birds. RONS Project No. 99010

Strategy 2.7.2:   Conduct regular surveys of water conditions within the Districts as identified in the Monitoring Plan. RONS Project No. 99011

Strategy 2.7.3:   Monitor the impact of wetlands on hydrology within the watershed as identified in the Monitoring Plan. RONS Project No. 99011

Strategy 2.7.4:   Conduct water analysis to monitor changes in contaminants and other key chemicals over time as identified in the Monitoring Plan. RONS Project No. 99016

Objective 2.8:   Cooperation. Attend and participate in watershed district meetings.

Strategy 2.8.1:   Watersheds: Continue regular participation in Bois de Sioux and Upper Minnesota River watershed district activities and participate in other watersheds as appropriate. RONS: None

Objective 2.9:   Research. Encourage and cooperate in research on hydrological systems within the District.

Strategy 2.9.1:   Research: Continue to cooperate with others on hydrological research and offer Federal lands as potential research sites. RONS Project No. 99017

Strategy 2.9.2:   Pattern Tiling: Offer to participate with watershed and other groups to determine the watershed impact of increased pattern tiling. RONS Project No. 99011

Objective 2.10: Management. Increase use of hydrological data gathering in the overall management of the Districts following the guidance developed in the Monitoring Plan.

Strategy 2.10.1: Follow guidance developed in water monitoring plan.

Objective 2.11: Hydrologist. Hire a hydrologist to conduct hydrological monitoring program, analyze the data and present the information to management in a usable form.

Strategy 2.11.1: Have annual meetings for hydrologists throughout the Districts to share information, techniques, and results. RONS Project No. 99011

Strategy 2.11.2: The hydrologist should summarize hydrological data in an annual report and identify how the hydrological data can be incorporated in management decisions for the benefit of waterfowl and other target populations. RONS Project No. 99011

Strategy 2.11.3: Hydrologist should monitor contaminants in the wetlands within the District on a regular basis as outlined in the Monitoring Plan. RONS Project No. 99016

USFWS Photo

Objective 2.12: Plant Control. Reduce exotic plants including noxious weeds on state and county lists through an aggressive program including burning, mowing, chemical treatment, hand cropping, and interseeding. Primary targets include purple loosestrife, Canada thistle, and leafy spurge.

Strategy 2.12.1: Improve mechanical and chemical weed control. RONS Project Nos. 98031, 97004, and 97008

Objective 2.13: Minnow and Carp Control. Working with partners, by 2010 carp and undesirable minnow populations will be controlled on 90 percent of infested WPA wetlands through water level control, reduced minnow stocking, barriers, and chemical control.

Strategy 2.13.1: Monitoring and Control Plan. Work with Service and Minnesota DNR fisheries biologists to develop a control strategy and monitoring plan. RONS Project No. 99015

Objective 2.14:   Grasshopper Control: We will work with Minnesota Department of Agriculture to devise an appropriate emergency grasshopper control plan by 2008 so that future infestations are handled effectively and in a way that minimizes or eliminates insecticide use on WPAs for grasshopper control.

Strategy 2.14.1: Grasshoppers: Contact Minnesota Department of Agriculture in 2006 to begin planning process. RONS Project No. 97005

Objective 2.15:   Biological Control: Increase emphasis on biological control whenever feasible. The District will continue to release beetles for control of spurge and loosestrife as appropriate.

Strategy 2.15.1: Promote and use biological control. RONS Project Nos. 98031, 97004, and 97008

Strategy 2.15.2: Spurge: By 2003, eliminate chemical control of leafy spurge by releasing control beetles on 100 percent of known WPA infestations.

Goal 3: Acquisition

Within current acquisition acreage goals, identify the highest priority acres for acquisition taking into account block size and waterfowl productivity data. These priority areas should drive acquisition efforts whenever possible. Service land acquisition should have no negative impact on net revenues to local government. Understand and communicate the economic effects of federal land ownership on local communities.

Objective 3.1:   Evaluating Acquisition Priority. Review and update the current acquisition guidelines by the year 2003. Acquisition strategies for future acquisitions within the Districts will be based on site potential. Consideration should be given to size, quality, key species affected, habitat fragmentation, landscape scale complexes, potential productivity of restored wetlands, etc.

Strategy 3.1.1: Land Acquisition Guidelines: Staff making land acquisition decisions will consider issues presented in an acquisition form that highlights biological and management factors affecting acquisition decisions. RONS: None

Objective 3.2:   Goal Acres. By 2005, conduct a biological assessment to determine if current goal acres will be sufficient to reach waterfowl recruitment objectives for the District.

Strategy 3.2.1: Biological Assessment: Work with other districts to complete biological assessment. RONS Project No. 99004

Objective 3.3:   Coordination. The District will coordinate with the District Acquisition Office to insure rapid response to willing seller offers that meet the acquisition priorities. An offer will be made to the seller within 6 months of the decision to acquire the tract.

    Strategy 3.3.1:   Rapid Decision : If interested in acquiring a tract, the WMD staff will notify the Acquisition Office within 1 month of the initial land owner contact of their interest in proceeding with the acquisition. RONS Project No. 99005

    Strategy 3.3.2:   Rapid Offer: The Acquisition Office will make an offer within 5 months of receiving the statement of interest from the WMD staff. RONS: None

    Strategy 3.3.3:   Delineations on GIS: By 2004, all existing delineation information will be incorporated into the GIS, allowing better and faster delineation decisions. RONS Project No. 99005

Objective 3.4:   Acquisition. The District will meet current District goal acres within 15 years by acquiring an average of 1,630 acres in fee title, 3,335 acres of wetland easements and 1,660 acres of upland easements per year, for waterfowl breeding and use. This objective will be modified as appropriate if the goal acres are modified.

    Strategy 3.4.1:   Use GIS for Acquisition: Use GIS capabilities to analyze historic and current information to assist with identifying acquisition focus areas. RONS Project No. 99005

    Strategy 3.4.2:   Identify Willing Sellers: Contact landowners of key parcels to establish relationship and inform them of our interest in fee or easement acquisition if they are interested. RONS Project No. 97022

    Strategy 3.4.3:   Communicate with Counties: Improve communication with counties concerned about federal land acquisition. RONS Project No. 97022

Objective 3.5:   Advocate 100 percent of revenue sharing and a lump sum payment for past underpayment through a trust fund to the counties.

    Strategy 3.5.1:   Briefing: Regions 3 and 6 will participate in a briefing of top Fish and Wildlife Service leaders in 2003 to discuss revenue sharing issues. RONS: None

    Strategy 3.5.2:   Lump Sum Trust Payment: Inform agency leaders and outside parties that a one-time, lump sum trust fund payment to counties is a potential solution to revenue sharing problem. RONS: None

Objective 3.6:   Conduct a study that would provide the following information to managers so that they can better communicate the issue to the public:

1) A graph of revenue sharing for the last 20 years.

2) A detailed explanation of the impact of federal ownership on school taxes.

3) A detailed study of the trust fund payments to the state in relation to the revenue sharing shortfall.

4) How much money do we really need to make up the trust fund from 1993 and prior.

Strategy 3.6.1: Support Realty Search: Encourage and support examination of revenue sharing details to be conducted by regional realty office.

Objective 3.7:   Determine local economic value of Federal land ownership.

Strategy 3.7.1: Support research: Support ongoing research on economic effects of public land ownership.

Objective 3.8:   Demonstrate the hydrologic benefits of restored wetlands; determine cash value of wetland values.

Strategy 3.8.1: USGS and Red River Watershed Study: Participate in planned research by USGS and Red River Watershed working group to measure flood control values of wetlands. RONS Project No. 99017

Objective 3.9:   Determine social value of natural habitat in the landscape. Determine importance of wildlife to people in a community.

Strategy 3.9.1: Measure WPA Aesthetic Values: By 2008, estimate economic benefit of aesthetic values provided by public lands. RONS Project No. 99003

Goal 4: Monitoring

Collect baseline information on plants, fish and wildlife and monitor critical parameters and trends of key species and/or species groups on and around District units. Promote the use of coordinated, standardized, cost effective, and defensible methods for gathering and analyzing habitat and population data. Management decisions will be based on the resulting data.

Objective 4.1:   Inventory and Monitoring Workshop: Conduct an inventory and monitoring workshop by 2005 with recognized researchers in the field to identify monitoring needs, approaches, strategies and target species.

Strategy 4.1.1: Coordinate workshop with Regional Biologist.

Objective 4.2:   Inventory and Monitoring Plan. Develop an Inventory and Monitoring Plan by 2007 that will identify census needs and appropriate techniques as part of a coordinated monitoring program that will be used to evaluate species richness within the Districts by developing species data and accounts on selected sites.

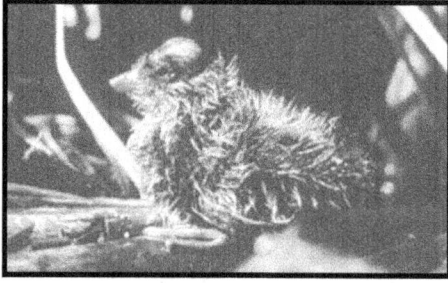

Strategy 4.2.1: Biologist will develop plan. RONS Project No. 97005

Objective 4.3:   Geographic Information System. Increase use of GIS technology in monitoring habitat and wildlife (See operations section for details). RONS Project No. 97009

Objective 4.5:   Increase the use of biological data in the overall management of the Districts by fulfilling the actions identified in the Inventory and Monitoring Plan and the following: .

Strategy 4.5.1: Annual Meeting. Have annual meetings for biologists and field personnel to share information, techniques and results of management strategies on target populations. RONS Project No. 97005

Strategy 4.5.2: Data Summaries. The biologist should summarize data concerning the impact of management strategies on target species and present to management so decisions can be based on monitoring information. RONS Project No. 97005

Objective 4.6:   Biological Inventory. As part of the Inventory and Monitoring Plan, inventory the biological resources on the Districts by the year 2010.

Strategy 4.6.1: Biological Monitoring: Conduct inventory and monitoring annually according to plan. RONS Project No. 99013

Objective 4.7:   Breeding Birds. Conduct regular surveys of breeding grassland and wetland migratory birds. Include information on reproductive success as well as abundance following techniques identified in the Inventory and Monitoring Plan.

> *Strategy 4.7.1:* Hire Technician to assist with monitoring. RONS Project No. 99013

Objectives 4.8:   Monitoring. Monitor the levels of external threats to the Waterfowl Production Units such as soil erosion, incoming water quality, pesticide use, and contaminants as identified in the Inventory and Monitoring Plan.

> *Strategy 4.8.1:* Contract Monitoring: Hire contaminants monitoring firm to conduct a thorough investigation of impacts to WPAs over a 4-year period. RONS Project No. 99016

Goal 5: Endangered Species / Unique Communities

Preserve enhance, and restore rare native northern tallgrass prairie, flora and fauna that are or may become endangered. Where feasible in both ecological and social/economic terms, reintroduce native species on WPAs in cooperation with the Minnesota DNR.

Objective 5.1:   Threatened and Endangered Species. Identify and survey threatened and endangered species within the District looking specifically for species of special interest.

> *Strategy 5.1.1:* Incorporate surveys into monitoring plan and implement. RONS Project Nos. 97005, 99013

Objective 5.2:   Invertebrates. Conduct regular surveys of invertebrate communities in grassland and wetland communities following the approaches identified in the Inventory and Monitoring Plan.

> *Strategy 5.2.1:* Incorporate surveys into monitoring plan and implement. RONS Project Nos. 97005, 99013

Objective 5.3:   Research. Encourage and cooperate in research that will further our understanding about management and habitat manipulations on the District.

> *Strategy 5.3.1:* Collaborative Research: We will encourage collaborative projects with research institutions. RONS Project No. 97005

Objective 5.4:   Partners for Fish and Wildlife. With the Partners for Fish and Wildlife staff in the Regional Office, develop clear guidance for upland and riparian restoration work so each District is managing the program consistently.

Strategy 5.4.1: Help develop guidance and implement upland and riparian restoration work. RONS Project No. 99014

Objective 5.5: Inventory and Monitoring. The District will identify the location of endangered and threatened species within the District boundaries through the Inventory and Monitoring Plan. The District will obtain baseline data including maps of all federally endangered and threatened species by 2005.

Strategy 5.5.1: Priority Inventory: Make threatened and endangered species inventories a high priority within District monitoring plan being developed.

Objective 5.6: Management. The District will protect and enhance populations of endangered, threatened, and special emphasis species indigenous on District lands. Management applications applied to these areas will be tailored to meet species management needs.

Strategy 5.6.1: Habitat Management: Examine habitat management practices and management unit block size for all units with endangered, threatened, or special emphasis species present. RONS Project No. 97005

Objective 5.7: Cooperation. The Districts will work with partners and other agencies to develop specific plans for target species occurring within the Districts.

Strategy 5.7.1: Special Concern Work Groups: Promote one or more multi-agency work groups to identify and promote management needs for special concern species. RONS Project No. 97005

Objective 5.8: Enforcement. The Districts will enforce all Endangered Species Act and Migratory Bird Treaty Act regulations within the District through increased contacts with hunters, neighbors and visitors.

Strategy 5.8.1: Hire enforcement officer. RONS Project No. 97012

Objective 5.9: Monitoring. The Districts will obtain baseline data including maps of all federally endangered and threatened species as well as all native prairie tracts, calcareous fens and oak savannah by 2005.

Objective 5.10: Cooperation. The Districts will identify threatened Northern Tallgrass Prairie unique communities and work through the Tall Grass Prairie Habitat Preservation Area project partners or other agencies and partners to acquire in fee title or protect through easement where the Small Wetlands Acquisition Program is not appropriate. All remaining native prairie remnants larger than 5 acres will by identified by 2005 and strategies for their protection will be developed by the year 2005.

Strategy 5.10.1: Scorecard Team: Serve on existing multi-agency "scorecard team" which identifies prairie remnants, ranks them, and assigns a responsible partner for action. RONS: None

Objective 5.11: Enforcement. The Districts will prohibit the introduction of wildlife species that are not native to the Northern Tallgrass Prairie Ecosystem.

Strategy 5.11.1: Maintain policy of prohibiting introduction of exotics on WPAs. RONS: None

Objective 5.12: Develop priority actions to be implemented by the Partners for Fish and Wildlife Program with the strategies to be developed in a joint effort by all districts by 2004 with the Morris Wetland Management District taking the lead and responsible for the documentation.

Strategy 5.12.1: Identify Actions: Participate in a statewide Partners for Fish and Wildlife Meeting in 2003 which identifies priority actions. RONS: None

People

Goal 6: Public Use/ Environmental Education

Provide opportunities for the public to use the WPAs in a way that promotes understanding and appreciation of the Prairie Pothole Region. Promote greater understanding and awareness of the Wetland Management District's programs, goals, and objectives. Advance stewardship and understanding of the Prairie Pothole Region through environmental education, outreach and partnership development.

Objective 6.1: Each Wetland Management District will strive to meet the National Visitor Service Standards for the Refuge System by the year 2005:

Strategy 6.1.1: Develop a Visitor Services Plan by 2005. RONS Project No. 99003

Strategy 6.1.2: Interpret key resources and issues by updating visitor center displays by 2004. RONS Project No. 97014 plus existing MMS project proposal.

Strategy 6.1.3: Provide quality wildlife observation and photography opportunities through continued trail development and at least one photographic blind on a WPA. RONS Project No. 97002

Strategy 6.1.4: Improve hunter access through parking area upgrades and informational signs. RONS Project No. 98018

Strategy 6.1.5: Investigate opportunities for improved recreational fishing opportunities by monitoring fish populations in each WPA. RONS Project No. 99015

Strategy 6.1.6: By 2003, cultivate a Friends Group focusing on the relationship between the City of Morris and the Long Lake-Edwards WPA. RONS Project No. 97006

Objective 6.2: Each Wetland Management District should have a full-time public use specialist by 2004.

Strategy 6.2.1: By 2004, hire an Outdoor Recreation Planner to develop and implement a quality environmental education program. RONS Project No. 97006

Objective 6.3: Each Wetland Management District should designate a Waterfowl Production Area in each county that will be handicapped accessible.

Strategy 6.3.1: Accessible WPAs: By 2010, provide enhanced accessibility to one WPA in each county and inform public. RONS Project No. 98033

Objective 6.4: Develop maps for each Wetland Management District that can be easily provided upon request by the public by 2003.

Strategy 6.4.1: Implement GIS generated maps in 2003.

Objective 6.5: Develop an outreach plan for the Morris Wetland Management District, following the Public Use Plan developed by Fergus Falls Wetland Management District. Address internal (within the Service) and external audiences by 2003.

Strategy 6.5.1: Write an Outreach Plan for the Morris WMD by 2005. RONS Project No. 99003

Objective 6.6: Promote greater understanding of the WMD program; implement the Public Use Plan for each District by 2006.

Strategy 6.6.1: Coordination Meeting: Identify outreach needs and opportunities during cross-regional wetland management district coordination meeting.

Strategy 6.6.2: Agency Leaders: Coordinate with other offices to invite and encourage current and future Service Directors, Deputy Directors, Refuge Division Chiefs, Regional Directors, and Refuge Programmatic Assistant Regional Directors to visit at least one wetland management district within one year of assuming their leadership position.

Objective 6.7: Increase environmental visits to WMD headquarters by 2006.

Strategy 6.7.1: Schools: Maintain and seek to increase environmental education visits by nearby elementary and secondary school students. Enhance use of headquarters area by University of Minnesota-Morris students for scholastic and recreational visits. RONS Project No. 97014

Operations

Goal 7: Development Plan

Preparation of WPA Development Plans: Complete Geographic Information System (GIS) based WPA Development Plans for each unit in each District. Provide Districts with GIS to assist with acquisition, restoration, management and protection of public and private lands.

Objective 7.1: The WMD will have computer support staff by 2005.

Strategy 7.1.1: Hire Computer and GIS Support: By 2005, hire a computer support specialist to oversee GIS and other office computer support and data entry. RONS Project No. 97009

Goal 8: Staff, Facilities and Equipment

Provide necessary levels of maintenance, technician and administrative support staff to achieve other Wetland Management District goals: Provide all Districts with adequate and safe office, maintenance and equipment storage facilities Acquire adequate equipment and vehicles to achieve other District goals. Maintain District equipment and vehicles at or above Service standards.

Objective 8.1: The staffing needs identified in this CCP are added as identified elsewhere in the plan.

Objective 8.2: Identify all buildings that do not meet service standards or needs by 2005.

Strategy 8.2.1: Space Needs Analysis: By 2005, conduct a comprehensive analysis of shop, storage, and office space and configuration needs expected for the next 15 years. RONS Project No. 99019

Objective 8.3: Construct, replace or modify buildings so that all buildings meet service standards and needs by 2010. RONS Project No. 99019

Objective 8.4: Ensure that all Wetland District vehicles are replaced when their mileage reaches normal industry replacement standards (6 years or 60,000). RONS: Existing MMS projects.

Objective 8.5:   Ensure that Wetland Management District office and field tools and equipments are adequate to fulfill this plan. RONS: Existing MMS projects.

Goal 9: Annual Capital Development Funds

Ensure that annual capital development funds are large enough to meet necessary development of new WPA land: Have adequate funds available each year to permit completion of maintenance needs for each Wetland Districts current land base of Waterfowl Production Areas.

USFWS Photo

Objective 9.1:   Educate and provide adequate information to Regional, Washington, departmental and congressional staffs of need for capital improvement funding of an ongoing acquisition program.

    Strategy 9.1.1: By 2004, identify costs of adding new lands to O&M budgets and communicate information. RONS Project No. 99036

Objective 9.2:   Maintain a current inventory of all maintenance needs, updating it annually.

    Strategy 9.2.1: Maintenance Management System: Analyze and modify maintenance management system lists of identified maintenance backlog. RONS: None

    Strategy 9.2.2: Erase Maintenance Backlog: By 2015, eliminate backlog of maintenance needs. RONS: Existing MMS list

Objective 9.3:   The Refuge Supervisor will summarize accomplishments combining all districts to demonstrate the work done through previous funding. RONS: None

Goal 10: Consistency Goal

Develop and apply consistent policies for habitat, public use, and resource protection and ensure frequent coordination among Districts, both in Minnesota and in neighboring states with WPAs (North and South Dakota, Iowa, and Wisconsin).

Objective 10.1:   All existing WPAs will have Development Plans completed by 2008.

    Strategy 10.1.1: Shift 100 percent of manual plans to GIS by 2005. RONS Project No. 97009

Objective 10.2:   Ensure that newly acquired land receives timely, effective unit planning to meet trust responsibilities within 2 years of taking possession of area.

Strategy 10.2.1: Shift to GIS based planning. RONS Project No. 97009

Objective 10.3: Quarterly coordination meetings for the WMDs will be held to discuss common issues and practices. The meetings will include all District managers and District supervisors.

Strategy 10.3.1: Attend and assist with coordination.

Objective 10.4: Once a year a regional meeting will be held to compare notes with managers in Region 6 and other Wetland Management Districts in Region 3 that are not included in this Comprehensive Conservation Plan.

Strategy 10.4.1: Coordinate 2002 cross-regional meeting.

Chapter 5: Plan Implementation

Essential Staffing, Mission-Critical Projects and Major Maintenance Needs

The Service relies on two systems to track the needs of the Wetland Management Districts and other units of the National Wildlife Refuge System. These systems are the Refuge Operating Needs System and the Maintenance Management System. Each station has scores of projects in each system, representing a need which is often beyond the realities of funding. However, each station has identified its most critical needs which form a realistic assessment of funding needed to meet many of the goals, objectives, and strategies identified in the CCP. These needs also form the basis for the President's budget request to Congress. These critical needs are listed below in the categories of essential staff, mission-critical projects, and major maintenance projects. A complete listing of projects in the Operating Needs System is found in Appendix F and it represents the long-term needs of Morris Wetland Management District to operate at optimum levels.

Essential Staffing Needs

Wildlife Biologist
Visitor Services Specialist

Mission-Critical Projects

Prairie Chicken Reintroductions
Native Prairie Restoration
Water Level Management
Visitor Services

Major Maintenance Projects

Replace Storage Building at Benson Site
Replace Roof on Maintenance Building
Replace Boundary Fences
Replace Tractor
12 Additional Projects

Total Funding Needs: $1,435,000

Step-down Management Plans

The draft list of Step-Down Management Plan necessary to implement the direction of the CCP include only the Inventory and Monitoring Plan, which will be completed December 2002.

Figure 11: Staffing Chart

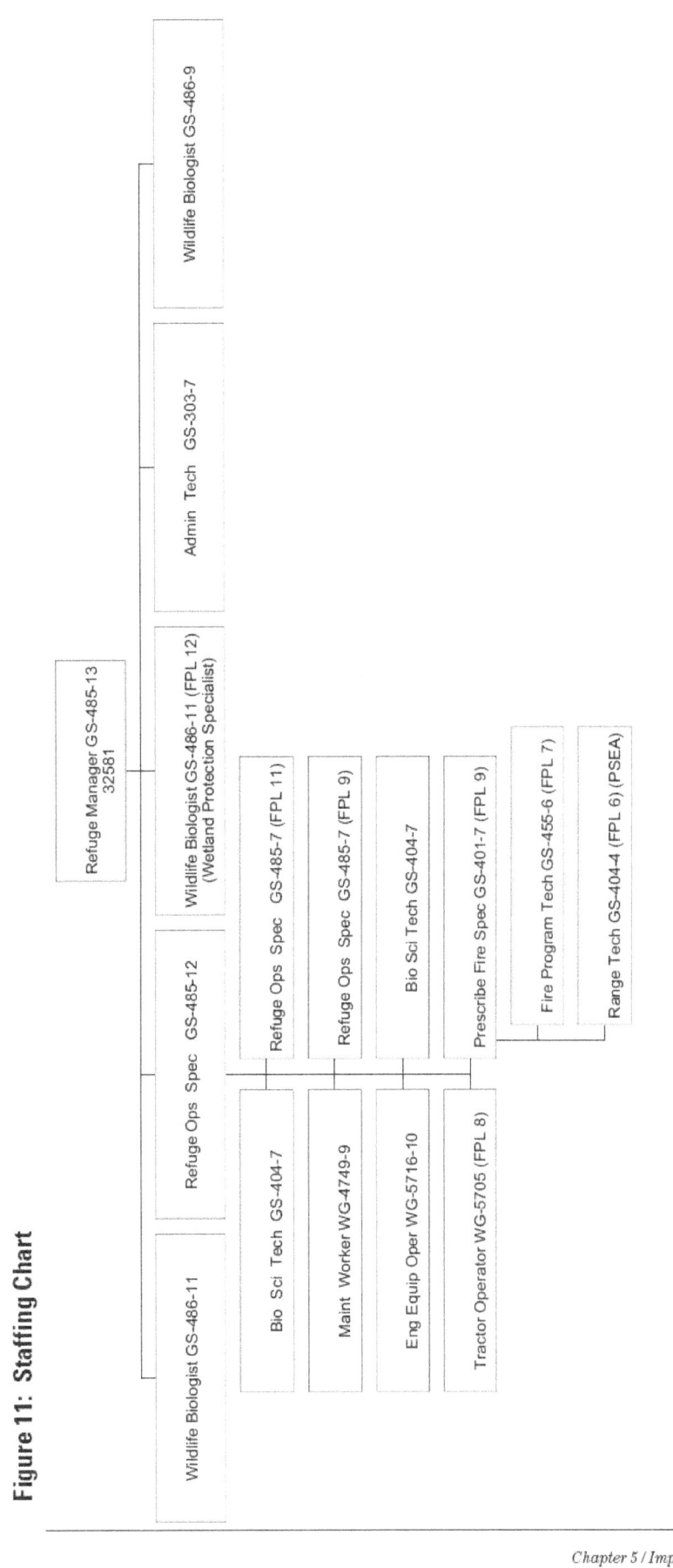

A cultural resource management plan will also be prepared to meet the requirements of Section 14 of the Archaeological Resources Protection Act and Section 110(a)(2) of the National Historic Preservation Act.

Partnership Opportunities

Within the Private Lands Program, the Refuge maintains partnerships with all eight county Soil and Water Conservation Districts, and local, state, other federal agencies, and other groups such as Ducks Unlimited, Pheasants Forever and Minnesota Waterfowl Association and watershed districts.

We will seek to develop partnerships with additional public and private groups as opportunities arise.

Monitoring and Evaluation

Monitoring is critical to successful implementation of this plan. Monitoring is necessary to evaluate the progress toward objectives and to determine if conditions are changing.

Accomplishment of the objectives described in this CCP will be monitored annually by the District Manager's supervisor. Successful performance will be tied to the accomplishment of objectives that are scheduled for that year. The public will be informed about the activities of the District staff through news releases and information on each District's web site.

The techniques and details for monitoring related to specific objectives will be specified in the Inventory and Monitoring Step Down Plan.

Substantial changes are likely to occur within the Service and the local community during the next 15 years. The Plan and its objectives will be examined at least every 5 years to determine if any modifications are necessary to meet the changing conditions.

Appendices

Appendix A: Authority and Legal Compliance

Appendix A
Authority And Legal Compliance

Wetland Management Districts Legal Mandate

The Migratory Bird Conservation Act was established on February 18, 1929, (45 Stat. 1222), as amended, 16 (U.S.C. 715d, 715e, 715f, to 715k and 715l to 715r). The Act provides for the acquisition of lands determined to be suitable as an inviolate sanctuary for migratory birds.

The Migratory Bird Hunting Stamp Act of March 16, 1934 was amended in 1958 and authorized the "...acquisition by gift, devise, lease, purchase, or exchange of, small wetland and pothole areas, interest therein, and right-of-way to provide access thereto. Such small areas to be designated as 'Waterfowl Productions Areas', may be acquired without regard to the limitations and requirements of the Migratory Bird Conservation Act,..."

"...As Waterfowl Production Areas" subject to "...all of the provisions of such Act...except the inviolate sanctuary provisions...."16 U.S.C. 718(c) (Migratory Bird Hunting and Conservation Stamp).

Mandate for FMHa Easements and Fee title Transfers. ."...for conservation purposes..." 7 U.S.C. at 2002 (Consolidated Farm and Rural Development Act).

Legal Context

In addition to the 1958 Ammendment to the Migratory Bird Hunting and Conservation Stamp Act 16 U.S.C. 718 (d) (c) and the National Wildlife Refuge System Improvement Act of 1997, the legal and policy guidance for the operation of national wildlife refuges are contained in the following documents or acts:

The work done by the Fish and Wildlife Service is largely mandated by a number of laws (Acts) and Executive Orders which pertain to the conservation and protection of natural and cultural resources. Those Acts and Executive Orders which are most important in establishing and administering the Wetland Management Districts (Districts) are listed below.

Migratory Bird Hunting and Conservation Stamp Act 16 U.S.C. 718 (d) (c)
National Wildlife Refuge System Improvement Act of 1997
Omnibus Parks and Public Lands Management Act of 1996 (Sec. 305, P.L. 104-333).
Title 50 of the Code of Federal Regulation, Subchapters B and C
Migratory Bird Hunting and Conservation Stamp Act (16 USC 718-718-h).
Migratory Bird Treaty Act of 1918 (16 USC 703-712).
National Environmental Policy Act of 1969 (PL 91-190, 42 USC 4321-4347).
Bald Eagle Protection Act of 1940 (16 USC 668-668d)
American Indian Religious Freedom Act (PL 95-341, [1978], 92 Stat. 42 USC 1996).
Antiquities Act (P.L. 59-209, approved 6/8/1906, 34 Stat. 225, 16 USC 431-433).
Reservoir Salvage Act, 16 USC 469).
Executive Order 13007 – Sacred Sites (5/24/1996).

National Environmental Policy Act of 1969 (NEPA). The purposes of the NEPA are to: declare a national policy which will encourage productive and enjoyable harmony between man and his environment; promote efforts which will prevent or eliminate damage to the environment and biosphere and stimulate the health and welfare of man; enrich the understanding of the ecological systems and natural resources important to the Nation; and establish a Council on Environmental Quality.

The Endangered Species Act of 1973, as amended. This Act ensures that projects not affect the continued existence of any endangered or threatened species in the project area or result in destruction or adverse modification of their critical habitats.

Executive Order 11988. E.O. 11988 directs Federal agencies to (1) avoid development in the floodplain unless it is the only practical alternative, (2) reduce the hazards and risks associated with floods, (3) minimize the impact of floods on human safety, health, and welfare, and (4) restore and preserve the natural and beneficial values of the floodplain.

Executive Order 11990. E.O. 11990 directs Federal agencies to (1) minimize destruction, loss, or degradation of wetlands and (2) preserve and enhance the natural and beneficial values of wetlands when a practical alternative exists.

Executive Order 12372 (Intergovernmental Review of Federal Programs). In compliance, the Service will send copies of the Environmental Assessment to State Planning Agencies for review.

Executive Order 12996 (Management and General Public Use of the National Wildlife Refuge System). E.O. 12996 provides directives to the Secretary of the Interior on compatible wildlife-dependent recreational activities (hunting, fishing, wildlife observation, photography, environmental education, and interpretation).

The Archeological Resources Protection Act of 1979. Section 14 of the Archaeological Resources Protection Act of 1979 requires an inventory program of all Federal lands. This Act expands upon the Antiquities Act to protect all archeological sites more than 100 years old on Federal land, and to ensure that archeological investigations on Federal land are performed in the public interest by qualified persons.

Uniform Relocation and Assistance and Real Property Acquisition Policies Act of 1970, as amended. This Act provides for uniform and equitable treatment of persons who sell their homes, businesses, or farms to the Service. The Act requires that any purchase offer be no less than the fair market value of the property.

The National Historic Preservation Act of 1966, as amended; Executive Order 11593 (Protection and Enhancement of the Cultural Environment); and Title 36, Code of Federal Regulations, Part 800 (Protection of Historic Properties). Section 106 of the National Historic Preservation Act of 1966 requires Federal agencies to consider the effects of their undertaking on properties meeting criteria for the National Register of Historic Places. The regulations in 36 CFR Part 800 describe how Federal agencies are to identify historic properties, determine effect on significant historic properties, and mitigate adverse effects. Section 110 of the 1966 Act codifies the salient elements from E.O. 11593, "to ensure that historic preservation is fully integrated into ongoing programs and missions of Federal agencies." Section 110 also requires each Federal agency to establish a program leading to inventory of all historic properties on its lands.

The Native American Graves Protection and Repatriation Act of 1990. Directs Federal agencies to protect Native American human remains and associated burial items located on or removed from Federal land.

Federal Farmland Protection Policy Act of 1981, as amended. The Act, is intended to minimize the extent to which a project would contribute to the conversion of farmland to nonagricultural uses.

Clean Water Act (Section 401 and 404). Section 404 of the Act is intended to protect access to and quality of the nation's waters by preventing the unnecessary loss of wetlands and other sensitive aquatic areas. Section 401 of the Act requires water quality certification prior to the issuance of a 404 permit and for other activities discharging into a water body.

Rivers and Harbor Act (Section 10 of 1899). Section 10 of this Act regulates the placement of fill in navigable waters of the United States.

Refuge Revenue Sharing Act of 1935, as amended. This act requires revenue sharing provisions to all fee-title ownerships that are administered solely or primarily by the Secretary through the Service.

Migratory Bird Conservation Act of 1929. The Act established the Migratory Bird Conservation Commission which consists of the Secretaries of the Interior (chairman), Agriculture, and Transportation, two members from the House of Representatives, and an ex-officio member from the state in which a project is located. The Commission approves acquisition of land and water, or interests therein, and sets the priorities for acquisition of lands by the Secretary for sanctuaries or for other management purposes. Under this Act, to acquire lands, or interests therein, the state concerned must consent to such acquisition by legislation. Such legislation has been enacted by most states.

Archaeological and Historic Preservation Act of 1974. This Act amends the Reservoir Salvage Act of 1960 to expand its provisions to the preservation of historic and archaeological data in all Federal or federally assisted or licensed construction projects that might otherwise be lost. This Act directs Federal agencies to notify the Secretary of the Interior whenever they find a Federal or federally assisted, licensed or permitted project may cause loss or destruction of significant scientific, prehistoric or archaeological data. Funds may be appropriated, donated and/or transferred for the recovery, protection and preservation of such data.

Fish and Wildlife Act of 1956. This Act initially established the Fish and Wildlife Service underthe Assistant Secretary for Fish and Wildlife and a Commissioner for Fish and Wildlife. The Service consisted of the Bureau of Sport Fisheries and Wildlife and a Bureau of Commercial Fisheries, each having a Director. In 1970, the Bureau of Commercial Fisheries was transferred to the Department of Commerce. The Act was amended by Public Law 93-271 to abolish the office of Commissioner and establish the U.S. Fish and Wildlife Service under a Director. Under this Act, the Secretary is authorized to take such steps as may be required for the development, advancement, management, conservation, and protection of fish and wildlife resources including but not limited to research, development of existing facilities, and acquisition by purchase or exchange of land and water or interests therein. The Act also authorizes the Service to accept gifts of real or personal property for its benefit and use in performing its activities and services. Such gifts qualify under Federal income, estate, or gift tax laws as a gift to the United States.

Fish and Wildlife Improvement Act of 1978. This act was passed to improve the administration of fish and wildlife programs and amends several earlier laws including the Refuge Recreation Act, the National Wildlife Refuge System Administration Act, and the Fish and Wildlife Act of 1956. It authorizes the Secretary to accept gifts and bequests of real and personal property on behalf of the United States. It also authorizes the use of volunteers on Service projects and appropriations to carry out a volunteer program.

Land and Water Conservation Fund Act of 1965. This Act provides funding through receipts from the sale of surplus Federal land, appropriations from oil and gas receipts from the outer continental shelf, and other sources for land acquisition under several authorities. Appropriations from the Fund may be used for matching grants to states for outdoor recreation projects and for land acquisition by various Federal agencies, including the Fish and Wildlife Service.

National Wildlife Refuge System Administration Act of 1966. This Act defines the National Wildlife Refuge System as including wildlife refuges, areas for the protection and conservation of fish and wildlife which are threatened with extinction, wildlife ranges, game ranges, wildlife management areas, and waterfowl production areas. The Secretary is authorized to permit any use of an area provided such use is compatible with the major purposes for which such area was established. The purchase consideration for rights-of-way go into the Migratory Bird Conservation Fund for the acquisition of lands. By regulation, up to 40 percent of an area acquired for a migratory bird sanctuary may be opened to migratory bird hunting unless the Secretary finds that the taking of any species of migratory game birds in more than 40 percent of such area would be beneficial to the species. The Act requires an Act of Congress for the divestiture of lands in the system, except (1) lands acquired with Migratory Bird Conservation Commission funds, and (2) lands can be removed from the system by land exchange, or if brought into the system by a cooperative agreement, then pursuant to the terms of the agreement.

Refuge Recreation Act of 1962. This Act authorizes the Secretary of the Interior to administer refuges, hatcheries, and other conservation areas for recreational use, when such uses do not interfere with the areas' primary purposes. It authorizes construction and maintenance of recreational facilities and the acquisition of land for incidental fish and wildlife oriented recreational development or protection of natural resources. It also authorizes the charging of fees for public use.

Appendix B: Priority Bird Species

Appendix B
Priority Bird Species

Appendix B contains a list of bird species that occur within the Morris WMD and have been designated as species of concern at three geographic scales.

(1) Region 3's Resource Conservation Priorities list includes rare/declining, federally-listed, recreationally important, and superabundant bird species that are of high concern in the Upper Midwest.

(2) The U. S. Fish and Wildlife Service's Birds of Conservation Concern list identifies priority species at the Bird Conservation Region (BCR) level (BCRs are ecological regions designated as conservation planning units by the North American Bird Conservation Initiative); the Morris WMD lies within BCR(s) 11 and 23.

(3) Bird species within the WMD that are on the Minnesota Department of Natural Resources list of endangered, threatened, and special concern species are noted because the Service and the DNR share management responsibility for them. The bird species on these collective lists are those that are of highest concern within the Morris WMD, and by focusing on these species, the WMD will address local, regional, and national priorities.

PRIORITY BIRD SPECIES OF THE MORRIS WETLAND MANAGEMENT DISTRICT

SPECIES	REGION 3 2002 RCP	BCR 11 2002 BCC	BCR 23 2002 BCC	MN DNR
Common Loon	X			
Horned Grebe				X
American White Pelican				X
Double-crested Cormorant	X			
American Bittern	X	X		
Least Bittern	X			
Black-crowned Night-Heron	X			
Snow Goose	X			
Canada Goose (residents)	X			
Canada Goose (migrants)	X			
Trumpeter Swan	X			X
Wood Duck	X			
Mallard	X			
Blue-winged Teal	X			
Northern Pintail	X			
Canvasback	X			
Lesser Scaup	X			
Bald Eagle	X			X
Northern Harrier	X	X		
Northern Goshawk	X			
Red-shouldered Hawk	X			X
Swainson's Hawk	X	X		
Peregrine Falcon	X	X	X	X
Greater Prairie-Chicken				X
Yellow Rail	X	X		X
King Rail	X			X
Piping Plover				X
Greater Yellowlegs	X		X	
Solitary Sandpiper		X		
Willet		X		
Upland Sandpiper	X	X	X	
Whimbrel	X			
Hudsonian Godwit	X	X	X	
Marbled Godwit	X	X	X	X
Sanderling		X		
White-rumped Sandpiper		X		
Stilt Sandpiper	X		X	
Buff-breasted Sandpiper	X	X	X	
Short-billed Dowitcher	X		X	
American Woodcock	X			
Wilson's Phalarope	X	X	X	X
Franklin's Gull				X
Common Tern	X		X	X
Forster's Tern	X			X
Black Tern	X		X	
Black-billed Cuckoo	X	X	X	
Long-eared Owl	X		X	

PRIORITY BIRD SPECIES OF THE MORRIS WETLAND MANAGEMENT DISTRICT

SPECIES	USFWS			MN DNR
	REGION 3 2002 RCP	BCR 11 2002 BCC	BCR 23 2002 BCC	
Short-eared Owl	X	X	X	X
Whip-poor-will	X			
Red-headed Woodpecker	X	X	X	
Northern Flicker	X			
Olive-sided Flycatcher	X			
Loggerhead Shrike	X	X	X	X
Bell's Vireo			X	
Sedge Wren	X		X	
Wood Thrush	X		X	
Blue-winged Warbler			X	
Golden-winged Warbler	X		X	
Cerulean Warbler			X	X
Connecticut Warbler	X			
Canada Warbler	X			
Field Sparrow	X			
Grasshopper Sparrow	X	X		
Henslow's Sparrow	X	X	X	X
LeConte's Sparrow	X	X		
Nelson's Sharp-tailed Sparrow	X	X		X
Chestnut-collard Longspur		X		
Dickcissel	X		X	
Bobolink	X		X	
Eastern Meadowlark	X			
Western Meadowlark	X			
Orchard Oriole	X			

KEY

REGION 3 2002 RCP: Species is on the U. S. Fish and Wildlife Service's 2002 Regional Resource Conservation Priorities list.

BCR 11 2002 BCC: Species is on the U. S. Fish and Wildlife Service's 2002 Birds of Conservation Concern list for the Prairie Potholes Bird Conservation Region (BCR 11).

BCR 23 2002 BCC: Species is on the U. S. Fish and Wildlife Service's 2002 Birds of Conservation Concern list for the Prairie Hardwood Transition Bird Conservation Region (BCR 23).

MN DNR: Species is on the Minnesota Department of Natural Resources species of concern list.

Appendix C: Species List

Appendix C: Species List

Plants of the Morris Wetland Management District, Minnesota

Note: this should be considered a working list of the plant species in the Morris Wetland Management District. It was compiled using plant species lists from Big Stone National Wildlife Refuge and the Fergus Falls Wetland Management District, along with the list of species that have been collected in the Morris District. An updated and accurate plant species list will be created in coming years as the District's Biological Inventory and Monitoring Program gets underway.

Grasses

Agrostis alba	red top
Agrostis stolonifera var. *palustris*	creeping bentgrass
Alopecurus carolinianus	Carolina foxtail
Andropogon gerardii	big bluestem
Aristida purpurea var. *longiseta*	red threeawn, Fendler threeawn
Bouteloua curtipendula	sideoats grama
Bouteloua gracilis	blue grama
Bouteloua hirsuta	hairy grama
Bromus commutatus	hairy chess, meadow brome
Bromus inermis	smooth brome
Bromus kalmii	Kalm's brome, prairie brome
Buchloe dactyloides	buffalo grass
Calamagrostis canadensis	bluejoint
Calamagrostis montanensis	plains reedgrass
Calamovilfa longifolia	sand reedgrass
Deschampsia caespitosa	tufted hairgrass
Dichanthelium leibergii	Leiberg's panic grass
Dichanthelium oligosanthes	Scribner's panic grass
Digitaria sanguinalis	large crabgrass, hairy crabgrass
Distichlis spicata	inland saltgrass
Elymus canadensis	Canada wildrye
Elymus repens	quackgrass
Elymus trachycaulus	slender wheatgrass
Elymus virginicus	Virginia wildrye
Eragrostis cilianensis	stinkgrass
Eragrostis spp.	Lovegrass
Hesperostipa comata	needleandthread
Hesperostipa spartea	porcupine grass
Hordeum jubatum	foxtail barley
Hordeum pusillum	little barley
Koeleria macrantha	Junegrass
Leersia oryzoides	rice cutgrass
Muhlenbergia cuspidata	plains muhly
Muhlenbergia richardsonis	mat muhly
Nassella viridula	green needlegrass
Panicum capillare	witchgrass
Panicum virgatum	switchgrass
Phalaris arundinacea	reed canarygrass

Phleum pratense	timothy
Phragmites australis	common reed
Poa arida	plains bluegrass, bunch speargrass
Poa compressa	Canada bluegrass
Poa pratensis	Kentucky bluegrass
Puccinellia nuttalliana	Nuttall alkaligrass
Schedonnardus paniculatus	tumblegrass
Schizachyrium scoparium	little bluestem
Setaria glauca	yellow foxtail
Sorghastrum nutans	Indiangrass
Spartina pectinata	prairie cordgrass
Sporobolus cryptandrus	sand dropseed
Sporobolus heterolepis	prairie dropseed
Torreyochloa pallida	pale false mannagrass

Aquatic Monocots

Caltha palustris	marsh marigold
Carex atherodes	slough sedge, wheat sedge
Carex hallii	Hall's sedge, deer sedge
Carex pseudocyperus	cypress-like sedge
Carex sterilis	sterile sedge
Carex tenera	quill sedge
Ceratophyllum demersum	coontail
Cyperus acuminatus	short-pointed umbrella sedge
Cyperus esculentus	yellow nutsedge, chufa
Eleocharis parvula	dwarf spikerush
Eleocharis quinqueflora	few-flowered spikerush
Juncus balticus	Baltic rush
Juncus dudleyi	Dudley's rush
Lemna spp.	duckweeds
Myriophyllhum spp.	watermilfoils
Potamogeton spp.	pondweeds
Rhynchospora capillacea	hair-like beak-rush
Sagittaria latifolia	arrowhead, duck potato
Schoenoplectus acutus	hardstem bulrush
Schoenoplectus fluviatilis	river bulrush
Schoenoplectus pungens	common three-square
Schoenoplectus tabernaemontani	softstem bulrush
Scirpus pallidus	pale bulrush
Scleria verticillata	whorled nutrush, low nutrush
Sparganium spp.	burreed
Typha angustifolia	narrow-leaved cattail
Typha latifolia	broad-leaved cattail
Vallisneria americana	wild celery, eelgrass
Zizania aquatica	wild rice

Trees and Shrubs

Acer negundo	boxelder
Acer saccharinum	silver maple
Alnus spp.	alder
Amelanchier spp.	serviceberry

Amorpha canescens	lead plant
Amorpha fruticosa	false indigo
Betula nigra	river birch
Betula pumila	bog birch
Carya cordiformis	bitternut hickory
Cephalanthus occidentalis	buttonbush
Cornus racemosa	grey-stemmed dogwood
Cornus sericea	redosier dogwood
Corylus americana	American hazel
Crataegus pruinosa	frosted hawthorn
Elaeagnus angustifolia	Russian olive
Fraxinus pennsylvanica	green ash
Juglans nigra	black walnut
Populus deltoides	cottonwood
Populus tremuloides	trembling aspen
Prunus americana	wild plum
Prunus virginiana	chokecherry
Quercus coccinea	scarlet oak
Quercus ellipsoidalis	northern pin oak
Quercus macrocarpa	bur oak
Quercus rubra	northern red oak
Rhus glabra	smooth sumac
Ribes americanum	currant
Rosa arkansana	prairie rose
Rubus spp.	raspberry
Salix amygdaloides	peachleaf willow
Salix interior	sandbar willow
Salix nigra	black willow
Symphoricarpos occidentalis	wolfberry, snowberry
Tilia americana	American basswood
Ulmus americana	American elm
Ulmus pumila	Siberian elm
Zanthoxylum americanum	common prickly-ash

Vines

Calystegia sepium	hedge false bindweed
Clematis virginiana	virgin's bower, devil's darning needles
Convolvulus arvensis	field bindweed
Cuscuta spp.	dodder
Menispermum canadense	Canada moonseed
Vitis riparia	riverbank grape

Forbs

Achillea millefolium	common yarrow
Agalinis auriculata	eared false foxglove
Agoseris glauca	prairie dandelion
Allium canadense	wild garlic, meadow garlic
Allium cernuum nodding	wild onion
Allium stellatum	prairie onion
Allium tricoccum	wild leek

Ambrosia artemisiifolia	common ragweed
Ambrosia psilostachya	western ragweed
Anemone canadensis	meadow anemone, Canada anemone
Anemone cylindrica	thimbleweed
Antennaria parvifolia	small-leaved pussytoes
Apocynum cannabinum	Indian hemp, dogbane
Aquilegia canadensis	columbine
Aralia nudicaulis	wild sarsaparilla
Artemisia absinthium	wormwood sage, absinth wormwood
Artemisia campestris	green sagewort, western sagewort
Artemisia dracunculus	green sagewort, tarragon
Artemisia frigida	prairie sagewort, fringed sagewort
Artemisia ludoviciana	white sage, cudweed sagewort
Asclepias amplexicaulis	blunt-leaved milkweed
Asclepias hirtella	green milkweed
Asclepias incarnata	swamp milkweed
Asclepias speciosa	showy milkweed
Asclepias sullivantii	Sullivant's milkweed, prairie milkweed
Asclepias syriaca	common milkweed
Asclepias verticillata	whorled milkweed
Astragalus agrestis	field milkvetch
Astragalus crassicarpus	groundplumb, prairie plumb
Astragalus flexuosus	slender milkvetch
Astragalus lotiflorus	low milkvetch, lotus milkvetch
Astragalus missouriensis	Missouri milkvetch
Bacopa rotundifolia	water-hyssop
Bidens tripartita	beggarticks
Brassica nigra	black mustard
Brassica rapa	field mustard
Callitriche heterophylla	larger water-starwort
Caltha palustris	marsh marigold
Calylophus serrulatus	toothed primrose, yellow evening primrose
Campanulastrum americanum	tall bellflower
Cardamine bulbosa	spring cress, bulbous bittercress
Castilleja sessiliflora	downy painted cup
Centaurea biebersteinii	spotted knapweed
Cerastium arvense	prairie chickweed
Cerastium brachypodum	mouse-ear chickweed
Chenopodium album	goosefoot, lambsquarters
Heterotheca villosa	hairy false goldenaster
Cicuta maculata	water hemlock
Cirsium arvense	Canada thistle
Cirsium discolor	field thistle
Cirsium flodmanii	Flodman's thistle
Cirsium hillii	Hill's Thistle
Comandra umbellata	bastard toadflax
Coronilla varia	crown vetch
Coreopsis palmata	prairie coreopsis, stiff tickseed
Corydalis aurea	golden corydalis
Cypripedium candidum	white lady's slipper
Dalea candida	white prairie clover
Dalea purpurea	purple prairie clover
Dalea villosa	silky prairie clover
Delphinium carolinianum	prairie larkspur, Carolina larkspur

Desmanthus illinoensis	prairie mimosa
Echinaceae angustifolia	purple coneflower
Elatine triandra	waterwort
Equisetum hyemale	scouring rush
Equisetum laevigatum	smooth horsetail
Erigeron strigosus	daisy fleabane
Eupatorium maculatum	Joe-Pye weed
Eupatorium perfoliatum	common boneset
Euphorbia agraria	leafy spurge
Fragaria virginiana	wild strawberry
Galium boreale	northern bedstraw
Galium concinnum	shining bedstraw
Gaura coccinea	scarlet gaura
Gentiana andrewsii	closed bottle gentian
Gentiana puberulenta	downy gentian
Geranium carolinianum	Carolina crane's-bill
Geum triflorum	prairie smoke
Glechoma hederacea	ground ivy
Glycyrrhiza lepidota	wild licorice
Grindelia squarrosa	gumweed
Hedeoma hispida	rough false pennyroyal
Helianthus annuus	annual sunflower
Helianthus giganteus	giant sunflower
Helianthus grosseserratus	saw-toothed sunflower
Helianthus helanthoides	ox-eye, false sunflower
Helianthus maximiliani	Maxmillian's sunflower
Helianthus pauciflorus	prairie sunflower
Hepatica acutiloba	sharp-lobed hepatica
Hesperis matronalis	dame's rocket
Heuchera richardsonii	prairie alum-root
Hieracium longipilum	long-bearded hawkweed
Houstonia longifolia	long-leaved bluets
Hydrophyllum virginianum	Virginia waterleaf
Hypoxis hirsuta	yellow star grass
Lactuca canadensis	wild lettuce
Lathyrus palustris	marsh vetchling
Lepidium virginicum	wild pepper-grass
Liatris aspera	rough blazing star
Liatris punctata	dotted blazing star
Liatris pycnostachya	prairie blazing star
Lilium philadelphicum	prairie lily
Limosella aquatica	mudwort
Lithospermum canescens	hoary puccoon
Lithospermum incisum	fringed puccoon
Lobelia spicata	pale spiked lobelia
Lotus unifoliolatus	bird's-foot treefoil
Lycopus americanus	cut-leaved waterhorehound
Lycopus asper	western waterhorehound
Lygodesmia juncea	rush skeleton plant
Lythrum salicaria	purple loostrife
Machaeranthera pinnatifida	cutleaf ironplant
Medicago lupulina	black medic
Medicago sativa	alfalfa
Melilotus alba	white sweet-clover

Melilotus officinalis	yellow sweet-clover
Mentha arvensis	wild mint
Mimulus ringens	monkeyflower
Mirabilis nyctaginea	four o'clock
Monarda fistulosa	wild bergamot
Myosotis verna	forget-me-not
Myosurus minimus	mousetail
Nelumbo lutea	american lotus
Nepeta cataria	catnip
Nymphaea odorata	white water lily
Oenothera biennis	evening primrose
Onosmodium molle	false gromwell
Orobanche fasciculata	clustered broomrape
Orobanche ludoviciana	Louisiana broomrape
Oxalis stricta	common yellow wood-sorrel
Oxalis violacea	violet wood-sorrel
Pedicularis canadensis	wood betony
Pedicularis lanceolata	swamp lousewort
Pediomelum esculentum	prairie turnip
Penstemon albidus	white beardtongue
Penstemon cobea	showy beardtongue
Penstemon gracilis	slender beardtongue
Penstemon grandiflorus	large-flowered beardtongue
Penstemon pallidus	pale beardtongue
Penthorum sedoides	ditch stonecrop
Phlox pilosa	downy phlox, prairie phlox
Physalis virginiana	ground cherry
Plantago spinulosa	large-bracted, sand plantain
Polygonum coccineum	smartweed
Polygonum pensylvanicum	pinkweed
Polygonum punctatum	white smartweed
Polygonum tenue	slim knotweed
Portulacea oleracea	purslane
Potentilla anserina	silverweed
Potentilla arguta	Prairie, tall cinquefoil
Potentilla paradoxa	bushy cinquefoil
Prenanthes alba	white lettuce
Prenanthes racemosa	rattlesnake root
Psoralea argophylla	silverleaf scurfpea
Psoralidium tennuiflorum	scurfy pea
Pulsatilla patens	pasqueflower
Ranunculus cymbalaria	seaside buttercup
Ratibida columnifera	prairie coneflower
Ratibida pinnata	gray-headed coneflower
Rhus radicans	poison ivy
Rotala ramosior	toothcup
Rudbeckia hirta	black-eyed susan
Rumex crispus	curly dock
Rumex altissimus	pale dock
Salicornia rubra	red saltwort
Sanguinaria canadensis	bloodroot
Senecio aereus	golden ragwort
Sium suave	water-parsnip
Silphium perfoliatum	cup plant

Silphium terebinthinaceum	prairie dock
Sisyrinchium campestre	prairie blue-eyed grass
Smilax herbacea	carrion flower
Solanum nigrum	black nightshade
Solidago canadensis	Canada goldenrod
Solidago gigantea	late goldenrod
Solidago juncea	early goldenrod
Solidago mollis	soft goldenrod
Solidago nemoralis	oldfield goldenrod
Solidago ridellii	Riddell's goldenrod
Solidago rigida	hard-leaved goldenrod
Sonchus arvensis	perennial sow-thistle
Sonchus asper	spiny-leaved sow-thistle
Stachys palustris	woundwort
Symphyotrichum ericoides	white heath aster
Symphyotrichum lanceolatum	panicled aster
Symphyotrichum oblongifolium	aromatic aster
Symphyotrichum sericeum	silky aster
Talinum teretifolium	fame flower
Thalictrum dasycarpum	meadow rue
Tofieldia glutinosa	false asphodel
Tradescantia virginiana	Virginia spiderwort
Tragopogon dubius	goatsbeard
Trifolium pratense	red clover
Triglochin palustris	marsh arrow-grass
Urtica dioica	stinging nettle
Utricularia vulgaris	common bladderwort
Vagnera stellata	star-flowered Solomon's seal
Verbascum spp. *mullein*	
Verbena hastata	blue vervain
Verbena stricta	wooly verbena
Veronia fasiculata	common ironweed
Veronica peregrina	purslane speedwell
Vicia americana	American vetch
Viola canadensis	white Canada violet
Viola nuttallii	yellow prairie violet
Viola pedata	birdfoot violet
Viola pedatifida	prairie violet
Viola pubescens	downy yellow violet
Viola soroia	woolly blue violet
Woodsia oregana	Oregon woodsia
Zigadenus elegans	white camass
Zizia aptera	heart-leaved alexanders
Zizia aurea	golden alexanders

Cacti

Escobaria vivipara	ball cactus
Opuntia fragilis	prickly pear
Opuntia macrorhiza	plains prickly pear

Ferns

Botrychium campestre	prairie moonwort
Cheilanthes llanosa	hairy-lip fern
Cystopteris fragilis	fragile fern
Woodsia ilvensis	rusty woodsia fern

Mosses

Lycopodium spp.	club moss

Mammals of the Morris Wetland Management District, Minnesota

Note: This is a working list of mammal species that are likely to occur in the Morris Wetland Management District. The list was compiled using species records and ranges from the sources listed at the end. An updated and accurate mammal species list will be created in coming years as the District's Biological Inventory and Monitoring Program gets under way. Scientific names follow Jones, et al. (1997).

Class Mammalia
Order Didelphimorphia – Opossums
      Family Didelphidae – Opossums
            Didelphis virginiana – Virginia Opossum

Order Insectivora – Insectivores
      Family Soricidae – Shrews
            Sorex cinereus – Masked Shrew
            Sorex haydeni – Hayden's Shrew
            Sorex hoyi – Pygmy Shrew
            Blarina brevicauda – Short-tailed Shrew
      Family Talpidae – Moles
            Scalopus aquaticus – Eastern or Prairie Mole
Order Chiroptera – Bats

      Family Vespertilionidae – Vespertilionid Bats
            Myotis lucifugus – Little Brown Bat
            Myotis septentrionalis – Northern Myotis or Northern Long-eared
Bat   *Lasiurus borealis* – Eastern Red Bat
            Lasiurus cinereus – Hoary Bat
Lasionycteris noctivagans – Silver-haired Bat
            Pipistrellus subflavus – Eastern Pipistrelle
            Eptesicus fuscus – Big Brown Bat
Order Lagomorpha – Lagomorphs
      Family Leporidae – Hares and Rabbits
            Sylvilagus floridanus – Eastern Cottontail
            Lepus townsendii – White-tailed Jackrabbit
Order Rodentia – Rodents
      Family Sciuridae – Squirrels
            Tamias striatus – Eastern Chipmunk
            Marmota monax – Woodchuck
            Spermophilus franklinii – Franklin's Ground Squirrel
            Spermophilus richardsonii – Richardson's Ground Squirrel
            Spermophilus tridecemlineatus – Thirteen-lined Ground Squirrel
            Sciurus carolinensis – Gray Squirrel
            Sciurus niger – Fox Squirrel
            Tamiasciurus hudsonicus – Red Squirrel

      Family Geomyidae – Pocket Gophers
            Geomys bursarius – Plains Pocket Gopher
      Family Heteromyidae – Heteromyids
            Perognathus flavescens – Plains Pocket Mouse
      Family Castoridae – Beaver
            Castor canadensis – Beaver

Family Muridae – Mice, Rats, and Voles
    Reithrodontomys megalotis – Western Harvest Mouse
    Peromyscus leucopus – White-footed Mouse
    Peromyscus maniculatus – Deer Mouse
    Onychomys leucogaster – Northern Grasshopper Mouse
    Rattus norvegicus – Norway Rat
    Mus musculus – House Mouse
    Clethrionomys gapperi – Southern Red-backed Vole
    Microtus ochrogaster – Prairie Vole
    Microtus pennsylvanicus – Meadow Vole
    Ondatra zibethicus – Muskrat
Family Zapodidae – Jumping Mice
    Zapus hudsonius – Meadow Jumping Mouse
    Zapus princeps – Western Jumping Mouse
Order Carnivora – Carnivores
    Family Canidae – Canids
        Canis latrans – Coyote
        Vulpus vulpes – Red Fox
    Family Procyonidae – Procyonids
        Procyon lotor – Raccoon
    Family Mustelidae – Mustelids
        Mustela erminea – Ermine or Short-tailed Weasel
        Mustela frenata – Long-tailed Weasel
        Mustela nivalis – Least Weasel
        Mustela vison – Mink
        Taxidea taxus – Badger
        Lontra canadensis – Northern River Otter
    Family Mephitidae – Mephitids
        Mephitis mephitis – Striped Skunk
Order Artiodactyla – Even-toed Ungulates
    Family Cervidae – Cervids
        Odocoileus hemionus – Mule Deer
        Odocoileus virginianus – White-tailed Deer

Resources:
Burt, W. H. and R. P. Grossenheider. 1980. A field guide to the mammals, 3rd ed. Boston, Houghton Mifflin Company. 289 pp.

Harvey, M. J., J. S. Altenbach, and T. L. Best. 1999. Bats of the United States. Arkansas Game and Fish Commission. 64 pp.

Hazard, E. B. 1982. The mammals of Minnesota. University of Minnesota Press, Minneapolis. 280 pp.

Jones, C., R. S. Hoffmann, D. W. Rice, M. D. Engstrom, R. D. Bradley, D. J. Schmidly, C. A. Jones, and R. J. Baker. 1997. Revised checklist of North American Mammals north of Mexico, 1997. Occasional Papers Museum of Texas Tech University No. 173. 19 pp.

Birds of the Morris Wetland Management District, Minnesota

Note: This should be considered a working list of bird species in the Morris Wetland Management District. It was last officially updated in August 1991, though the below list includes some changes recommended by district staff. An updated and accurate bird species list will be created in coming years as the District's Biological Inventory and Monitoring Program gets under way.

Abbreviations used in the checklist:
a = Abundant - Common species that is numerous
c = Common - Certain to be seen or heard in suitable habitat
u = Uncommon - Present, but not certain to be seen
r = Rare - Seen at intervals of 2 to 5 years
ac = Accidental
* = Species that nests in the District

	Spring	Summer	Fall	Winter
Common Loon *	c	c	c	ac
Pied-billed Grebe *	c	c	c	r
Horned Grebe	c		u	
Red-necked Grebe *	c	c	u	
Eared Grebe *	u	u	u	
Western Grebe *	c	u	c	
Clark's Grebe *	ac	r	ac	
American White Pelican*	a	c	c	
Double-crested Cormorant *	a	a	a	
American Bittern *	u	u	r	
Least Bittern *	r	u	r	
Great Blue Heron *	c	c	c	r
Great Egret *	c	c	c	
Snowy Egret	u	u	ac	
Little Blue Heron	ac			
Cattle Egret *	u	r	r	
Green Heron *	c	c	u	
Black-crowned Night Heron *	u	c	u	
Yellow-crowned Night Heron		ac		
White-faced Ibis	ac			
Turkey Vulture *	u	u	u	
Greater White-fronted Goose	u		r	
Snow Goose	c		u	r
Ross's Goose	ac		ac	
Canada Goose *	a	a	a	a
Mute Swan	ac		ac	
Trumpeter Swan	r	ac	ac	
Tundra Swan	a	ac	a	ac
Wood Duck *	c	c	c	ac
Gadwall *	c	u	c	ac
American Wigeon *	c	u	c	
American Black Duck	ac	ac	u	
Mallard *	a	a	a	a
Blue-winged Teal *	a	a	a	
Cinnamon Teal	r		r	

	Spring	Summer	Fall	Winter
Northern Shoveler *	c	c	c	
Northern Pintail *	u	u	u	
Green-winged Teal *	c	u	c	
Canvasback *	c	u	c	
Redhead *	c	c	c	
Ring-necked Duck *	a	c	c	
Greater Scaup	u		u	
Lesser Scaup *	a	u	c	
Surf Scoter	ac		ac	
White-winged Scoter	ac		ac	
Black Scoter	ac		ac	
Long-tail Duck			ac	ac
Bufflehead	c		c	u
Common Goldeneye	a		c	ac
Hooded Merganser *	c	u	c	
Common Merganser	c	ac	c	r
Red-breasted Merganser	u	ac	r	
Ruddy Duck *	c	c	c	
Osprey *	u	u	u	
Bald Eagle *	c	c	c	r
Northern Harrier *	c	c	c	ac
Sharp-shinned Hawk	u	u	u	r
Cooper's Hawk *	c	c	u	r
Northern Goshawk	r		r	r
Red-shouldered Hawk	ac	u	ac	
Broad-winged Hawk	u	u	u	
Swainson's Hawk *	u	u	u	
Red-tailed Hawk *	c	a	c	r
Rough-legged Hawk	u		u	r
Ferruginous Hawk	ac	r	ac	
Golden Eagle	r		r	ac
American Kestrel *	c	a	c	r
Merlin	u		u	r
Gyrfalcon	r		r	ac
Peregrine Falcon	r		r	
Prairie Falcon	r		r	ac
Gray Partridge *	u	u	u	u
Ring-necked Pheasant *	c	c	c	u
Ruffed Grouse *	u	u	u	u
Greater Prairie Chicken *	u	u	u	u
Wild Turkey *	u	u	u	u
Yellow Rail *	r		r	
Virginia Rail *	u	c	u	
Sora *	c	c	c	
Common Moorhen	ac	r		
American Coot *	a	a	a	ac
Sandhill Crane	u		u	
Black-bellied Plover	u	r	u	
American Golden Plover	u	r	u	
Semipalmated Plover	u	u	u	
Killdeer *	c	a	c	
American Avocet	r		r	
Greater Yellowlegs	c	u	c	

	Spring	Summer	Fall	Winter
Lesser Yellowlegs	c	u	c	
Solitary Sandpiper	u	u	u	
Willet	r	ac	r	
Spotted Sandpiper *	c	c	c	
Upland Sandpiper *	u	c	u	
Whimbrel	ac			
Hudsonian Godwit	u		u	
Marbled Godwit *	c	u	u	
Ruddy Turnstone	u		u	
Sanderling	u		u	
Semipalmated Sandpiper	c		c	
Western Sandpiper	ac			
Least Sandpiper	c		c	
White-rumped Sandpiper	u		u	
Baird's Sandpiper	u		u	
Pectoral Sandpiper	c		c	
Dunlin	c		u	
Stilt Sandpiper	u		u	
Buff-breasted Sandpiper	r			
Short-billed Dowitcher	c		c	
Long-billed Dowitcher	u		u	
Common Snipe *	c	c	c	ac
American Woodcock *	u	u	u	
Wilson's Phalarope *	c	u	c	
Red-necked Phalarope	u		u	
Franklin's Gull	a	r	a	
Bonaparte's Gull	c	r	c	
Ring-billed Gull	a	c	a	
Herring Gull	u	r	u	
Glaucous Gull	ac		ac	
Sabine's Gull	ac		ac	
California Gull	ac			
Caspian Tern	u	r	u	
Common Tern	r	ac	r	
Forster's Tern *	c	c	c	
Black Tern *	c	c	c	
Rock Dove *	a	a	a	a
Mourning Dove *	c	a	a	r
Black-billed Cuckoo *	r	u	r	
Yellow-billed Cuckoo *	r	r	r	
Eastern Screech Owl *	u	u	u	u
Great Horned Owl *	c	c	c	c
Snowy Owl	u		u	r
Barred Owl *	u	u	u	u
Long-eared Owl	r	r	r	r
Short-eared Owl *	u	u	u	ac
Northern Saw-whet Owl	r		r	r
Common Nighthawk *	c	a	c	
Whip-poor-will	u	u	u	
Chimney Swift *	c	c	c	
Ruby-throated Hummingbird *	u	c	u	
Belted Kingfisher *	c	c	c	r
Red-Headed Woodpecker *	u	c	u	

	Spring	Summer	Fall	Winter
Red-bellied Woodpecker *	u	u	u	u
Yellow-bellied Sapsucker *	c	c	c	
Downy Woodpecker *	c	c	c	c
Hairy Woodpecker *	c	c	c	c
Northern Flicker *	c	c	c	r
Pileated Woodpecker *	u	u	u	u
Olive-sided Flycatcher	u		u	
Eastern Wood Pewee *	u	u	u	
Yellow-bellied Flycatcher	r			
Alder Flycatcher *	u	u	u	
Willow Flycatcher *	u		u	
Least Flycatcher *	c	c	c	
Eastern Phoebe *	c	c	c	
Say's Phoebe *	ac			
Great Crested Flycatcher *	c	c	c	
Western Kingbird *	u	c	u	
Eastern Kingbird *	c	c	c	
Loggerhead Shrike *	r	r	r	
Northern Shrike	u		u	u
Yellow-throated Vireo *	u	u	u	
Blue-headed Vireo	u		u	
Warbling Vireo *	c	c	c	
Philadelphia Vireo	r		r	
Red-eyed Vireo *	c	c	c	
Gray Jay				ac
Blue Jay *	c	c	c	c
American Crow *	a	c	a	u
Common Raven	u		u	
Horned Lark *	a	a	a	r
Purple Martin *	c	c	c	
Tree Swallow *	a	a	a	
Northern Rough-winged Swallow *	c	c	c	
Bank Swallow *	c	c	c	
Cliff Swallow *	a	a	a	
Barn Swallow *	a	a	a	
Black-capped Chickadee *	c	c	c	c
Boreal Chickadee				ac
Red-breasted Nuthatch	u		u	u
White-breasted Nuthatch	c	c	c	c
Brown Creeper *	u	r	u	u
House Wren *	c	c	c	
Winter Wren	r		r	
Sedge Wren *	c	c	c	
Marsh Wren *	c	c	c	
Golden-crowned Kingletc		c	r	
Ruby-crowned Kinglet	c		c	ac
Blue-gray Gnatcatcher *	u	u	u	
Eastern Bluebird *	c	c	c	
Townsend's Solitaire			ac	ac
Veery *	c	c	u	
Gray-cheeked Thrush	u		u	
Swainson's Thrush	c		c	

	Spring	Summer	Fall	Winter
Hermit Thrush	u		u	ac
Wood Thrush *	r			
American Robin *	a	a	a	u
Varied Thrush				ac
Gray Catbird *	c	c	c	
Northern Mockingbird	r	r		
Brown Thrasher *	c	c	c	ac
European Starling *	a	a	a	u
American Pipit	u		u	
Sprague's Pipit	ac			
Bohemian Waxwing	u		u	u
Cedar Waxwing *	c	c	c	u
Blue-winged Warbler	r			
Golden-winged Warbler	r		r	
Tennessee Warbler	a		c	
Orange-crowned Warbler	c		c	
Nashville Warbler	c		c	
Northern Parula	u		r	
Yellow Warbler *	c	c	c	
Chestnut-sided Warbler	c		c	
Magnolia Warbler	c		c	
Cape May Warbler	r		r	
Black-throated Blue Warbler	u		ac	
Yellow-rumped Warbler	a		a	ac
Black-throated Green Warbler	u		u	
Blackburnian Warbler	u		u	
Pine Warbler	r			
Palm Warbler	a		a	
Bay-breasted Warbler	r		r	
Blackpoll Warbler	c		c	
Cerulean Warbler	u		u	
Black-and-white Warbler	c		c	
American Redstart *	c	c	c	
Prothonotary Warbler	u			
Ovenbird *	c	c	c	
Northern Waterthrush	u		u	
Connecticut Warbler	u			
Mourning Warbler	u		r	
Common Yellowthroat *	a	a	c	
Wilson's Warbler	u		u	
Canada Warbler	u		u	
Scarlet Tanager *	u	u	u	
Spotted Towhee	r			
Eastern Towhee	r		r	ac
American Tree Sparrow	c		c	u
Chipping Sparrow *	c	c	c	
Clay-colored Sparrow *	c	c	c	
Field Sparrow *	u	u	u	
Vesper Sparrow *	c	c	c	
Lark Sparrow	r	r	r	
Savannah Sparrow *	c	a	c	
Grasshopper Sparrow *	u	u	u	
Henslow's Sparrow *	r	u		

	Spring	Summer	Fall	Winter
Le Conte's Sparrow *	u	u	u	
Nelson's Sharp-tailed Sparrow	r		r	
Fox Sparrow	c		u	
Song Sparrow *	c	c	c	ac
Lincoln's Sparrow	u		u	
Swamp Sparrow *	c	c	c	
White-throated Sparrow	a		a	r
Harris' Sparrow	c		c	u
White-crowned Sparrow	u		u	
Dark-eyed Junco	a		a	c
Lapland Longspur	c		c	r
Smith's Longspur	r		u	
Snow Bunting	c		c	c
Lark Bunting	ac	ac		
Northern Cardinal *	u	u	u	u
Rose-breasted Grosbeak *	c	c	c	
Blue Grosbeak	ac			
Indigo Bunting *	c	c	c	
Dickcissel *	u	c	r	
Bobolink *	c	c	c	
Red-winged Blackbird *	a	a	a	r
Eastern Meadowlark *	r	r		
Western Meadowlark *	c	c	c	ac
Yellow-headed Blackbird *	a	a	a	r
Rusty Blackbird	c		c	r
Brewer's Blackbird *	c	c	c	
Common Grackle *	a	a	a	r
Brown-headed Cowbird *	c	c	c	r
Orchard Oriole *	u	u	u	
Baltimore Oriole *	c	c	c	
Pine Grosbeak	r		r	r
Purple Finch *	u	r	u	u
House Finch *	c	c	c	c
Red Crossbill	u	u	u	u
White-winged Crossbill	u	u	u	u
Common Redpoll	c		c	c
Hoary Redpoll	r		r	r
Pine Siskin	u	r	u	u
American Goldfinch *	c	c	c	u
Evening Grosbeak	u		u	u
House Sparrow *	a	a	a	a

Reptile and Amphibian List

REPTILES

Common Snapping Turtle	*Chelydra serpentina*
Western Painted Turtle	*Chrysemys picta*
Western Spiny Softshell Turtle	*Trionyx spiniferus*
Northern Prairie Skink	*Eumeces septentrionalis*
Western Hognose Snake	*Heterodon nasicus*
Eastern Hognose Snake	*Heterodon platyrhinos*
Bullsnake, Gopher Snake	*Pituophis melanoleucus*
Texas Brown Snake	*Storeria dekayi*
Northern Redbelly Snake	*Storeria occipitomaculata*
Western Plains Garter Snake	*Thamnophis radix*
Red-sided Garter Snake	*Thamnophis sirtalis*
Smooth Green Snake	*Opheodrys vernalis*

AMPHIBIANS

Mudpuppy	*Necturus maculosus*
Eastern Newt	*Diemictylus viridescens*
Tiger Salamander	*Ambystoma tigrinum*
Blue-spotted Salamander	*Ambystoma laterale*
American Toad	*Bufo americanus*
Great Plains Toad	*Bufo cognatus*
Canadian Toad	*Bufo hemiophrys*
Gray Treefrog	*Hyla versicolor*
Green Frog	*Rana clamitans*
Western Chorus Frog	*Pseudacris triseriata*
Northern Leopard Frog	*Rana pipiens*
Wood Frog	*Rana sylvatica*
Northern Spring Peeper	*Hyla crucifer*
Mink Frog	*Rana septentrionalis*

Appendix D: National Wetlands Inventory – Minnesota Counties Wetland Types

National Wetlands Inventory – Minnesota Counties Wetland Types

County	Total Wetland (small, shallow wetlands)	Palustrine Acres	%	Riverine Acres	%	Lacustrine Acres (Lakes and deep water reservoirs)	%
Becker	149,248	73,056	34	260	<1	75,932	35
Big Stone	59,347	44,475	70	71	<1	14,801	23
Blue Earth	23,577	14,542	48	2,723	9	6,312	21
Brown	16,498	11,431	52	1,516	7	3,551	16
Chippewa	11,401	7,843	52	853	6	2,705	18
Clay	30,483	25,600	68	916	2	3,967	10
Clearwater	104,255	87,146	47	452	<1	16,657	9
Cottonwood	12,700	7,078	50	506	4	5,116	36
Douglas	95,323	44,819	42	203	<1	50,301	47
Faribault	9,975	5,702	51	806	7	3,467	31
Freeborn	18,681	9,762	50	192	1	8,727	44
Grant	35,696	19,265	50	97	<1	16,334	42
Jackson	22,129	11,783	50	734	3	9,612	41
Kandiyohi	82,499	44,939	48	57	<1	37,503	40
Kittson	49,981	49,094	69	352	1	535	1
Lac qui Parle	26,751	18,653	59	594	2	7,504	24
LeSueur	42,417	27,703	61	580	1	14,134	31
Lincoln	20,988	14,557	66	3	0	6,428	29
Lyon	16,105	11,930	64	11	<1	4,164	22
Mahnomen	48,206	34,050	51	476	1	13,680	20
Marshall	112,892	102,291	50	1,301	1	9,300	5
Martin	21,434	10,503	45	24	<1	10,907	46
McLeod	37,088	29,760	75	50	<1	7,278	18
Meeker	65,808	44,874	58	416	1	20,518	26
Murray	21,703	13,094	56	9	0	8,600	37
Nicollet	20,949	15,200	57	1,340	5	4,409	17
Nobles	10,946	6,984	60	46	1	3,916	33
Norman	14,176	12,465	60	1,544	7	167	1
Otter Tail	261,870	114,210	33	1,132	1	146,538	43
Pennington	22,759	21,097	67	1,253	4	409	1
Pipestone	4,760	4,520	87	88	2	152	3
Polk	78,325	60,479	57	2,608	2	15,238	14
Pope	72,474	43,011	50	55	<1	29,408	34

National Wetlands Inventory – Minnesota Counties Wetland Types

County	Total Wetland (small, shallow wetlands)	Palustrine Acres	%	Riverine Acres	%	Lacustrine Acres (Lakes and deep water reservoirs)	%
Red Lake	9,321	7,832	54	1,450	10	39	0.5
Redwood	8,204	7,171	66	728	7	305	3
Renville	17,856	14,937	72	713	3	2,206	11
Rock	3,383	2,422	59	848	21	113	3
Roseau	133,897	131,076	37	633	<1	2,188	1
Sibley	27,241	21,758	71	55	2	5,428	18
Steele	6,344	5,293	69	99	1	952	12
Stevens	26,832	19,610	68	304	1	6,918	24
Swift	24,752	19,695	64	449	1	4,608	15
Traverse	28,009	20,828	71	211	1	6,970	24
Waseca	17,150	12,416	67	9	<1	4,725	25
Watonwan	7,033	4,830	20	103	1	2,100	23
Wilkin	11,568	10,201	79	1,201	9	166	1
Yellow Medicine	11,696	9,547	65	632	4	1,517	10
TOTALS	1,954,730	1,329,532		28,703		596,495	

Appendix E: Compatibility Determinations

COMPATIBILITY DETERMINATION

Use: Permit Archeological Investigations

Station Name: Morris Wetland Management District

Establishing and Acquisition Authority(ies):

Waterfowl Production Areas - The Migratory Bird Hunting and Conservation Stamp Act, March 16, 1934, (16 U.S.C. Sec. 718-718h, 48 Stat. 452) as amended August 1, 1958, (P.L. 85-585; 72 Stat. 486) for acquisition of "Waterfowl Production Areas"; the Wetlands Loan Act, October 4, 1961, as amended (16 U.S.C. 715k-3 - 715k-5, Stat. 813), funds appropriated under the Wetlands Loan Act are merged with duck stamp receipts in the fund and appropriated to the Secretary for the acquisition of migratory bird refuges under provisions of the Migratory Bird Conservation Act, February 18, 1929, (16 U.S.C. Sec. 715, 715d - 715r, as amended.

FmHA fee title transfer properties - Consolidated Farm and Rural Development Act 7 U.S.C. 2002.

Refuge Purpose(s):

Waterfowl Production Areas - "...as Waterfowl Production Areas" subject to "...all of the provisions of such Act [Migratory Bird Conservation Act]....except the inviolate sanctuary provisions..." and "...for any other management purpose, for migratory birds".

FmHA fee title transfer properties - "for conservation purposes..."

National Wildlife Refuge System Mission:

"...To administer a national network of lands and waters for the conservation, management, and where appropriate, restoration of the fish, wildlife, and plant resources and their habitats within the United States for the benefit of present and future generations of Americans."

Description of Use:

Permitted archeological investigations on the Minnesota Wetland Management Districts, Minnesota, are those requested by archeologists who are not performing the investigation for District management purposes (e.g., not for Section 106 of the National Historic Preservation Act). Rather, permitted archeologists are pursuing their own or institutional research or are working for other parties that will be conducting activities on FWS land, or as requested by the Governor of Minnesota, and similar third party activities on lands of the National Wildlife Refuge System. Permitted investigations can occur at any time of the year although usually not during the winter. Investigations may be as short as a few hours or go on for months, depending on the research objective. These permitted investigations occur on the District because the District is where the resource is found or where the resource could be disrupted.

Archeologists request Archaeological Resources Protection Act (ARPA) permits or Antiquities Act permits to conduct "Surveys and limited testing and limited collections on lands identified" and "Excavation, collection and intensive study of specific sites described" on District land. Permits are issued by the Regional Director to qualified archeologists.

Permits can be for anyplace on FWS owned and managed lands, but each permit is for specific lands; i.e., no general archeological permits are authorized.

The District Manager issues a special use permit to archeologists prior to investigation on lands managed by the District, to define allowable dates and times for the investigation, and other management controls.

Availability of Resources:

The District has resources available to administer this use. This activity will require the District Manager to develop and issue a Special Use Permit and random inspections of the project area. ARPA/Antiquities permits are received by the Regional Historic Preservation Officer and issued by the Regional Director as part of normal duties.

Anticipated Impacts of the Use:

Impacts from routine pedestrian surveys, soil coring, shovel tests, and land form analysis are limited to short-term disturbance to wildlife using the immediate area and disruption of vegetative cover for the growing season on an extremely small area affected by shovel tests.

Impacts from a large scale excavation are potentially longer term (several growing seasons) with associated wildlife disturbance impacts affecting animals in the immediate area and vegetation cover disruption severe enough to require site regrading and reseeding of the area to desired native species.

Public Review and Comment:

During the Scoping phase of the preparation of the Comprehensive Conservation Plan (CCP), six open houses were held to solicit public input and comment on all aspects of district management. Draft copies of the CCP will be distributed during a 30-day comment period and an additional six public meetings will be held to garner public comments, written and verbal, on the draft plan including all Compatibility Determinations.

Determination:

___ Use is Not Compatible

_X_ Use is Compatible With Following Stipulations

Stipulations Necessary to Ensure Compatibility:

Applicant must obtain a Special Use Permit issued by the District Manager. The Special Use Permit is to prescribe administrative or management restrictions required by the District Manager.

Permittee will shore up walls of test pits and trenches in accordance with OSHA standards; will flag, barricade, and sign testing areas as necessary to prevent injury to the public; will refill shovel tests as soon as excavated and data recorded including replacing the vegetative plug to restore original conditions; will backfill excavations as soon as data recording is completed and seed the surface with a grass or other vegetative mix approved by the District Manager.

Predetermined stipulations on ARPA/Antiquities permits and the requirements in 43 CFR Part 7, "Protection of Archaeological Resources: Uniform Regulations," contain protective measures to be accomplished by archeologists.

Justification:

Although temporary disruption of habitat and wildlife routine could occur, this disruption is limited in scope and duration. Due to stipulations and the issuance of a permit, managers will have control on when the activitity will occur so sensitive habitat, or sensitive nesting times, can be avoided as needed. With stipulations in place, the use would not materially interfere with or detract from the purpose of WPAs. No long-term harm should come to the natural resources managed by the District.
In addition, the archeological investigations would be conducted in the public interest for which Federal agencies protect archeological sites; and the results may be included in public interpretive exhibits and other public dissemination. The results of the study could increase District understanding of prior human activities on the District and could be part of District interpretive program.

Signature: Project Leader s/Steven J. Delehanty 3/26/03

Concurrence: Regional Chief s/Nita M. Fuller 4/9/03

Mandatory 10- or 15-year Re-evaluation Date: 2012

COMPATIBILITY DETERMINATION

Use: Collection of Edible Wild Plant Foods for Personal Use

Station Name: Morris Wetland Management District

Establishing and Acquisition Authority(ies):

Waterfowl Production Areas - The Migratory Bird Hunting and Conservation Stamp Act, March 16, 1934, (16 U.S.C. Sec. 718-718h, 48 Stat. 452) as amended August 1, 1958, (P.L. 85-585; 72 Stat. 486) for acquisition of "Waterfowl Production Areas"; the Wetlands Loan Act, October 4, 1961, as amended (16 U.S.C. 715k-3 - 715k-5, Stat. 813), funds appropriated under the Wetlands Loan Act are merged with duck stamp receipts in the fund and appropriated to the Secretary for the acquisition of migratory bird refuges under provisions of the Migratory Bird Conservation Act, February 18, 1929, (16 U.S.C. Sec. 715, 715d - 715r, as amended.

FmHA fee title transfer properties - Consolidated Farm and Rural Development Act 7 U.S.C. 2002.

Refuge Purpose(s):

Waterfowl Production Areas - "...as Waterfowl Production Areas" subject to "...all of the provisions of such Act [Migratory Bird Conservation Act]....except the inviolate sanctuary provisions..." and "...for any other management purpose, for migratory birds".

FmHA fee title transfer properties - "for conservation purposes..."

National Wildlife Refuge System Mission:

"...To administer a national network of lands and waters for the conservation, management, and where appropriate, restoration of the fish, wildlife, and plant resources and their habitats within the United States for the benefit of present and future generations of Americans".

Description of Use:

Allow public to collect plant food products on WPAs for personal use.

Some plants growing on WPAs produce edible products such as fruits and nuts. Apples, raspberries and walnuts are examples these products. These plants grow in the uplands, occupy a small percentage of the total upland acreage, and are often found at abandoned building sites which have been reclaimed by the U.S. Fish and Wildlife Service. Harvest occurs during the daylight hours, usually in the late summer or fall and typically is of short duration. These foods are hand harvested by picking the products from the plant or gathering what has fallen to the ground.

Mushrooms, asparagus and wild mint are examples of plants that are collected and consumed or used as tea. These are cut by hand during harvest.

Wild rice grows in permanent wetlands. With a license from the State of Minnesota, it can be hand harvested from July 15 through September 30 using non-motorized watercraft. Harvest time is restricted to 9:00 a.m. to 3:00 p.m.

Access to harvest sites is accomplished by walking from a designated parking area or public roadway. Canoes used to harvest wild rice are launched at boat ramps or carried to the wetland from parking areas or public roadways.

Collection of these foods is not a wildlife-dependent recreational use and occurs infrequently. For a small number of people, this is a traditional, family oriented activity which provides an opportunity for those participating to collect wholesome, healthy foods while enjoying the beauty of the natural environment.

Availability of Resources:

Waterfowl Production Areas have been open to hunting since they were acquired. As a result, access trails, parking lots, signage and other facilities as well as staff to enforce regulations and maintain these facilities have been provided by the Service. These facilities will be maintained to meet the needs of the hunting public and will be used incidentally by those who are collecting edible wild plant foods. This use will not require a significant increase in additional maintenance or enforcement staff expenditures. The Service will not have to provide special equipment.

Anticipated Impacts of the Use:

Historically, public participation in the collection of plant food products on WPAs was low, and future participation is also expected to be low. The quantity and frequency of plant food products removed is not expected to significantly diminish wildlife food sources or jeopardize wildlife survival.

Short-term disturbance to wildlife may occur during these activities, but will be insignificant. Most of these activities occur in the late summer or fall, after ground-nesting birds have completed the nesting season. This activity should not result in short or long-term impacts that adversely affect the purpose of WPAs or the mission of the National Wildlife System.

Public Review and Comment:

Six open houses were held and written comments were solicited from the public about Wetland Management District operations during the drafting of Comprehensive Conservation Plans. This process identified 22 issues of concern. The collection of plant food products was not identified as an issue of concern.

This Compatibility Determination was prepared concurrently with, and included in the Draft Comprehensive Conservation Plans for Wetland Management Districts in Minnesota. Public review and comment was solicited during the CCP comment period.

Determination (check one below):

_____ Use is Not Compatible

__X__ Use is Compatible With Following Stipulations

Stipulations Necessary to Ensure Compatibility:

- The use of motorized vehicles or motorized water craft is prohibited except by permit or in designated parking areas, access trails or public roads.
- Camping, overnight use and fires are prohibited.
- Digging of plants or their roots is prohibited.
- Plant food products cannot be sold.
- Damage to trees is prohibited.
- Wild rice will be harvested according to state regulations

Justification:

This use will have limited and localized impacts when conducted within the stipulations above. Administration of the use will require little to no administrative time or funding. This use will not diminish the primary purposes of waterfowl production, or the conservation of other migratory birds and wildlife.

Signature: Project Leader s/Steven J. Delehanty 3/26/03

Concurrence: Regional Chief s/Nita M. Fuller 4/9/03

Mandatory 10- or 15-year Re-evaluation Date: 2012

COMPATIBILITY DETERMINATION

Use: Cooperative Farming for Cover Enhancement

Refuge Name: Morris Wetland Management District

Establishing and Acquisition Authority(ies):

Waterfowl Production Areas - The Migratory Bird Hunting and Conservation Stamp Act, March 16, 1934, (16 U.S.C. Sec. 718-718h, 48 Stat. 452) as amended August 1, 1958, (P.L. 85-585; 72 Stat. 486) for acquisition of "Waterfowl Production Areas"; the Wetlands Loan Act, October 4, 1961, as amended (16 U.S.C. 715k-3 - 715k-5, Stat. 813), funds appropriated under the Wetlands Loan Act are merged with duck stamp receipts in the fund and appropriated to the Secretary for the acquisition of migratory bird refuges under provisions of the Migratory Bird Conservation Act, February 18, 1929, (16 U.S.C. Sec. 715, 715d - 715r, as amended.

FmHA fee title transfer properties - Consolidated Farm and Rural Development Act 7 U.S.C. 2002.

Refuge Purpose(s):

Waterfowl Production Areas - "...as Waterfowl Production Areas" subject to "...all of the provisions of such Act [Migratory Bird Conservation Act]....except the inviolate sanctuary provisions..." and "...for any other management purpose, for migratory birds."

FmHA fee title transfer properties - "for conservation purposes..."

National Wildlife Refuge System Mission:

"...To administer a national network of lands and waters for the conservation, management, and where appropriate, restoration of the fish, wildlife, and plant resources and their habitats within the United States for the benefit of present and future generations of Americans."

Description of Use:

Cooperative farming is the term used for cropping activities done by a third party on land that is owned by the Service in fee title or controlled by the Service through a restrictive easement. This type of activity is usually done on a short-term basis (3 years or less) to prepare an optimum seed bed for the establishment of native prairie species.

The cropping is done under the terms and conditions of a Cooperative Farming Agreement or Special Use Permit issued by the Wetland District Manager. The terms of the Agreement or Permit insure that all current Service and District restrictions are followed.

Cooperative farming activities are only compatible on previously disturbed areas that have unacceptable levels of chemical residue, noxious weeds, or non-native plant species or ecotypes or to honor the land use clauses of a purchase agreement. To ensure that all Service policies are met, all such land use clauses must be approved by the Wetland District Manager prior to Service acceptance of the purchase agreement.

Waterfowl Production Areas in Minnesota average less than 200 acres in size and are intermingled with private and other public lands. Although the specific acreage of fields to be cooperatively farmed will vary by unit, they will typically range from 5 to 160 acres.

Availability of Resources:

The needed staff time for development and administration of cooperative farming programs is already committed and available. Most of the needed work to prepare for this use would be done as part of routine grassland management duties. The decision to use a cooperative farmer would occur as part of strategies developed under grass-land development and management discussions. The additional time needed to coordinate issuance and oversight of the needed Special Use Permit or Cooperative Farming Agreement is relatively minor and within existing District resources.

The cooperative farming of Service land will in most cases generate income for the Service. In accordance with Service policy, all income is submitted for deposit in the Refuge Revenue Sharing Account and is not available at the district level to offset station costs incurred in administration of this use. However, all Service employees involved in the administration of the program must be sensitive to the primary purpose of cooperative farming: providing an optimum seed bed for native prairie plant species. The Service should receive a fair market value from cooperative farmers, but generation of income is a secondary consideration when developing the terms and conditions of a cooperative farming agreement.

To lessen any appearance of favoritism or impropriety, District Managers should document how cooperators were selected and how rental rates were derived (see Refuge Manual).

Anticipated Impacts of the Use:

Cooperative farming to prepare suitable seed beds for native prairie plantings will result in short-term disturbances and long-term benefits to both resident and migra-tory wildlife using Waterfowl Production Areas and Service-managed upland ease-ments. Short-term impacts will include disturbance and displacement typical of any noisy heavy equipment operation. Cropping activities in old fields or abandoned croplands will also result in short-term loss of habitat for any animal or insect species using those areas for nesting, feeding, or perching. Long-term benefits are extremely positive due to establishment of diverse nesting cover including native tallgrass species. The resulting habitat will greatly improve conditions for most of the same species affected by the short-term negative impacts. Strict time constraints placed on this use will limit anticipated impacts to these relatively minor areas.

Public Review and Comment:

During the Scoping phase of the preparation of the Comprehensive Conservation Plan (CCP), six open houses were held to solicit public input and comment on all aspects of district management. Draft copies of the CCP will be distributed during a 30-day comment period and an additional six public meetings will be held to garner public comments, written and verbal, on the draft plan including all Compatibility Determi-nations.

Determination:

____ Use is Not Compatible

_X_ Use is Compatible With Following Stipulations

Stipulations Necessary to Ensure Compatibility:

1. Cooperative farming agreements will be limited to 3 years or less and comply with all appropriate Service regulations on chemical application and use.

Justification:

The cooperative farming of previously disturbed areas that are owned or under easement by the Service and have unacceptable levels of chemical residue, noxious weeds, or non-native plant species or ecotypes or are being farmed to honor the land use clauses of a purchase agreement to prepare an optimum seed bed for the establishment of native prairie species, will not materially interfere with or detract from the fulfillment of the National Wildlife Refuge System mission or the purposes of Waterfowl Production Areas or FmHA transfer lands for the following reasons:

1) Only areas that have already been significantly manipulated or altered by cropping activities will be affected. These areas contain few if any native plants and offer extremely limited value to the ecological integrity of the unit or landscape.

2) Cooperative farming activities in most cases, provide the fastest, most cost effective way to establish native prairie species on areas that have unacceptable levels of chemical residue, noxious weeds, or non-native plant species or ecotypes. District staff could complete all work, but for most districts that would required additional equipment and/or staff to efficiently break up non-native brome sod, or to cultivate and control weeds on small, widely scattered tracts of land. Hiring contractors to do this work at rates that can approach $100/acre is a possibility, but would require additional funds in years when the farming acres were high. By using local farmers to conduct these farming activities, district budgets and staff time can be better allocated to completing the needed restoration (seeding of native grasses and forbs) on lands that have completed the farming cycle and are in good condition for seeding.

3) Short-term impacts of farming small tracts of land are minor. No wildlife or habitat losses occur when land purchased in row crop is farmed for an additional period of 2-3 years. Low quality grasslands that are farmed as a first step to conversion to higher-value native grasslands will result in habitat loss for trust resources during the farming period. The long-term benefits to the ecological integrity of the district and landscape by restoring these degraded or row cropped areas to native prairie plant species are significant and exceed the short-term losses incurred through the cropping process.

Signature: Project Leader s/Steven J. Delehanty 3/26/03

Concurrence: Regional Chief s/Nita M. Fuller 4/9/03

Mandatory 10- or 15-year Re-evaluation Date: 2012

COMPATIBILITY DETERMINATION

Use: Disability Access to Waterfowl Production Areas

Refuge Name: Morris Wetland Management District

Establishing and Acquisition Authority(ies):

Waterfowl Production Areas - The Migratory Bird Hunting and Conservation Stamp Act, March 16, 1934, (16 U.S.C. Sec. 718-718h, 48 Stat. 452) as amended August 1, 1958, (P.L. 85-585; 72 Stat. 486) for acquisition of "Waterfowl Production Areas"; the Wetlands Loan Act, October 4, 1961, as amended (16 U.S.C. 715k-3 - 715k-5, Stat. 813), funds appropriated under the Wetlands Loan Act are merged with duck stamp receipts in the fund and appropriated to the Secretary for the acquisition of migratory bird refuges under provisions of the Migratory Bird Conservation Act, February 18, 1929, (16 U.S.C. Sec. 715, 715d - 715r, as amended.

FmHA fee title transfer properties - Consolidated Farm and Rural Development Act 7 U.S.C. 2002.

Refuge Purpose(s):

Waterfowl Production Areas - "...as Waterfowl Production Areas" subject to "...all of the provisions of such Act [Migratory Bird Conservation Act]....except the inviolate sanctuary provisions..." and "...for any other management purpose, for migratory birds."

FmHA fee title transfer properties - "for conservation purposes..."

National Wildlife Refuge System Mission:

"...To administer a national network of lands and waters for the conservation, management, and where appropriate, restoration of the fish, wildlife, and plant resources and their habitats within the United States for the benefit of present and future generations of Americans."

Description of Use:

Disability access is the term used to describe the process of granting exemptions to current Refuge Regulations that assist persons with disabilities in engaging in compatible activities on Waterfowl Production Areas. The most common type of exemption given will be Special Use Permits of limited duration which allow the use of motorized vehicles on existing roads and trails. All exemptions granted will comply with the general public safety regulations of the Department of Interior and the specific public safety guidance of the Service Compatibility Policy. Based on experience to date, it is expected that most disability access requests will be for hunting, but this policy also applies to the other priority public uses on refuges; wildlife observation, wildlife photography, environmental education, interpretation, and fishing. Waterfowl Production Areas in Minnesota average less than 200 acres in size and are intermingled with private and other public lands. Although the specific locations and sizes of areas affected will vary by Permit disturbances will typically vary from 0.5 to 3.0 acres.

Availability of Resources:

The needed staff time for development and administration of Special Use Permits authorizing motorized vehicle use on existing roads and trails is already committed and available. Most of the work needed to prepare for this use would be done as part of routine Waterfowl Production Area management duties. The decision to allow such use would occur as part of normal facility management and inspection programs. The additional time needed to coordinate issuance and oversight of the needed Special Use Permit is relatively minor and within existing District resources.

Anticipated Impacts of the Use:

A small amount of additional motorized use on established roads and trails will result in short-term disturbances to both resident and migratory wildlife using Waterfowl Production Areas. Short-term impacts will include disturbance and displacement typical of any motorized intrusion into wildlife habitat. Long-term impacts are not anticipated as most of the use will involve travel on roadways already used by Refuge staff to conduct management surveys and activities throughout the year.

Public Review and Comment:

During the Scoping phase of the preparation of the Comprehensive Conservation Plan (CCP), six open houses were held to solicit public input and comment on all aspects of district management. Draft copies of the CCP will be distributed during a 30-day comment period and an additional six public meetings will be held to garner public comments, written and verbal, on the draft plan including all Compatibility Determinations.

Additionally, a news release will be sent to local newspapers each fall prior to hunting seasons describing the disability access policy and soliciting public comments to Refuge offices.

Determination:

_____ Use is Not Compatible

__X__ Use is Compatible With Following Stipulations

Stipulations Necessary to Ensure Compatibility:

1. Motorized access will be limited to existing roads and trails in good condition.

2. Access is limited to persons who qualify for disability access as described in the Comprehensive Conservation Plan for the Minnesota Wetland Management Districts.

Justification:

The Americans With Disabilities Act and ensuing Service policy require that all Service programs and facilities meet the needs of the disabled. Offering special access as described in this determination is one way that the Service can meet that obligation to the American public.

Authorizing motorized vehicle use on established roads and trails for persons with disabilities engaged in compatible uses will cause minimal disturbance and provide appropriate recreational opportunities for people who might otherwise not be able to visit Waterfowl Production Areas.

Issuance of permits for disability access will not be limited to a set number as it is expected that meeting the requested demand will still result in a small amount of permits with only minimal wildlife disturbance as a consequence. At the expected level of use, this use is compatible as it will be below the threshold where unacceptable wildlife disturbance will occur. If demand far exceeds expectations within the time period covered by this determination and the disturbance threshold is exceeded, District staff will reevaluate the program and may limit the number of permits issued.

Signature: Project Leader s/Steven J. Delehanty 3/26/03

Concurrence: Regional Chief s/Nita M. Fuller 4/9/03

Mandatory 10- or 15-year Re-evaluation Date: 2012

COMPATIBILITY DETERMINATION

Use: Interpretation and Environmental Education

Station Name: Morris Wetland Management District

Establishing and Acquisition Authority(ies):

Waterfowl Production Areas - The Migratory Bird Hunting and Conservation Stamp Act, March 16, 1934, (16 U.S.C. Sec. 718-718h, 48 Stat. 452) as amended August 1, 1958, (P.L. 85-585; 72 Stat. 486) for acquisition of "Waterfowl Production Areas"; the Wetlands Loan Act, October 4, 1961, as amended (16 U.S.C. 715k-3 - 715k-5, Stat. 813), funds appropriated under the Wetlands Loan Act are merged with duck stamp receipts in the fund and appropriated to the Secretary for the acquisition of migratory bird refuges under provisions of the Migratory Bird Conservation Act, February 18, 1929, (16 U.S.C. Sec. 715, 715d - 715r, as amended.

FmHA fee title transfer properties - Consolidated Farm and Rural Development Act 7 U.S.C. § 2002.

Refuge Purpose(s):

Waterfowl Production Areas - "...as Waterfowl Production Areas" subject to "...all of the provisions of such Act [Migratory Bird Conservation Act]...except the inviolate sanctuary provisions...." and "...for any other management purpose, for migratory birds"

FmHA fee title transfer properties - "...for conservation purposes...."

National Wildlife Refuge System Mission:

"...To administer a national network of lands and waters for the conservation, management, and where appropriate, restoration of the fish, wildlife, and plant resources and their habitats within the United States for the benefit of present and future generations of Americans."

Description of Use:

To allow wildlife interpretation and environmental education programs to be conducted on Waterfowl Production Areas. Formal programs include activities prepared, scheduled, and organized for school-aged children and organized groups by U.S. Fish and Wildlife Service staff. Programs conducted by the Prairie Wetlands Learning Center would be included in this category. In most cases, curriculums and program schedules are prepared in advance. These curriculums address a number of wildlife conservation issues including wetland and grassland conservation, migratory bird management, and the conservation of endangered species. Informal programs include self-guided auto tour routes and nature trails, impromptu presentations and discussions of wildlife conservation issues with interested citizens, casual visitors, and unscheduled groups. The visitation and use of a Waterfowl Production Area by local educators and their classes on their own for the purposes of furthering their understanding of natural resource management issues would also classified as an informal program.

In addition, this use includes the development of indoor interpretive areas within Wetland Management District offices. There are many purposes for these exhibits, including telling the story of waterfowl conservation and the National Wildlife Refuge System.

Availability of Resources:

Some staff and funding are available for a limited amount of interpretation and environmental education programming on Waterfowl Production Areas. Currently, however, staffing levels and funding are not adequate to fully capitalize on all the opportunities to interpret wildlife conservation issues within these rural communities. The individual station Comprehensive Conservation Plans detail the needed funding and staff to bring these programs up to Service standards.

Anticipated Impacts of the Use:

The overall impacts to Waterfowl Production Areas and their associated wildlife populations from this use will be minimal. There will be some disturbance to waterfowl and other wildlife, but at levels that will not likely interfere with waterfowl production. School buses and personal vehicles will utilize parking areas and access trails already constructed for use by waterfowl hunters and Service employees conducting habitat management activities. The limited number of nature trails that will be developed will minimize disturbance to vegetation and wildlife use of these areas. Any auto tour routes are designed to minimize disturbance to waterfowl during the spring breeding/nest season.

Public Review and Comment:

Six open houses were held in preparation for the Comprehensive Conservation Plans for the Minnesota Wetland Management Districts. Public comments have also been solicited about Service operations including public use programs such as interpretation and environmental education. The Service has also contracted with the University of Minnesota to conduct a visitor use study of Waterfowl Production Areas in western Minnesota. Upon completion, this survey will yield additional public input into the use of Waterfowl Production Areas for interpretation and environmental education.

Determination:

_____ Use is Not Compatible

_X_ Use is Compatible With Following Stipulation

Stipulation Necessary to Ensure Compatibility:

1. Use of motorized vehicles and water craft is prohibited except by permit or in designated parking areas, access trails, or public roads/tour routes.

2. Managers will monitor use patterns and densities and make adjustments in timing, location and duration as needed to limit disturbance.

Justification:

This use has been determined compatible provided the above stipulation is implemented. This use is being permitted as a priority public use and will not diminish the primary purposes of waterfowl production as well as conservation of migratory birds and other wildlife. This use will meet the mission of the NWRS by furthering understanding and knowledge of this Nation's migratory bird conservation needs by the general public.

Signature: Project Leader s/Steven J. Delehanty 3/26/03

Concurrence: Regional Chief s/Nita M. Fuller 4/9/03

Mandatory 10- or 15-year Re-evaluation Date: 2017

COMPATIBILITY DETERMINATION

Use: Recreational Fishing

Refuge Name: Morris Wetland Management District

Establishing and Acquisition Authority(ies):

Waterfowl Production Areas - The Migratory Bird Hunting and Conservation Stamp
Act, March 16, 1934, (16 U.S.C. Sec. 718-718h, 48 Stat. 452) as amended August 1,
1958, (P.L. 85-585; 72 Stat. 486) for acquisition of "Waterfowl Production Areas"; the
Wetlands Loan Act, October 4, 1961, as amended (16 U.S.C. 715k-3 - 715k-5, Stat.
813), funds appropriated under the Wetlands Loan Act are merged with duck stamp
receipts in the fund and appropriated to the Secretary for the acquisition of migratory
bird refuges under provisions of the Migratory Bird Conservation Act, February 18,
1929, (16 U.S.C. Sec. 715, 715d - 715r, as amended.

FmHA fee title transfer properties - Consolidated Farm and Rural Development Act
7 U.S.C. § 2002.

Refuge Purpose(s):

Waterfowl Production Areas - "....as Waterfowl Production Areas" subject to "....all of
the provisions of such Act [Migratory Bird Conservation Act]....except the inviolate
sanctuary provisions...." and "...for any other management purpose, for migratory
birds"

FmHA fee title transfer properties - "for conservation purposes...."

National Wildlife Refuge System Mission:

"...To administer a national network of lands and waters for the conservation, management, and where appropriate, restoration of the fish, wildlife, and plant resources and
their habitats within the United States for the benefit of present and future generations of Americans."

Description of Use:

Allow public fishing on Waterfowl Production Areas (WPAs) in accordance with State
regulations and seasons. Minnesota recreational fishing regulations allow the traditional taking of game fish species with rod and reel from shore, a boat or through the
ice, removal of rough fish by spear, harpoon, archery and dip net as well as the taking
of limited quantities of mussels, crayfish, frogs, minnows and turtles for personal use.
All WPAs will be open to public fishing, provided that all forms of fishing or entry on
all or any part of individual areas may be temporarily suspended by posting upon
occasions of unusual or critical conditions of, or affecting land, water, vegetation, or
wildlife populations. As of March 1999 the U.S. Fish and Wildlife Service owns a total
of 56,693 acres of wetlands on WPAs in Minnesota. Although the entire wetland
acreage is open to fishing approximately one (1) percent provide waters deep enough
to support viable fisheries. Acquisition of WPAs is ongoing and as lands are purchased they will be opened to fishing. The game fish season ordinarily runs from the
second Sunday in May through the third Sunday in February while other season for
taking of aquatic species run from April or May through November to February.
Generally WPAs have access trails from public roads and for safety reasons parking

lots of less than 1 acre are provided where sufficient traffic exists. This use is being proposed as (1) "The Procedural Agreement between the Minnesota Department of Natural Resources and Service for the Coordination of the Small Wetlands Acquisition Program in Minnesota" states "it is the policy of the Regional Director to cooperate with the Department in providing habitat for resident wildlife and for public access and use, including hunting." and (2) Fishing is a priority public use on National Wildlife Refuge System Lands. WPAs average approximately 210 acres in size and are intermingled across the landscape with other public and private lands. The few WPAs with viable fisheries are generally connected to adjacent streams or lakes that are located off Service lands and aquatic species move between these bodies of water. The State of Minnesota manages these species over the larger bodies of water maintaining healthy populations by allowing harvest of surpluses though recreational fishing.

Availability of Resources:

WPAs by statute and regulation are open to waterfowl hunting and as a result access trails, parking lots, signage and other facilities as well as staff to enforce regulations and maintain these facilities have been provided by the Service. With the exception of additional enforcement staff time these facilities will be used by the public while engaged in recreational fishing. Given the anticipated light fishing pressure, staff are deemed adequate to administer and enforce laws related to fishing.

Anticipated Impacts of the Use:

Fishing activities and harvest of other aquatic species may cause temporary disturbance to waterfowl and other wildlife using WPAs. This disturbance may displace individual animals to other parts of the WPA, however, this disturbance will be limited in scope due to: (1) the small number of WPAs with viable fisheries; (2) prohibition on use of motorized boats; (3) access which is predominately via foot travel; (4) lack of boat launching facilities. Installation and use of parking areas and access trails will result in minimal impacts as these parking areas and trails are used by waterfowl hunters as well as by Service employees conducting refuge management activities.

Public Review and Comment:

During drafting of the Comprehensive Conservation Plans six open houses were held and written comments were solicited from the public about Wetland Management District operations including public use programs such as fishing. Comments were received, compiled and addressed as issues in the Plan as well as the Environmental Assessment. No comments regarding fishing on WPAs were received. This determination was also included in the final draft distributed to the public for review and comment. Additionally the Service has contracted with the University of Minnesota to conduct a visitor use study of Waterfowl Production Areas in western Minnesota. This study is in its second year and will yield a wide array of public input on Service programs including fishing.

Determination (check one below):

_____   Use is Not Compatible

___X___   Use is Compatible With Following Stipulations

Stipulations Necessary to Ensure Compatibility:

1. Use of motorized vehicles and water craft is prohibited except by permit or in designated parking areas, access trails or public roads.

2. Camping, overnight use and fires are prohibited.

3. Littering or disposal of entrails is prohibited.

4. All applicable State and Federal Regulations will apply.
Justification: Fishing at anticipated levels and on small areas of relatively few WPAs will have localized and short-duration impacts and will not materially interfere with the waterfowl production purpose of WPAs. Stipulations will help reduce or eliminate any unwanted impacts of the use. State regulations and monitoring help ensure that harvest levels of fish do not harm long-term populations.

Signature: Project Leader s/Steven J. Delehanty 3/26/03

Concurrence: Regional Chief s/Nita M. Fuller 4/9/03

Mandatory 10- or 15-year Re-evaluation Date: 2017

COMPATIBILITY DETERMINATION

Use: Establishing Food Plots and Placing Feeder Cribs for Resident Wildlife

Station Name: Morris Wetland Management District

Establishing and Acquisition Authorities:

Waterfowl Production Areas - The Migratory Bird Hunting and Conservation Stamp Act, March 16, 1934, (16 U.S.C. Sec. 718-718h, 48 Stat. 452) as amended August 1, 1958, (P.L. 85-585; 72 Stat. 486) for acquisition of "Waterfowl Production Areas"; the Wetlands Loan Act, October 4, 1961, as amended (16 U.S.C. 715k-3 - 715k-5, Stat. 813), funds appropriated under the Wetlands Loan Act are merged with duck stamp receipts in the fund and appropriated to the Secretary for the acquisition of migratory bird refuges under provisions of the Migratory Bird Conservation Act, February 18, 1929, (16 U.S.C. Sec. 715, 715d - 715r, as amended.

FmHA fee title transfer properties - Consolidated Farm and Rural Development Act 7 U.S.C. § 2002.

Refuge Purpose(s):

Waterfowl Production Areas - "....as Waterfowl Production Areas" subject to "....all of the provisions of such Act [Migratory Bird Conservation Act]....except the inviolate sanctuary provisions...." and "...for any other management purpose, for migratory birds"

FmHA fee title transfer properties - "for conservation purposes...."

National Wildlife Refuge System Mission:

"...To administer a national network of lands and waters for the conservation, management, and where appropriate, restoration of the fish, wildlife, and plant resources and their habitats within the United States for the benefit of present and future generations of Americans."

Description of Use:

Allow the establishment of food plots and the placement of feeder cribs on Waterfowl Production Areas (WPAs) throughout Minnesota in accordance with the attached stipulations section. Food plots are small fields of agricultural crops with some or all of the crop left standing through the winter. Feeder cribs are either containers or bales containing grain or forage designed for use by resident wildlife during the winter. Certain WPAs have been identified as critical wintering areas for resident wildlife. Allowing the establishment of food plots or placement of feeder cribs provides winter cover and food sources during harsh winter conditions. Particularly during severe winters, food plots and feeder cribs are widely recognized as important to maintain populations of resident wildlife, especially pheasants, deer, and prairie grouse. The food plots and feeder cribs are maintained by private individuals (under cooperative farming agreements), sporting clubs, or other agencies such as the Minnesota Department of Natural Resources (DNR). Typically, these food plots or feeder cribs are used each year on the same WPA. Food plots are sometimes rotated onto different sites within the same WPA to reduce the build-up of insect or plant pests within the food plot or to manage a stand of non-native vegetation through the use of periodic re-seeding following use as a food plot. The use of food plots and feeder cribs also cultivates a strong sense of cooperation between the U.S. Fish and Wildlife Service and its partners.

Feeder cribs and food plots are not a priority public use as identified in the Refuge Improvement Act. Feeder cribs and food plots are a non-essential but helpful tool to facilitate two priority uses (hunting and wildlife observation) since they help maintain high populations of species widely viewed as desirable to view and hunt.

Availability of Resources:

Establishment of food plots and placement of feeder cribs maintained by private organization or other agencies requires limited Service resources. Food plots are managed under cooperative farming agreement with private individuals or by local sporting clubs. Likewise, feeder cribs are placed and maintained by volunteers or the DNR requiring little to no Service involvement. There is a modest administrative cost associated with developing cooperative farming agreements with private coordinators. These costs typically involve a few hours of staff time for each food plot agreement with most agreements lasting 2 or 3 years. Feeder crib placement requires less administrative oversight.

Anticipated Impacts of the Use:

Feeder crib placement will result in minimal impacts as they are generally placed during the winter months and are very small in size. (Typically, a pallet-sized feeding platform or hay bale rests on the ground.) There will be some temporary disturbance to resident wildlife when feeder cribs are placed on the unit or when additional food is added once or twice per winter. There is an aesthetic cost associated with allowing placement of an artificial structure in a natural setting. Waterfowl impacts are small since the cribs are usually installed after fall migration is complete. Cribs are normally removed before spring nesting begins. If they are left in place during the nesting season, there is a small plot of ground under the crib unavailable for nesting or other migratory bird use. There is likely an inconsequential benefit to a few migratory bird species that use the feeder cribs during winter months. There is some opportunity for enhanced wildlife observation since resident wildlife, particularly pheasants, tend to frequent the area around the feeder cribs and are visible from adjacent roads.

Food plots have more significant impacts in that most plots are approximately 10 acres in size, effectively eliminating that land from use by nesting waterfowl or other migratory birds. Grassland bird research suggests that agricultural crops do not create the same harmful barrier to grassland bird use as tree plantings. (Some grassland birds avoid not only the trees but also a zone around the trees or are prevented from making normal daily movements from one side of a tree line to another.) Many grassland bird species, possibly including waterfowl, have better nest success when nesting in large contiguous blocks of grassland. Careful siting of food plots can avoid breaking up a large grassland block into smaller fragments. Some migratory birds actually benefit from the effect of adding more vegetative edges and encouraging some annual weed growth in and around a grassland block. However, these tend to be species whose populations are less imperiled than those requiring large grassland blocks. Waterfowl impacts due to food plots can be reduced but not eliminated by siting the food plots strategically and confining their use to critical areas. Stipulations identified later in this document will prevent critical resources such as native prairie remnants or large, contiguous blocks of grassland habitat from being degraded or destroyed by food plots.

Agricultural chemical impacts due to food plots will be reduced with restrictions on allowable herbicides used. No insecticide use will be allowed on food plots. Runoff and erosion are minimized with proper food plot siting.

Food plots tend to be popular areas for hunting and the increased levels of hunting around food plots will cause increased levels of disturbance due to hunter activity. These periodic disturbances should be mainly limited to autumn and early winter hunting seasons. The impact to waterfowl should be small.

The planting, tending, and partial harvest of food plots creates brief episodes of intrusion with agricultural tractors and implements but the impact to wildlife and public use should be minor.

Public Review and Comment:

During drafting of the Comprehensive Conservation Plans six open houses were held and written comments were solicited from the public about Wetland Management District operations including management techniques such as food plots and feeder cribs. Additionally the Service has contracted with the University of Minnesota to conduct a Visitor use study of WPA's in western Minnesota. This study is in its second year and will yield a wide array of public input on Service programs including land management issues.

This determination is being made as part of a Comprehensive Conservation Plan. Additional opportunity for public review will occur during review of the Comprehensive Conservation Plan.
Determination:

_____Use is Not Compatible

___X___Use is Compatible With Following Stipulations

Stipulations Necessary to Ensure Compatibility:

1. Areas for food plots must be identified as critical wintering sites for resident wildlife.

2. Food plots and feeder cribs will not have negative impacts on critical habitats such as wetlands and native prairie remnants.

3. Food plots will be sited to minimize grassland fragmentation.

4. Allowable species for planting in food plots will include: corn, soybeans, sunflowers, wheat, barley, oats, rye, buckwheat, millet, and sorghum.

5. Food plots will be no greater than ten (10) acres and will occupy no more than 5 percent of the total acreage of the WPA on which the plot will be located.

6. No more than 20 percent of the WPAs in any Wetland Management District will contain a food plot.

7. No WPA will contain more than one food plot in any year.

Justification:

Restricted use of food plots and feeder cribs will not materially interfere with or detract from the purposes for which the units were established. The use of feeder cribs creates negligible interference. Food plots create more significant interference with unit purposes and are thus more stringently controlled to ensure that they remain compatible. Allowing the use of food plots leads to higher and more stable resident wildlife populations by reducing catastrophic population crashes during severe winters. These higher populations facilitate two priority public uses, hunting and wildlife observation. The impacts to waterfowl and other migratory birds are modest based on limiting the size and location of food plots, and the stipulations in place.

Signature: Project Leader s/Steven J. Delehanty 3/26/03

Concurrence: Regional Chief s/Nita M. Fuller 4/9/03

Mandatory 10-year Re-evaluation Date: 2012

COMPATIBILITY DETERMINATION

Use: Controlled grazing on waterfowl production areas and conservation easements

Station Name: Morris Wetland Management District

Establishing and Acquisition Authorities:

Waterfowl Production Areas - The Migratory Bird Hunting and Conservation Stamp Act, March 16, 1934, (16 U.S.C. Sec. 718-718h, 48 Stat. 452) as amended August 1, 1958, (P.L. 85-585; 72 Stat. 486) for acquisition of "Waterfowl Production Areas"; the Wetlands Loan Act, October 4, 1961, as amended (16 U.S.C. 715k-3 - 715k-5, Stat. 813), funds appropriated under the Wetlands Loan Act are merged with duck stamp receipts in the fund and appropriated to the Secretary for the acquisition of migratory bird refuges under provisions of the Migratory Bird Conservation Act, February 18, 1929, (16 U.S.C. Sec. 715, 715d - 715r, as amended.

FmHA fee title transfer properties - Consolidated Farm and Rural Development Act 7 U.S.C. § 2002.

Refuge Purpose(s):

Waterfowl Production Areas - "....as Waterfowl Production Areas" subject to "....all of the provisions of such Act [Migratory Bird Conservation Act]....except the inviolate sanctuary provisions...." and "...for any other management purpose, for migratory birds"

FmHA fee title transfer properties - "for conservation purposes...."

National Wildlife Refuge System Mission:

"...To administer a national network of lands and waters for the conservation, management, and where appropriate, restoration of the fish, wildlife, and plant resources and their habitats within the United States for the benefit of present and future generations of Americans."

Description of Use:

Allow the limited grazing by domestic livestock, chiefly cattle but potentially including other domestic livestock, on waterfowl production areas and easements to improve grassland vigor and health. Controlled grazing is recognized as a valuable tool to remove standing vegetation, reduce vegetative litter, and suppress woody vegetation.

Grazing may take place anytime from April through November. Most commonly, we will use short duration grazing pulses lasting 4 to 8 weeks and then require livestock removal. We will use three typical seasons of use. One season will be early spring (mid April to late May) on native prairie or seeded native grasses designed to reduce the vigor of exotic species and increase the vigor of native species. Summer grazing (July 15 - September 1) may be used, especially on non-native grasslands, to stimulate the grassland after the peak nesting season yet allow vegetative regrowth in the fall. Fall grazing (September 1 - October 31) will be designed to have effects similar to spring grazing, mostly on native prairie remnants or fields seeded with native tallgrass prairie species.

Fencing and control of livestock will be the responsibility of the cooperating private party. Market rate grazing fees will be required of permittees. Market grazing fees will include typical market deductions for unusual fencing requirements, required cattle movement, or other factors limiting economic return for the permittees. In 2001, we anticipate these market rates to be $2.75 per animal unit month (AUM). One AUM is the amount of forage consumed by a cow/calf pair in a 30-day grazing period. Thus, the grazing fee for each cow/calf pair will be $2.75 for each 30 days of grazing. Market rates will determined annually in consultation with USDA on prevailing local grazing rates.

Frequency of grazing on any unit will be based on site-specific evaluation of the grassland unit being managed. Historically, we have frequently grazed units for two consecutive years and then eliminated grazing from the unit for several years before resuming grazing.

Grazing is not a priority public use as identified in the Refuge Improvement Act. As an economic use of Refuge System lands, a compatibility determination for grazing is mandatory.

Availability of Resources:

Developing grazing agreements and monitoring compliance and biological effects requires some Service resources. Most grazing costs (fencing, monitoring herd health, and so on) are assumed by the permittee. Some alternative grassland management is required if we do not use grazing as a tool for grassland management. Typically, these other tools are prescribed burning, mowing, and haying. Haying has comparable costs to controlled grazing since it also requires administering special use permits. Mowing is more expensive since all costs are assumed by the agency. Prescribed burning is an effective grassland management tool but staff limitations prevent us from burning as many acres as desirable each year. Plus, there is likely an ecological benefit to rotating grassland management techniques and seasons over time so that a given field may be grazed one year and burned another.

Anticipated Impacts of the Use:

Grazing by domestic livestock has severe short-term effects on grassland communities. Many of these effects are desirable and are designed to maintain and improve healthy grassland communities. Some of these effects include removing standing vegetation, trampling of other vegetation, and reducing populations of pioneering woody plants. Other effects of grazing are more harmful but generally short-lived. Grazing in the spring can cause direct loss of grassland bird nests due to trampling and loss of standing vegetation. Grazing at any time of year creates an aesthetic issue of concern for some people who enjoy using WPAs; seeing public land being grazed by domestic livestock reduces the appeal of the visit for many people. Fortunately, our controlled grazing is typically of short duration and does not occur annually on any unit. Grazing livestock can create minor direct disturbance of wildlife but any harm should be negligible. There is a slight potential for conflict between members of the public and livestock or the permittee, particularly in the autumn when most WPAs receive their heaviest use. All permittees will be advised that the unit is open to the public for hunting and other recreation. There is a very slight risk of injury to the public caused by livestock. Most visitors who are uncomfortable using property containing livestock are likely to select another unit or another time of year for their visit.

Public Review and Comment:

During drafting of the Comprehensive Conservation Plans six open houses were held and written comments were solicited from the public about Wetland Management District operations including management techniques such as grazing. Additionally the Service has contracted with the University of Minnesota to conduct a visitor use study of WPAs in western Minnesota. This study is in its second year and will yield a wide array of public input on Service programs including land management issues.

A draft version of this compatibility determination will be posted at the headquarters of the Morris Wetland Management District for public review and comment.

Determination:

_____ Use is Not Compatible

___X__ Use is Compatible With Following Stipulations

Stipulations Necessary to Ensure Compatibility:

1. Grazing will not occur more frequently than 3 out of every 5 years on any tract without the preparation of a site-specific compatibility determination.

2. All fencing costs will be borne by the permittee.

3. No insecticides, including insecticidal dusting bags, will be used on WPAs or easements.

4. No supplemental feeding will be allowed without specific authorization of the Wetland District Manager.

5. Control and confinement of the livestock will be the responsibility of the permittee.

Justification:

Controlled grazing by domestic livestock will not materially interfere with or detract from the purposes for which the units were established. Limited livestock grazing creates temporary disturbances to vegetation. Many of these disturbances are desirable for grassland management. Grazing produces an undesirable but short-term impact to grassland bird nesting and site aesthetics. Controlled grazing is an alternative management tool that can be used to replace or complement prescribed burning, mowing, or haying on grasslands. Without occasional disturbance caused by mowing, haying, burning, or grazing, the health of the grassland community would decline, as would an areas potential for waterfowl production.

Signature: Project Leader s/Steven J. Delehanty 3/26/03

Concurrence: Regional Chief s/Nita M. Fuller 4/9/03

Mandatory 10-year Re-evaluation Date: 2012

COMPATIBILITY DETERMINATION

Use: Haying

Station Name: Morris Wetland Management District

Establishing and Acquisition Authority(ies):

Waterfowl Production Areas - The Migratory Bird Hunting and Conservation Stamp Act, March 16, 1934, (16 U.S.C. Sec. 718-718h, 48 Stat. 452) as amended August 1, 1958, (P.L. 85-585; 72 Stat. 486) for acquisition of "Waterfowl Production Areas"; the Wetlands Loan Act, October 4, 1961, as amended (16 U.S.C. 715k-3 - 715k-5, Stat. 813), funds appropriated under the Wetlands Loan Act are merged with duck stamp receipts in the fund and appropriated to the Secretary for the acquisition of migratory bird refuges under provisions of the Migratory Bird Conservation Act, February 18, 1929, (16 U.S.C. Sec. 715, 715d - 715r, as amended.

FmHA fee title transfer properties - Consolidated Farm and Rural Development Act 7 U.S.C. § 2002.

Refuge Purpose(s):

Waterfowl Production Areas - "....as Waterfowl Production Areas" subject to "....all of the provisions of such Act [Migratory Bird Conservation Act]....except the inviolate sanctuary provisions...." and "...for any other management purpose, for migratory birds"

FmHA fee title transfer properties - "for conservation purposes...."

National Wildlife Refuge System Mission:

"...To administer a national network of lands and waters for the conservation, management, and where appropriate, restoration of the fish, wildlife, and plant resources and their habitats within the United States for the benefit of present and future generations of Americans."

Description of Use:

Haying is the cutting and removal, by baling and transport to an off-refuge location, of grass, either nonnative cools season species such as brome or native warm or cool season species. Haying of this type is typically done by a cooperative farmer acting under authority of a Cooperative Farming Agreement or Special Use Permit issued by the Wetland District Manager.

Haying can be an effective management tool as part of an overall grassland management plan to improve and maintain district grasslands for the benefit of migratory birds. Grasslands need periodic renovation to maintain vigor, diversity, and the structure necessary for migratory bird use. Haying is an effective alternative to burning or grazing, which are two other means used by district staff to maintain grassland vigor. If local site conditions preclude use of prescribe fire due to hazards to neighboring property or a similar problem, removal of accumulated biomass through haying does serve to reduce unwanted overstory, reduce woody plant invasion, etc. Such removal will allow for more vigorous regrowth of desirable species following the haying, although results are neither as dramatic nor positive as with prescribed fire.

Haying may also be used as part of a native grass seeding strategy on newly acquired lands needing restoration. To reduce weed competition and minimize herbicide applications, a cooperative farmer may be used to seed the native grass mix and interseed it with oats. As a requirement of the permit, the cooperator would be required to cut, bale, and remove the oats before maturation. Such silage is useful for dairy operations and serves the biological purpose of releasing the young native grasses for vigorous midsummer growth with minimal competition.

A third possible use of haying on district grasslands involves the initial steps of removing unwanted vegetation prior to seeding the area to native grasses. Haying of a nonnative cool season field is an effective step in advance of spraying the field with Round Up or a similar chemical designed to kill all existing vegetation. Removal of the heavy grass overstory by haying allows the chemical spray to more effectively treat the target plants. Better removal of the unwanted grasses will in turn ensure better success of the planted native grasses whether they are interseeded into the sod or the soil turned over and leveled prior to seeding.

A more limited application for haying on Waterfowl Production Areas involves its use for establishing fire breaks for the prescribed fire program. A cooperative farmer would hay the grassland strips in early fall. That area would then green up earlier in the spring and would have no dead overstory biomass, allowing its use as a fire break.

Waterfowl Production Areas in Minnesota average less than 200 acres in size and are intermingled with private and other public lands. Although specific acreages for fields to be hayed will vary by unit, they will typically range from 5 to 40 acres with only rare exceptions exceeding 75 acres. Newly seeded areas with oats as a nurse crop may be larger as new units are frequently seeded in entirety. In that case, haying could possibly cover the entire unit and cover several hundred acres. Hay acreages for fire breaks would be very small, estimated at less than 5 acres per WPA per event.

Availability of Resources:

No additional fiscal resources are needed to conduct this use. The needed staff time is already committed and available. Most of the work needed to prepare for this use would be done as part of routine grassland management duties. The decision to use a cooperative farmer for haying would only follow as part of strategies developed under grassland management discussions. The additional time needed to coordinate issuance and oversight of the needed Special Use Permit or Cooperative Farming Agreement for haying is relatively minor and within existing district resources.

Anticipated Impacts of the Use:

Haying will result in short-term disturbances and long-term benefits to both resident and migratory wildlife using Waterfowl Production Areas. Short-term impacts will include disturbance and displacement typical of any noisy heavy equipment operation. Cutting and removal of standing grasses will also result in short-term loss of habitat for those species requiring tall grasses for feeding and perching such as obligatory grassland species such as the bobolink or dickcissel. Long-term benefits will accrue due to the increased vigor of the regrown grasses or the establishment of highly desirable native tallgrass species, which will improve conditions for those same species affected by the short-term negative impacts. Longer-term negative impacts may occur to resident wildlife species such as pheasant that would lose overwintering habitat in the hay areas. Strict time constraints placed on this use will limit anticipated impacts to these relatively minor areas.

Public Review and Comment:

During the Scoping phase of the preparation of the Comprehensive Conservation Plan (CCP), six open houses were held to solicit public input and comment on all aspects of district management. Draft copies of the CCP will be distributed during a 30-day comment period and an additional six public meetings will be held to garner public comments, written and verbal, on the draft plan including all compatibility determinations.

Determination:

_____ Use is Not Compatible

___X__ Use is Compatible With Following Stipulations

Stipulations Necessary to Ensure Compatibility:

1. Haying will only be allowed after July 15 to minimize disturbance to nesting migratory birds. In normal years, most birds are off the nest by this date.

2. Bales must be removed from the WPA within 2 days of baling.

3. Windrowed grass left lying to dry prior to baling must be raked and moved every 2 days if left on newly seeded native grass and in no cases should remain on the ground more than 6 days prior to baling.

Justification:

Haying will not materially interfere with waterfowl production if done within the necessary stipulations. Use of haying as a management tool can be a valuable technique for providing long-term habitat improvements to grassland that otherwise would degrade through natural succession or dominance of non-native plants. Without this tool, the areas would suffer encroachment of undesirable woody species such as box elder or ash or would remain in unwanted non-native cool season grasses such as brome. Use of the areas by trust species such as waterfowl or grassland obligate species such as bobolink, dickcissel, or grasshopper sparrow would slowly decline in the absence of haying or other similar management.

Signature: Project Leader s/Steven J. Delehanty 3/26/03

Concurrence: Regional Chief s/Nita M. Fuller 4/9/03

Mandatory 10- or 15-year Re-evaluation Date: 2012

COMPATIBILITY DETERMINATION

Use: Hunting of Resident Game and Furbearers

Station Name: Morris Wetland Management District

Establishing and Acquisition Authority(ies):

Waterfowl Production Areas - The Migratory Bird Hunting and Conservation Stamp
Act, March 16, 1934, (16 U.S.C. Sec. 718-718h, 48 Stat. 452) as amended August 1,
1958, (P.L. 85-585; 72 Stat. 486) for acquisition of "Waterfowl Production Areas"; the
Wetlands Loan Act, October 4, 1961, as amended (16 U.S.C. 715k-3 - 715k-5, Stat.
813), funds appropriated under the Wetlands Loan Act are merged with duck stamp
receipts in the fund and appropriated to the Secretary for the acquisition of migratory
bird refuges under provisions of the Migratory Bird Conservation Act, February 18,
1929, (16 U.S.C. Sec. 715, 715d - 715r, as amended.

FmHA fee title transfer properties - Consolidated Farm and Rural Development Act
7 U.S.C. § 2002.

Refuge Purpose(s):

Waterfowl Production Areas - "....as Waterfowl Production Areas" subject to "....all of
the provisions of such Act [Migratory Bird Conservation Act]....except the inviolate
sanctuary provisions...." and "...for any other management purpose, for migratory
birds"

FmHA fee title transfer properties - "for conservation purposes...."

National Wildlife Refuge System Mission:

"...To administer a national network of lands and waters for the conservation, management, and where appropriate, restoration of the fish, wildlife, and plant resources and
their habitats within the United States for the benefit of present and future generations of Americans."

Description of Use:

Allow public hunting of resident game and furbearers on Waterfowl Production Areas
in accordance with State regulations and seasons. All Waterfowl Production Areas
will be open to public hunting, provided that all forms of hunting or entry on all or any
part of individual areas may be temporarily suspended by posting upon occasions of
unusual or critical conditions of, or affecting land, water, vegetation, or wildlife
populations. Hunting is a priority public use on National Wildlife Refuge System
Lands and as of March 1999 the U.S. Fish and Wildlife Service owns a total of 171,863
acres of Waterfowl Production Areas in Minnesota. Acquisition of Waterfowl Production Areas is ongoing and as lands are purchased they will be opened to hunting of
resident game and furbearers. Although open to all state seasons the majority of use
occurs from mid September though the end of December. Many Waterfowl Production Areas have trails necessary to gain access from public roads and for safety
reasons, in high traffic areas, parking lots of less than 1 acre are provided. This use is
being proposed as: (1) "The Procedural Agreement between the Minnesota Department of Natural Resources and Service for the Coordination of the Small Wetlands
Acquisition Program in Minnesota" states "it is the policy of the Regional Director to

cooperate with the Department in providing habitat for resident wildlife and for public access and use, including hunting."; (2) hunting is a priority public use on National Wildlife Refuge system Lands. Waterfowl Production Areas average less than 200 acres in size and are intermingled with private and other public lands. The State of Minnesota manages resident game and furbearers over these broad landscapes and maintains healthy populations by allowing harvest of surpluses though recreational hunting.

Availability of Resources:

Waterfowl Production Areas are by statute and regulation open to waterfowl hunting. These lands have been open to hunting since they were acquired and as a result access trails, parking lots, signage and other facilities, as well as staff to enforce regulations and maintain these facilities, have been provided by the Service. With the exception of additional enforcement staff time, these facilities will be used by those who hunt resident game and furbearers as well as waterfowl.

Anticipated Impacts of the Use:

Installation and use of parking areas and access trails will result in minimal impacts as these parking areas and trails are used by waterfowl hunters as well as by Service employees conducting refuge management activities. Although hunting causes mortality and temporary disturbance to waterfowl and other wildlife, harvesting populations to the carrying capacity of existing habitat insures long-term health and survival of the species. Hunting occurs well after the breeding season for waterfowl so no disturbance to this central purpose is anticipated.

Public Review and Comment:

During drafting of the Comprehensive Conservation Plans six open houses were held and written comments were solicited from the public about Wetland Management District operations, including public use programs such as hunting. This determination was also included in the final draft distributed to the public for review and comment. Additionally the Service has contracted with the University of Minnesota to conduct a visitor use study of Waterfowl Production Areas in western Minnesota. This study is in its second year and will yield a wide array of public input on Service programs including hunting of resident game and furbearers.

Determination (check one below):

_____ Use is Not Compatible

__X__ Use is Compatible With Following Stipulations

Stipulations Necessary to Ensure Compatibility:

1. Nontoxic shot must be used in accordance with current regulations.
2. Use of motorized vehicles and water craft is prohibited except by permit or in designated parking areas, access trails or public roads.
3. Camping, overnight use and fires are prohibited.
4. All applicable State and Federal Regulations will apply.

Justification:

This use has been determined compatible provided the above stipulations are implemented. This use is being permitted as it is a priority public use and will not diminish the primary purposes of waterfowl production as well as conservation of migratory birds and other wildlife. This use will meet the mission of the NWRS by providing renewable resources for the benefit of the American public while conserving fish, wildlife and plant resources on these lands.

Signature: Project Leader s/Steven J. Delehanty 3/26/03

Concurrence: Regional Chief s/Nita M. Fuller 4/9/03

Mandatory 10- or 15-year Re-evaluation Date: 2017

COMPATIBILITY DETERMINATION

Use: Irrigation travelways on Waterfowl Management Wetland Easements and/or FmHA type "C" Wetland Easements

Station Name: Morris Wetland Management District

Establishing and Acquisition Authority(ies):

Waterfowl Production Areas - The Migratory Bird Hunting and Conservation Stamp Act, March 16, 1934, (16 U.S.C. Sec. 718-718h, 48 Stat. 452) as amended August 1, 1958, (P.L. 85-585; 72 Stat. 486) for acquisition of "Waterfowl Production Areas"; the Wetlands Loan Act, October 4, 1961, as amended (16 U.S.C. 715k-3 - 715k-5, Stat. 813), funds appropriated under the Wetlands Loan Act are merged with duck stamp receipts in the fund and appropriated to the Secretary for the acquisition of migratory bird refuges under provisions of the Migratory Bird Conservation Act, February 18, 1929, (16 U.S.C. Sec. 715, 715d - 715r, as amended.

FmHA fee title transfer properties - Consolidated Farm and Rural Development Act 7 U.S.C. § 2002.

Refuge Purpose(s):

Waterfowl Production Areas - "....as Waterfowl Production Areas" subject to "....all of the provisions of such Act [Migratory Bird Conservation Act]....except the inviolate sanctuary provisions...." and "...for any other management purpose, for migratory birds"

FmHA fee title transfer properties - "for conservation purposes...."

National Wildlife Refuge System Mission:

"...To administer a national network of lands and waters for the conservation, management, and where appropriate, restoration of the fish, wildlife, and plant resources and their habitats within the United States for the benefit of present and future generations of Americans."

Description of Use:

Allow irrigation travelways through wetland areas protected by an easement that prohibits burning, draining, filling, or leveling. This use of travelways in wetland areas may be permitted via four techniques: (1) Placement of 4-foot to 5-foot wide wooden beams laced together with cable in "railroad bed" style; (2) placement of 4-foot to 5-foot wide metal mats made of corrugated, expanded or punched metal; (3) removal of the muck layer not to exceed 10 foot in width in the bottom of the wetland and replacing it with sand or gravel to the natural bottom contour; (4) exposure of hard substrate by removal of the muck layer not to exceed 10 foot in width in the bottom of the wetland (only permitted in high water table wetlands). More specific details for allowing this use are found in the Service's Administrative and Enforcement Procedures for Waterfowl Management Easement Manual.

Availability of Resources:

Wetland easements are currently monitored by Service employees via aerial and ground inspection to ensure that landowners comply with the provisions of the easement document. Little additional cost will be incurred to monitor this use while inspecting other easements. Additional staff, equipment, and supplies are needed to map and better monitor all easements. The individual station Comprehensive Conservation Plans detail the needed funds and staffing levels to properly monitor these easements.

Anticipated Impacts of the Use:

The construction phase of the project will cause temporary disturbance to wildlife using the wetland easement areas. Installation of properly constructed travelways will result in no long-term impacts to the wetlands or wildlife using them. Disturbance by the irrigation equipment itself is expected to be minimal due to the slow rate of movement and acclimatization by wildlife.

Public Review and Comment:

During drafting of the Comprehensive Conservation Plans six open houses were held and written comments were solicited from the public related to Wetland Management District operations including easement acquisition and management operations. This determination was also included in the final draft distributed to the public for review and comment.

Determination (check one below):

___   Use is Not Compatible

_X_   Use is Compatible With Following Stipulations

Stipulations Necessary to Ensure Compatibility:

1. The landowner must demonstrate that equipment and/or topography modifications cannot be accomplished to avoid wetlands, and equipment is incapable of traversing wetlands in their natural condition.
2. No pesticides, fertilizers or other compounds except water may be passed through the irrigation system while traversing the wetland area.

3. Permits to allow the use must be issued by the Regional Director, will not exceed 10 years in duration and will not be issued where groundwater withdrawal negatively impacts the water levels of surface wetlands.

4. Permits will limit construction of travelways to times of low waterfowl/wildlife use and require Service presence during installation or subsequent maintenance activities.

5. Only travelways approved in the Service's Administrative and Enforcement Procedures for Waterfowl Management Easements Manual may be installed.

Justification:

With the above stipulations, impacts of this use will be temporary during the construction phase and little to none during operation. This use will not diminish the long-term productivity of easement wetlands for waterfowl production or other wildlife. Thus, the use will not materially interfere with the waterfowl production or conservation purpose of the units.

Signature: Project Leader s/Steven J. Delehanty 3/26/03

Concurrence: Regional Chief s/Nita M. Fuller 4/9/03

Mandatory 10- or 15 year Re-evaluation Date: 2012

COMPATIBILITY DETERMINATION

Use: Installation of Bluebird Boxes, other Nest Boxes, or Nesting Structures by Public or Groups

Station Name: Morris Wetland Management District

Establishing and Acquisition Authorities:

Waterfowl Production Areas - The Migratory Bird Hunting and Conservation Stamp Act, March 16, 1934, (16 U.S.C. Sec. 718-718h, 48 Stat. 452) as amended August 1, 1958, (P.L. 85-585; 72 Stat. 486) for acquisition of "Waterfowl Production Areas"; the Wetlands Loan Act, October 4, 1961, as amended (16 U.S.C. 715k-3 - 715k-5, Stat. 813), funds appropriated under the Wetlands Loan Act are merged with duck stamp receipts in the fund and appropriated to the Secretary for the acquisition of migratory bird refuges under provisions of the Migratory Bird Conservation Act, February 18, 1929, (16 U.S.C. Sec. 715, 715d - 715r, as amended.

FmHA fee title transfer properties - Consolidated Farm and Rural Development Act 7 U.S.C. § 2002.

Refuge Purpose(s):

Waterfowl Production Areas - "....as Waterfowl Production Areas" subject to "....all of the provisions of such Act [Migratory Bird Conservation Act]....except the inviolate sanctuary provisions...." and "...for any other management purpose, for migratory birds"

FmHA fee title transfer properties - "for conservation purposes...."

National Wildlife Refuge System Mission:

"...To administer a national network of lands and waters for the conservation, management, and where appropriate, restoration of the fish, wildlife, and plant resources and their habitats within the United States for the benefit of present and future generations of Americans."

Description of Use:

Allow the installation of nest structures such as bluebird nest boxes and wood duck boxes by individuals or groups on Waterfowl Production Areas throughout Minnesota. Site-by-site authorization will be made by the Refuge Manager via a letter of authorization. Requests for installing nesting structures are occasionally made by individuals and sporting groups. The majority of requests are for bluebird and wood duck boxes to be placed along roads near the edges of WPA boundaries. Some requests could be for artificial mallard nesting sites or other artificial nest sites for migratory birds. The structures are usually placed in late winter or early spring. Structures are affixed using either floating rafts (less common) or poles or posts. Structures are occasionally mounted to existing trees although this is less desirable due to increased nest predation.

In all cases, the intention of the requestors is to enhance wildlife populations through providing safe nesting sites.

Placing artificial nesting structures on WPAs is not a priority public use as defined in the Refuge Improvement Act. The use is a non-essential contributor to other priority uses such as wildlife observation, wildlife photography, and environmental education.

Availability of Resources:

Installation of artificial nest structures on Waterfowl Production Areas by private individuals or groups requires minimal resources. Monitoring and maintenance of structures is required by the private individual or group as well as all associated costs of the installation. Should cooperators fail to adequately maintain the structures, there will be some cost associated with removing abandoned structures.

Anticipated Impacts on Refuge Purpose(s):

The installation of artificial nesting structures has a minimal impact on the purposes for which Waterfowl Production Areas were established. Waterfowl nesting structures will increase the production of waterfowl by providing sites for nests where predators are less likely to destroy the nests. Waterfowl nests in nesting structures are far likelier to be successful than nests in uplands. Other structures such as bluebird houses will provide nesting sites for other migratory birds. Artificial nesting boxes are widely credited with helping increase the population of eastern bluebirds in North America.

There is some small, temporary wildlife disturbance caused during placement and maintenance of the structures. This disturbance is minor.

There are some aesthetic costs associated with placing artificial structures in natural settings. These costs are minimized by requiring placement of non-waterfowl structures along the edges of WPAs in areas already appearing unnatural due to fences, signs, and adjacent crop fields. Wood duck boxes and other waterfowl nesting devices are typically placed in or near wetlands, although private parties typically prefer to place the structures adjacent to roads. No access by motorized vehicles or other special access will be provided for installing nest structures.

Public Review and Comment:

During drafting of the Comprehensive Conservation Plans six open houses were held and written comments were solicited from the public about Wetland Management District operations including public use programs such as the installation of artificial nesting structures. Additionally the Service has contracted with the University of Minnesota to conduct a visitor use study of WPAs in western Minnesota. This study is in its second year and will yield a wide array of public input on Service programs including wildlife nesting structures.

This determination is being made as part of a Comprehensive Conservation Plan. Additional review will occur as part of the public review of the Comprehensive Conservation Plan.

Determination:

_____ Use is Not Compatible

___X___ Use is Compatible With Following Stipulations

Stipulations Necessary to Ensure Compatibility:

1. Approval from Project Leader via a letter of authorization is required prior to installation.

2. Annual maintenance is required.

3. Structures may be removed upon Project Leaders' request. Some possible reasons include: lack of maintenance, poor placement, and variation from approved installation plan.

4. Ownership of any nest structure placed on any Waterfowl Production Areas by private individuals or groups will be forfeited to the Service upon installation.

Justification:

Artificial nesting structures do not materially interfere with or detract from the purposes for which the units were acquired. In fact, these structures likely contribute to the purposes of Waterfowl Production Areas by providing secure nesting sites for waterfowl and other migratory birds. Nest success for ducks using artificial nest structures is higher than for ducks nesting in grasslands. Nesting boxes for cavity nesting birds like bluebirds and wood ducks can increase populations when natural cavities are scarce. At worst, nesting structures are neutral in their effect; likely there is a positive effect. The aesthetic costs of artificial nest structures are modest and can be minimized through appropriate siting.

Signature: Project Leader s/Steven J. Delehanty 3/26/03

Concurrence: Regional Chief s/Nita M. Fuller 4/9/03

Mandatory 10-year Re-evaluation Date: 2012

COMPATIBILITY DETERMINATION

Use: Wildlife Observation and Photography (Including the means of access such as hiking, snowshoeing, cross-country skiing, and canoeing)

Station Name: Morris Wetland Management District

Establishing and Acquisition Authorities:

Waterfowl Production Areas - The Migratory Bird Hunting and Conservation Stamp Act, March 16, 1934, (16 U.S.C. Sec. 718-718h, 48 Stat. 452) as amended August 1, 1958, (P.L. 85-585; 72 Stat. 486) for acquisition of "Waterfowl Production Areas"; the Wetlands Loan Act, October 4, 1961, as amended (16 U.S.C. 715k-3 - 715k-5, Stat. 813), funds appropriated under the Wetlands Loan Act are merged with duck stamp receipts in the fund and appropriated to the Secretary for the acquisition of migratory bird refuges under provisions of the Migratory Bird Conservation Act, February 18, 1929, (16 U.S.C. Sec. 715, 715d - 715r, as amended.

FmHA fee title transfer properties - Consolidated Farm and Rural Development Act 7 U.S.C. § 2002.

Refuge Purpose(s):

Waterfowl Production Areas - "....as Waterfowl Production Areas" subject to "....all of the provisions of such Act [Migratory Bird Conservation Act]....except the inviolate sanctuary provisions...." and "...for any other management purpose, for migratory birds"

FmHA fee title transfer properties - "for conservation purposes...."

National Wildlife Refuge System Mission:

"...To administer a national network of lands and waters for the conservation, management, and where appropriate, restoration of the fish, wildlife, and plant resources and their habitats within the United States for the benefit of present and future generations of Americans."

Description of Use:

Allow general public access during anytime of the year to Waterfowl Production Areas (WPAs) for the observation and photographing of associated flora and fauna. All WPAs will be open to the public for the observation and photography of wildlife and their habitats unless specifically closed by the manager. Allowable forms of access to WPAs include hiking, snowshoeing, cross-country skiing, canoes, and non-motorized boats. Limited access by bicycle, horses, and motorized vehicles will be allowed on designated driving routes only. Motorized boats, including those with electric motors, will not be allowed within WPAs. Wildlife observation and photography are priority public uses on National Wildlife Refuge System Lands as identified in the Refuge Improvement Act of 1997. Entry on all or portions of individual areas may be temporarily suspended by posting upon occasions of unusual or critical conditions affecting land, water, vegetation, wildlife populations, or public safety.

Access for wildlife observation and photography will allow public access and enjoyment of scenic views and an array of wildlife including waterfowl, other migratory birds, tallgrass prairie plants, and resident wildlife. WPAs provide opportunities for wildlife enjoyment not usually available on adjacent private land.

Waterfowl Production Areas will be open 24 hours per day although overnight camping will not be allowed.

Availability of Resources:

Wildlife observation and photography require minimal resources. These lands have been open to public use since they were acquired. Thus, access trails, parking lots, signs, and other facilities as well as staff to enforce regulations and maintain these facilities have been provided by the Service.

Some public use facilities are sub-standard. The WMD Comprehensive Conservation Plan recognizes these problems and recommends solutions to improve public access opportunities. Some enhanced wildlife observation and photography opportunities will only be provided upon implementation of the Comprehensive Conservation Plan.

Anticipated Impacts on Refuge Purpose(s):

Wildlife observation and photography pose minimal impacts on the purposes for which Waterfowl Production Areas were established. Access is typically by individuals or small groups on foot or using snowshoes or skies. Damage to habitat by walking is minimal and temporary. There is some temporary disturbance to wildlife due to human activity on the land. The most likely impact to WPA purposes would be during spring and early summer nesting and brood rearing but the expected sporadic and limited use by the public should not create unreasonable impacts. Winter activities pose no impacts to nesting waterfowl and little to impact to vegetation. The winter disturbance to resident wildlife is temporary and minor. Large groups typically use established foot trails with little impact on vegetation. Disturbance to wildlife, such as flushing a nesting bird, is inherent to these activities; however, the disturbance is temporary and generally not malicious. Any unreasonable harassment would be grounds for the manager to close the area to these uses or restrict the uses to minimize harm.

Access by motorized vehicles, bicycles, and horses is limited to established trails, public roads and parking lots. Parking lots and access trails have minimal impacts because they are relatively small in size, generally have established cover on them, and typically are mowed after the nesting season is complete. They also allow for safe use of these public lands.

Use of most WPAs for the purpose of wildlife observation and photography is minimal. The established wildlife viewing trails on a handful of WPAs are more heavily used for wildlife observation and photography but they have been designed to minimize harmful impacts.

Public Review and Comment:

During drafting of the Comprehensive Conservation Plans six open houses were held and written comments were solicited from the public about Wetland Management District operations including public use programs such as wildlife observations and photography. Additionally, the Service has contracted with the University of Minnesota to conduct a visitor use study of WPAs in western Minnesota. This study is in its second year and will yield a wide array of public input on Service programs, including wildlife observations and photography.

This determination is being developed as part of the WMD Comprehensive Conservation Plan and will be subject to further public review during the review phase of the overall plan.

Determination:

_____ Use is Not Compatible

__X__ Use is Compatible With Following Stipulations

Stipulations Necessary to Ensure Compatibility:

1. Certain modes of access such as motorized vehicle, bicycles, and horses will be limited to designated trails, public roads, and parking lots.

2. Camping, overnight use, and fires are prohibited.

3. No photo or viewing blinds may be left over night.

4. Harassment of wildlife or excessive damage to vegetation is prohibited.

Justification:

This use has been determined compatible because wildlife viewing and photography will not materially interfere with or detract from unit purposes, including waterfowl production. The level of use for wildlife observation and photography is moderate on most WPAs. The associated disturbance to wildlife is temporary and minor. Wildlife observation and photography are priority public uses and inculcate visitors with the joys of abundant wildlife and wild lands. These uses also help fulfill the mission of the National Wildlife Refuge System. Those WPAs with increased activities generally have facilities present to accommodate the public use with minor impacts to the habitat.

Signature: Project Leader s/Steven J. Delehanty 3/26/03

Concurrence: Regional Chief s/Nita M. Fuller 4/9/03

Mandatory 10-year Re-evaluation Date: 2017

COMPATIBILITY DETERMINATION

Use: One-time Fruits of the Soil Harvest

Station Name: Morris Wetland Management District

Establishing and Acquisition Authority(ies):

Waterfowl Production Areas - The Migratory Bird Hunting and Conservation Stamp
Act, March 16, 1934, (16 U.S.C. Sec. 718-718h, 48 Stat. 452) as amended August 1,
1958, (P.L. 85-585; 72 Stat. 486) for acquisition of "Waterfowl Production Areas"; the
Wetlands Loan Act, October 4, 1961, as amended (16 U.S.C. 715k-3 - 715k-5, Stat.
813), funds appropriated under the Wetlands Loan Act are merged with duck stamp
receipts in the fund and appropriated to the Secretary for the acquisition of migratory
bird refuges under provisions of the Migratory Bird Conservation Act, February 18,
1929, (16 U.S.C. Sec. 715, 715d - 715r, as amended.

FmHA fee title transfer properties - Consolidated Farm and Rural Development Act
7 U.S.C. § 2002.

Refuge Purpose(s):

Waterfowl Production Areas - "....as Waterfowl Production Areas" subject to "....all of
the provisions of such Act [Migratory Bird Conservation Act]....except the inviolate
sanctuary provisions...." and "...for any other management purpose, for migratory
birds"

FmHA fee title transfer properties - "for conservation purposes...."

National Wildlife Refuge System Mission:

"...To administer a national network of lands and waters for the conservation, management, and where appropriate, restoration of the fish, wildlife, and plant resources and
their habitats within the United States for the benefit of present and future generations of Americans."

Description of Use:

Allow one-time collection of plants or their seeds for personal use.

Plants growing on WPAs provide important wildlife habitat and can also be desirable
for landscaping or decorative uses. Individuals occasionally request permission to
harvest seeds from WPAs in order to establish these plants on private property. The
cutting and removal of some plants is occasionally requested for use in floral decora-
tions.

Hand harvest of native prairie plant seed is used to collect seed to re-establish small
plots of native plants. These plots can be for landscaping purposes or to develop
habitat for wildlife. Prairie plant seed harvest occurs during daylight hours, primarily
in September and October, but can occur for individual species throughout the summer.

The decorative portion of some plants can be used in floral arrangements or for other
decorative purposes. Cattails (Typha sp.), Baby's-breath (Gypsophila paniculata),

Asters (Aster sp.) and grapevines (Vitis sp.) are examples of some species which are occasionally used in decorative floral arrangements.

Access to harvest sites is accomplished by walking from a designated parking area or public roadway. If non-motorized watercraft are used, they should be launched at boat ramps or carried to the wetland from parking areas or public roadways.

Collection of these plants and seeds is not a wildlife-dependent recreational use. For a small number of people, this is a traditional, family oriented activity that provides an opportunity for those participating to enjoy the beauty of the natural environment. These uses also enable people to enjoy the beauty of WPA plants in or around their homes and provides small patches of habitat for wildlife.

Availability of Resources:

Waterfowl Production Areas have been open to hunting since they were acquired. As a result, access trails, parking lots, signage and other facilities as well as staff to enforce regulations and maintain these facilities have been provided by the Service. These facilities will be maintained to meet the needs of the hunting public and will be used incidentally by those who are hand harvesting plants or their seeds. This use will not require a significant increase in additional maintenance or enforcement staff expenditures. The Service will not have to provide special equipment.

Anticipated Impacts of the Use:

Historically, public participation in the hand collecting of plants or seeds on WPAs was low, and future participation is also expected to be low. The quantity and frequency of hand harvesting plants or their seeds is not expected to result in significant distur-bance, diminish wildlife food sources or jeopardize wildlife survival.

Short-term disturbance to wildlife may occur during these activities, but will be insignificant. Most of these uses occur in the late summer or fall, after ground nesting birds have completed the nesting season. This uses should not result in short or long-term impacts that adversely affect the purpose of WPAs or the mission of the National Wildlife System.

Public Review and Comment:

Six open houses were held and written comments were solicited from the public about Wetland Management District operations during the drafting of Comprehensive Conservation Plans. This process identified 22 issues of concern. One-time Fruits of the Soil Harvest on WPAs was not identified as an issue of concern.

This Compatibility Determination was prepared concurrent with, and included in, the Draft Comprehensive Conservation Plans for Wetland Management Districts in Minnesota. Public review and comment was solicited during the CCP comment period.

Determination (check one below):

_____ Use is Not Compatible

__X__ Use is Compatible With Following Stipulations

Stipulations Necessary to Ensure Compatibility:

- Camping, overnight use and fires are prohibited.
- Digging of plants or their roots is prohibited.
- Cutting trees or noxious weeds is prohibited.
- Grass/forb seed harvest is limited to 10 pounds.
- 20 plants per species can be cut and removed for decorative purposes.
- No threatened or endangered species may be harvested or cut.
- The use of motorized vehicles or motorized watercraft is prohibited except by permit or in designated parking areas, access trails or public roads.

Justification:

This use will have limited and localized impacts when conducted within the stipulations above. Administration of the use will require little to no administrative time or funding. This use will not diminish the primary purposes of waterfowl production, or the conservation of other migratory birds and wildlife.

Signature: Project Leader s/Steven J. Delehanty 3/26/03

Concurrence: Regional Chief s/Nita M. Fuller 4/9/03

Mandatory 10- or 15-year Re-evaluation Date: 2012

COMPATIBILITY DETERMINATION

Use: Placement of new, small parking areas on Waterfowl Production Areas

Station Name: Morris Wetland Management District

Establishing and Acquisition Authority(ies):

Waterfowl Production Areas - The Migratory Bird Hunting and Conservation Stamp
Act, March 16, 1934, (16 U.S.C. Sec. 718-718h, 48 Stat. 452) as amended August 1,
1958, (P.L. 85-585; 72 Stat. 486) for acquisition of "Waterfowl Production Areas"; the
Wetlands Loan Act, October 4, 1961, as amended (16 U.S.C. 715k-3 - 715k-5, Stat.
813), funds appropriated under the Wetlands Loan Act are merged with duck stamp
receipts in the fund and appropriated to the Secretary for the acquisition of migratory
bird refuges under provisions of the Migratory Bird Conservation Act, February 18,
1929, (16 U.S.C. Sec. 715, 715d - 715r, as amended.

FmHA fee title transfer properties - Consolidated Farm and Rural Development Act
7 U.S.C. § 2002.

Refuge Purpose(s):

Waterfowl Production Areas - "....as Waterfowl Production Areas" subject to "....all of
the provisions of such Act [Migratory Bird Conservation Act]....except the inviolate
sanctuary provisions...." and "...for any other management purpose, for migratory
birds"

FmHA fee title transfer properties - "for conservation purposes...."

National Wildlife Refuge System Mission:

"...To administer a national network of lands and waters for the conservation, management, and where appropriate, restoration of the fish, wildlife, and plant resources and
their habitats within the United States for the benefit of present and future generations of Americans."

Description of Use:

Allow the placement and construction of small parking areas on any Waterfowl
Production Area where the Wetland Manager considers necessary to provide safe off-
road parking and access to the general public for the following permitted activities:
hunting of migratory birds and resident game animals, hiking, wildlife observation,
photography, fishing, and/or interpretation, all priority public uses on National
Wildlife Refuge System Lands. In addition, these parking areas will be used by
Service personnel in conducting management activities or biological surveys and
assessments on each of the Waterfowl Production Areas.

The U.S. Fish and Wildlife Service owns, as of March 1999, nearly 172,000 acres of
Waterfowl Production Areas in Minnesota. Acquisition of Waterfowl Production
Areas is ongoing and as new lands are acquired they will be opened to priority public
uses. A procedural agreement between the Minnesota Department of Natural Resources and the Service states "it is the policy of the Regional Director to cooperate
with the Department in providing habitat for resident wildlife and for public access
and use (emphasis added), including hunting."

These parking areas will be less than an acre and will be relatively primitive facilities such as grass or gravel surfaced. Barriers to restrict motorized vehicles within the parking areas and to identify the parking area boundary generally will be constructed of wood posts, wire fence or rock barriers, appropriate and available on a site specific basis.

Availability of Resources:

Waterfowl Production Areas are open to all priority public uses and as a result access trails, signage and other facilities, as well as staff to enforce regulations and maintain these facilities, have been provided by the Service. Currently the staffing levels and facilities required for public programs and accessibility on Waterfowl Production Areas do not meet Service public use standards. The individual station Comprehensive Conservation Plans detail the needed funds and manpower to bring these programs up to Service standards.

Anticipated Impacts of the Use:

Installation and use of these parking areas and access trails will result in minimal impacts as these parking areas are used infrequently during most of the year by either the general public participating in authorized and permitted activities or by Service personnel. Peak use of these areas will generally occur during fall hunting seasons when no disturbance to nesting or young animals will result. Impacts to habitat will be minimal due to their relatively small size (< 1 acre) by comparison to the average size of the Waterfowl Production Area (average < 200 acres). Impacts will be lessened by selection of sites away from any wetland or native prairie. Generally, parking areas will be constructed at or near abandoned farm sites utilizing existing graveled driveways or previously constructed farm field approaches immediately off of public roadways. Parking lots constructed within the interior of a unit will be avoided when ever possible to minimize wildlife disturbance, impacts to unique or critical habitats and conflicts with other authorized public uses.

Public Review and Comment:

During the drafting of the Comprehensive Master Plans, six open houses were held and written comments were solicited from the public about Wetland District Operations including public use programs. Additionally, the Service has contracted with the University of Minnesota to conduct a visitor use study of Waterfowl Production Areas in western Minnesota. This study, in its second year, will provide public input on Service programs and facilities on Waterfowl Production Areas.

Determination:

_____ Use is Not Compatible

_X_ Use is Compatible With Following Stipulations

Stipulations Necessary to Ensure Compatibility:

1. Parking areas must not be constructed in areas where negative wetland impacts will result.

2.Parking areas must not be constructed on native prairie habitat.

3. Camping, overnight use and fires are prohibited.

4. Location of parking areas within the interior of each unit should be avoided whenever possible.

5.An archaeological review of each selected site shall be made through the State Historic Preservation Officer and Regional Historic Preservation Officer prior to construction.

Justification:

This use has been determined compatible provided the above stipulations are implemented. This use is permitted as it is deemed necessary to provide safe off-road access by the public to participate in appropriate and permitted priority uses and will not diminish the primary purposes of waterfowl production and the conservation of migratory birds and other wildlife. This use will meet the mission of the National Wildlife Refuge System by providing resources for the benefit of the American public while conserving fish, wildlife and plant resources on these lands.

Signature: Project Leader s/Steven J. Delehanty 3/26/03

Concurrence: Regional Chief s/Nita M. Fuller 4/9/03

Mandatory 10- or 15-year Re-evaluation Date: 2012

COMPATIBILITY DETERMINATION

Use: Short-term Upland Disturbance for Highway or Other Public Interest Projects with No ROW Expansion and Full Restoration.

Station Name: Morris Wetland Management District

Establishing and Acquisition Authorities:

Waterfowl Production Areas - The Migratory Bird Hunting and Conservation Stamp Act, March 16, 1934, (16 U.S.C. Sec. 718-718h, 48 Stat. 452) as amended August 1, 1958, (P.L. 85-585; 72 Stat. 486) for acquisition of "Waterfowl Production Areas"; the Wetlands Loan Act, October 4, 1961, as amended (16 U.S.C. 715k-3 - 715k-5, Stat. 813), funds appropriated under the Wetlands Loan Act are merged with duck stamp receipts in the fund and appropriated to the Secretary for the acquisition of migratory bird refuges under provisions of the Migratory Bird Conservation Act, February 18, 1929, (16 U.S.C. Sec. 715, 715d - 715r, as amended.

FmHA fee title transfer properties - Consolidated Farm and Rural Development Act 7 U.S.C. § 2002.

Refuge Purpose(s):

Waterfowl Production Areas - "....as Waterfowl Production Areas" subject to "....all of the provisions of such Act [Migratory Bird Conservation Act]....except the inviolate sanctuary provisions...." and "...for any other management purpose, for migratory birds"

FmHA fee title transfer properties - "for conservation purposes...."

National Wildlife Refuge System Mission:

"...To administer a national network of lands and waters for the conservation, management, and where appropriate, restoration of the fish, wildlife, and plant resources and their habitats within the United States for the benefit of present and future generations of Americans."

Description of Use:

Allow short-term disturbance to uplands for highway or other public interest projects with no right-of-way expansion and full restoration. Every year, requests are made by state and local government agencies and utility companies to do repairs and improvements to existing road ways and utility facilities associated with existing rights-of-way on WPAs throughout Minnesota. Many of these requests require temporary work outside existing right-of-way boundaries, generally resulting in temporary disturbance to the associated vegetation. Frequently, the temporary work requested is required to reshape a slope immediately adjacent to a road right-of-way to improve transportation safety. Other times, the requested action can be merely for permission to turn around heavy equipment on land immediately adjacent to the right-of-way. Most often, the temporary work outside of the right-of-way is conducted during the summer and fall, when construction conditions are optimal. The work typically involves temporary disturbance to previously farmed uplands that are then reseeded to native vegetation by the requesting organization. This determination will allow approved work and temporary habitat disturbance outside the right-of-way boundary when long-term impacts are either beneficial or not significantly harmful.

Availability of Resources:

Minimal expense is required of the Service for these projects. Authorization of the projects will require the requesting organization to cover habitat restoration costs. There is a modest administrative cost to issuing and monitoring this work.

Anticipated Impacts on Refuge Purpose(s):

The impacts to the associated uplands with this use will be minimal and temporary. When the request includes unavoidable destruction of vegetation, approval will be limited to sites previously tilled or otherwise disrupted. No native prairie remnants or wetlands may be destroyed. Any areas with disturbed vegetation will be seeded by the requesting organization to a diverse mix of native species that will lead to better long-term habitat than the vegetation originally disturbed.

Most of this work occurs in summer and fall, after the waterfowl nesting season. The duration of any single project is usually 1 to 8 weeks. Occasionally, work may occur during the nesting season but the size of the disturbance zone will be minimal. The quality of the habitat in the disturbed zone may be diminished for up to 3 years following the project but the disturbed zone will provide some migratory bird value by the year following the project. The long-term productivity of the disturbed zone will frequently increase due to the replacement of exotic, less desirable cover with native vegetation.

Most of the impacts will be along existing roads in areas already subject to significant habitat and aesthetic deterioration due to existing transportation rights-of-way. Rarely, a utility right-of-way can split an otherwise contiguous block of quality habitat. In these settings, the disturbance will still be temporary but the impact to waterfowl and other migratory birds is likely greater. The existing right-of-way already authorizes disturbance within the right-of-way so the larger impact of creating a disturbance within quality habitat will likely occur anyway. The decision to authorize temporary disturbance outside the right-of-way will slightly increase the magnitude of the disturbance.

Public Review and Comment:

During drafting of the Comprehensive Conservation Plans six open houses were held and written comments were solicited from the public about Wetland Management District operations including management programs such as right-of-way issues.

This determination is being considered as part of a larger Comprehensive Conservation Plan subject and will be subject to additional public review during the public review of the entire plan.

Determination:

_____ Use is Not Compatible

__X__ Use is Compatible With Following Stipulations

Stipulations Necessary to Ensure Compatibility:

1. All work done outside of existing rights-of-way must be approved by the Project Leader in the form of a letter of authorization.

2. Conditions stipulated in a letter of authorization such as seeding mixes, weed control, etc. must be followed to remain a compatible use.

3. No work that leads to permanent loss of wetlands or native prairie remnants will be allowed without a site-specific compatibility determination.

Justification:

This use will not materially interfere with or detract from the purposes for which the units were established with the above stipulations in place. Almost all WPAs are constrained by one or more rights-of-way that were in place before acquisition by the federal government. Temporary disturbances to land adjacent to these rights-of-way will have only small, temporary harmful effects on wildlife and may lead to improved long-term productivity by replacing degraded, exotic vegetation with vigorous native vegetation. Work within the rights-of-way is beyond the authority of the Fish and Wildlife Service to regulate other than influencing the timing and scope to minimize wildlife harm. Allowing temporary work outside the right-of-way does little or no long-term harm to wildlife resources and allows the holder of the right-of-way to provide essential human services to our rural communities. Restoration of the disturbed sites can actually increase productivity by providing more robust vegetation.

Signature: Project Leader s/Steven J. Delehanty 3/26/03

Concurrence: Regional Chief s/Nita M. Fuller 4/9/03

Mandatory 10-year Re-evaluation Date: 2012

COMPATIBILITY DETERMINATION

Use: Wood Cutting/Timber Harvest

Station Name: Morris Wetland Management District

Establishing and Acquisition Authority(ies):

Waterfowl Production Areas - The Migratory Bird Hunting and Conservation Stamp Act, March 16, 1934, (16 U.S.C. Sec. 718-718h, 48 Stat. 452) as amended August 1, 1958, (P.L. 85-585; 72 Stat. 486) for acquisition of "Waterfowl Production Areas"; the Wetlands Loan Act, October 4, 1961, as amended (16 U.S.C. 715k-3 - 715k-5, Stat. 813), funds appropriated under the Wetlands Loan Act are merged with duck stamp receipts in the fund and appropriated to the Secretary for the acquisition of migratory bird refuges under provisions of the Migratory Bird Conservation Act, February 18, 1929, (16 U.S.C. Sec. 715, 715d - 715r, as amended.

FmHA fee title transfer properties - Consolidated Farm and Rural Development Act 7 U.S.C. § 2002.

Refuge Purpose(s):

Waterfowl Production Areas - "....as Waterfowl Production Areas" subject to "....all of the provisions of such Act [Migratory Bird Conservation Act]....except the inviolate sanctuary provisions...." and "...for any other management purpose, for migratory birds"

FmHA fee title transfer properties - "for conservation purposes...."

National Wildlife Refuge System Mission:

"...To administer a national network of lands and waters for the conservation, management, and where appropriate, restoration of the fish, wildlife, and plant resources and their habitats within the United States for the benefit of present and future generations of Americans."

Description of Use:

The removal of standing or fallen trees by private individuals. This Compatibility Determination applies to all wood removal activities regardless of the ultimate use of the wood (e.g. firewood, pulp, etc.). Differences in scope and necessary equipment will occur depending on the amount and type of wood available for removal. Impacts to the purpose of the WPAs and System mission are similar regardless of why the wood is removed. This activity will only occur where the Service has determined that a management need exists to remove wood from WPAs consistent with the WPA Development Plan or other document.

Wood cutting is not a priority public use, as defined by the Refuge Improvement Act of 1997, of the National Wildlife Refuge System.

Wood removal may be done within former homesites, along existing windbreaks/shelter belts, and in other areas on WPAs where trees are encroaching on the prairie. Harvest sites will vary in size from a portion of an acre up to several hundred acres depending on the site and management objectives.

Wood removal activities may be authorized throughout the year. Most often, wood removal activities will occur during the winter months when frozen ground will facilitate access and afford protection to underlying soils and vegetation.

The scope of the activity will be determined by the management objective for the area and by the quantity and quality of available wood. Equipment used for harvest may range from chainsaws and axes, to traditional logging equipment such as feller-bunchers and log skidders. Access may be by snow machine, ATV, pick-up truck, farm tractor, or larger traditional logging equipment.

Harvest of wood products may be permitted on WPAs to stop, reduce, or reverse the encroachment and presence of trees on prairie habitats. The Tallgrass Prairie habitat is arguably the most endangered of all North American ecosystems, with less than 1 percent of the historic habitat remaining. Encroachment of woody vegetation due to fire suppression, absence of landscape-scale grazing, and tree planting practices continue to threaten this habitat type. Waterfowl Production Areas are established to produce waterfowl, and managing woody vegetation to enhance prairie habitat generally facilitates that purpose. In accordance with the System mission, restoration of the tallgrass prairie habitat is appropriate over most of the acreage in the Minnesota wetland districts. Managing woody vegetation is an important means to that end.

Availability of Resources:

The time required to plan, issue permits, and monitor the implementation of a wood product harvest program would require the dedication of some existing staff hours to this activity. In permitting a wood products harvest, the manager has identified a management need and presumably has secured and prioritized station resources to that end.

Anticipated Impacts of the Use:

In permitting this type of activity, the potential exists to directly impact waterfowl production by displacement of birds from localized areas due to disturbance, or crushing of nests as a result of access for this activity. These impacts are easily avoided by timing of the activity in accordance with site specific characteristics. In limited and rare instances, a small number of individuals of tree-nesting species (e.g. wood duck, hooded merganser, etc.) may be displaced from a local area for obvious reasons.

Indirect impacts to waterfowl production will occur as a result of removing woody vegetation. In nearly every instance, these impacts will be positive. The removal of woody vegetation from historic prairie habitats impacts waterfowl production and the System mission by facilitating the restoration of tallgrass prairie and removing artificially created predator habitat from within the WPAs.

Access for the purpose of removing wood may impact habitat by rutting soils, destroying ground cover, creating weed seed beds, and increasing sedimentation due to runoff in nearby wetlands. These impacts can again be avoided by timing of the activity.

Public Review and Comment:

This Compatibility Determination is provided in draft form along with the Minnesota Wetland Management Districts' Comprehensive Conservation Plan and Environmental Assessment. Opportunity for public review and comment is concurrent with the public review process for the EA.

Determination (check one below):

_____ Use is Not Compatible

__X__ Use is Compatible With Following Stipulations

Stipulations Necessary to Ensure Compatibility:

1. Work will generally be restricted to areas where soil types indicate that pre-settlement habitat was comprised of native prairie vegetation.

2. If work is in an area where waterfowl nesting is likely, no cutting operations will be permitted from April through July 15.

3. Vehicle access for wood removal will be limited to existing trails or restricted to the frozen ground period when rutting and damage to growing vegetation would occur.

4. A special use permit will be issued so that site specific impacts can be reduced or eliminated and Service management goals are met.

Justification:

Any direct impacts on waterfowl production (take, disturbance, etc.) can be largely avoided by timing the activity so that it is not coincident with the waterfowl production season. Removal of trees in certain instances will, on occasion, eliminate wood duck, hooded merganser, or other cavity-nesting species habitat. This would be an irregular and occasional impact and, since most wood harvest will be associated with restoration sites, it is unlikely that these areas would have provided historic nesting sites. Due to the benefits that would be realized by other waterfowl species, and the abundance of artificial and natural nest sites for cavity-nesting species in the area, these impacts would not significantly detract from the WPAs' purpose or System mission.

Impacts to the habitat as a result of access to WPAs for wood removal purposes are potentially significant, but also easily avoided. Areas where woody species are removed for the purpose of conversion of the habitat type to prairie will likely receive follow-up treatments of burning, farming, or both. Ground disturbance in these areas is less problematic and possibly desirable depending on the specific site. Access to and from these areas will need to be carefully controlled (via special use permit) to avoid impacts such as rutting and increased sedimentation in area wetlands due to run-off. If existing roads are not present, access can be restricted to periods of frozen ground to avoid or minimize impacts to underlying vegetation and soils.

Other indirect impacts are generally considered positive and thus do not materially interfere with or detract from the purpose of waterfowl production or the System mission. The removal of trees along trails, in shelter belts, and within old home sites will benefit waterfowl production by assisting with the restoration of prairie habitat and eliminating predator habitat and perch sites. Individuals participating in the wood harvest program will be under special use permit and thus site specific stipulations will ensure resource protection and achievement of management goals. Control of woody species encroachment on prairie habitats is a necessary management activity for the Minnesota wetland districts in converting areas back to their historical grassland condition and directly supports the mission of the National Wildlife Refuge System.

Signature: Project Leader s/Steven J. Delehanty 3/26/03

Concurrence: Regional Chief s/Nita M. Fuller 4/9/03

Mandatory 10- or 15-year Re-evaluation Date: 2012

COMPATIBILITY DETERMINATION

Use: Trapping of Furbearers

Station Name: Morris Wetland Management District

Establishing and Acquisition Authority(ies):

Waterfowl Production Areas - The Migratory Bird Hunting and Conservation Stamp Act, March 16, 1934, (16 U.S.C. Sec. 718-718h, 48 Stat. 452) as amended August 1, 1958, (P.L. 85-585; 72 Stat. 486) for acquisition of "Waterfowl Production Areas"; the Wetlands Loan Act, October 4, 1961, as amended (16 U.S.C. 715k-3 - 715k-5, Stat. 813), funds appropriated under the Wetlands Loan Act are merged with duck stamp receipts in the fund and appropriated to the Secretary for the acquisition of migratory bird refuges under provisions of the Migratory Bird Conservation Act, February 18, 1929, (16 U.S.C. Sec. 715, 715d - 715r, as amended.

FmHA fee title transfer properties - Consolidated Farm and Rural Development Act 7 U.S.C. § 2002.

Refuge Purpose(s):

Waterfowl Production Areas - "....as Waterfowl Production Areas" subject to "....all of the provisions of such Act [Migratory Bird Conservation Act]....except the inviolate sanctuary provisions...." and "...for any other management purpose, for migratory birds"

FmHA fee title transfer properties - "for conservation purposes...."

National Wildlife Refuge System Mission:

"...To administer a national network of lands and waters for the conservation, management, and where appropriate, restoration of the fish, wildlife, and plant resources and their habitats within the United States for the benefit of present and future generations of Americans."

Description of Use:

Public trapping of resident furbearers on Waterfowl Production Areas (WPA) in Minnesota in accordance with State regulations. This Compatibility Determination does not apply to "commercial" trapping activities where the Service awards a contract, or permit, for the removal of a specie or species to facilitate management, i.e. the Service needs 3,000 muskrats removed from an area to protect a dike system.

Trapping is not a priority public use, as defined by the Refuge Improvement Act of 1997, of the National Wildlife Refuge System.

By regulation (50 CFR 31.16), lands acquired as WPAs are open to public trapping unless closed under the authority of 50 CFR 25.21. Within the Minnesota wetland management districts, only eight WPAs have been closed to trapping: three in the Detroit Lakes District and five in the Fergus Falls District. Using 1999 data, trapping is permitted on approximately 170,000 acres of WPAs in Minnesota. Trapping is permitted for a wide variety of species; however, mink, racoon, muskrat, red fox, and beaver are the primary target species. As a result, most trapping activity on WPAs is concentrated in wetland areas.

The Minnesota Department of Natural Resources maintains information on numbers of trappers, harvest, and population trends of furbearers on a statewide basis. Based on license sales and mail surveys of licensees, it is estimated that approximately 4,100 people participated in trapping during the 1999-2000 season on a statewide basis. A percentage of these trappers use WPAs. The trend in the number of people participating in trapping in Minnesota is down, and it is assumed that activity on WPAs mirrors the statewide trend. For the 3-year period ending in 1988, the annual estimated average number of trappers was more than 13,700. For the 3-year period ending in 2000, this number had declined to less than 5,300.1

Trapping seasons for various species of wildlife generally run from mid-September through mid-March, with beaver trapping extending until mid-May. Several species of unprotected mammals (weasel, coyote, striped skunk, gophers, and porcupine) may be trapped on a year-around basis. While State regulations technically permit such activity, there is no known trapping activity, excluding March and April beaver trapping, outside of the traditional winter "season." Minnesota regulations have established trap tending hours of 5 a.m. until 10:00 p.m.

Trappers may utilize leghold traps, snares, and body-gripping ("Conibear"type) traps for the purpose of trapping various furbearers, small game, and unprotected species of wildlife. Each method is qualified under State regulation as to trap size and types of allowable sets in order to protect non-target species, and provide for the safe use of the area by others.

Access for trapping on WPAs is almost exclusively by foot. Walking and snowshoeing are the primary means of access. When conditions allow, some limited, non-motorized boat access may occur for the purpose of trapping. Travel on WPAs by highway vehicles, ATVs (3 and 4-wheelers), and snowmachine is prohibited at all times. Many WPAs have parking lots to facilitate all allowed public uses, including trapping.

Availability of Resources:

There is no incremental increase in administering this activity, as allowed, above the stations' general operating costs that we can attribute directly to the public trapping program.

Anticipated Impacts of the Use:

Public trapping can potentially impact the waterfowl production of WPAs through both direct and indirect impacts. Direct impacts are those where there is an immediate cause and effect relationship between the activity and the resources required to fulfill the waterfowl production purpose and System mission. Direct impacts may include such effects as killing or displacing of waterfowl during the pair bonding/ nesting season, or destruction of nests by trampling. Indirect impacts are those where the effects of the permitted activity affect other populations or habitats that in turn have direct impacts on waterfowl production and the System purpose. Indirect impacts may include catch of target and non-target species that are predators on waterfowl and/or nests, or removal of species that induce habitat change (i.e. beaver). Impacts, either direct or indirect, may be negative, neutral, or positive.

Because of the temporal separation of trapping activities and waterfowl using the areas for production, direct impacts to waterfowl production by trappers is negligible. Beaver trappers using WPAs after early March, undoubtedly disturb individuals on occasion, and cause temporary displacement of waterfowl from specific and limited areas. These impacts would be occasional, temporary, and isolated to small geographic areas. Any habitat change as a result of the physical impacts of trapping activity (trampling, etc.) is undetectable and insignificant.

Indirect impacts to waterfowl production do result from the removal of animals under a trapping program. In many instances, these impacts are positive. Many species that may be trapped are predators on waterfowl at various stages in the production cycle. Controlling populations of predators on waterfowl has generally positive impacts on the waterfowl purpose which vary in significance among areas. Timing of the removal of predators, size of the WPA, and adjacent land use all affect the degree to which predator management, through a public trapping program, benefits waterfowl production.

Impacts to waterfowl production habitat occur as a result of removal of species such as beaver and muskrat. Due to the societal requirements to intensively manage water levels on WPAs, managing beaver and muskrat populations at reasonable levels through a public trapping program results in positive impacts to waterfowl production and minimizes the need to commit Service resources to the same end.

When considering impacts to the System mission, impacts also include those to the furbearer populations themselves. Individual animals are harvested and removed, yet data indicates these furbearer populations, with the exception of red fox, are increasing. The red fox population has shown a slight decline in the western and southern portions of the state for roughly the past 8 years. Concurrently, the red fox estimated trapping harvest has declined from over 20,000 annually through the mid-1990s, to less than 10,000 for the past two seasons.[1] In spite of the recent decline, the red fox population is comparable to that of the mid-1980s. Minnesota DNR still considers the red fox population healthy, and views slowly declining populations in the south and west as an effect of a slowly increasing coyote population in this same area and not a result of trapping.[2]

Public Review and Comment:

This Compatibility Determination is provided in draft form along with the Minnesota Wetland Management Districts' Draft Comprehensive Conservation Plan and Environmental Assessment. Opportunity for public review and comment is concurrent with the public review process for the EA.

Determination:

_____ Use is Not Compatible

_X_ Use is Compatible With Following Stipulations

Stipulations Necessary to Ensure Compatibility:

- Trapping activity must be conducted in compliance with existing State regulations.
- Trappers must comply with existing WPA access and use regulations.

Justification:

Direct impacts to the waterfowl production purpose are negligible due to the temporal separation of most trapping activity and the use of WPAs by waterfowl for production. Limited disturbance of individuals and pairs undoubtedly occurs from beaver trapping activity occurring after early March. These temporary and isolated disturbance events result in temporary displacement of birds from a specific location. Due to the duration of these events, the small number of individual waterfowl involved, and the limited geographic area impacted by the presence of one or a few individuals, these impacts on waterfowl production and the System mission are negligible.

Indirect impacts to waterfowl production occur as a result of the effects of trapping on the target, or non-target, species' populations. Most species of interest to trappers and common "non-target" catches (i.e. skunk, free-ranging house cat) are predators on waterfowl at some point in the production cycle. Management of red fox, racoon, mink, otter, and skunk populations, through a regulated trapping program is, at worst, a neutral impact, and likely a positive one in most cases on the waterfowl production purpose. Due to edge effects and concentrations of nesting waterfowl, the impacts of predator management are likely inversely related to WPA size. The average size of Minnesota's WPAs is less than 200 acres. In these small parcels, the effects of only a few individual predators can be highly significant on waterfowl production in the local area. Timing of the removal of predators also affects the impact that this activity has on waterfowl production. Again, depending on the time of year, impacts on waterfowl production may be neutral or positive. While there is considerable debate about the effects of the presence of coyotes on waterfowl production, the density and subsequent harvest of coyotes through the trapping program is insignificant. Likewise is the harvest of other species that are permitted under State regulations (i.e. gray fox, badger, opossum, martin, fisher, otter, bobcat).

Other indirect impacts on waterfowl production occur as a result of the manipulation of populations of species that affect habitat. Beaver and muskrat, by their nature, affect habitat that, in turn, may affect waterfowl production. Upon initial analysis, we often think of beaver and their wetland construction activities, and muskrat with their propensity to maintain open water, as beneficial to waterfowl production. In exceptionally large marshes and in pre-settlement times, this is/was likely the case. However, the landscape of western and southern Minnesota has been so altered through agricultural conversion that few historic ecosystem functions remain intact. Other than the fact that water continues to flow downhill, the hydrology of this landscape bears little resemblance to its pre-settlement conditions. Dikes, levees, roads, culverts, tile lines, pumps, and water control structures work to move and confine water with calculated purpose. Ramifications of disruption to this system can include private property damage, public safety hazards, disgruntled neighbors, and legal liability. As a result, the U.S. Fish and Wildlife Service intensely manages water on WPAs to provide for waterfowl production and to fulfill the mission of the National Wildlife Refuge System, while remaining within societal constraints. Left unchecked, beaver activity results in disruption to the water flow when culverts and water control structures are blocked. High muskrat populations are detrimental to levees and dikes as individuals burrow into these structures and compromise the structural integrity. Without the ability to control water levels, our waterfowl production purpose would suffer as would our ability to contribute to the System mission. A public trapping program facilitates management of beaver and muskrat populations at such levels that many benefits created by these species are realized, yet the ability of the Service to manage water levels is not compromised. On a statewide basis, beaver harvest has remained fairly stable over the past decade in spite of the decline in the number of trappers participating in the activity. The muskrat harvest fluctuates widely driven by fur prices and the natural fluctuations in muskrat populations.

Overall, trapping is a very minor public use of WPAs but is an important management tool in localized areas. The public trapping program on WPAs allows for public opportunity and management of furbearer populations. Consistent with the System mission, trapping on WPAs results in management of populations and is not a "control" program intending to eliminate components of the ecosystem for the benefit of others. Data from the State of Minnesota, DNR, on trapping activity and wildlife populations indicates removal of individuals, under the current management scheme is not resulting in harm to the target populations. The public trapping program, as managed, does not materially interfere with or detract from the Service's ability to meet our purpose of waterfowl production or the mission of the National Wildlife Refuge System.

Signature: Project Leader s/Steven J. Delehanty 3/26/03

Concurrence: Regional Chief s/Nita M. Fuller 4/9/03

Mandatory 10- or 15-year Re-evaluation Date: 2012

---

[1] Dexter, M.H., compiler. 2000. Status of wildlife populations, fall 2000. Unpub. Rep., Division of Wildlife, Minn. Dept. Nat. Res., St. Paul, Minnesota. 180pp

[2] Berg, B., Minn. Dept. Nat. Res., Grand Rapids, Minnesota. Personal Communication.

COMPATIBILITY DETERMINATION

Use: Placement of Wetland Accesses/Ramps in Support of Priority Public Uses

Station Name: Morris Wetland Management District

Establishing and Acquisition Authority(ies):

Waterfowl Production Areas - The Migratory Bird Hunting and Conservation Stamp Act, March 16, 1934, (16 U.S.C. Sec. 718-718h, 48 Stat. 452) as amended August 1, 1958, (P.L. 85-585; 72 Stat. 486) for acquisition of "Waterfowl Production Areas"; the Wetlands Loan Act, October 4, 1961, as amended (16 U.S.C. 715k-3 - 715k-5, Stat. 813), funds appropriated under the Wetlands Loan Act are merged with duck stamp receipts in the fund and appropriated to the Secretary for the acquisition of migratory bird refuges under provisions of the Migratory Bird Conservation Act, February 18, 1929, (16 U.S.C. Sec. 715, 715d - 715r, as amended.

FmHA fee title transfer properties - Consolidated Farm and Rural Development Act 7 U.S.C. § 2002.

Refuge Purpose(s):

Waterfowl Production Areas - "....as Waterfowl Production Areas" subject to "....all of the provisions of such Act [Migratory Bird Conservation Act]....except the inviolate sanctuary provisions...." and "...for any other management purpose, for migratory birds"

FmHA fee title transfer properties - "for conservation purposes...."

National Wildlife Refuge System Mission:

"...To administer a national network of lands and waters for the conservation, management, and where appropriate, restoration of the fish, wildlife, and plant resources and their habitats within the United States for the benefit of present and future generations of Americans."

Description of Use:

Allow the placement and/or construction of accesses/ramps on any Waterfowl Production Area where the Wetland Manager considers necessary to provide access to the general public for the following permitted activities: hunting of migratory birds and resident game animals, hiking, wildlife observation, photography, fishing, and/or interpretation, all priority public uses on National Wildlife Refuge System Lands. In addition, these ramps will be used by Service personnel in conducting management activities or biological surveys and assessments on each of the Waterfowl Production Areas.

The U.S. Fish and Wildlife Service owns, as of March 1999, nearly 172,000 acres of Waterfowl Production Areas in Minnesota. Acquisition of Waterfowl Production Areas is ongoing and as new lands are acquired they will be opened to priority public uses. A procedural agreement between the Minnesota Department of Natural Resources and the Service states "it is the policy of the Regional Director to cooperate with the Department in providing habitat for resident wildlife and for public access and use (emphasis added), including hunting."

These accesses will be small, single ramp structures and will be relatively primitive facilities such as grass or gravel surfaced. In rare cases where a very high level of use or site conditions dictate, the placement of a concrete ramp my be warranted.

Availability of Resources:

Waterfowl Production Areas are open to all priority public uses and as a result access trails, informational and interpretive signs and other facilities as well as staff to enforce regulations and maintain these facilities have been provided by the Service. Currently the staffing levels and facilities required for public programs and accessibility on Waterfowl Production Areas do not meet Service public use standards. The individual station Comprehensive Conservation Plans detail the needed funds and manpower to bring these programs up to Service standards.

Anticipated Impacts of the Use:

Installation and use of these accesses/ramps will result in minimal impacts as these areas are used infrequently during most of the year by either the general public participating in authorized and permitted activities or by Service personnel. Peak use of these areas will generally occur during fall hunting seasons when no disturbance to nesting or young animals will result. Impacts to habitat will be minimal due to their relatively small size by comparison to the average size of the Waterfowl Production Area (average < 200 acres). Impacts will be lessened by selection of sites that minimize the need for any wetland alterations and/or avoidance of native prairie. Accesses/ramps constructed within the interior of a unit will be avoided when ever possible to minimize wildlife disturbance, impacts to unique or critical habitats and conflicts with other authorized public uses.

Public Review and Comment:

During the drafting of the Comprehensive Master Plans, six open houses were held and written comments were solicited from the public about Wetland District Operations including public use programs. Additionally, the Service has contracted with the University of Minnesota to conduct a visitor use study of Waterfowl Production Areas in western Minnesota. This study, in its second year, will provide public input on Service programs and facilities on Waterfowl Production Areas.

Determination:

_____ Use is Not Compatible

__X__ Use is Compatible With Following Stipulations

Stipulations Necessary to Ensure Compatibility:

1. Accesses/ramps must not be constructed in areas where negative wetland impacts or loss will result.

2 Accesses/ramps must not be constructed on native prairie habitat.

3. Camping, overnight use and fires are prohibited.

4. Location of ramps within the interior of each unit should be avoided whenever possible.

5. An archaeological review of each selected site shall be made through the State Historic Preservation Officer and Regional Historic Preservation Officer prior to construction.

Justification:

This use has been determined compatible provided the above stipulations are implemented. This use is permitted as it is deemed necessary to provide safe off-road access by the public to participate in appropriate and permitted priority uses. The footprint of the access site is small and will not diminish the primary purposes of waterfowl production and the conservation of migratory birds and other wildlife. This use will meet the mission of the National Wildlife Refuge System by providing resources for the benefit of the American public while conserving fish, wildlife and plant resources on these lands.

Signature: Project Leader s/Steven J. Delehanty 3/26/03

Concurrence: Regional Chief s/Nita M. Fuller 4/9/03

Mandatory 10- or 15-year Re-evaluation Date: 2012

Appendix F: RONS Lists

Morris Wetland Management District

RONS No.	Title	First Year Cost	Recurring Base ($000)
97005	Implement Science-Based Land Management (biologist)	139	74
00002	Increase education/outreach and customer service efforts (outreach specialist)	118	53
99035	Increase project to reintroduce imperiled prairie chickens	76	
99006	Local Ecotype Seed for Native Prairie Reconstruction	45	45
99036	Improve upkeep of wildlife management and public use facilities	100	100
98027	Upgrade wildlife drive	267	6
97001	Install artificial waterfowl nesting structures	42	11
97002	Improve Public Service	357	76
97003	Wetland restorations	204	54
97004	Noxious weed control	217	27
97006	Increased outreach efforts	95	43
97008	Protection of native prairie ecosystem	119	
97009	Implement Geographic Information System	388	130
98010	Improve safety and quality of prescribed burn program for habitat management	93	6
97011	Restoration of Tallgrass Prairie	204	23
97012	Increased law enforcement monitoring	105	10
97013	Private lands enhancement	164	10
97014	Increase public information and education	22	20
97015	Enhance native prairie management	28	22
97016	Enhance native prairie management	331	23
97017	Reestablishment of native grasslands	533	26
98018	Improve public accessibility to Federal lands	150	
97019	Reestablishment of native grasslands	562	5
97020	Private lands enhancement	65	23
97021	Private land wetland restorations	59	3
97023	Aerial surveys/photographic documentation	30	6
97024	Increase predator fence enclosures	137	10
97025	Purchase native grass seed drying box	24	
97026	Post boundaries of Federal land	49	8
97027	Purchase Bobcat machine for maintenance work	42	
97028	Purchase All-Terrain Vehicle	26	
98030	Improve habitat quality on Federal WPA's for public safety	69	
98031	Improve employee safety and control Exotic Weeds	182	
98032	Improve safety of transporting equipment for habitat management	119	
98033	Construct accessible hunting blinds	193	54
98034	Enhance disease monitoring and control	30	
97022	Land Acquisition	41	5
97029	Aerial Photographs	22	
99001	Update MAAPE Process and Monitoring Techniques	22	
99002	Nesting Island Construction	162	
99003	Visitor Service and Outreach	141	76
99004	Cooperative Biological Assessment for Waterfowl Recruitment	108	
99005	GIS Delineations for Acquisitions and Management	253	20
99007	Expanding Burning Season and Monitoring	95	10

RONS No.	Title	First Year Cost	Recurring Base ($000)
99008	Contract Prescribed Fire Crews	108	
99009	Grassland Management by Mowing	296	48
99010	Water Control Structure Installation and Monitoring	85	4
99011	Hydrology Monitoring	129	64
99013	Biological Monitoring and Inventory Assistance	75	10
99014	Upland and Riparian Restoration Work	96	10
99015	Fish Monitoring on WPA's	38	5
99016	Contaminants Monitoring	108	
99017	USGS and Red River Watershed Study	38	5
99019	Space Needs Analysis and Construction	27	1
99020	Partner Coordination	65	32
99021	Tree Inventory and Management	300	110
99022	Winter Food Source and Cover Monitoring	45	6
99023	Reintroduction of Native Species	75	10
99024	Canada Goose Control	97	53
00001	Law Enforcement Equipment	80	

Appendix G: Existing Partnerships

Appendix G: Existing Partnerships

All the Wetland Management Districts have an extensive network of partnerships covering the counties within their management areas. Partners include:

Minnesota Department of Natural Resources
   Area Wildlife Managers
   Area Fisheries Managers
   Area Hydrologists
   Trails and Waterways Specialists
   Waterfowl Specialists
   Prairie Biologists
   Ecological Services Specialists
County Soil and Water Conservation Districts
Natural Resource Conservation Service
USGS - Biological Resources Division
U.S. Army Corps of Engineers
Local Watershed Districts
Farm Service Agency
County Commissions
County Land and Resource Offices
Township Boards of Supervisors
City Governments
Ducks Unlimited
Minnesota Waterfowl Association
Pheasants Forever Chapters
Minnesota Deer Hunters Chapters
Izaak Walton League
The Nature Conservancy
Minnesota Wildlife Federation
White Earth Chippewa Tribe
Lake Associations
Local Sportsmen and Conservation Organizations
Local School Districts
Regional Universities and Colleges

Other Programs

The Wetland Management Districts support and benefit, or are benefitted by other programs which are presented under the categories of: Federal, State, Local, and Private Habitat Restoration and Preservation Mechanisms.

Federal Mechanisms

North American Waterfowl Management Plan (Prairie Pothole Joint Venture)
The North American Waterfowl Management Plan (NAWMP), signed in 1986, outlines a broad framework for waterfowl management strategies and conservation efforts in the United States, Canada, and Mexico (for additional information see section 3.9.3.1). The NAWMP is designed to reach its objectives through key joint venture areas and state implementation plans within these joint ventures. The Wetland Management

Districts of Western Minnesota (Districts) are located in the U. S. Prairie Pothole Joint Venture (PPJV) area. The PPJV was identified in the NAWMP as the highest priority Joint Venture area in the United States and Canada.

Partnerships play a key role in funding the PPJV. During the PPJV's first seven years, partners raised more than $139,386,609 to protect, restore, or enhance more than 1,896,310 habitat acres. Additionally, the North American Wetlands Conservation Act (NAWCA) has been a major source of funding for PPJV projects and has provided 20 grants to projects in Minnesota and Iowa from 1991 through 1996. The two recent projects that fall within the Districts are described in the following paragraphs.

A 1996 NAWCA $1 million grant and $2.3 million in partner funds to aid restoration of tallgrass prairie and wetlands in 19 northwestern Minnesota counties of the Red River Basin. The 10 year project will be administered by The Nature Conservancy.

Prairie Heritage Project - Proposal for $1 million NAWCA grant in April 1997 for the acquisition of native grassland tracts that are adjacent or in proximity to existing and/ or restorable wetlands in Minnesota. If approved, Pheasants Forever would administer the grant along with partner dollars totaling $2.15 million in late 1997.

Endangered and Threatened Species Recovery Program

Partners in Flight Program for Migratory Neotropical Birds

USFWS Ecosystem Planning
The northern tallgrass prairie has been identified as one of its top priorities within the Service's Upper Mississippi/Tallgrass Prairie and Mississippi Headwaters/ Tallgrass Prairie ecosystem plans. These plans are intended to assist the Service identify resource priorities and action strategies necessary to meet trust responsibilities within specified geographic areas.

COE Red River EIS
The U.S. Army Corps of Engineers is involved in a major Environmental Impact Statement involving water retention sites in the Red River Watershed working with the Red River Watershed Management Board and member watershed districts in Minnesota.

National Water Quality Assessment
The Red River Basin is one of 60 hydrologic systems being assessed by the U.S. Geological Survey through the National Water Quality Assessment program (NAWQA). The basin was selected because its water is of vital importance to the region's economy, and of international concern. NAWQA is using a multidisciplinary approach to assess water quality. The ecology of aquatic biological communities is one of the disciplines for the assessment.

Conservation Reserve Program (CRP)
U.S. Department of Agriculture (USDA). Pursuant to the Conservation Title of the Food Security Act of 1985 (Farm Bill) and later versions of that bill, the program sponsors activities designed to provide protection of soil and water quality through direct payments to farmers for retiring eligible cropland and environmentally sensitive lands for a period of 10 to 15 years. The program encourages protection of highly erodible uplands and filter strips along wetlands, which can reduce pesticide and sediment runoff.

FSA CRP Conservation Priority Areas

The Minnesota State FSA Committee, in conjunction with the State Technical Committee, received approval for the Lake Agassiz Interbeach Area to be designated a State Conservation Priority Area (CPA) for implementing the Conservation Reserve Program (CRP) in Minnesota. Approval came in accordance with guidance provided in FSA CRP Notice 269. A National CPA was designated for the prairie pothole area bordering the Lake Agassiz Interbeach Area. The CPA's will maximize benefits to wildlife and their associated habitats by protecting and enhancing state, Federal, and locally threatened, endangered or candidate listed species of concern, and native plant communities, and, by restoring and enhancing biologically significant terrestrial and aquatic habitats.

Wetland Reserve Program (WRP)

U.S. Department of Agriculture (USDA). The 1996 re-authorization of the Farm Bill reestablished a Wetlands Reserve Program that provides financial incentives for restoration and protection of up to 975,000 acres through long-term agreements. Easements are for 30 years or more, depending on the maximum amount of time allowed by state law, and provide landowners with 75 percent to 100 percent cost-sharing for permanent easements, 50 percent to 75 percent for 30 year easements and restoration cost-sharing agreements.

Set-aside Programs

Farmers participating in Federal price support programs have been required to set aside a certain percentage of their base acreage in most years. Conservation measures are required to provide soil erosion protection, water quality enhancement, wildlife production, and natural beauty. Millions of acres of cropland are retired each year often benefiting wildlife.

Environmental Quality Incentives

U.S. Department of Agriculture (USDA). A new program which combines the functions of the Agricultural Conservation Program, Water Quality Incentives Program, Great Plains Conservation Program, and the Colorado River Basin Salinity Control Program. EQIP is funded at $200 million annually to encourage the establishment of long-lasting conservation practices that will conserve soil, water, forest, and wildlife resources. Livestock-related conservation practices will receive 50 percent of program funding. The program provides cost-sharing to farmers up to 75 percent of the cost of conservation practices with a maximum payment to any one person of $10,000 annually, and to $50,000 for the life of the contract.

Wildlife Habitat Incentives Program (WHIP)

USDA. WHIP, authorized in the Federal Agriculture Improvement and Reform Act, is a new voluntary program for people to develop and improve wildlife habitat on private lands. It provides both technical assistance and cost sharing to help establish and improve fish and wildlife habitat. Participants who own or control land work with the USDA (Natural Resources Conservation Service) to prepare and implement a wildlife habitat development plan. The Natural Resources Conservation Service provides technical and financial assistance for the initial establishment of wildlife habitat development practices. In addition, if the landowner agrees, State wildlife agencies or private organizations may also provide expertise or additional funding to help complete a project.

FmHA Wetland-Related Programs

U.S. Department of Agriculture, Farmers Home Administration. Building on an earlier program prompted by E.O. 11990, the 1990 Farm Bill requires the USDA to establish perpetual conservation easements on wetlands in the FmHA inventory of foreclosed farmland. The act also allows for cancellation or reduction of debt in exchange for conservation easements on wetlands.

Partners for Wildlife Program

U.S. Department of Interior, Fish and Wildlife Service (Service). Drawing on several legal authorities, the Service effort assists private landowners voluntarily restore converted and degraded wetlands and associated upland habitats. The Service provides technical assistance and cost-sharing to complete the work if the landowner agrees to maintain the area for a period of 10 years. The program focuses on restoring and enhancing habitats that provide wildlife, fisheries, water quality, aesthetic, and recreation benefits.

Appendix H: Glossary

Appendix H: Glossary

Block Size

Block size is the term used to describe the size of a contiguous piece of wildlife habitat. A block may have more than one kind of habitat; for example, grassland and wetlands, but not developments such as plowed agricultural fields. A large block size for grassland nesting birds could be 2,000 to10,000 acres depending on the species of bird.

Brood parasites

In the prairie, the main brood parasite of grassland birds is the cowbird. Female cowbirds do not build their own nest, they lay eggs in the nests of other birds. Often the young cowbirds will push other nestlings from the nest and will dominate the time and care of the foster parents. Cowbirds are attracted to woodlands and have the greatest impact on grassland birds that nest near woodlots.

Comprehensive Conservation Plan (CCP)

The National Wildlife Refuge System Improvement Act of 1997 requires that each refuge must be managed in accordance with an approved CCP that will guide management decisions and set forth strategies for achieving refuge purposes and contributing to the mission of the Refuge System.

Conservation Reserve Program (CRP)

A U.S. Department of Agriculture program that takes highly erodible or environmentally sensitive cropland out of production for 10 to 15 years. Farmers receive annual rental payments and most of the erodible land is planted in perennial grasses and grass/legume mixtures.

Cool-season grass

Grass species that green early in the spring and flower before July. Often these plants are dormant during the heat of the summer. Most cool-season grasses are not native to the prairie ecosystem.

Edge effects

When ground nesting birds nest near habitat edges, their chances for success are reduced because the nest is easy to locate for predators and nest parasites. Predators such as hawks, fox, skunk, and raccoon and nest parasites such as cowbirds, hunt along habitat edges. This "edge effect" has been observed at the interface of woodlands and grasslands, grasslands and water, and roads and grasslands.

Federal Trust Species	Species that cross state and international boundaries or are afforded national protection through various laws and treaties, such as the Migratory Bird Treaty Act and the Endangered Species Act. The well-being of waterfowl populations is a classic Federal trust responsibility and the main purpose for the creation of the Small Wetland Acquisition Program in the 1960s.
Fragmentation	The process by which habitats are broken up into smaller, isolated parcels dominated by human activity is called habitat fragmentation. Habitat fragmentation reduces an ecosystem's biological diversity because small, isolated patches of habitat have fewer species than larger, less isolated patches. In the prairie grasslands, fragmentation occurred when the prairie was converted to agriculture.
Forbs	Flowering plants that are not grass-species, usually they are broad-leaved, green plants with attractive flowers.
Goal	For the purpose of the Comprehensive Conservation Plan, "goals" are defined as broad, open-ended statements of desired future conditions (vision) that convey a purpose, but not measurable units. These are directional statements for a specific program, often qualitative and expressed in terms of benefits. They have been described as "where the rubber meets the sky."
Grassland	Habitat that is dominated by grass, but may contain hundreds of other species of plants such as flowering asters and legumes. "Grassland" is a term that is used to describe planted cover, as well as natural virgin prairie. The term does not imply that the habitat is natural.
Lucustrine Wetland	Deep water lakes and reservoirs. The Lucustrine System is a deepwater dominated system, and includes standing waterbodies like lakes, reservoirs, and deep ponds.
Mesic (dry-mesic, wet-mesic)	This term is used to describe species that occur where there is an average level of moisture within a habitat. The land is not too dry or too wet. Usually, it refers to the nature of the entire area; for example, mesic prairie.
Objective	For the purpose the Comprehensive Conservation Plan, the term, "objective" is defined as, a concise statement of what will be achieved (specificity), how much will be achieved (quantified), when it will be achieved (time bound), and who is responsible for the

work (accountability). Objectives are where the rubber meets the road.

Project — For the purpose of the Comprehensive Conservation Plan, the term, "project" is defined as a work plan proposal that shows budget and staff time needed to implement a strategy.

Pulustrine Wetland — Shallow water wetlands. The Pulustrine System encompasses the vast majority of the country's inland marshes, bogs and swamps and does not include any deepwater habitat.

Riverine — The Riverine System is limited to freshwater river and stream channels and is mainly a deepwater habitat system.

Refuge Operation Needs System (RONS) — This is the system that is used within the U.S. Fish and Wildlife Service to identify projects to be included for possible future funding. When money becomes available from a variety of sources, it can be used to address identified RONS projects.

Strategy — For the purpose of the Comprehensive Conservation Plan, the term, "strategy" is defined as a solution or approach to achieving an objective (more detailed and often includes the how).

Warm-season grass — Grass species that green later in the spring, often reaching their peak growth in the warm summer months and flower in July. Many native bunch grass species such as big-blue stem and little-blue stem are warm season grasses.

Waterfowl Production Areas (WPA) — Upland grasslands and wetlands that are purchased by the Federal government to provide nesting habitat for waterfowl and hunting areas for waterfowl and upland game hunters.

Waterfowl — The group of water birds, known scientifically as Anseriformes, including ducks, geese and swans. Many state hunting regulations also refer to cormorants which are not truly a member of the waterfowl group. Cranes, grebes, herons and pelicans are also not waterfowl.

Wetland — Wetlands are lands transitional between terrestrial and aquatic systems where the water table is usually at or near the surface or the land is covered by shallow water. For the purposes of this classification, wetlands must have one or more of the following three attributes: 1) at least periodically, the land supports predominantly hydrophytes (water plants); 2) the substrate is predominantly undrained hydric soil; and 3) the substrate is nonsoil and is saturated with water or covered by shallow water at some time during the growing season of each year (Cowardin, et al. 1979).

Wetland Management Districts (District)

The Federal administrative unit that is charged with acquiring, overseeing and managing the Waterfowl Production Areas and easements within a specified group of counties. Most Districts are large, covering several counties.

Appendix I: Bibliography

Appendix I: Bibliography

Aaseng, Norman E., John C. Almendinger, Robert P. Dana, Barbara C. Delaney, Hannah L. Dunevitz, Kurt A. Rusterholz, Nancy P. Sather, and Daniel S. Wovcha. 1993. Minnesota's native vegetation, a key to natural communities, version 1.5. Biological Report No. 20. Minnesota Dept. Natural Resources, Natural Heritage Program.

Ball, I.J., Eng, R. L., and Ball, S. K. 1995. Population density and productivity of ducks on large grassland tracts in northcentral Montana. Wildl. Soc. Bull. 23: 767-773.

Burger, L.D., L.W. Burger, Jr. and J. Faaborg. 1994. Effects of prairie fragmentation on predation of artificial nests. J. Wild. Manage. 58:249-254.

Coffin, B. and L. Pfannmuller, 1988. Minnesota's Endangered Flora and Fauna. University of Minnesota Press. Minneapolis, MN.

Cowardin, L. M., V. Carter, F. C. Golet, and E. T. LaRoe. 1979. Classification of wetlands and deepwater habitats of the United States. U.S. Fish and Wildlife Service FWS/OBS-79/31. Washington. D.C.

Dahl, T.E. 1990. Wetland losses in the United States: 1780-1980. U.S. Department of the Interior. Fish and Wildlife Service. Washington D.C.

Defenders of Wildlife. 1999. The Citizen's Wildlife Refuge Planning Handbook: Charting the future of conservation on the national wildlife refuge near you. Defenders of Wildlife. Washington D.C. 1999.

Eckert, K.R. 1994. A birder's guide to Minnesota. Williams Publications, Plymouth, MN.

Ensor, K. and S. Smith. 1994. Herbicide concentrations in select waterfowl production area wetlands in west central Minnesota, 1993. Report to the U.S. Fish and Wildlife Service. Office of Environmental Contaminants. Federal Building, Fort Snelling, Twin Cities.

Fitzgerald J. D. N. Pashley, S. J. Lewis, and B. Pardo 1998. Partners in Flight Bird Conservation Plan for the Northern Tallgrass Prairie (Physiographic Area 40). MO Department of Conservation.

Freemark, K. and M. Csizy. 1993. Effect of different habitats vs. agricultural practices on breeding birds. Pages 284-285 (abstract) in Agricultural Research to Protect Water Quality: Proceeding of the Conference. Feb. 21-24, 1993. Minneapolis, MN Soil and Water Conservation Society.

Galatowitsch, S. M. and A. G. van der Valk. 1994. Restoring prairie wetlands; an ecological approach. Iowa State University Press, Ames Iowa.

Green, J. C. and R. B. Janssen. 1975. Minnesota Birds. University of Minnesota Press, Minneapolis.

Grue, C.E., L. R. DeWeese, P. Mineau, G.A. Swanson, J.R. Foster and P. M. Arnold, J. Huckins, P. J. Sheechan and W. K. Marshall, A. P. Ludden. 1986. Potential impacts of agricultural chemicals on waterfowl and other wildlife inhabiting prairie wetlands: an evaluation of research needs and approaches. Trans. 51st N. A. Wildl. And Nat. Res. Conf. 357-383.

Hanson and Zimmer 1999

Hargrave, Bryan. 1993. The upper levels of an ecological classification system for Minnesota. Draft. State of Minnesota, Department of Natural Resources Forestry.

Hazard, E.B. 1982. Mammals of Minnesota. University of Minnesota Press. Minneapolis, MN

Henderson, C. L., A.L. Lambrecht, 1997. Traveler's Guide to Wildlife in Minnesota. Minnesota Department of Administration Communications. Media Division. St. Paul, Minnesota.

Janssen, B. 1987. Birds of Minnesota. University of Minnesota Press, Minneapolis, MN.

Jannssen, R.B., and A.X. Hertzel. 1996. County occurrences of Minnesota birds. Minnesota Ornithologist's Union Occasional Papers No. 1.

Johnson, R.G. and S. A. Temple. 1986. Assessing habitat quality for birds nesting in fragmented tallgrass prairies. Pp. 245-49. In J. Verner, M.L. Morrison, and C.J. Ralph, eds. Wildlife 2000: modeling habitat relationships of terrestrial vertebrates. University of Wisconsin Press, Madison.

Johnson, R.G., and S. A. Temple. 1990. Nest predation and brood parasitism of tallgrass prairie birds. Journal of Wildlife Management 54:106-11.

Knopf, F. L. 1994. Avian assemblages on altered grasslands. Studies in Avian Biology 15:247-57.

Lariviere, S., L. R. Walton, and F. Messier. 1999. Selection by Striped Skunks (Mephistis mephitis) of farmsteads and buildings as denning sites. American Midland Naturalist. (In press).

Lariviere, S. and F. Messier. 1998. Denning ecology of the striped skunk in the Canadian prairies: implications for waterfowl nest predation. Journal of applied ecology 35: 207-213.

Lariviere, S. and F. Messier. 1998. Spatial organization of a prairie striped skunk population during the waterfowl nesting season. J. Wild. Manage. 62:199-204.

Moyle, J.B. and E.W. Moyle, 1977. Northland Wildflowers - A Guide for the Minnesota Region. University of Minnesota Press. Minneapolis, MN.

Noss, R.F., et al. 1995. Endangered Ecosystems of the United States: A Preliminary Assessment of Loss and Degradation. Biological Report 28: Washington, D.C.: U.S. Department of Interior, National Biological Service.

Oldfield, B. and J.J. Moriarty, 1994. Amphibians and Reptiles Native to Minnesota. University of Minnesota Press. Minneapolis, MN.

Ojakangas, R.W. and C. L. Matsch. 1982. Minnesota's geology. University of Minnesota Press. University of Minnesota, Minneapolis, Minnesota.

Ostlie, W.R., R. E. Schneider, J. M. Aldrich, T.M. Faust, R.L.B. McKim, and H.M. Watson. 1996. The status of biodiversity in the Great Plains. The Nature Conservancy, Arlington, VA.

Paton, P.W. C. 1994. The effect of edge on avian nest success: how strong is the evidence? Conservation Biology 8:17-26.

Pasitschniak-Arts, M. and F. Messier. 1996. Predation on artificial duck nests in a fragmented prairie landscape. Ecoscience 3:436-441.

Sample, David W. and M. J. Mossman. 1997. Managing Habitat for Grassland Birds: a guide for Wisconsin. Wisconsin Department of Natural Resources. Bureau of Integrated Science Services. Madison, Wisconsin.

Roberts, 1932. Birds of Minnesota. University of Minnesota, Minneapolis, Vols 1 and 2.

Sampson, F. B. and F. L. Knopf. Prairie conservation: preserving North America's most endangered ecosystem. Island Press, Washington D.C.

Strangis, J.M. 1996. Birding Minnesota. Falcon Press, Helena, MT.

Tester, J. R. 1995. Minnesota's Natural Heritage-an Ecological Perspective. University of Minnesota Press. Minneapolis, MN.

Tilman, D. and J. A. Downing. 1994. Biodiversity and stability in grasslands. Nature 367:363-365.

Tome , M. W., C. Grue, L. R. DeWeese. 1991. Ethyl parathion in wetlands following aerial application to sunflowers in North Dakota. Wildl. Soc. Bull. 19:450-457.

U. S. Fish and Wildlife Service. 1999. Fulfilling the Promise: The National Wildlife Refuge System. Visions for Wildlife, Habitat, People and Leadership. Department of the Interior; Washington D.C.

Weller, M. W. 1982. Freshwater Marshes: University of Minnesota Press, Minneapolis, MN.

Wendt, Keith M., and Barbara Coffin. 1988. Natural vegetation of Minnesota at the time of the public land survey, 1847-1907. Biological Report No. 1. Minnesota Dept. of Natural Resources, Natural Heritage Program.

Appendix J: List of Preparers

Appendix J: List of Preparers

Don Hultman
Former Refuge Supervisor (Area 3)
USFWS Regional Office, Ft. Snelling, Minnesota

Kevin Brennan
Wetlands District Manager
Fergus Falls Wetland Management District

Barry Christenson
Wetlands District Manager
Litchfield Wetland Management District

Rick Julian
Refuge Manager
Rydell National Wildlife Refuge

Mark Chase
Wetlands District Manager
Detroit Lakes Wetland Management District

Thomas Bell
Refuge Manager
Big Muddy National Wildlife Refuge

Steve Delehanty
Wetlands District Manager
Morris Wetland Management District

Ron Bell
Refuge Manager
Big Stone National Wildlife Refuge

Rich Papasso
Refuge Operation Specialist
Big Stone National Wildlife Refuge

Steve Kallin
Wetlands District Manager
Windom Wetland Management District

John Dobrovolny
Regional Historic Preservation Officer
USFWS Regional Office, Ft. Snelling, Minnesota

Mike Marxen
CCP Coordinator
USFWS, Pacific Northwest Region

Mary Mitchell
Wildlife Biologist/Regional GIS Coordinator
USFWS Regional Office, Ft. Snelling, Minnesota

Sean Killen
Cartographer
USFWS Regional Office, Ft. Snelling, Minnesota

John Schomaker, Ph.D.
Refuge Planning Specialist/CCP Coordinator
USFWS Regional Office, Ft. Snelling, Minnesota

Jane Hodgins
Technical Writer/Editor
USFWS Regional Office, Ft. Snelling, Minnesota

Jan Eldridge, Ph.D.
Wildlife Biologist
USFWS, Ascertainment and Planning, Ft. Snelling, Minnesota

Appendix K: Guidance for Acquisition

U.S. Fish and Wildlife Service (Service) - Region 3
Strategic Growth of the Small Wetland Acquisition Program (SWAP)
Guidelines for Fee and Easement Purchase

Introduction

Project Leaders on Wetland Management Districts (WMD) within the major waterfowl breeding habitats of the United States are charged with the responsibility to identify tracts of land that meet the goals of the SWAP for inclusion in the National Wildlife Refuge System (NWRS). Of all the responsibilities Project Leaders carry, identifying lands to include in the NWRS has the longest lasting implications and is by far the most important.

The main goal of the SWAP has been, and still is, to purchase a complex of wetlands and uplands that provide habitat in which waterfowl can successfully reproduce. The basic concept has been to purchase in fee title key brood marshes that include adequate nesting cover on adjacent uplands while protecting under easement surrounding temporary and seasonal wetland basins as breeding pair habitat. It is important that lands purchased under the SWAP are the **preeminent waterfowl production habitats** within a Wetland Management District.

Delineation of lands for purchase as waterfowl production habitat is as much an art as it is a science. This requires meshing the opportunity to purchase and manage a particular tract of land with the biological needs of breeding waterfowl in a socially acceptable, cost effective and efficient manner.

History

The SWAP began in 1958 and accelerated rapidly in the early 1960's with passage of the Wetlands Loan Act. The original 1960's delineations were prepared for each fee title parcel based on their suitability to provide brood rearing habitat for waterfowl. These delineations designated wetlands as priority A, B, and C for fee title purchase. These tracts had few upland acres and only existing wetlands with no drainage facilities were considered for fee or easement purchase. In some locations, these original delineations have been reevaluated and revised. In Minnesota, a 1974 exercise produced maps showing proposed boundaries of each fee title delineation, as well as wetlands within a two-mile radius that were eligible for easement purchase. A 1984 effort produced maps of "significant wetland areas" for fee title purchase. Although dated, these efforts were biologically sound and provide valuable information in deciding which properties to purchase today.

Over the years our understanding of breeding waterfowl biology has increased and the landscape of the Upper Midwest has changed dramatically. The SWAP itself has evolved to include purchase of drained wetlands, increased upland acreage, and grassland easements along with new counties that include lands within intensely agricultural and urbanized landscapes.

Since the inception of the SWAP, most State Fish and Wildlife Agencies in primary waterfowl breeding habitats also conducted land acquisition programs that protected wetlands for waterfowl production.

In recent years, many new programs have been launched by Service partners that compliment the SWAP including U.S. Department of Agriculture's Conservation Reserve Program (CRP), Conservation Reserve Enhancement Program (CREP), Wetland Reserve Program (WRP), Farmers Home Administration Inventory and Debt Restructure programs, State programs such as Reinvest in Minnesota (RIM) and the Permanent Wetland Preserve (PWP), as well as non government organization programs such as The Nature Conservancy (TNC) Preserves. In addition, the Service has recently established National Wildlife Refuges to protect native prairie tracts over an area that is closely aligned with the Prairie Pothole Region.

Project Leaders must consider these program changes when determining which lands to purchase under the SWAP.

Biological Considerations

The following guidelines for the SWAP have been developed with the goal of directing acquisition of waterfowl production habitat for prairie nesting species ducks.

As one moves through the major waterfowl breeding habitats from Wisconsin to Iowa to Montana, the primary biological factor limiting waterfowl production varies with the landscape. In Iowa and southern Minnesota, the simple lack of any wetlands or upland cover tends to limit the occurrence of breeding waterfowl. In parts of Wisconsin, Michigan and western Minnesota, the low number of temporary and seasonal wetlands and diminished upland cover limit the number of breeding pairs that settle and successfully nest. In the parts of the eastern Dakotas where the wetland base is fairly intact, breeding waterfowl settle, but production can be limited by the lack of secure upland cover. In the central Dakotas and northern Montana, generally the wetland base and grassland cover are sufficient to attract and insure adequate nest success rates for breeding waterfowl populations. Acquisition programs should focus on providing the missing components for that particular landscape.

The first credo of breeding waterfowl habitat is "the abundance of wetlands (especially temporary and seasonal) within a given landscape during the spring/summer correlates directly with the number of breeding duck pairs."

The second credo of breeding waterfowl habitat is "as grassland acreage (idle grassland, hayland, pasture, road rights-of-ways, etc.) within a given landscape increases, waterfowl nest success increases.

The third credo of breeding waterfowl habitat is "as the predator component within a given landscape approaches the naturally occurring compliment (i.e., coyotes vs. red fox), waterfowl nest success increases."

When delineating lands for purchase under the SWAP, Project Leaders must view current conditions as well as anticipated future developments. Since the home range of most prairie nesting species of waterfowl covers roughly four-square miles, delineations need to be viewed as part of a larger landscape within a two-mile radius. The "perfect" 4-square mile tract would consist of a complex of wetlands spread across the landscape intermingled with greater than 30% grassland cover on the uplands and few, if any, trees or forested areas. The wetland complex on this "perfect" 4-square mile landscape would be made up of four or more larger brood marshes and 150 or more temporary and seasonal wetlands.

Delineation Criteria for Fee Title Purchases

Delineations will be prepared to show the eventual boundary of a Waterfowl Production Area after all tracts have been acquired.

Size of WPA: 80 - 1,000 acres

Upland/Wetland Ratio: 4:1

Wetland Types: Delineate only a wetland complex. This complex will have at least one PEMF brood marsh of significant size. There must be a scattering of PEMA and PEMC wetlands throughout the area.

Soils: Heavy, fertile, alkaline clay loam, or loam Mollisol soils. These soil types evolved under geographic regions that were predominantly prairie grassland.

1. Omit buildings and building sites when they are not critical to the management of the WPA.

2. A minimum of 20 percent of the entire delineation should be wet. (Use restorable drained, as well as existing basins in determining percent wetland.)

3. Maximum of 50 percent of the entire delineation may be wetland.

4. Written justification and approval of the Refuge Supervisor is needed when the size of the WPA purchased is under 80 acres or exceeds 1,000 acres.

5. Limit number of Waterfowl Production Areas to 4-5 per township.

Delineation Criteria for Habitat Easements

Grassland easements should be obtained on lands where a suitable wetland complex exists, but additional upland cover is necessary to provide adequate waterfowl breeding habitat (i.e., overlying a wetland easement).

Grassland easements must be within 2,600 feet of a wetland that provides brood habitat.
If requested by the owner, delineations may exclude one small tract (1-5 acres) on the exterior boundary and/or in a corner for parking and/or a building.

Generally roads and trails should not be allowed on habitat easements. If an access trail is absolutely necessary, the delineation should show the approximate route.

Delineation Criteria for Wetland Easements

It is preferred that wetland easements be obtained on all PEMA, PEMC, PEMF, and PEMG wetlands within two miles of fee title Waterfowl Production Areas or any other permanently protected brood marsh. Wetland easement maybe taken to permanently protect good brood marshes that would be otherwise unprotected.

Wetlands should be delineated to water levels that approximate the Ordinary High Water mark (i.e 100 year rainfall event).

All drained wetlands restored under the Partners for Wildlife, CRP, or other similar wetland restoration programs that are lacking permanent protection should be considered for wetland easement protection. Where easements include wetland restorations structures (ditch plugs, tile risers, culverts, etc) Project Leaders should consider requesting recorded mean sea level elevations.

Wetlands with drainage facilities (i.e. un-maintained ditches or tiles) that exhibit PEMC, PEMF or PEMG characteristics maybe delineated for easement purchase. In these situations the landowner(s) forfeit their rights to maintain the drainage facilities so the entire wetland should be placed under easement to eliminate any third party drainage rights. Restoration of partially drained wetlands to historic water levels is preferred and should be explored with the landowner prior to taking an easement.

Do not place artificial or created wetlands under easement (i.e., dugouts, stock dams, dams on natural streams/riparian areas).

Delineation Criteria Applicable to all SWAP Acquisitions

Avoid purchasing land with problems that will significantly affect the tract's biological integrity, diversity, and environmental health.

1. Try to avoid purchasing lands within city limits or adjacent to commercial or rural housing developments. Do not use the SWAP just to prevent commercial or rural development.

2. Do not purchase lands when a legal ditch(s) passes through the major brood marsh unless specific detail is provided that insures future water levels will be adequate (i.e., cleanout depths are agreed to by drainage authority or legal process for impoundment of water, or abandonment occurs concurrently with purchase).

3. Evaluate any recorded or unrecorded outstanding third party rights (i.e., ditches, tiles, access trails, mineral rights) and do not purchase lands when these rights substantially affect future management.

4. Avoid purchasing tracts without access.

5. Avoid purchasing tracts with costly future management problems (i.e., contaminants, flashy watershed with frequent flood damages, fish lakes, extensive invasions of exotic species, etc.).

6. Avoid purchasing tracts that are the recipient of sewage lagoon discharge or feedlot runoff.

7. Where management problems may develop and public uses significantly differ, avoid intermingling Service lands with other agency/NGO lands.

8. As they approve tracts for purchase, Project Leaders should consider the goal acres for each county to insure they are not exceeded before all essential tracts are purchased.

Prioritizing Acquisitions & Other Considerations

Priority should be given to fee title and habitat easement purchases using the SWAP Acquisition Priority Scorecard (Exhibit 2). Round-outs to existing fee title Waterfowl Production Areas should receive priority over other tracts. Wetland Easements will be assigned a high, medium or low priority and should be based on criteria similar to habitat easements and fee title tracts. Priority will be give to wetland easements covering previously drained wetlands that have been restored.

In targeting and prioritizing SWAP tracts Project Leaders should use Geographic Information System data including thunderstorm maps, land cover maps (grassland acreage), landscape characteristic maps and data on predator populations. Project Leaders also need to evaluate potential purchases for tracts where future management actions will significantly contribute to increased waterfowl production (i.e., purchase of a 100+ acre drained wetland that will be restored and managed for hemi-marsh conditions and over water nesting species of ducks).

In prioritizing tracts for purchase under the SWAP other wildlife benefits may help determine priority. These may include presence of large tracts of native prairie, endangered or threatened species, or colonial nesting birds, expanding and protecting large tracts of grassland as Grassland Bird Conservation Areas and resident species benefits (i.e., pheasant wintering marsh).

Format

All SWAP acquisitions will have the SWAP Acquisition Proposal cover sheet with fee title and habitat easement tracts including the SWAP Acquisition Priority Scorecard (Exhibit 2). The Project Leader's signature at the bottom of the SWAP Acquisition Proposal form represents approval for inclusion of the lands into the NWRS.

All SWAP delineations will be made on the most recent digital ortho quadrangles using the Wetland Management District Geographic Information System (GIS) acquisition format with the following standard colors (during FY02, field stations will transition from the pen and ink format to GIS.):

Boundary: Proposed Purchases (Fee or Easement): White

WPA: Existing - green   Wetland Easement: Existing - yellow
Habitat Easement: Existing - dark blue   Flowage Easement: Existing - light blue
FmHA Easement: Existing - red   Wetlands: blue

Show all drainage (tile, open ditch, county, and judicial ditches) with lines and arrows.

Show roads, railroads, and other rights-of-ways.

Show building sites within and adjacent to delineated areas.

All wetland easement delineations will have the USFWS Wetland Easement Field Form attached (Exhibit 3).

Suggested Reading

Greenwood, Raymond J., Alan B. Sargeant, Douglas H. Johnson, Lewis M. Cowardin, and Terry L. Shaffer. 1995. Factors associated with duck nest success in the Prairie Pothole Region of Canada. Wildlife Monographs 128:1-57. Jamestown, ND: Northern Prairie Wildlife Research Center Home Page. http://www.npwrc.usgs.gov/resource/othrdata/nestsuc/nestsucc.htm (Version 02JUN99).

Krapu, Gary L., Raymond J. Greenwood, Chris P. Dwyer, Kathy M. Kraft, and Lewis M. Cowardin. 1997. Wetland use, settling patterns, and recruitment in mallards. Journal of Wildlife Management 61(3):736-746. Northern Prairie Wildlife Research Center Home Page. http://www.npwrc.usgs.gov/resource/othrdata/wetlndus/wetlndus.htm (Version 14NOV97).

Johnson, Douglas. H. and James W. Grier. 1988. Determinants of breeding distributions of ducks. Wildlife Monographs 100:1-37. Jamestown ND: Northern Prairie Wildlife Research Center Home Page. http://www.npwrc.usgs.gov/resource/distr/birds/distduck/distduck.htm (Version 15APR98).

Cowardin, Lewis M., Terry L. Shaffer, and Kathy M. Kraft. 1995. How much habitat management is needed to meet mallard production objectives? Wildlife Society Bulletin 23(1):48-55. Jamestown, ND: Northern Prairie Wildlife Research Center Home Page. http://www.npwrc.usgs.gov/resource/othrdata/marshbrd/marshbrd.htm (Version 16JUL97).

Reynolds, Ronald E., Danny R. Cohan, and Michael A. Johnson. 1996. Using
     landscape information approaches to increase duck recruitment in the
     Prairie Pothole Region. Transactions of the North American Wildlife and
     Natural Resource Conference 61:86-93. Jamestown, ND: Northern Prairie
     Wildlife Research Center Home Page.
     http://www.npwrc.usgs.gov/resource/othrdata/incduck/incduck.htm
     (Version 16JUL97).

Johnson, Douglas. H. and James W. Grier. 1988. Determinants of breeding
     distributions of ducks. Wildlife Monographs 100:1-37. Jamestown ND:
     Northern Prairie Wildlife Research Center Home Page.
     http://www.npwrc.usgs.gov/resource/distr/birds/distduck/distduck.htm
     (Version 15APR98).

Sargeant, Alan B., Raymond J. Greenwood, Marsha A. Sovada, and Terry L. Shaffer.
     1993. Distribution and abundance of predators that affect duck production -
     Prairie Pothole Region. U.S. Fish and Wildlife Service, Resource
     Publication 194. Jamestown, ND: Northern Prairie Wildlife Research Center Home Page.
     http://www.npwrc.usgs.gov/resource/distr/others/predator/predator.htm
     (Version 16JUL97).

Cowardin, Lewis M., David S. Gilmer, and Charles W. Shaiffer. 1985. Mallard
     recruitment in the agricultural environment of North Dakota. Wildlife
     Monographs 92:1-37. Jamestown, ND: Northern Prairie Wildlife Research Center Home
Page.http://www.npwrc.usgs.gov/resource/othrdata/recruit/recruit.htm
     (Version 02JUN99).

Winter, Maiken, Douglas H. Johnson, Therese M. Donovan, and W. Daniel
     Svedarsky. 1998. Evaluation of the Bird Conservation Area Concept
     in the Northern Tallgrass Prairie. Annual Report: 1998. Northern
     Prairie Wildlife Research Center, U.S. Geological Survey, Jamestown,
     ND: Northern Prairie Wildlife Research Center Home Page.
     http://www.npwrc.usgs.gov/resource/1999/bcarprt/bcarprt.htm
     (Version 18MAY99).

Kantrud, Harold A., Gary L. Krapu, and George A. Swanson. 1989. Prairie basin
     wetlands of the Dakotas: A community profile. U. S. Fish and Wildlife
     Service, Biological Report 85(7.28). Jamestown, ND: Northern Prairie
     Wildlife Research Center Home Page.
     http://www.npwrc.usgs.gov/resource/othrdata/basinwet/basinwet.htm
     (Version 16JUL97).

SWAP ACQUISITION PROPOSAL

Exhibit 1

To:

From:

Tract Name:_____Size:_____

County:_____Township/Section:_____

Owner's Name:_____

Address:_____

_____

Phone Number:_____

Interested Individual when not owner:_____

Acquisition Type: Fee_____   Wet Ease_____   Flow Ease_____

            Habitat Ease: Total_____Hay_____Graze_____Hay and Graze_____

Priority:Fee & Habitat Easement: Round-out_____   Score_____

            Wetland Easement: Restoration_____High_____Medium_____Low_____

Comments:

Delineation Contact:

Name:_____Phone:_____

Address:_____

E-mail:_____Fax:_____

Approved_____ Date_____

            Project Leader

Landscape Setting Score - within 2 mile radius of center of delineation (maximum of 40) _____
PEMA + PEMC - Include existing and permanently protected restorable temporary & seasonal wetlands.

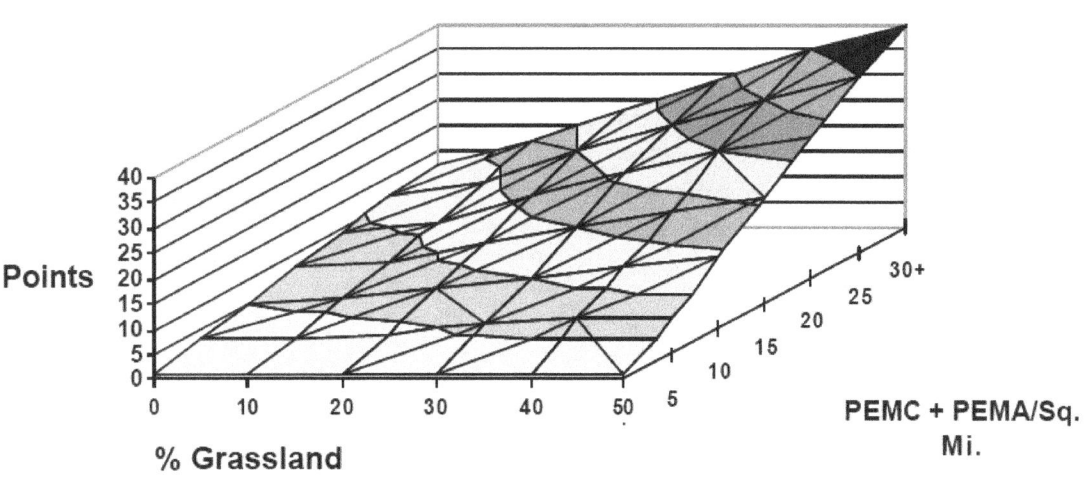

Points

% Grassland

PEMC + PEMA/Sq. Mi.

% Grassland - Include all pasture, hay land, CRP, idle grass and other grassland.

WPA Delineation Score (maximum of 50) _____
Final Size of WPA

    80-160 ac. - 2 pts   160-320 ac. - 5 pts   320-640 ac - 8 pts 640+ ac - 10 pts

Wetland Density (existing + restorable within eventual boundary)

    0-10/sq mi - 2 pts   10-20/sq mi - 5 pts   20-30/sq mi - 8 pts   30+/sq mi.- 10 pts

Wetland to Upland Ratio (within eventual boundary)

    1:1 - 2 pts   1:2 - 5 pts   1:3 - 8 pts   1:4 - 10pts

Wetland Type Ratio (number of PEMF to PEMA+PEMC basins)

    ≤1:10 - 1 pt   1:10 - 1:20 - 2 pts   1:20 - 1:30 - 4 pts   ≥1:30 - 5 pts

    100+ acre PEMF that naturally or with a w/c structure installed provides
    hemi-marsh conditions for over-water nesting species of diving ducks -   10 pts

Soils:
    Tract contains 75% or greater Mollisol Series Soils -   5 pts

Other Factors Score (5 pts. each maximum of 10 pts.) _____
    Native Prairie within delineation (minimum size 40 acres)
    Presence of Endangered or Threatened Species
    Presence of breeding population of Colonial Nesting Birds
    Within Boundary of Identified GBCA or Shorebird CA
    Provides "Substantial Benefit" to local population(s) of Resident Species
    Adjacent to permanently protected waterfowl habitat (i.e. WRP, RIM, state easement)

Total Score (maximum of 100) _____

USFWS WETLAND EASEMENT FIELD FORM   Exhibit 3

Date:_____ County:_____ Township Name:_____

Legal Description of Proposed Easement: (**Attach photo with numbered basins**)
T. _____N., R. _____W., section _____, _____

Contact made by: _____ Mapped by:_____

Owner's Name: _____

Interested individual when not owner:_____

Easement Program Explained?   Y   N   N/A

Basin No.	Type	Present Condition*				Basin No.	Type	Present Condition*			
1	____	1	2	3	4	21	____	1	2	3	4
2	____	1	2	3	4	22	____	1	2	3	4
3	____	1	2	3	4	23	____	1	2	3	4
4	____	1	2	3	4	24	____	1	2	3	4
5	____	1	2	3	4	25	____	1	2	3	4
6	____	1	2	3	4	26	____	1	2	3	4
7	____	1	2	3	4	27	____	1	2	3	4
8	____	1	2	3	4	28	____	1	2	3	4
9	____	1	2	3	4	29	____	1	2	3	4
10	____	1	2	3	4	30	____	1	2	3	4
11	____	1	2	3	4	31	____	1	2	3	4
12	____	1	2	3	4	32	____	1	2	3	4
13	____	1	2	3	4	33	____	1	2	3	4
14	____	1	2	3	4	34	____	1	2	3	4
15	____	1	2	3	4	35	____	1	2	3	4
16	____	1	2	3	4	36	____	1	2	3	4
17	____	1	2	3	4	37	____	1	2	3	4
18	____	1	2	3	4	38	____	1	2	3	4
19	____	1	2	3	4	39	____	1	2	3	4
20	____	1	2	3	4	40	____	1	2	3	4

*Legend: 1 - Existing basin qualifies in present condition   3 - Basin qualifies with restoration
          2 - Basin qualifies with no maintenance of drainage facility   4 - Does not qualify for easement
Comments:

Appendix L: Goal Acres

Appendix L: Goal Acres

	Purchase Options			Easements		
County	Procedural Agreement Total Acres	Total Acres Approved To Date	Current Balance	Procedural Agreement Total Acres	Total Acres Approved To Date	Current Balance
Becker	19,220.00	12,014.49	7,205.51	31,900.00	7,798.47	24,101.53
Big Stone	15,600.00	11,140.81	4,459.19	42,640.00	25,629.35	17,010.65
Clay	23,960.00	10,374.43	13,585.57	35,400.00	19,598.24	15,801.76
Cottonwood	6,446.38	3,184.78	3,261.60	4,000.00	398.92	3,601.08
Douglas	17,120.00	9,605.37	7,514.63	31,226.00	26,747.69	4,478.31
Faribault	5,920.00	806.24	5,113.76	4,000.00	269.28	3,730.72
Freeborn	3,610.00	1,396.63	2,213.37	4,000.00	379.10	3,620.90
Grant	18,854.00	9,977.96	8,876.04	20,737.00	14,618.07	6,118.93
Jackson	8,500.00	4,161.89	4,338.11	3,000.00	425.85	2,574.15
Kandiyohi	16,800.00	13,254.47	3,545.53	32,660.00	14,677.34	17,982.66
Lac qui Parle	6,600.00	4,005.00	2,594.01	23,540.00	4,491.24	19,048.76
LeSueur	4,230.00	412.76	3,817.24	9,100.00	450.86	8,649.14
Mahnomen	14,000.00	5,406.94	8,593.06	35,250.00	18,026.09	17,223.91
McLeod	5,380.00	951.66	4,428.34	5,093.00	2,425.04	2,667.96
Meeker	15,440.00	4,619.28	10,820.72	14,700.00	8,035.58	6,664.42
Morrison	6,320.00	466.00	5,854.00	4,900.00	-	4,900.00
Norman	9,400.00	1,119.00	8,281.00	4,900.00	-	4,900.00
Otter Tail	35,704.62	20,825.73	14,878.89	75,290.00	70,516.57	4,773.43
Polk	22,700.00	11,161.77	11,538.23	46,460.00	7,829.18	38,630.82
Pope	21,000.00	13,289.22	7,710.78	44,180.00	33,570.49	10,609.51
Stearns	14,900.00	9,063.18	5,836.82	15,810.00	4,818.83	10,991.17
Stevens	12,850.00	9,371.15	3,478.85	6,090.00	4,007.55	2,082.45
Swift	10,800.00	6,904.60	3,895.40	14,540.00	4,931.85	9,608.15
Todd	6,560.00	803.35	5,756.65	4,800.00	112.00	4,688.00
Traverse	6,720.00	4,103.98	2,616.02	8,440.00	3,983.31	4,456.69
Wilkin	2,997.00	2,197.00	800.00	1,430.00	1,066.00	364.00
Wright	17,140.00	2,180.14	14,959.86	7,515.00	1,920.58	5,594.42
Yellow Medicine	1,260.00	963.85	296.15	7,860.00	637.27	7,222.73
Other Counties*	41,428.00	9,485.22	31,942.78	47,859.00	7,986.39	39,872.61
Totals	391,460.00	183,247.89	208,212.11	587,320.00	285,351.14	301.968.86

*Other Counties

Blue Earth	888.45			87.00		
Carver				48.00		
Chippewa	246.47			120.00		
Clearwater				4,582.68		

Continued Next Page

Appendix L: Goal Acres

County	Procedural Agreement Total Acres	Purchase Options Total Acres Approved To Date	Current Balance	Procedural Agreement Total Acres	Easements Total Acres Approved To Date	Current Balance
*Other Counties Continued						
Dakota		73.90			0.18	
Lincoln		754.26			739.33	
Lyon		1,574.48			231.00	
Martin		74.00			437.88	
Murray		1,886.63			86.00	
Nobles		508.27			94.44	
Renville		1,091.23				
Rice		615.00			783.82	
Rock					60.14	
Scott		40.00			164.00	
Sibley		797.92			307.83	
Steele		630.13				
Waseca		248.78				
Watonwan		55.70			244.09	
Totals / Other Counties		9,485.22			7,986.39	

Appendix M: Environmental Assessment

Finding of No Significant Impact

Environmental Assessment and Comprehensive Conservation Plan for Morris Wetland Management District, Minnesota

An Environmental Assessment (EA) has been prepared to identify management strategies to meet the conservation goals of the Morris Wetland Management District (District). The EA examined the environmental consequences that each management alternative could have on the quality of the physical, biological, and human environment, as required by the National Environmental Policy Act of 1969 (NEPA). The EA presented and evaluated three alternatives for managing wildlife and habitats as well as visitor services on the District over the next 15 years:

Alternative 1 – Maintain Management on Current Acres With No Additional Land Acquisition. Under this alternative we would manage fee title land already in the system and would not increase the holdings to the agreed goal acres for each county within the District. We would restore native grasslands, improve wetlands and evaluate our approach to waterfowl production. We would maintain recruitment rate of waterfowl and we would continue our present monitoring approach. We would avoid any actions that would harm threatened or endangered species. We would maintain public access and continue current staffing levels.

Alternative 2 – Increase Land Holdings to Goal Acres and Maintain Current Management Practices (No action). Under this alternative we would continue acquiring land up to the negotiated goal acres within each county in the District. We would expand the size of Waterfowl Production Areas (WPAs) in areas of prime waterfowl use through easements and working with partners. We would restore native grasslands and restore and improve wetlands. We would maintain recruitment rates of waterfowl and continue monitoring programs. We would avoid actions that would harm threatened or endangered species. We would continue current public access and staffing levels.

Alternative 3 – Increase Land Holdings to Goal Acres and Expand Management for Waterfowl, Other Trust Species and the Public (Preferred). Under this alternative we would acquire land up to the negotiated goal acres for each county within the District. We would expand the size of WPAs in areas of prime waterfowl use and we would focus on prime habitat as identified by monitoring and GIS mapping. We would follow Strategic Growth guidelines for acquisition which will focus on: 1) wetland complexes, surrounding grasslands and natural predator component. 2) unit size, location, and ratio of upland to wetlands, 3) prioritize according to the benefit to waterfowl., but other wildlife benefits will be considered. We would avoid actions that would harm threatened or endangered species. We would expand and improve public access to WPAs. Management of the District will be consistent with other Districts throughout Minnesota, Wisconsin and the Dakotas.

The alternative selected for implementation is Alternative 3. The strategies presented in the Comprehensive Conservation Plan (CCP) were developed as a direct result of the selection of this alternative.

For reasons presented above and based on an evaluation of the information contained in the Environmental Assessment, we have determined that the action of adopting Alternative 3 as the management alternative for the Morris Wetland Management District CCP is found to have special environmental conditions as described in the attached Environmental Assessment. This Finding of No Significant Impact will not be final nor any actions taken pending a 30-day period for public review.

Additional Reasons:

1. The fire management section within the Environmental Assessment was expanded as a result of comments and will be acted on after a 30-day period of public review.
2. Future management actions will have a neutral or positive impact on the local economy.
3. A cultural resource inventory completed prior to this CCP included recommendations for the protection of cultural, archaeological and historical resources.
4. This action will not have an adverse impact on threatened or endangered species.

Supporting References:

Environmental Assessment
Comprehensive Conservation Plan

_____   7/17/03
Regional Director   Date

Contents

Figures:

Tables:

1.0 Purpose and Need for Action

1.1 Purpose and Need for Action

1.1.1 Purpose

The U.S. Fish and Wildlife Service (Service) is proposing to prepare and implement a Comprehensive Conservation Plan (CCP) for the Minnesota Wetland Management Districts, which include the Big Stone Wetland Management District, the Detroit Lakes Wetland Management District, the Fergus Falls Wetland Management District, the Litchfield Wetland Management District, the Morris Wetland Management District, and the Windom Wetland Management District.

The purpose of the proposed action is to establish the management direction of the Districts for the next 15 years. The action is needed because adequate and cohesive long-term management direction does not exist for the District. Management is now guided by several general policies and short-term plans. Future management direction will be defined in a detailed set of goals, objectives, and strategies described in the CCP.

Refuge Purpose Statements are primary to the management of each refuge within the System. The Purpose Statement is derived from the legislative authority used to acquire specific refuge lands and is, along with Refuge System goals, the basis on which primary management activities are determined. Additionally, these statements are the foundation from which "allowed" uses of refuges are determined through a defined "compatibility process." Purpose Statements for the Wetland Management Districts are:

> "...as Waterfowl Production Areas" subject to "all of the provisions of such Act [Migratory Bird Conservation Act]...except the inviolate sanctuary provisions..." 16 U.S. C. 718(d)(c) [Migratory Bird Hunting and Conservation Stamp Act],
>
> "...for any other management purpose, for migratory birds." 16 U.S.C. 715D [Migratory Bird Conservation Act],
>
> "...for conservation purposes..."7 U.S.C. 2002 [Consolidated Farm and Rural Development Act].

The action is also needed to assess existing management issues, opportunities and alternatives, and then determine the best course for managing the natural resources in each District. Further, this action will satisfy the legislative mandate of the National Wildlife Refuge System Improvement Act of 1997 which requires the preparation of a CCP for all National Wildlife Refuges, including Wetland Management Districts. An additional purpose of the Environmental Assessment (EA) is to provide direction and consideration of the Wetland Management Districts' fire management program, which is integral to the CCP.

This EA was prepared using guidelines of the National Environmental Policy Act of 1969. The Act requires us to examine the effects of proposed actions on the natural and human environment. This EA describes three alternatives for future Complex

Figure 1: Minnesota Wetland Management Districts Location

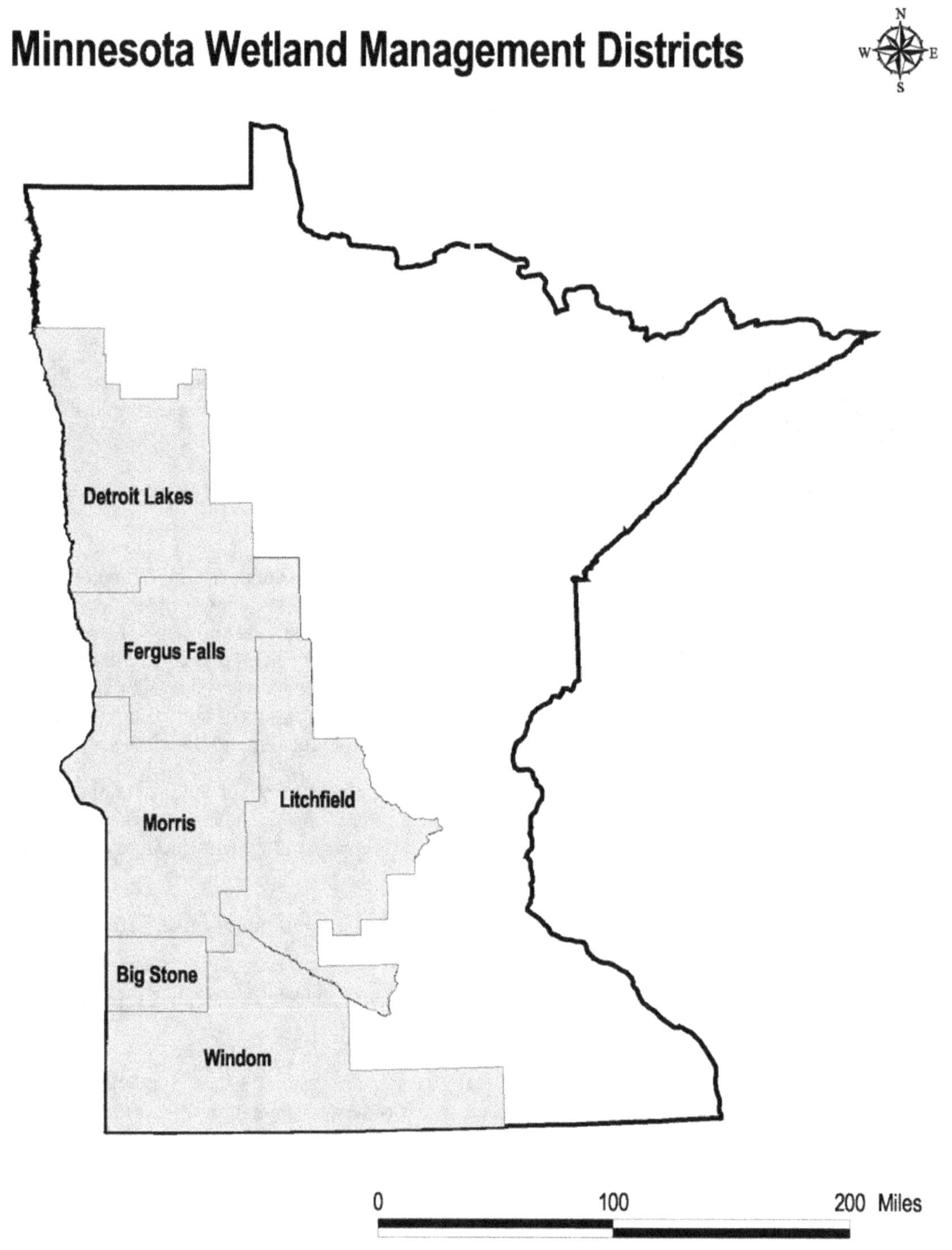
Minnesota Wetland Management Districts
N
W
E
S
Detroit Lakes
Fergus Falls
Litchfield
Morris
Big Stone
Windom
0
100
200 Miles

management, the environmental consequences of each alternative, and our preferred management direction. Each alternative has a reasonable mix of fish and wildlife habitat prescriptions and wildlife-dependent recreational opportunities. Selection of the identified preferred alternative was based on its environmental consequences and ability to achieve the Complex's purpose.

1.1.2 Need for Action

The CCP ultimately derived from this EA will set the management direction for the Districts for the next 15 years. This EA will present three management alternatives for the future of the Districts. One of the alternatives will be selected based on its ability to meet identified goals. These goals may also be considered as the primary need for action. They reflect Service trust responsibilities and priorities based upon species needs, environmental conditions and Service policy. Goals for the Districts were developed by the planning team and encompass all aspects of wetland management district management including public use, habitat management and maintenance operations. Each of the three management alternatives described in this EA will be able to at least minimally achieve these goals.

The goals for the Minnesota Wetland Management Districts include:

Wildlife Goal:	Strive to preserve and maintain diversity and increase the abundance of waterfowl and other key wildlife species in the Northern Tallgrass Prairie Ecosystem. Seek sustainable solutions to the impact of Canada Geese on adjacent private croplands. Preserve, restore, and enhance resident wildlife populations where compatible with waterfowl and the preservation of other trust species.
Habitat Goal:	Restore native prairie plant communities of the Northern Tallgrass Prairie Ecosystem using local ecotypes of seed and maintain the vigor of these stands through natural processes. Restore functioning wetland complexes and maintain the cyclic productivity of wetlands. Continue efforts for long-term solutions to the problem of invasive species with increased emphasis on biological control to minimize damage to aquatic and terrestrial communities. Continue efforts to better define the role of each District in assisting private landowners with wetland, upland and riparian restorations.
Acquisition Goal:	Within current acquisition acreage goals, identify the highest priority acres for acquisition taking into account block size and waterfowl productivity data. These priority areas should drive acquisition efforts whenever possible. Service land acquisition should have no negative impact on net revenues to local government. Understand and communicate the economic effects of federal land ownership on local communities.
Monitoring Goal:	Collect baseline information on plants, fish and wildlife and monitor critical parameters and trends of key species and/or species groups on and around District units. Promote the use of coordinated, standardized, cost effective, and defensible methods for gathering and analyzing habitat and population data. Management decisions will be based on the resulting data.

Endangered Species / Unique Communities Goal:	Preserve enhance, and restore rare native northern tallgrass prairie, flora and fauna that are or may become endangered. Where feasible in both ecological and social/economic terms, reintroduce native species on WPAs in cooperation with the Minnesota DNR.
Public Use / Environmental Education Goal:	Provide opportunities for the public to use the WPAs in a way that promotes understanding and appreciation of the Prairie Pothole Region. Promote greater understanding and awareness of the Wetland Management District's programs, goals, and objectives. Advance stewardship and understanding of the Prairie Pothole Region through environmental education, outreach and partnership development.
Development Plan Goal:	Preparation of WPA Development Plans: Complete Geographic Information System (GIS) based WPA Development Plans for each unit in each District. Provide Districts with GIS to assist with acquisition, restoration, management and protection of public and private lands.
Staff, Facilities and Equipment Goal:	Provide necessary levels of maintenance, technician and administrative support staff to achieve other Wetland Management District goals: Provide all Districts with adequate and safe office, maintenance and equipment storage facilities Acquire adequate equipment and vehicles to achieve other District goals. Maintain District equipment and vehicles at or above Service standards.
Annual Capital Development Funds Goal:	Ensure that annual capital development funds are large enough to meet necessary development of new WPA land: Have adequate funds available each year to permit completion of maintenance needs for each Wetland Districts current land base of Waterfowl Production Areas.
Consistency Goal:	Develop and apply consistent policies for habitat, public use, and resource protection and ensure frequent coordination among Districts, both in Minnesota and in neighboring states with WPAs (North and South Dakota, Iowa, and Wisconsin).

1.2 Decision Framework

In compliance with the National Environmental Policy Act of 1969, the Regional Director for the Great Lakes-Big Rivers Region of the Service will use this Environmental Assessment to select one of three alternatives (Chapter 2) and determine whether the alternative selected will have a significant impact on the quality of the human environment. Specifically, analysis and findings described in this EA will help the Regional Director decide whether to adopt the District's management direction pursuant to the goals, objectives, and strategies in the CCP (see CCP).

1.3 Background

1.3.1 The United States Fish and Wildlife Service

The United States Fish and Wildlife Service (Service) is the primary Federal agency responsible for conserving, protecting, and enhancing the Nation's fish and wildlife resources and their habitats for the continuing benefit of the American people. Some responsibilities are shared with Federal, state, tribal, and local entities, but the Service has specific responsibilities for "trust species" - endangered species, migratory birds, interjurisdictional fish, and certain marine mammals - as well as managing and protecting lands and waters administered by the Service.

The Service's mission is "Working with others to conserve, protect, enhance and, where appropriate restore fish, wildlife and plants and their habitats for the continuing benefit of the American people."

Service goals are:

- Sustainability of fish and wildlife populations: Conserve, protect, restore and enhance fish, wildlife and plant populations entrusted to our care.

- Habitat Conservation: A Network of Land and Waters: Cooperating with others, we will conserve an ecologically diverse network of lands and waters – of various ownerships – providing habitats for fish, wildlife and plant resources.

- Public Use and Enjoyment: Provide opportunities to the public to enjoy, understand and participate in use and conservation of fish and wildlife resources.

- Partnerships in Natural Resources: Support and strengthen partnerships with tribal, state and local governments and others in their efforts to conserve and enjoy fish, wildlife, plants and their habitats.

1.3.2 The National Wildlife Refuge System

The National Wildlife Refuge System (System) is an integral component of the Service with the mission of "administering a national network of lands and waters for the conservation, management, and where appropriate, restoration of the fish, wildlife and plant resources and their habitats within the United States for the benefit of present and future generations of Americans."

The Service manages more than 500 national wildlife refuges covering more than 93 million acres that are specifically managed for fish and wildlife and their habitats. The majority of these lands, almost 83 percent of the land in the Refuge System is found in the 16 refuges in Alaska, with the remaining acres spread across the remaining 49 states and several territories. More than 88 per cent of the acreage in the System was withdrawn from the Public Domain. The remainder has been acquired through purchase, from other Federal agencies, as gifts, or through easement/lease agreements.

Goals of the National Wildlife Refuge System are to:

■ Fulfill our statutory duty to achieve refuge purposes and further the System mission.

■ Conserve, restore where appropriate, and enhance all species of fish, wildlife, and plants that are endangered or threatened with becoming endangered.

■ Perpetuate migratory bird, interjurisdictional fish, and marine mammal populations.

■ Conserve a diversity of fish, wildlife, and plants.

■ Conserve and restore, where appropriate, representative ecosystems of the United States, including ecological processes characteristic of those ecosystems.

■ Foster understanding and instill appreciation of fish, wildlife, and plants, and their conservation, by providing the public with safe, high-quality, and compatible wildlife-dependent public use. Such use includes hunting, fishing, wildlife observation and photography, and environmental education and interpretation.

1.3.3 Minnesota Wetland Management Districts

Located in western Minnesota, the Wetland Management Districts of Minnesota are set in a landscape that was once a mosaic of prairie and wetlands. From north to south the land varied between woodland, sandy ridges and hills covered by prairie flowers, dotted with small, blue wetlands and oak savannah. The combination of prairie grasslands and small wetlands made it among the most biologically productive landscapes in the world; supporting many people and an abundance of wildlife.

When European settlers arrived on the prairies, they recognized the land's productivity and rapidly turned it to agriculture. In a few decades it ranked among the richest agricultural land in the world. The landscape changed so rapidly, little of the original prairie was saved. Today, only fragments remain in isolated, small blocks. With fragmentation and the loss of large predators, smaller predators such as raccoon, striped skunks and fox increased, much to the detriment of ground-nesting birds and other native grassland species.

Perhaps no other ecosystem on earth as been so dramatically altered, in such a short time, as the tallgrass prairie ecosystem of the Midwest. As the prairie wetlands were being drained at an unprecedented rate, early surveys of the Prairie Pothole Region revealed a strong correlation between prairie wetlands and waterfowl breeding habitat. The Duck Stamp Act was passed in 1934 as an early step in stemming the loss of prairie wetlands. Although the original Act did not allow purchase of small wetlands, it created a way for hunters to actively participate in maintaining waterfowl populations. In 1958 the Act was amended, making it possible for the Service to buy small wetlands and uplands for breeding waterfowl and for hunting. The acquired wetlands became Waterfowl Production Areas, or WPAs, and formed the core of the Wetland Management Districts. Wetland management districts are the federal administrative unit that is responsible for acquiring, overseeing, and managing the Waterfowl Production Areas and easements within a specified group of counties. Most Districts are large and cover several counties.

At the time the Small Wetland Acquisition Program (SWAP) began in 1962, the Service entered into a Procedural Agreement with the State of Minnesota. This document laid out the rules for the purchase of wetlands as required by the Wetland Loan Act of 1961. The agreement was amended in 1976 when the number of counties authorized for acquisition increased from 19 to 28, and the goal acreage was increased. In 1991, the Minnesota Land Exchange Board gave the Service approval to expand its land acquisition program to all 87 counties of the State. The State goal of 231,000 acres in fee title and 365,170 acres in easements, as established in 1976, remains unchanged.

In western Minnesota, as of March 31, 1999, the Service owned 171,863 acres. Of these acres, 56,693 are wetlands. In addition, the Service administers perpetual easement agreements on 266,171 acres, of which 62,098 acres are wetlands. Wetlands that were once drained have been restored; on Waterfowl Production Areas, 4,064 wetland restorations have impounded 15,900 wetland acres.

The Wetland Management Districts combine to form a greater land mass than the largest national wildlife refuge in the lower 48 states. On average, each District has 23,000 to 73,400 breeding ducks each year. Combined, the Districts average 240,600 breeding ducks each year.

1.3.4 Minnesota WMD Vision Statement for Desired Future Condition

The Districts will emphasize waterfowl production and ensure the preservation of habitat for migratory birds, threatened and endangered species, and resident wildlife. The Districts will provide opportunities for the public to hunt, fish, observe and photograph wildlife and increase public understanding and appreciation of the Northern Tallgrass Prairie Ecosystem.

1.4 Project Inception

Several Federal, State, and local resource management plans provide the framework for the Service's proposed action, including the North American Waterfowl Management Plan - U.S. Prairie Pothole Joint Venture and the Minnesota Prairie Pothole Joint Venture Implementation Plan, the National Wetlands Priority Conservation Plan, the Service's Regional Wetlands Concept Plan, the Service's Ecosystem Plan for the Mississippi Headwater/Tallgrass Prairie ecosystem, the Partners in Flight Northern Tallgrass Prairie Bird Conservation Plan and the U.S. Shorebird Conservation Plan and strategic planning efforts of numerous local governments, which identifies preservation and protection of land and water resources as important public needs.

To address the declining status of North American waterfowl populations, the United States and Canada signed the North American Waterfowl Management Plan (NAWMP) in 1986. The purpose of the NAWMP is to restore a continental breeding population of 62 million ducks, including 8.7 million mallards, 6.3 million pintails, and a fall flight of 100 million ducks during years of average environmental conditions. Of late, the NAWMP has added objectives and activities for nongame birds. The NAWMP is designed to reach these objectives through key joint venture areas and state implementation plans within these joint venture areas.

Minnesota is one of five states (Minnesota, South Dakota, North Dakota, Montana, and Iowa) located in the U.S. portion of the Prairie Pothole Joint Venture (PPJV)

Area of the NAWMP. The objective of the PPJV is to produce 6.8 million breeding ducks and a fall flight of 13.6 million birds by the year 2000.

In 1986, the U.S. Congress authorized the Emergency Wetlands Resources Act to protect critical wetlands and promote wetland conservation. One of the requirements of the Act was the preparation of a national plan to identify high priority wetlands for protection. In 1989 the Department of the Interior developed the National Wetlands Priority Conservation Plan, as directed by the Act.

In 1990, the Service developed a Regional Wetlands Concept Plan for the Great Lakes-Big Rivers Region (Minnesota, Iowa, Missouri, Illinois, Indiana, Wisconsin, Michigan, and Ohio). The purpose of the plan was to identify wetlands that are valuable for protection in conformance with the Emergency Wetlands Resources Act of 1986.

Photo Copyright by Jan Eldridge

In 1994, the Service developed an Ecosystem Plan for the Mississippi Headwaters/Tallgrass Prairie ecosystem. The overall goal of that plan is to form creative and productive partnerships to restore some of the natural processes and a measure of the former biological diversity that once characterized this ecosystem.

Henceforth, in 1997 the Service initiated detailed management planning on Minnesota Wetland Management Districts. An interdisciplinary planning team was assembled to reaffirm the purpose and significance of the Districts, determine the scope of the planning effort, and define a protocol for carrying out the project. The protocol has included an information gathering phase, an information analysis phase, an information transfer phase, and a planning and implementation phase (current phase). A geographic information system (GIS) was developed to aid in the analysis and transfer of information.

1.5. Scoping and Public Involvement

Scoping is the process of identifying opportunities and issues related to a proposed action. The planning process for this CCP began October 1, 1997, when a Notice Of Intent to prepare a comprehensive management plan was published in the Federal Register (Vol. 62: 51482).

Initially, members of the planning team identified a list of issues and concerns that were likely to be associated with the management of the refuge. These preliminary issues and concerns were based on the team members' knowledge of the area, contacts with citizens in the community, and ideas already expressed to the refuge staff. Refuge staff and Service planners then began asking refuge neighbors, organizations, local government units, schools and interested citizens to share their thoughts in a series of open house events. Open houses were conducted on the following schedule:

November 17 – Detroit Lakes Wetland Management District, 7 attended
November 18 – Fergus Falls Wetland Management District, 9 attended
November 19 – Morris Wetland Management District, 9 attended
November 20 – Litchfield Wetland Management District, 1 attended
November 25 – Windom Wetland Management District, 15 attended
February 4 – Regional Office, Twin Cities, 62 attended

People were also invited to send in written comments describing their concerns as well as what they like about the refuge. Fifty-one written comments were received.

The range of issues identified by members of the public is as diverse as the individuals voicing them. However, several common themes emerged. Issues fall into broad categories of wildlife, habitat and people. These comments formed the basis of the issues addressed by the CCP. Dealing with these issues is at the core of the development of goals and objectives for the management of the Wetland Management Districts.

1.5.1 Issues and Concerns

The following list of needs were identified through our scoping process and were used to develop criteria for evaluating Alternatives in the Environmental Assessment.

Wildlife & Habitat

Waterfowl Productivity
- How do we increase waterfowl production on District lands?

- How do we ensure the Districts are buying the highest priority land in the most efficient and cost-effective manner?

Other Migratory Birds
- How should we manage wetlands on District lands to optimize migrational, breeding and nesting habitat for migratory birds.

- How do we stem the loss of migratory birds on District lands?

Threatened / Endangered Species
- How should the Districts address listed and rare and declining species?.

Native Species
- How should we improve native prairie restorations on District lands?

- Under what circumstances should the Districts introduce rare native species on District lands?

Biological Inventories/Monitoring
- How do we improve biological inventories and monitoring on District lands?.

Federal Trust vs. Resident Wildlife
- How should the Districts balance the needs of federal trust species with those of resident wildlife?

Invasive Species
- How should the Districts control invasive species on District lands?

Habitat Restoration and Management
- How should the Districts reduce the amount of crop depredation by foraging Canada Geese on private lands adjacent to WPAs?

- What are the long-term goals of the Districts Partners for Wildlife Private Lands Program?

- How can the Districts mitigate negative external influences (e.g., contaminants) on WPAs and reduce its impact on long-term health and productivity of District land?

Partners for Fish & Wildlife Program
- What is the long range goal of the Partners for Fish and Wildlife Program (Private Lands) on Wetland Management Districts?

People

Wildlife-dependent Recreation and Education
- How can the Districts better communicate the benefits of federal land to a community.

- How can the Districts provide adequate facilities and programs for the public to fully enjoy wildlife-dependent recreation in a way that is compatible with the Service and National Wildlife Refuge mission?

Operations

Land Acquisition
- Funding is needed to develop and manage newly acquired WPA land and facilities.

Staffing
- Districts need sufficient staff in critical areas to fully meet resource challenges and opportunities.

Facilities and Equipment
- Districts need office, maintenance and storage facilities to carry out their mission.

- Vehicles and other necessary equipment need to be replaced on a regular basis according to Service standards.

Management Consistency Among Districts
- The Districts need to be consistent in their application of policy and resource protection efforts.

1.6 Legal, Policy, And Administrative Guidelines

1.6.1 Legal Mandates

Service resource management and land acquisition is done in accordance with authority delegated by Congress and interpreted by regulations and guidelines established in accordance with such delegations (Appendix A).

1.6.2 Endangered Species Act Section 7 Review

The proposed action may affect but is not likely to affect any federally listed threatened or endangered species or species proposed for listing. This precludes the need for further action on the project as required under Section 7 of the Endangered Species Act of 1973, as amended.

Chapter 2: Description of Alternatives

2.1 Development of Alternatives

Project Leaders on Wetland Management Districts (WMD) within the major water-fowl breeding habitats of the United States have been charged with the responsibility to identify tracts of land that meet the goals of the Small Wetland Acquisition Program (SWAP) for inclusion in the National Wildlife Refuge System (NWRS). Of all the responsibilities Project Leaders carry, identifying lands to include in the NWRS

Photo Copyright by Ian Eldridge

has the longest lasting implications and is by far the most important. The land, once acquired needs to be managed intensively with a variety of tools available to the managers. The intensity of management is limited by the number of staff available and the scattered distribution of the land holdings across a wide landscape in 28 counties of Western Minnesota. The following Alternatives identify three approaches meeting the goals and responsibilities of land ownership and management.

The main goal of the SWAP has been, and still is, to purchase a complex of wetlands and uplands that provide habitat in which waterfowl can successfully reproduce. The basic concept has been to purchase in fee title key brood marshes that include adequate nesting cover on adjacent uplands while protecting under easement surrounding temporary and seasonal wetland basins as breeding pair habitat. Once this is accomplished the land must be managed through seeding with native grasses and forbs, burning, and spraying for exotic and/or invasive vegetation and insects, and dispose abandoned buildings and wells. In addition, the areas must be fenced, signed and made accessible to the public.

The SWAP began in 1958 and accelerated rapidly in the early 1960's with passage of the Wetlands Loan Act. The original 1960's delineations were prepared for each fee title parcel based on their suitability to provide brood rearing habitat for waterfowl. These delineations designated wetlands as priority A, B, and C for fee title purchase. These tracts had few upland acres and only existing wetlands with no drainage facilities were considered for fee or easement purchase. In some locations, these original delineations have been reevaluated and revised. In Minnesota, a 1974 exercise produced maps showing proposed boundaries of each fee title delineation, as well as wetlands within a two-mile radius that were eligible for easement purchase. A 1984 effort produced maps of "significant wetland areas" for fee title purchase. Although dated, these efforts were biologically sound and provide valuable information in deciding which properties to purchase today.

Over the years our understanding of breeding waterfowl biology has increased and the landscape of the Upper Midwest has changed dramatically. The SWAP itself has evolved to include purchase of drained wetlands, increased upland acreage, and grassland easements along with new counties that include lands within intensely agricultural and urbanized landscapes.

Three possible alternatives to acquisition and management were considered as we thought about the future of the programs for the Wetland Management Districts. The three alternatives were (1) manage what lands we currently own, (2) acquire additional lands and manage them as we currently manage the lands that we own and (3) acquire additional lands and expand management beyond the present level of intensity.

In the following sections we summarize what we would do under each alternative. The alternatives are described in the following paragraphs, but more detail is provided in Table 2 on page 21. The third alternative is our preferred alternative, which is developed in more detail as the Comprehensive Conservation Plan.

2.2 Elements Common To All Alternatives

2.2.1 Fire

2.2.11 Prescribed Fire
Prescribed fire is a habitat management tool that is used on the Districts regularly. District staff annually burn WPAs to enhance habitat for upland game, waterfowl, and other species of interest. The periodic burning of grasslands, and sedge meadows reduces encroaching vegetation such as willow. It also encourages the growth of desirable species such as native prairie grasses and forbes.

All prescribed burns are carried out by highly trained and qualified personnel who perform the operation under very precise plans. The Wetland Management Districts have approved fire management plans that describe in detail how prescribed burning will be conducted on District land. No burning takes place unless it meets the qualifications of the prescription for each unit. A prescription is a set of parameters that define the air temperature, fuel moisture, wind direction and velocity, soil moisture, relative humidity, and several other environmental factors under which a prescribed burn may be ignited. This insures that there is minimal chance the fire will escape the unit boundaries and that the fire will have the desired effect on the plant community.

Prescribed burns will occasionally be conducted within or near development zones, sensitive resources, and boundary area to reduce the risk from wildfire damage. To the greatest extent possible, hazard reduction prescribed fires will only be used when they compliment resource management objectives.

Combustion of fuels during prescribed fire operations may temporarily impact air quality, but the impacts are mitigated by small burn unit size, the direction of winds the burns are conducted with, and the distance from population centers. All efforts will be taken to assure that smoke does not impact smoke sensitive areas such as roads and local residences.

Burn frequency will vary on established grassland, savanna, and wet meadow units dependent on management objectives, historic fire frequency, and funding. As part of the prescribed fire program, a literature search will be conducted to determine the effects of fire on various plant and animal species, and a monitoring program will be instituted to verify that objectives are being achieved. Collectively, the Wetland Management Districts conduct an average of 121 prescribed fires covering approximately 16,113 acres each year (5-year average, 1998-2002). The District's goal will be to burn every 4 to 7 years. Under the preferred alternative, the collective goal of the Districts is to burn 30,000 to 32,000 acres per year. This frequency replicates the wildfire frequency that historically occurred and is needed to maintain the grassland biome. Approximately 95 percent of burning occurs in the spring from April through May. The balance of burning occurs in the fall, generally in late September through mid-October.

Prescribed fires cannot and will not be ignited when the area is at an extreme fire danger level and/or the National Preparedness level is V, without the approval of the Regional Fire Management Coordinator. In addition, the Districts will not ignite prescribed fires when adjacent counties or the State in which the burn unit is located have instituted burning bans without the applicable State DNR concurrence. Drought can have an effect on fire severity and control. One or more drought indicators (PDI - KBI) will be used to determine the degree of drought. These indicators can be accessed on the web at *http://www.boi.noaa.gov/fwxweb/fwoutlook.htm*

Spot fires, slop-overs, and escapes can be an expected occurrence on any prescribed fire. They can be caused by any of a number of factors that can not always be accounted for in the planning process. A few minor occurrences of these events on a prescribed burn can usually be controlled by holding forces of the burn crew. If so, they do not constitute a wildfire. The burn boss is responsible for evaluating the frequency and severity of these events and taking mitigating measures such as slowing down or stopping the burn operation, ordering additional holding forces from within District staff, or taking measures to extinguish the prescribed burn. Should an escape event exceed the ability of existing holding forces to control, and additional assistance become necessary in the form of DNR involvement, the event will be classified a wildfire and controlled accordingly. Once controlled by these forces the prescribed burning operation will be stopped for the burning period. A fire number will be obtained to implement wildfire funding to cover the cost of control, a wildfire report will be generated and a Wildland Fire Situation Analysis will be prepared.

Prescribed burns can be conducted at any time of year depending on resource objectives and prescription. However, the normal prescribed fire season begins approximately April 1, and ends by May 31, due to early bird nesting. Fall burning may begin again August 15, and end October 31.

Precautions will be taken to protect threatened and endangered species during prescribed burning. Nesting trees for Bald Eagles will be protected and burning will not be conducted at a time or in a way to negatively impact any nesting eagles. If any of the known disjunct populations of listed plant species are in or near a burn unit, precautions will be taken to avoid the plants.

Existing firebreaks will be used. They may undergo minor improvements such as graveling or rotovation (vegetation disruption). General policy dictates that any new firebreaks or below surface improvements to existing firebreaks will be approved by the Regional Historic Preservation Officer.

The District Managers will be responsible for supervising the development of resource management objectives for individual units. The District staff will provide assistance in the selection of the appropriate management tool needed to meet objectives. Prescribed fire is just one of a combination of tools available. If needed, the Zone Fire Management Officer (Zone FMO) will be consulted for assistance in developing a prescription that will achieve the desired results.

Burn plans (The Fire Management Plan) are written that document the treatment objectives, the prescription, and the plan of action for carrying out the burn. Burn plans are written by or under the guidance of a qualified burn boss. The burn plan

Table 1: Fee Title Acres Approved, and Goal Acres for each District as per Land Exchange Board (LEB)

Wetland Management Districts	Fee Title Acres Approved for Purchase by LEB	Goal Acres	Remainder
Detroit Lakes	41,615	89,280	47,665
Fergus Falls	43,417	74,675	31,258
Litchfield	33,213	76,220	46,007
Big Stone	2,343	0	0
Morris	51,208	74,830	23,622
Windom	12,669	24,476	11,807

follows the format in the Service's Fire Management Handbook or a format approved by the Regional Fire Management Coordinator and addresses all aspects as specified in the Service's Fire Management Handbook. Details regarding fire resources and procedures may be found in the individual fire plans for each District. All burn plans are reviewed by the Refuge Supervisor, Zone FMO, and approved by the individual Refuge Managers prior to implementation.

2.2.12 Fire Prevention and Detection

Although fire may have historically played a role in the development of habitats on the Districts, human ignited fires and natural ignitions burning without a prescription are likely to result in unwanted damage to cultural and/or natural resources. In order to prevent wildfire, an educational program will be utilized to reduce the threat of human caused fires. Ongoing monitoring will be conducted by staff, visitors, and cooperators to detect fire ignitions. Actions taken to implement this include:

- Fire prevention will be discussed at safety meetings, prior to the fire season, and during periods of high fire danger. Periodic training of staff in regards to fire prevention will be conducted.

- During periods of extreme fire danger, warnings will be posted at visitor information stations.

- Public contacts will be made via press releases and verbal contacts during periods of extreme fire danger.

- A thorough investigation will be conducted of all fires suspected to have been illegally set. Upon completion of the investigation, appropriate action will be taken.

- The Districts rely on neighbors, visitors, cooperators, and staff to detect and report fires. In addition, the step-up plan provides for increased patrols by District personnel during periods of very high and extreme fire danger.

- All fires occurring within or adjacent to (within two miles) the individual WPAs will be reported to the respective District headquarters. The person receiving the report will be responsible for implementing the Fire Dispatch Plan.

- Requests for assistance by cooperators on fires not threatening an individual WPA must be made to the District Manager or designee. Only qualified and properly equipped resources meeting NWCG standards will be dispatched off of the District.

- Firefighter and public safety always take precedence over property and resource protection during any fire management activity. Under moderate to severe fire danger index ratings, flaming fronts are capable of moving at fast speeds in all fuel models. In order to eliminate safety hazards to the public, all public access into the burn units will be closed the day of the burn. Fire crews will be briefed that should an individual who is not a member of the fire crew be observed in the prescribed burn unit, they will be immediately escorted out of the area. The fire crew will keep the fire scene clear of people except for Service firefighters and cooperating fire crews.

2.2.13 Fire Suppression

Service policy requires the District to utilize the Incident Command System (ICS) and firefighters meeting NWCG qualifications for fires occurring on District property. All suppression efforts will be directed towards safeguarding life while protecting the District=s resources and property from harm. Mutual aid resources responding from Cooperating Agencies will not be required to meet NWCG standards, but must meet the standards of their Agency. Mutual aid resources will report to the Incident Commander (IC) in person or by radio and receive their duty assignment. Mutual aid forces will be first priority for release from the fire. If additional firefighters are needed, appropriate procedures will be used to acquire them.

All fires occurring on the District and staffed with Service employees will be supervised by a qualified IC. The IC will be responsible for all management aspects of the fire. If a qualified IC is not available, one will be ordered through the appropriate area office dispatch center. All resources will report to the IC (either in person or by radio) prior to deploying to the fire and upon arrival to the fire. The IC will be responsible for: (1) providing a size-up of the fire to dispatch as soon as possible; (2) determine the resources needed for the fire; and (3) advising dispatch of resource needs on the fire. The IC will receive general suppression strategy from the Fire Management Plan, but appropriate tactics used to suppress the fire will be up to the IC to implement. Minimum impact suppression tactics (MIST) will be used whenever possible.

Severity funding may be essential to provide adequate fire protection for the District during periods of drought, as defined by the Palmer Drought Index or other appropriate drought indicators. Severity funds may be used to hire additional firefighters, extend firefighter seasons, or to provide additional resources. The Service Fire Management Handbook provides guidelines for use of severity funding.

The incident commander (IC) on a wildland fire or the prescribed fire burn boss on a prescribed burn will be responsible for the completion of a DI-1202 Fire Report as well as Crew Time Reports for all personnel assigned to an incident and return these reports to the Assistant Manager. The IC or burn boss should include a list of all expenses and/or items lost on the fire and a list of personnel assignments on the DI-1202. The Zone FMO will enter all data into the FMIS computer database within 10 days after the fire is declared out. The Zone FMO will also inform the timekeeper of all time and premium pay to be charged to the fire and ensure expended supplies are replaced. In addition, the following provisions will apply:

- Utilize existing roads and trails, bodies of water, areas of sparse or non-continuous fuels as primary control lines, anchor points, escape routes, and safety zones.

- When appropriate, conduct backfiring operations from existing roads and natural barriers to halt the spread of fire.

- Use burnouts to stabilize and strengthen the primary control lines.

- Depending upon the situation, either direct or indirect attack methods may be employed. The use of backfire in combination with allowing the wildfire to burn to a road or natural firebreak would be least damaging to the environment. However direct attack by constructing control lines as close to the fire as possible may be the preferred method to establish quicker control.

- Retardants may be used on upland areas.

- Constructed fire line will be rehabilitated prior to departure from the fire or scheduled for rehabilitation by other non-fire personnel.

- The Incident Commander will choose the appropriate suppression strategy and technique. As a guide: On low intensity fires (generally flame lengths less than 4 feet) the primary suppression strategy will be direct attack with hand crews and engines. If conditions occur that sustain higher intensity fires (those with flame lengths greater than 4 feet) then indirect strategies which utilize back fires or burning out from natural and human-made fire barriers may be utilized. Those barriers should be selected to safely suppress the fire, minimize resource degradation and damage and be cost effective.

- The use of earth moving equipment for suppression activities (dozers, graders, plows) on the District land will not be permitted without the approval of the individual District Manager or his/her designated representative in the event of their absence.

- All areas in which wildfires occur on the District or District administered lands will be evaluated prior to the aerial or ground application of foams and/or retardants. Only approved chemical foams and retardants will be used (or not used) in sensitive areas such as those with riparian vegetation.

- Hazard reduction prescribed fires may be used in fire adapted communities that have not had significant fire for more than twice the normal fire frequency for that community type.

- Utilization of heavy equipment during high intensity fires will be allowed only with the approval of the individual managers of the Districts.

- Wild fire use for resource benefit will not be utilized.

- Engines will remain on roads and trails to the fullest extent possible.

- Whenever it appears a fire will escape initial attack efforts, leave Service lands, or when fire complexity exceeds the capabilities of command or operations, the IC will take appropriate, proactive actions to ensure additional resources are ordered. The IC, through dispatch or other means, will notify the Complex FMO of the situation. With Zone FMO assistance the Refuge Manager at each Complex Refuge will complete a Wildland Fire Situation Analysis (WFSA) and Delegation of Authority.

- The IC will be responsible for mop-up and rehabilitation actions and standards on District fires. District fires will be monitored until declared out.

- Rehabilitation of suppression actions will take place prior to firefighters being released from the fire. Action to be taken include: 1) All trash will be removed; 2) Fire lines will be refilled and water bars added if needed; 3) Hazardous trees and snags cut and all stumps cut flush; and 4) Damage to improvements caused by suppression efforts will be repaired, and a rehabilitation plan completed if necessary. Service policy states that only damage to improvements caused by suppression efforts can be repaired with fire funds. Service funds cannot be used to repair damage caused by the fire itself (i.e. burnt fence lines). If re-seeding is necessary, it will be accomplished according to Service policy and regulations

2.2.2 Cultural Resources

The District Manager will, during early planning, provide the Regional Historic Preservation Officer a description and location of all projects, activities, routine maintenance and operations that affect ground and structures, requests for permitted uses, and alternatives being considered. The RHPO will analyze these undertakings for potential to affect historic properties and enter into consultation with the public and local government officials to identify concerns about impacts by the undertaking. This notification will be at least equal to, preferably with, public notification accomplished for NEPA and compatibility.

2.2.3 Listed Species

Prior to the burning season, Ecological Services will review each District's Fire Management Plan to ensure that prescribed burning will not negatively impact listed species.

2.3 Alternative 1 – Discontinue Acquiring Additional Land and Maintain Management on Current Land

Under this alternative we would manage fee title land already in the system and would not increase the holdings to the agreed goal acres for each county within the District. We would restore native grasslands using local ecotypes of mixed native grasses and forbs and improve wetlands by increasing water control and improving watersheds. We would regularly evaluate our approach to waterfowl production. We would maintain the recruitment rate of waterfowl and the current level of inspection of our lands and easements. We would continue to conduct the 4-square-mile monitoring program and the monitoring of nesting structures under this alternative. We would continue routine surveys such as the scent post survey and bird counts and non-routine surveys when requested, such as the deformed frog survey. We would continue to avoid any actions that would harm endangered or threatened species, and we would note the presence of any species that is federally listed as endangered or threatened.

We would maintain the public access to WPA's that currently exists. We would complete and document development plans for every WPA on the District as time and staffing permit. The development plans would be recorded in a geographic information system and document ownership boundaries, habitat, facilities and history of management.

Each District would continue with the current level of staffing. We would identify and replace facilities and equipment that do not meet Service standards. We would expect that the maintenance backlog would be reduced, but not eliminated, over the life of the CCP.

Management would continue to be inconsistent among Districts. There would be limited coordination with the Districts in Iowa, Wisconsin, and the Dakotas.

Currently, the Districts manage the following lands:

Big Stone WMD	Acres
Native Prairie (virgin)	25
Other Grasslands/Farmland	1,445
Forested/Brushland	34
Wetland/Riverine	839
Total	*2,343*

Detroit Lakes WMD	Acres
Native Prairie (virgin)	4,051
Other Grasslands/Farmland	15,262
Forested/Brushland	4,178
Wetland/Riverine	18,124
Total	*41,615*

Fergus Falls WMD	Acres
Native Prairie (virgin)	2,294
Other Grasslands/Farmland	20,881
Forested/Brushland	3,828
Wetlands and Rivers	16,309
Total	*43417*

Litchfield WMD	Acres
Native prairie (virgin)	2,653
Other grasslands/farmland	14,310
Forested/brushland	2,969
Wetland/riverine	13,281
Total	*33,213*

Morris WMD	Acres
Native Prairie (virgin)	7,035
Other Grasslands/Farmland	23,969
Forested/Brushland	2,268
Wetland/Riverine	17,936
Total	*51,208*

Windom WMD	Acres
Native prairie	422
Other grasslands/farmland	7,564
Forested/brushland	543
Wetland/riverine	4,140
Total	*12,669*

2.4 Alternative 2: Increase Land Holdings to Goal Acres and Maintain Current Management Practices (No Action Alternative)

Under this alternative we would continue acquiring land up to the goal acres agreed to by each county within the District (See Table 1). We would expand the size of Waterfowl Production Areas in areas of prime waterfowl use through easements and working with partners.

We would restore native grasslands using local ecotypes of mixed native grasses and forbs and improve wetlands by increasing water control and improving watersheds. We would regularly evaluate our approach to waterfowl production. We would maintain the recruitment rate of waterfowl and the current level of inspection of our lands and easements. We would continue to conduct the 4-square-mile monitoring program and the monitoring of nesting structures under this alternative. We would continue routine surveys such as the scent post survey and bird counts and non-routine surveys when requested, such as the deformed frog survey. We would continue to avoid any actions that would harm endangered or threatened species. We would note the presence of any species that is federally listed as endangered or threatened.

We would continue current public access on existing areas and add access to new acquisitions slowly over several years. We would complete and document development plans for every WPA on the District as time and staffing permit. The development plans would be recorded in a geographic information system and document ownership boundaries, habitat, facilities and history of management.

Each District would continue with the current level of staffing. We would identify and replace facilities and equipment that do not meet Service standards. We would expect that the maintenance backlog would be reduced, but not eliminated, over the life of the CCP.

Management would continue to be inconsistent among Districts. There would be limited coordination with the Districts in Iowa, Wisconsin, and the Dakotas.

2.5 Alternative 3 – Increase Land Holdings to Goal Acres and Expand Management for Waterfowl, Other Trust Species and the Public (Preferred Alternative)

Under this alternative we would continue acquiring land up to the goal acres agreed to by each county within the District (See Table 1). We would expand the size of Waterfowl Production Areas in areas of prime waterfowl use through easements and working with partners. We would focus whenever possible on prime habitat as outlined in the Habitat and Population Evaluation Team (HAPET) "thunderstorm" maps. These maps reveal high density waterfowl populations and, because the results are color coded, look somewhat like weather maps.

We would follow the Strategic Growth of the Small Wetland Acquisition Program (SWAP) Guidelines for Fee and Easement Purchase (Appendix K). These Guidelines specify that:

1) The program will focus on providing the mission components for the WMD landscape: wetland complexes, surrounding grasslands and a predator component that approaches a naturally occurring complement (i.e., coyotes vs. red fox).

2) The program will focus on established delineation criteria (size, location, ratio of upland to wetlands, soil composition, etc.) for all fee title, habitat and wetland easements (Appendix K).

3) The program will prioritize acquisition based on "thunderstorm maps," land cover (grassland acres), landscape characteristics and data on predator

populations. Prioritization will be given to tracts that benefit waterfowl, but other wildlife benefits will be considered in the priorities such as native prairie, endangered or threatened species, colonial nesting birds and expanding and protecting large tracts of grassland as Grassland Bird Core Conservation Areas as proposed by Fitzgerald et al. (1998).

We would restore native grasslands using local ecotypes of mixed native grasses and forbs and improve wetlands by increasing water control and improving watersheds. We would, where possible, follow HAPET recommendations for nesting platforms and predator management (electric fencing, predator control, islands, etc). Cooperating landowners within the District's watershed would be offered incentives and/or compensated through cost-sharing agreements for applying conservation and environmental farming practices on their lands and for creating, maintaining, or enhancing habitat for wildlife.

We would regularly evaluate our approach to waterfowl production and improve waterfowl monitoring. We would increase the recruitment rate of waterfowl and increase inspection of our lands and easements. We would work to prohibit the introduction of wildlife species that are not native to the Northern Tallgrass Prairie Ecosystem.

We would employ a scientifically defensible means to monitor and evaluate habitats and populations under this alternative. We would increasingly use geographic information systems in our monitoring. We would inventory the hydrological systems within the Districts, invertebrate communities, and monitor contaminant levels in water flowing into District wetlands. We would increase our surveys and monitoring of threatened and endangered species, invertebrates, and unique communities under this alternative. We would seek opportunities to enhance and reintroduce native species in the districts.

Under this alternative we would expand and improve opportunities for public use through construction of additional parking lots and interpretive kiosks on existing and acquired lands.

We would complete and document development plans for every WPA on the District within three years under this alternative. The development plans would be recorded in a geographic information system and document ownership boundaries, habitat, facilities and history of management.

Staff would be added to the Districts under this alternative. Implementation of the CCP would rely on partnerships formed with landowners in the watershed, volunteers and interested citizens, farm and conservation organizations, and with appropriate government agencies. We would identify and replace facilities and equipment that do not meet Service standards. Our goal would be to meet the standards by 2010.

Management of the Districts would be more consistent among the Minnesota Districts and with the Districts in Iowa, Wisconsin and the Dakotas.

Table 2: CCP Objectives Compared by Management Action

Alternative 1: Maintain Management on Current Acres with no additional land acquisition	Alternative 2: Increase Land Holdings to Goal Acres and Maintain Current Management Practices (No Action)	Alternative 3: Improve Wetland Management Districts for Waterfowl and Other Trust Species (Preferred Alternative)
Goal 1: Wildlife *Strive to preserve and maintain diversity and increase the abundance of waterfowl and other key wildlife species in the Northern Tallgrass Prairie Ecosystem. Seek sustainable solutions to the impact of Canada Geese on adjacent private croplands. Preserve, restore, and enhance resident wildlife populations where compatible with waterfowl and the preservation of other trust species.*		
Continue to use the MAAPE process to increase waterfowl production on the Districts. If updates are made in the process, it will likely be on an intermittent basis.	Same as Alternative 1.	Update MAAPE Process. The District will request the Fergus Falls Habitat and Population Evaluation Team (HAPET) to review the "Multi-Agency Approach to Planning and Evaluation" (MAAPE) process every 5 years to incorporate monitoring results and reevaluate strategies for increasing waterfowl production within the Districts.
Current waterfowl monitoring techniques using the four-square-mile monitoring program will continue to be the primary monitoring mechanism to determine waterfowl abundance and productivity estimates.	Same as Alternative 1.	Alternative Waterfowl Monitoring. The District will develop alternative monitoring techniques by the year 2007 for waterfowl abundance and productivity estimates in areas of Districts that are not well-covered by the four-square-mile monitoring program.
Recruitment Rate. Districts will strive to maintain the 2001 recruitment rate of mallards (approximately 0.52) or increase it slightly as additional operations funding is focused on current lands under Service control.	Recruitment Rate. Districts will strive to maintain the 2001 recruitment rate of mallards (approximately 0.52).	Recruitment Rate. The Districts will strive to increase potential recruitment rate of mallards in an average year from the current level of 0.52 to 0.60 by 2015.
Violations. Each year, the Districts will inspect all WPA, FmHA Conservation Easement and Habitat Easement for compliance to insure protection of migratory waterfowl and other habitats. Any illegal activity will be responded to immediately and restored as soon as possible.	Same as Alternative 1.	Same as Alternative 1.
Working With Partners. Increased effort over current levels due to reduction of land acquisition program on the Districts	Working With Partners. The District will cooperate with all USDA, Minnesota DNR and any other local agency programs as well as participate as a partner with local conservation groups which would increase waterfowl habitat and production.	Same as Alternative 2.

Table 2: CCP Objectives Compared by Management Action

Alternative 1: Maintain Management on Current Acres with no additional land acquisition	Alternative 2: Increase Land Holdings to Goal Acres and Maintain Current Management Practices (No Action)	Alternative 3: Improve Wetland Management Districts for Waterfowl and Other Trust Species (Preferred Alternative)
Goal 1: Wildlife continued		
Native species reintroductions will consist of native plant materials used to restore cropland to native grassland. No restoration of vertebrates or invertebrates will occur.	Same as Alternative 1.	Identify, evaluate, and prioritize opportunities to reintroduce native species documenting the needs in a plan by 2007.
Increase efforts to reintroduce native species. Small increases would be possible as operations and maintenance funding gradually increases without a corresponding increase in new lands to manage.	No reintroduction of new species will occur. The reintroduction of the current compliment of native plant materials will continue as part of the ongoing cropland restorations.	By 2010 begin a reintroduction program to reintroduce one species per year until all goal species identified under Objective 1.6 are reintroduced.
No memorandum of Understanding would be developed with the Minnesota DNR.	Same as Alternative 1.	Develop a Memorandum of Understanding with the Minnesota DNR which clearly articulates the responsibilities of Wetland Districts for the handling of landowner complaints originating from geese on WPA wetlands.
Same as Alternative 3 but only as funds and resources are available basis	Same as Alternative 1.	Cooperation. The Districts will cooperate with state wildlife offices and local organizations to provide winter food sources on documented wintering areas to benefit resident species of wildlife.

Table 2: CCP Objectives Compared by Management Action

Alternative 1: Maintain Management on Current Acres with no additional land acquisition	Alternative 2: Increase Land Holdings to Goal Acres and Maintain Current Management Practices (No Action)	Alternative 3: Improve Wetland Management Districts for Waterfowl and Other Trust Species (Preferred Alternative)
Goal 2: Habitat *Restore native prairie plant communities of the Northern Tallgrass Prairie Ecosystem using local ecotypes of seed and maintain the vigor of these stands through natural processes. Restore functioning wetland complexes and maintain the cyclic productivity of wetlands. Continue efforts for long-term solutions to the problem of invasive species with increased emphasis on biological control to minimize damage to aquatic and terrestrial communities. Continue efforts to better define the role of each District in assisting private landowners with wetland, upland and riparian restorations.*		
Same as Alternative 2. Restoration of native grasslands would diminish since few if any new lands would be added to the Districts over time.	An average of 250 acres in fee title per District will be restored to native grassland species each year. Other aspects of this objective will be similar to Alternative 3.	Prairie Restoration. Restore an average of 500 acres in fee title per District to native seeded grassland species each year. Begin the process on all new acquisitions within 5 years of purchase. Seed a diverse mix of predominantly native grasses and forbes using the ecotype recommendations of the Mississippi Headwater Tallgrass Prairie Ecosystem Team. Replicate, to the extent possible, the structure, species composition, and processes of native ecological communities in the Tallgrass Prairie to improve migratory bird habitat and improve existing soil and water quality within respective watersheds. Judiciously use non-native plantings when desirable to meet waterfowl and migratory bird population objectives.
Grassland Management. Renovate and seed or interseed 1000 acres of existing grasslands per District to improve diversity and vigor. Diminishing land acquisition will allow for a gradual increase in existing seeded acreage.	Grassland Management. Renovate and seed or interseed 250 acres of existing grasslands per District to improve diversity and vigor.	Grassland Management. Renovate and seed or interseed 500 acres of existing grasslands per District to improve diversity and vigor.
Prescribed Burn. Plan and conduct prescribed burns on over 5,000 acres annually per District to maintain and restore native prairie plant species. Diminishing land acquisition will allow for a gradual increase in burned acreage on existing lands.	Prescribed Burn. Plan and conduct prescribed burns on 2,000–4,000 acres annually to maintain and restore native prairie plant species to improve waterfowl and wildlife use, and to prepare selected sites for native seed harvest.	Prescribed Burn. Plan and conduct prescribed burns on 3,000–5,000 acres annually to maintain and restore native prairie plant species to improve waterfowl and wildlife use, and to prepare selected sites for native seed harvest.
Manage existing WPA and easement grasslands so that each acre is treated at least once every 6 years by burning, mowing, haying, grazing, or other management.	Manage existing WPA and easement grasslands so that each acre is treated at least once every 7 years by burning, mowing, haying, grazing, or other management.	Same as Alternative 2.

Table 2: CCP Objectives Compared by Management Action

Alternative 1: Maintain Management on Current Acres with no additional land acquisition	Alternative 2: Increase Land Holdings to Goal Acres and Maintain Current Management Practices (No Action)	Alternative 3: Improve Wetland Management Districts for Waterfowl and Other Trust Species (Preferred Alternataive)
Goal 2: Habitat, continued		
Restoration. Restore an average of 120 wetlands per year off refuge system land to serve migratory birds as migration, breeding and nesting habitat.	Restoration. Restore an average of 80 wetlands per year both on and off refuge system land to serve migratory birds as migration, breeding and nesting habitat.	Restoration. Restore an average of 100 wetlands per year both on and off refuge system land to serve migratory birds as migration, breeding and nesting habitat.
Management. Manage water levels on 100 percent of the wetlands that have built-in water control structures to increase vegetation and nutrient recycling for the benefit of waterfowl. Consider increasing the number of wetlands with control structures.	Management. Manage water levels on 100 percent of the wetlands that have built-in water control structures to increase vegetation and nutrient recycling for the benefit of waterfowl.	Same as Alternative 2.
Monitoring. Inventory hydrological systems in the Districts as identified in the monitoring plan, including chemical water analysis, water level, water flow and the interaction of Federal lands and private lands within the watershed.	Same as Alternative 1.	Same as Alternative 1.
Cooperation. Attend and participate in watershed district meetings.	Same as Alternative 1.	Same as Alternative 1.
Research. Encourage and cooperate in research on hydrological systems within the District.	Same as Alternative 1.	Same as Alternative 1.
Management. Increase use of hydrological data gathering in the overall management of the Districts following the guidance developed in the Monitoring Plan.	Same as Alternative 1.	Same as Alternative 1.
Hydrologist. Hire a hydrologist to conduct hydrological monitoring program, analyze the data and present the information to management in a useable form.	Same as Alternative 1.	Same as Alternative 1.

Table 2: CCP Objectives Compared by Management Action

Alternative 1: Maintain Management on Current Acres with no additional land acquisition	Alternative 2: Increase Land Holdings to Goal Acres and Maintain Current Management Practices (No Action)	Alternative 3: Improve Wetland Management Districts for Waterfowl and Other Trust Species (Preferred Alternative)
Goal 2: Habitat, continued		
Plant Control. Reduce exotic plants including noxious weeds on state and county lists through an aggressive program including burning, mowing, chemical treatment, hand cropping, and interseeding. Primary targets include purple loosestrife, Canada thistle, and leafy spurge.	Same as Alternative 1.	Same as Alternative 1.
Minnow and Carp Control. Working with partners, by 2008 carp and undesirable minnow populations will be controlled on 90 percent of infested WPA wetlands through water level control, reduced minnow stocking, barriers, and chemical control.	Same as Alternative 1, except that completion date would be 2010 and control will be on 70 percent of infested WPA wetlands.	Same as Alternative 1, except that completion date would be 2010 and control will be on 90 percent of infested WPA wetlands.
Grasshopper Control: We will work with Minnesota Department of Agriculture to devise an appropriate emergency grasshopper control plan by 2008 so that future infestations are handled effectively and in a way that minimizes or eliminates insecticide use on WPAs for grasshopper control.	Same as Alternative 1.	Same as Alternative 1.
Biological Control: Increase emphasis on biological control whenever feasible. The District will continue to release beetles for control of spurge and loosestrife as appropriate.	Same as Alternative 1.	Same as Alternative 1.
Goal 3: Acquisition *Within current acquisition acreage goals, identify the highest priority acres for acquisition taking into account block size and waterfowl productivity data. These priority areas should drive acquisition efforts whenever possible. Service land acquisition should have no negative impact on net revenues to local government. Understand and communicate the economic effects of federal land ownership on local communities.*		
Evaluating Acquisition Priority. No additional land would be acquired beyond 2003 target levels.	Evaluating Acquisition Priority. Review and update the current acquisition guidelines by the year 2003. Acquisition strategies for future acquisitions within the Districts will be based on site potential. Consideration should be given to size, quality, key species affected, habitat fragmentation, landscape scale complexes, potential productivity of restored wetlands, etc.	Same as Alternative 2.

Table 2: CCP Objectives Compared by Management Action

Alternative 1: Maintain Management on Current Acres with no additional land acquisition	Alternative 2: Increase Land Holdings to Goal Acres and Maintain Current Management Practices (No Action)	Alternative 3: Improve Wetland Management Districts for **Waterfowl and Other Trust Species** (Preferred Alternative)
Goal 3: Acquisition, continued		
Goal Acres. No or few new lands will be acquired beyond 2003. Habitat management efforts will be intensified to reach waterfowl recruitment objectives for the District.	Goal Acres. By 2005, conduct a biological assessment to determine if current goal acres will be sufficient to reach waterfowl recruitment objectives for the District.	Same as Alternative 2.
Coordination. The Districts will continue to insure a response to willing seller offers in high priority areas only.	Coordination. The Districts will coordinate with their District Acquisition Offices to insure rapid response to willing seller offers that meet the acquisition priorities. An offer will be made to the seller within 5 months of the decision to acquire the tract.	Same as Alternative 2.
Acquisition. Each District will meet 2003 Districe goal acres and will hold steady, or only minimally increase land holdings, over the next 15 years.	Acquisition. Each District will meet current District goal acres within 15 years by acquiring an average of 1,630 acres in fee title, 3,335 acres of wetland easements and 1,660 acres of upland easements per year, for waterfowl breeding and use. This objective will be modified as appropriate if the goal acres are modified.	Same as Alternative 2.
Advocate 100 percent of revenue sharing and a lump sum payment for past underpayment through a trust fund to the counties.	Same as Alternative 1.	Same as Alternative 1.
Continue to provide information to local governments and the public on the revenue sharing program for existing lands.	Conduct a study that would provide the following information to managers so that they can better communicate the issue to the public: 1)A graph of revenue sharing for the last 20 years, 2)A detailed explanation of the impact of federal ownership on school taxes, 3)A detailed study of the trust fund payments to the state in relation to the revenue sharing shortfall and 4)How much money do we really need to make up the trust fund from 1993 and prior.	Same as Alternative 2.
Determine local economic value of Federal land ownership.	Same as Alternative 1.	Same as Alternative 1.

Table 2: CCP Objectives Compared by Management Action

Alternative 1: Maintain Management on Current Acres with no additional land acquisition	Alternative 2: Increase Land Holdings to Goal Acres and Maintain Current Management Practices (No Action)	Alternative 3: Improve Wetland Management Districts for Waterfowl and Other Trust Species (Preferred Alternative)
Goal 3: Acquisition, continued		
Demonstrate the hydrologic benefits of restored wetlands; determine cash value of wetland values.	Same as Alternative 1.	Same as Alternative 1.
Determine social value of natural habitat in the landscape. Determine importance of wildlife to people in a community.	Same as Alternative 1.	Same as Alternative 1.
Goal 4. Monitoring *Collect baseline information on plants, fish and wildlife and monitor critical parameters and trends of key species and/or species groups on and around District units. Promote the use of coordinated, standardized, cost effective, and defensible methods for gathering and analyzing habitat and population data. Management decisions will be based on the*		
Inventory and Monitoring Plan. Develop an Inventory and Monitoring Plan by 2003 that will identify census needs and appropriate techniques as part of a coordinated monitoring program that will be used to evaluate species richness within the Districts by developing species data and accounts on selected sites.	Same as Alternative 1.	Same as Alternative 1.
Geographic Information System. Increase use of GIS technology in monitoring habitat and wildlife.	Same as Alternative 1.	Same as Alternative 1.
Maintain the current use of biological data in the overall management of the Districts.	Increase the use of biological data in the overall management of the Districts by fulfilling the actions identified in the Inventory and Monitoring Plan.	Same as Alternative 2.
Biological Inventory. As part of the Inventory and Monitoring Plan, inventory the biological resources on the Districts by the year 2010.	Same as Alternative 1.	Same as Alternative 1.
Breeding Birds. Conduct regular surveys of breeding grassland and wetland migratory birds.	Same as Alternative 1.	Same as Alternative 1.
Monitoring. Monitor the levels of external threats to the Waterfowl Production Units such as soil erosion, incoming water quality, pesticide use, and contaminants as identified in the Inventory and Monitoring Plan.	Same as Alternative 1.	Same as Alternative 1.

Table 2: CCP Objectives Compared by Management Action

Alternative 1: Maintain Management on Current Acres with no additional land acquisition	Alternative 2: Increase Land Holdings to Goal Acres and Maintain Current Management Practices (No Action)	Alternative 3: Improve Wetland Management Districts for Waterfowl and Other Trust Species (Preferred Alternative)
Goal 5: Endangered Species / Unique Communities *Preserve enhance, and restore rare native northern tallgrass prairie, flora and fauna that are or may become endangered. Where feasible in both ecological and social/economic terms, reintroduce native species on WPAs in cooperation with the Minnesota DNR.*		
Threatened and Endangered Species. Continue to avoid actions that would harm threatened and endangered species within the District.	Same as Alternative 1.	**Threatened and Endangered Species.** Identify and survey threatened and endangered species within the District looking specifically for species of special interest as listed in Appendix I.
Invertebrates. Maintain existing surveys of invertebrate communities in grassland and wetland communities.	Same as Alternative 1.	**Invertebrates.** Conduct regular surveys of invertebrate communities in grassland and wetland communities following the approaches identified in the Inventory and Monitoring Plan.
Research. Encourage and cooperate in research that will further our understanding about management and habitat manipulations on the District.	Same as Alternative 1.	Same as Alternative 1.
Partners for Fish and Wildlife. With the Partners for Fish and Wildlife staff in the Regional Office, develop clear guidance for upland and riparian restoration work so each District is managing the program consistently.	Same as Alternative 1.	Same as Alternative 1.
Management. The Districts will protect and enhance populations of endangered, threatened, and special emphasis species (Appendix E) indigenous on District lands. Management applications applied to these areas will be tailored to meet species management needs.	Same as Alternative 1.	Same as Alternative 1.
Cooperation. The Districts will work with partners and other agencies to develop specific plans for target species occurring within the Districts.	Same as Alternative 1.	Same as Alternative 1.
Enforcement. The Districts will enforce all Endangered Species Act and Migratory Bird Treaty Act regulations within their District through increased contacts with hunters, neighbors and visitors.	Same as Alternative 1.	Same as Alternative 1.

Table 2: CCP Objectives Compared by Management Action

Alternative 1: Maintain Management on Current Acres with no additional land acquisition	Alternative 2: Increase Land Holdings to Goal Acres and Maintain Current Management Practices (No Action)	Alternative 3: Improve Wetland Management Districts for Waterfowl and Other Trust Species (Preferred Alternative)
Goal 5: Endangered Species / Unique Communities, continued		
Monitoring. The Districts will obtain baseline data including maps of all federally endangered and threatened species as well as all native prairie tracts, calcareous fens and oak savanna by 2005.	Same as Alternative 1.	Same as Alternative 1.
Cooperation: The Districts will continue to support the efforts of the Northern Tallgrass Prairie NWR and project partners to protect native prairie remnants in the Wetland Districts.	Cooperation. The Districts will identify threatened Northern Tallgrass Prairie unique communities and work through the Northern Tallgrass Prairie NWR project partners or other agencies and partners to acquire in fee title or protect through easement where the Small Wetlands Acquisition Program is not appropriate. All remaining native prairie remnants larger than 5 acres will by identified by 2005 and strategies for their protection will be developed by the year 2005.	Same as Alternative 2.
Enforcement. The Districts will continue to prohibit the introduction of wildlife species that are not native to the Northern Tallgrass Prairie Ecosystem.	Enforcement. The Districts will prohibit the introduction of wildlife species that are not native to the Northern Tallgrass Prairie Ecosystem.	Same as Alternative 2.
Develop priority actions to be implemented by the Partners for Fish and Wildlife Program with the strategies to be developed in a joint effort by all districts by 2004 with the Morris Wetland Management District taking the lead and responsible for the documentation.	Same as Alternative 1.	Same as Alternative 1.
Goal 6: Public Use/Environmental Education *Provide opportunities for the public to use the WPAs in a way that promotes understanding and appreciation of the Prairie Pothole Region. Promote greater understanding and awareness of the Wetland Management District's programs, goals, and objectives. Advance stewardship and understanding of the Prairie Pothole Region through environmental education, outreach and partnership development.*		
Each Wetland Management District will strive to meet the National Visitor Service Standards for the Refuge System by the year 2005:	Same as Alternative 1.	Same as Alternative 1.

Table 2: CCP Objectives Compared by Management Action

Alternative 1: Maintain Management on Current Acres with no additional land acquisition	Alternative 2: Increase Land Holdings to Goal Acres and Maintain Current Management Practices (No Action)	Alternative 3: Improve Wetland Management Districts for Waterfowl and Other Trust Species (Preferred Alternative)
Goal 6: Public Use/ Environmental Education, continued		
Develop an outreach plan for each District, following the Public Use Plan developed by Fergus Falls Wetland Management District. Address internal (within the Service) and external audiences by 2003.	Same as Alternative 1.	Same as Alternative 1.
Each Wetland Management District should have a full-time public use specialist by 2004.	Same as Alternative 1.	Same as Alternative 1.
Each Wetland Management District should designate a Waterfowl Production Area in each county that will be handicapped accessible.	Same as Alternative 1.	Same as Alternative 1.
Develop maps for each Wetland Management District that can be easily provided upon request by the public by 2003.	Same as Alternative 1.	Same as Alternative 1.
Promote greater understanding of the WMD program; implement the Public Use Plan for each District by 2006.	Same as Alternative 1.	Same as Alternative 1.
Significantly increase visits for environmental education and interpretation to all District headquarters by 2006.	Same as Alternative 1	Slightly increase environmental visits to wetland management district headquarters by 2006. Land acquisition and restoration workloads will place limitations on the rate of increase.
Goal 7: Development Plan *Preparation of WPA Development Plans: Complete Geographic Information System (GIS) based WPA Development Plans for each unit in each District. Provide Districts with GIS to assist with acquisition, restoration, management and protection of public and private lands.*		
The WMD will have computer support staff by 2005.	Same as Alternative 1.	Same as Alternative 1.

Table 2: CCP Objectives Compared by Management Action

Alternative 1: Maintain Management on Current Acres with no additional land acquisition	Alternative 2: Increase Land Holdings to Goal Acres and Maintain Current Management Practices (No Action)	Alternative 3: Improve Wetland Management Districts for Waterfowl and Other Trust Species (Preferred Alternative)
Goal 8: Staff, Facilities and Equipment *Provide necessary levels of maintenance, technician and administrative support staff to achieve other Wetland Management District goals: Provide all Districts with adequate and safe office, maintenance and equipment storage facilities Acquire adequate equipment and vehicles to achieve other District goals. Maintain District equipment and vehicles at or above Service standards.*		
The staffing needs identified in this CCP are added as identified elsewhere in the plan.	Same as Alternative 1.	Same as Alternative 1.
Identify all buildings that do not meet service standards or needs by 2005.	Same as Alternative 1.	Same as Alternative 1.
Construct, replace or modify buildings so that all buildings meet service standards and needs by 2010.	Same as Alternative 1.	Same as Alternative 1.
Ensure that all Wetland District vehicles are replaced when their mileage reaches normal industry replacement standards (6 years or 60,000).	Same as Alternative 1.	Same as Alternative 1.
Ensure that Wetland Management District office and field tools and equipments are adequate to fulfill this plan.	Same as Alternative 1.	Same as Alternative 1.
Goal 9: Annual Capital Development Funds *Ensure that annual capital development funds are large enough to meet necessary development of new WPA land: Have adequate funds available each year to permit completion of maintenance needs for each Wetland Districts current land base of Waterfowl Production Areas.*		
Educate and provide adequate information to Regional, Washington, Departmental and Congressional staffs of need for capital improvement funding of an ongoing acquisition program.	Same as Alternative 1.	Same as Alternative 1.
Maintain a current inventory of all maintenance needs, updating it annually.	Same as Alternative 1.	Same as Alternative 1.
The Refuge Supervisor will summarize accomplishments combining all districts to demonstrate the work done through previous funding.	Same as Alternative 1.	Same as Alternative 1.

Table 2: CCP Objectives Compared by Management Action

Alternative 1: Maintain Management on Current Acres with no additional land acquisition	Alternative 2: Increase Land Holdings to Goal Acres and Maintain Current Management Practices (No Action)	Alternative 3: Improve Wetland Management Districts for Waterfowl and Other Trust Species (Preferred Alternative)
Goal 10: Consistency Goal *Develop and apply consistent policies for habitat, public use, and resource protection and ensure frequent coordination among Districts, both in Minnesota and in neighboring states with WPAs (North and South Dakota, Iowa, and Wisconsin).*		
All existing WPAs will have Development Plans completed by 2005.	All existing WPAs will have Development Plans completed by 2008.	Same as Alternative 2
Not Applicable. Acquisition of new lands would be limited to land exchanges.	Ensure that newly acquired land receives timely, effective unit planning to meet trust responsibilities within 2 years of taking possession of area.	Same as Alternative 2.
Quarterly coordination meetings for the WMDs will be held to discuss common issues and practices. The meetings will include all District managers and District supervisors.	Same as Alternative 1.	Same as Alternative 1.
Once a year a regional meeting will be held to compare notes with managers in Region 6 and other Wetland Management Districts in Region 3 that are not included in this Comprehensive Conservation Plan.	Same as Alternative 1	Same as Alternative 1

Table 3: Summary of Management Alternatives

		Alternatives	
Goals	Alternative 1 *Acquire no additional land and maintain management on current land*	Alternative 2 *Increase land holdings to goal acres and maintain current management practices (No Action)*	Alternative 3 *Increase land holdings to goal acres and expand management for waterfowl, other trust species and the public* *(Preferred Alternative)*
Wildlife Goal	■ Maintain recruitment rate of waterfowl ■ Regularly evaluate approach to waterfowl production.	Same as Alternative 1.	■ Increase recruitment rate of waterfowl. ■ Regularly evaluate approach to waterfowl production. ■ Where possible, follow HAPET recommendations for nesting platforms and predator management. ■ Seek opportunities to enhance and reintroduce native species within the Districts. ■ Work to prohibit introduction of non-native species.
Habitat Goal	■ Restore native grasslands using local grasses and forbs ■ Improve wetlands by increasing water control and improving watersheds.	Same as Alternative 1.	■ Restore native grasslands using local grasses and forbs; improve wetlands by increasing water control and improving watersheds. ■ Offer incentives to landowners for applying conservation and environmental farming practices on their land and for creating, maintaining or enhancing habitat on their land. ■ Work to prohibit introduction of non-native species.
Acquisition Goal	■ Manage existing fee title land and not increase holdings to the agreed goal acres for each county within the Districts.	■ Continue acquiring land up to goal acres. Expand the size of WPAs in areas of prime waterfowl use through easements and working with partners.	■ Continue acquiring land up to the goal acres. ■ Expand the size of WPAs in areas of prime waterfowl use through easements and working with partners. ■ Whenever possible, focus on prime habitat outlined by the Habitat and Population Evaluation Team maps. ■ Follow the Strategic Growth of the Small Wetland Acquisition Program Guidelines for fee and easement purchase.

Table 3: Summary of Management Alternatives

	Alternatives		
Goals	**Alternative 1** *Acquire no additional land and maintain management on current land*	**Alternative 2** *Increase land holdings to goal acres and maintain current management practices (No Action)*	**Alternative 3** *Increase land holdings to goal acres and expand management for waterfowl, other trust species and the public (Preferred Alternative)*
Monitoring Goal	■ Continue 4-square-mile monitoring program and monitoring nesting structures. ■ Routine surveys and non-routine surveys would be conducted when requested.	Same as Alternative 1.	■ Employ scientifically-defensible means to monitor and evaluate habitats and populations. ■ Increase use of GIS in monitoring. ■ Inventory hydrological systems with the Districts, inventory invertebrate communities, and monitor contaminant levels in water flowing into the Districts. ■ Increase surveys and monitoring of threatened and endangered species.
Endangered/Threatened Species Goal	■ Presence of federally listed threatened/endangered species would be noted. ■ Continue to avoid actions that would harm these species.	Same as Alternative 1.	■ Increase surveys and monitoring of threatened and endangered species, invertebrates, and unique communities. ■ Seek opportunities to enhance and reintroduce native species in the Districts.
Public Use / Environmental Education Goal	■ Existing public access to WPAs maintained.	■ Continue current public access on existing areas and add access to new acquisitions over several years.	■ Expand and improve public use opportunities through construction of parking lots and interpretive kiosks on existing and newly acquired lands.
Development Plan Goal	■ Development Plans completed for every WPA on each District as time and staffing permit. ■ Development Plans would be recorded in GIS.	Same as Alternative 1.	■ Complete and document development plans for every WPA within the District within 3 years. ■ Development plans would be recorded in GIS.

Table 3: Summary of Management Alternatives

Goals	Alternatives		
	Alternative 1 *Acquire no additional land and maintain management on current land*	Alternative 2 *Increase land holdings to goal acres and maintain current management practices (No Action)*	Alternative 3 *Increase land holdings to goal acres and expand management for waterfowl, other trust species and the public (Preferred Alternative)*
Staff, Facilities and Equipment Goal	■ Current level of staffing would continue on each District. ■ Facilities and equipment not meeting Service standards would be replaced. ■ Maintenance backlog would be reduced.	Same as Alternative 1.	■ Staff would be added to the Districts. ■ Implementation of the CCP would rely on partnerships formed with landowners in the watershed, volunteers and interested citizens, farm and conservation organizations, and appropriate government agencies. ■ Facilities and equipment not meeting Service standards would be replaced by 2010.
Annual Capital Development Funds Goal	■ No additional lands would be purchased, which would reduce mainte-nance needs.	■ Maintenance costs would increase with additional lands, however this would be balanced by WPA expansions accomplished through easements and work with partners.	Same as Alternative 2.
Consistency Goal	■ Existing inconsistencies in management of Districts would continue. ■ Coordination with Districts in surrounding states would be limited.	Same as Alternative 1.	■ Management would be more consistent among Minnesota Districts as well as Districts in Iowa, Wisconsin, North Dakota and South Dakota.

3.0 The Affected Environment

3.1 Detroit Lakes Wetland Management District

3.1.2 Introduction

Detroit Lakes WMD is the northernmost district in northwestern Minnesota and includes the counties of Becker, Clay, Mahomen, Norman and Polk. The headquarters is near Detroit Lakes, which is located in the southern portion of the District. The District is bordered on the west by the flat Red River flood plain and by the rolling hardwood forest-lake region on the east. The primary economic base of the area is agriculture, with a strong tourism industry centered on area lakes.

The rolling prairie zone and associated wetlands of this District, located between glacial Lake Agassiz's beach ridge and the hardwood forest, have not been spared from agricultural development. The tallgrass prairie, most of the wetlands, and much of the timberland have been converted to crop production.

The District currently manages 40,492 fee acres on 162 WPAs. In addition, 323 wetland easements totaling 12,715 wetland acres, three grassland easements totaling 156 acres and 18 FmHA conservation easements totaling 1,637 acres are administered by the WMD. These lands are scattered across five counties of northwest Minnesota.

3.1.2 Climate

District climate falls in the temperate zone with severely cold winters and warm summers. Temperatures can range from as low as -45 degrees Fahrenheit in January and February to the upper 90s (degrees Fahrenheit) during June through August. The warmest months are July and August with the average temperature near 70 degrees Fahrenheit.

Table 4: Major Habitat Types of Waterfowl Production Areas in the Detroit Lakes Wetland Management District

Habitat Types		Acres
Native prairie (virgin)		4,051
Other grasslands/farmland		15,262
Forested/brushland		4,178
Wetland/riverine		18,124
	Total	41,615

Normal annual precipitation is nearly 25 inches, most of which falls between April and September. The heaviest rainfall occurs in June, July and August when as much as 8 inches can fall in one month. Winter precipitation from snowfall is generally light (under 4 inches of measured precipitation).

3.1.3 Soils

District soils range from heavy silty clay in the flat Red River Valley to sand on the beach line of historic glacial Lake Agassiz to deep loam in the rolling grasslands of the prairie pothole area to shallow loam in the forested lakes region.

3.1.4 Natural Resources

The District is located in the transition area between the tallgrass prairie and big woods biomes. Habitat varies from virgin tallgrass prairie to cropland to forest, with thousands of wetlands and lakes scattered throughout. The result is an area that is rich in floral and faunal diversity. The only portion of the District that lacks diversity is the Red River Valley flood plain; however, there are remnant riverine habitats in the floodplain that are an oasis for wildlife, particularly migrating passerine birds.

3.1.4.1 Plants
Endangered/Threatened
A goblin fern population (Federal candidate species proposed for listing) has recently been located on the Hagen WPA in Polk County. Several Clay County WPAs are suspected of having the western prairie fringed orchid, which is Federally listed as endangered. In addition, Conservation Easement 10-C in Clay County protects a unique land feature on the glacial Lake Agassiz beachline that supports "short-grass" prairie species, and a portion of the only Minnesota breeding site for the chestnut-collared longspur.

Grassland
The native grasslands in the District have all of the species components of the tallgrass prairie, as many as 250 species of grasses, forbs and other prairie plants. The seeded native grasslands on District WPAs are dominated by four species of warm-season native grasses, big and little bluestem, switchgrass, and Indian grass. Non-native grasslands are a mixture of introduced cool-season grasses (primarily smooth brome, Kentucky bluegrass, and quackgrass) and native and introduced forbs.

Wetland
The District has wetland types I through VIII (Stewart and Kantrud 1971) and numerous lakes and rivers. About 60 percent of the original wetland habitat in the District has been lost through drainage or filling. The present wetland base could be classified as good to excellent. Through the Service's wetland restoration program, this wetland base is increasing and being enhanced annually. Wetland vegetation varies based on water conditions ranging from ephemeral to permanent open water wetlands and includes reed canary grass, cattail, bulrush, phragmites, burreed, coontail, bladderwort, waterlily, arrowhead, manna grass, duckweed, sedge, smart-weed, cord grass, and willow.

Forested
Forested areas occur primarily in the eastern half of the District. Composition is mixed hardwoods with species such as aspen, oak, basswood, ash, maple, etc. A few areas are dominated by white, red and jack pine. Fewer yet are composed of balsam

and white spruce stands. In the western half of the District, timbered areas are mainly farmstead and riparian habitats, dominated by boxelder, oak, cottonwood and ash. Some of the western most remaining tamarack stands in Minnesota occur on waterfowl production areas in Clay County. Nearly all American and red (rock) elms in the District have died from Dutch Elm Disease.

Noxious Weeds
All of the listed noxious weed species of Minnesota can be found in the District. The species most troublesome to District operations include plumeless thistle, leafy spurge, purple loosestrife, and Canada thistle and musk thistle.

3.1.4.2 Animals
Endangered/Threatened
Bald Eagles (threatened) commonly use WPAs during migration periods and throughout the summer. To date, no eagles are known to nest on WPAs; however, the number of area nests is increasing with some quite near WPAs.

The District is in the peripheral range of the gray wolf (threatened). Gray wolves are reproducing in eastern Becker County, including a denning sight located on Tamarac National Wildlife Refuge. Public reports of gray wolf sightings in the District are increasing annually.

The candidate species Dakota skipper also occurs on the District.

Birds
The District has a great diversity of bird species that are common to the grasslands, wetlands, and forests of Minnesota. Nesting waterfowl include Canvasback, Redhead, Blue-winged Teal, Mallard, Pintail, Wood Duck, Ring-necked Duck, and Ruddy Duck. Other noteworthy species include the Greater Prairie Chicken.

Trumpeter Swans have been reintroduced in the District. Nesting success has been steadily improving and some District WPAs are receiving increasing use.

Loons and Double-crested Cormorants frequent the deeper marshes of District WPAs; cormorants are steadily increasing. Abundant Sora and Common Snipe populations use WPA wetland habitat throughout the District.

Greater Sandhill Cranes, Great Egrets, Western, Pied-billed and Red-necked Grebes, Horned and Eared grebes, American and Least Bitterns, Great Blue Herons, Black-crowned Night Herons and White Pelicans are commonly observed during the migration and breeding seasons. Populations of Great Egrets and White Pelicans appear to be increasing in the District. Breeding pairs of Greater Sandhill Cranes also appear to be increasing dramatically. Cranes have been observed throughout the summer on Helliksen Prairie WPA in Becker County, Downing and Nelson Prairie WPAs in Mahnomen County, and on WPAs and private land throughout the eastern half of Polk County. There are also reports of crane production in southeastern Becker County in the Toad River Watershed.

Shorebirds common to the area include Killdeer, Marbled Godwit, Upland Plover (sandpiper), Spotted and Pectoral Sandpiper, Wilson's Phalarope, Greater and Lesser Yellowlegs, American Woodcock, and Common Snipe. These species and others are observed during migration and breeding seasons.

Herring, Ring-billed, Franklin and Bonepart's Gulls, Forester's and Common Terns are frequently observed during migration. Black Terns are summer residents of many WPAs.

At least 20 species of raptors utilize WPAs in this area. Marsh Hawks (Northern Harrier), Cooper's and Sharp-shinned Hawks, Red-tailed and rough-legged Hawks, American Kestrels, Broad-winged Hawks, Goshawks, Osprey and Great Horned Owls are among the most common. Peregrine Falcons use several WPAs during migration periods.

Mammals
All mammals endemic to Minnesota grasslands, transition zones, and forested areas are common in the District. The moose population is increasing throughout the District with an estimated 50 to 100 moose inhabiting District WPAs. The white-tailed deer population in this region of Minnesota is high. Other mammals commonly using WPA habitat include beaver, mink, muskrat, fox, coyote, skunks, raccoon, rabbits, otter, fisher and many rodent species.

Fish
While there is limited fish habitat on District WPAs, several of them are used by fish as spawning sites. Only one WPA has a resident fish population. Elsewhere in the District, there are numerous rivers and lakes with healthy fish populations.

Reptiles and Amphibians
Three snake species (garter, red-bellied, and smooth green), two salamanders (tiger and blue-spotted), four frog species (leopard, wood, tree, and spring peeper), two turtle species (snapper and painted), two toad species (Canadian and American) and the 13-lined skink are found in the District.

Other Wildlife
The Poweshiek Skipper, a State Special Concern Species butterfly, can be found on Flickertail Prairie WPA. This dry prairie site on the sandy beach-line of glacial Lake Agassiz may also hold a small population of the state-listed threatened Dakota Skipper butterfly.

3.1.5 Cultural Resources

The area encompassed by Detroit Lakes WMD exhibits evidence of human use and occupation for the past 6,000 years, possibly for the past 9,000 years. At least 700 prehistoric and historic period archeological sites and certain other cultural resources have been recorded; of which 100 sites are on District waterfowl production areas. With less than two per cent of the land having been surveyed for cultural resources, good potential exists for many unrecorded sites from the earliest Paleo Indian, Archaic, Woodland, Indian, and Euro-American cultures such as camps, villages, bison-kills, traditional cultural and sacred sites, subsistence procurement activities, trading posts, pioneer and other farmsteads, road and trails, and landscapes.

Cultural resources are important parts of the Nation's heritage: "those parts of the physical environment – natural and built – that have cultural value to some kind of sociocultural group ... [and] those non-material human social institutions...."King, p.9. The Service is committed to protecting valuable records of human interactions with each other and the landscape. Protection is accomplished in conjunction with the Service's mandate to protect fish, wildlife, and plant resources. (See the CCP for a complete review of cultural resource issues.)

3.1.6 Social and Economic Factors

The five counties of the District are intensely agricultural. Scattered farmsteads on large farms of predominantly small grain production with much smaller acreage devoted to hayland and pasture cover the area. Land use trends have been toward clean farming methods with fall tillage. In recent years, some conservation tillage has been occurring. Wetland drainage has been extensive with only the most permanent wetlands or those under perpetual easement protection remaining.

The agricultural community has suffered economically in recent years due to the general agricultural depression of the 1980s and dry growing seasons in 1988 and 1989. Some improvement in the farming economy has occurred in the 1990s as crop prices, yields, and land values have increased; however, the unusually wet summers of 1992, 1993 and 1999 caused it to slump again.

Recreation also provides important economic input into the District. Many of the recreational activities are centered around the many lakes and wetlands of the area with waterfowl hunting, fishing, and boating the main activities. Deer and upland bird hunting are other major recreational activities that provide important economic benefits.

3.2 Fergus Falls Wetland Management District

3.2.1 Introduction

The Fergus Falls Wetland Management District consists of Otter Tail, Grant, Douglas, Wilkin, and Wadena counties. These counties are in the Prairie Pothole Region generally on or west of the prairie-forest transition. This area was locked in glacial ice until about 12,000 years ago. By 8,000 years ago glacial Lake Agassiz was gone, leaving a basin that was flat with little topographic relief except for ancient beach ridges in an area of the Red River Valley we now know as Wilkin County. Douglas, Grant, and Otter Tail counties extend into the western prairie rolling topography known as glacial morain with numerous lakes. Wadena County is part of the Mississippi headwaters district, an area of geological complexity.

The woodlands to the east gradually begin as oak savannah phasing into oak-ash communities on the higher sites with willow-tamarack shrub swamps on the lower sites. Major rivers within the District include the Red River of the north; Otter Tail, Pelican, Mustinka and Rabbit, which flow west of the continental divide into the Hudson Bay drainage; and the Chippewa, Pomme de Terre, Long Prairie, Wing and Redeye Rivers, which flow east into the Mississippi drainage.

This region historically was covered by bluestem tallgrass prairie on the west phasing into oak savanna to the east. The coming of settlement in the late 1800s brought suppression of wildfires. Woodlands have moved west, taking over many areas that were once prairie or savanna.

The District currently manages 222 Waterfowl Production Areas (WPAs) totaling 42,671 acres. These WPAs are managed for optimum waterfowl production using techniques such as upland cover, water, and seasonal predator management. In addition, 916 wetland easements totaling 22,717 wetland acres, 4 grassland easements totaling 428 acres and 29 FmHA conservation easements totaling 2,967 acres are administered by the District.

3.2.2 Climate

Annual precipitation is about 22 inches per year. Temperatures range in extremes from as low as -40 degrees to highs of 90 degrees Fahrenheit or more. Winters are long and cold, with temperatures remaining below freezing for months at a time.

3.2.3 Soils

The soils in the eastern portion of the District are mainly formed in calcareous loamy glacial till, in outwash sediments, or in glacial drift overlying outwash. To the west, in the Red River Valley, the soils were formed in sandy to clayey lacustrine sediments or lacustrine modified glacial till overlying glacial till.

3.2.4 Natural Resources

Most of the District's remnant native prairie parcels are too small and have too many invasive trees and shrubs to support true indigenous populations of prairie species. These conditions do promote a wide variety of species with the added woody cover; however, the management philosophy is that maintaining biodiversity by protecting historical ecosystems (large treeless blocks of native prairie) is more important than maximizing local species diversity. In other words, harboring a smaller variety of indigenous prairie species is more important than having a higher diversity of species (some non-native) on unmanaged fragmented grassland that is being invaded by trees and brush.

3.2.4.1 Plants
Endangered/Threatened
The Western prairie fringed orchid is a federally threatened species. It is found in sedge meadows, especially in groundwater seeps at the base of ancient beach ridges, and has been documented in Douglas County. The federally listed threatened prairie bush clover may occur in the District; it is found in dry, gravelly hill prairies, often in association with big bluestem and Indian grass.

Grassland
Grassland areas consist mainly of former farm fields that have been seeded for nesting cover. Restoring these areas to their historic prairie appearance is difficult, if not impossible, because over 250 species of plants make up the native prairie plant community. Four to five species of warm season native grasses, often mixed with

---

Table 5: Major Habitat Types of Waterfowl Production Areas in the Fergus Falls Wetland Management District

Habitat Type	Acres
Native prairie (virgin)	2,294
Other grasslands/farmland	20,373
Forested/brushland	3,433
Wetland/riverine	16,571
Roads, buildings, misc.	105
Total	42,671

---

native forbs, are seeded on suitable upland sites. These warm season grasses include big bluestem, little bluestem, switchgrass, and Indian grass. The District has restored over 20,000 acres of grasslands on Service lands. Many upland acres remain in brome, quack or other cool season grasses which eventually will be converted to native warm season grasses.

The District currently owns 2,294 acres of unbroken native prairie and an additional 20,371 acres of other grassland on WPAs.

Wetland

Wetland vegetation varies based on water conditions ranging from ephemeral to permanent open water wetlands and includes reed canary grass, cattail, bulrush, phragmites, burreed, coontail, bladderwort, waterlily, arrowhead, manna grass, duckweed, sedge, smartweed, cord grass, and willow. There are currently 16,571 acres of wetlands on WPAs in the District, including riverine systems.

Forested

Because the primary objective of the District is the production of grassland nesting waterfowl species, few forested upland areas are purchased as WPA's. Where trees and brush do exist, as in the case of retired pasturelands, the dominant species include a mixture of burr oak, green ash, basswood, and ironwood with lesser amounts of white birch, aspen, maple, and American elm. Boxelder dominates most abandoned farmsteads. This species and green ash readily invade adjacent grasslands when control is not exercised. In general, most woodlands and brushlands are of irregular shape and size and occur more frequently in the eastern side of the District, which is the original prairie/hardwood transition zone. The Service currently owns 3,433 acres of forested and brushland habitat on WPAs in the District.

Noxious Weeds

Approximately 20 species have been declared noxious weeds in the District, but the main problem weeds on Service lands are plumeless thistle, Canada thistle, and leafy spurge. Smaller areas of wild millet, poison ivy, and marijuana have also been a problem. Methods of control used include ground spraying, mowing, and aerial spraying. Some experiments with biological control of leafy spurge have shown it to be a promising alternative.

3.2.4.2 Animals

Endangered and/or Threatened Species

For three straight years, there has been an active bald eagle nest on a WPA in the District. Thirty-five other known active eagle nests are present on private land. It is obvious that the bald eagle is expanding its range southward in the state, as witnessed by these recent nesting records. There are even more reports from the public of nesting eagles in the secluded lake and river country of eastern Otter Tail County, but these word-of-month reports have not been verified by Service personnel.

The Federally listed threatened piping plover (Great Plains population) is occasionally seen during the spring and fall. Reported sightings of gray wolves, both confirmed and unconfirmed, have been on the increase in recent years. With a near saturation population level of wolves in the northern timbered sections of the state, younger wolves are being forced into new areas. In 1992, Federal trappers removed a family of wolves that was killing cattle on a farm in eastern Otter Tail County. Wolves are no longer the rare sight that they were 5 years ago.

Birds
The District bird list contains 267 regularly occurring species, plus an additional list of nine accidental species.

Numerous species of waterfowl are common and 16 species nest in the District; the most common of these are the mallard, blue-winged teal, gadwall, and northern shoveler. Waterfowl production data for 1987-1990 indicates 0.13 pair per acre, leading to production of 0.11 ducks per acre.

Giant Canada geese continue to thrive and expand throughout most of the District. Captive flocks were started in Fergus Falls, Alexandria and Ashby and have readily expanded their breeding range. There is so much overlap in the breeding ranges of the various "flocks" that all the available habitat is now occupied by a homogenous mix from all three original flocks.

Marsh and water birds common to this District include the great blue heron, black tern, green-backed heron, great egret, coot, pied-billed grebe, sora and Virginia rail, black-crowned night heron, common snipe, American bittern and double-crested cormorant. Pelican Island, which is a 15-acre island located in Pelican Lake near Ashby, Minnesota, serves as a rookery for hundreds of herons, egrets and cormorants. The island is owned by the Nature Conservancy. Other smaller colonies of about 50 nests or less consisting mainly of great blue herons and great egrets are located in other parts of Otter Tail and Douglas counties. A large cormorant colony is located on three islands in Lye Lake in Otter Tail County; in 1994, it contained more than 2,000 breeding pairs.

Waterfowl Production Areas receive considerable use by shorebirds, especially during migration. Approximately 17 species of shorebirds are common or abundant during the spring migration. During the summer months, the most common are the killdeer, greater yellowlegs, and Wilson's snipe.

The red-tailed hawk, American kestrel, northern harrier, and great horned owl lead the list of the 16 common raptors in the District. The annual fall migration of hawks through the area normally runs from mid-September through the first week in October. At these times, as many as 50 hawks (mostly broadwings and/or red-tails) can be seen at one time. The peregrine falcon, which migrates through the District, has made a great recovery in recent years.

A survey of songbirds has been conducted on grasslands in WPAs in the District in 1993, and 51 species have been recorded. The most commonly observed birds, listed in descending order, were the red-winged blackbird, clay-colored sparrow, common yellowthroat, yellow-headed blackbird, and song sparrow. Grasshopper sparrows were found mainly on well-drained ground that lacked invasive shrubs. Due to the predominance of woody cover on many of the prairie parcels sampled, clay-colored sparrows and yellow warblers were two of the most frequently encountered species.

Mammals
White-tailed deer are the most abundant game animal in the District. Moose are becoming more common in Wilkin and East Otter Tail counties. Other common mammals include the fox, raccoon, snowshoe hare, cottontail and jackrabbit, mink, beaver, muskrat, weasel, and skunk. Periodically, a black bear, bobcat, or lynx is reported.

A small mammal diversity and abundance study was done in 1983 on warm season

grass fields on two WPAs in Otter Tail County. The most common small mammals found were shrews and mice in the genera Sorex, Blarina, and Peromyscus.
Fish

Because most wetlands on Service lands are shallow, the fishery resource is minimal. Bullheads, minnows, and northern pike are present on several WPAs. Many of the WPAs located along the Otter Tail and Pelican Rivers and those bordering meandered lakes provide an access for boat launching and some opportunity for bank fishing. High numbers of fathead minnows have become a problem in some wetlands in the District, leading to poor water quality and reduced invertebrate populations.

Reptiles and Amphibians
Numerous species of reptiles and amphibians are found in the District. One formal auditory frog and toad study is in progress in Grant County; preliminary results show the most common species to be the wood frog, chorus frog, and Canadian toad, with spring peepers and the American toad being less common. Leopard frogs are very common in other parts of the District, though they were not heard in this study. Little information is available on the salamanders, snakes, turtles, and skink that are found in the District.

3.2.5 Cultural Resources

The area encompassed by Fergus Falls WMD exhibits evidence of human use and occupation for the past 6,000 years, possibly for the past 9,000 years. At least 900 prehistoric and historic period archeological sites and certain other cultural resources have been recorded; of which 130 sites are on District waterfowl production areas. With less than 2 percent of the land having been surveyed for cultural resources, good potential exists for many unrecorded sites from the earliest Paleo Indian, Archaic, Woodland, Indian, and Euro-American cultures such as camps, villages, bison-kills, traditional cultural and sacred sites, subsistence procurement activities, trading posts, pioneer and other farmsteads, road and trails, and landscapes.

Cultural resources are important parts of the Nation's heritage: "those parts of the physical environment — natural and built — that have cultural value to some kind of sociocultural group ... [and] those non-material human social institutions...."King, p.9. The Service is committed to protecting valuable records of human interactions with each other and the landscape. Protection is accomplished in conjunction with the Service's mandate to protect fish, wildlife, and plant resources." (See the CCP for a complete review of cultural resource issues.)

3.2.6 Social and Economic Factors

The Northern Pacific and Great Northern Railroads arrived in 1871 and 1879, respectively. They provided vital links with grain markets in Minneapolis, St. Paul, and Duluth and helped farmers move from making a subsistence living to making a profit on their crops.

The five counties in the District are intensely agricultural. Scattered farmsteads of predominantly grain production with much smaller acreage devoted to hayland and pasture cover the area. Land use trends have been toward clean farming methods and intensive tillage, generally fall cultivated, although some conservation tillage (leaving crop residue) occurs. Drainage has been extensive, with less than half of the pre-settlement wetlands remaining. Wetland drainage is the preferred solution by farmers to cropland flooding, and grass cover is minimized by farmers because they believe it harbors weeds. Some wetlands on WPAs are the result of subirrigation and receive runoff from adjacent farmland.

Hunting, trapping, wildlife observation, photography, and cross-country skiing are among the public use activities permitted on WPAs. Public use is low, except during the opening weekends of the waterfowl hunting season.

The current economy of the area is heavily dependent upon agriculture, although tourism, light manufacturing, and recreation play an increasingly important role.

3.3 Morris Wetland Management District

3.3.1 Introduction

The Morris Wetland Management District (District), originally established in 1964 as the Benson Wetland Management District, now includes 246 Waterfowl Production Areas (WPAs) totaling 50,000 acres in fee title ownership. In addition, the District manages 591 wetland easements totaling 72,523 wetland acres, nine grassland easements totaling 605 acres and 21 Farmers Home Administration (FmHA) conservation easements totaling 1,224 acres. The fee and easement areas are scattered throughout Big Stone, Lac qui Parle, Pope, Stevens, Swift, Traverse, and Yellow Medicine counties.

The topography of west central Minnesota is extremely diversified, ranging from the granite outcrops of the Minnesota River bottoms to the rolling hills of Pope County. The flat agricultural land of the Red River Valley of the north blends into the transition zone between the tall grass prairie and the eastern deciduous forest. Soils of the region are generally productive, which contributed to the historically high concentrations of breeding waterfowl. With the advent of modern agriculture, over 60 percent of the original wetlands were drained and nearly 100 percent of the native grasslands were converted to cropland.

3.3.2 Climate

The continental climate of the District is characterized by cold, dry winters and warm, moist summers. The average annual rainfall is approximately 21-24 inches. More than 75 percent of the annual precipitation falls during the growing season, from April through September. Much of the rain during the growing season comes in thunderstorms, some of which are accompanied by hail and damaging winds. Records show that the average windspeed is nearly 12 miles per hour. The prevailing direction of the wind is from the northwest in winter and the south in summer. The average temperature is 42 degrees F. The coldest temperatures vary from -25 degrees to -35 degrees F. and summertime highs reach up to 100 degrees F. or more.

3.3.3 Soils

The soils within the seven counties of the district have been completely inventoried and detailed soil mapping is available. The geological classifications within the district range from lake (Glacial Lake Agassiz) deposits in the north, outwash deposits that occur primarily along river systems of the District, to glacial till deposits that cover most of the land in the District. The material classifications in these three geological classes are clay and silt in the lake deposits, sand and gravel in the outwash areas and mixed sand, silt, clay, gravel, and boulders in the glacial till. The glacial till areas consist of ground moraines and end or stagnation moraines. Ground moraines form flat to undulating land surfaces and the end or stagnation moraines form pitted to hilly land surfaces.

3.3.4 Natural Resources

3.3.4.1 Plants
Endangered/Threatened
The western prairie fringed orchid is a threatened species which may occur within the District.

Grassland
Grasslands comprise 31,665 acres of the District. This category includes 8,465 acres of reseeded native grasses and 7,012 acres of unbroken native prairie. The balance of the existing grassland contains various cover types including brome, quack and alfalfa.

Wetland
Wetlands make up 16,820 acres of the District. Most of the wetlands can be classified as Type I-V basins (Circular 39). Cattail, bulrush, phragmites, arrowhead, and smartweed are typical emergents found in the District. Duckweed, bladderwort and coontail are free-floating plants that occur frequently in wetland basins. Submergent plants such as pondweed and water milfoil also occur in District wetlands.

Forested
Morris lies within what was once the tall grass prairie. Less than 4 percent of the fee acreage is covered by timber. Of the 1,515 acres of timber and brush, the majority consists of old farm groves and shelterbelts.

Noxious Weeds
There are many noxious weeds that exist within the District; the primary ones are Canada thistle and leafy spurge. Purple loosestrife, trees invading the native prairie, and wild marijuana are also problems.

Table 6: Major Habitat Types of Waterfowl Production Areas in the Morris Wetland Management District

Habitat Type	Acres
Native prairie (virgin)	7,035
Other grasslands/farmlands	23,969
Forested/brushland	2,268
Wetland/riverine	17,936
Total	51,208

<u>3.3.4.2 Animals</u>
Endangered/Threatened
The piping plover (federally threatened Great Plains population) and the bald eagle (federally threatened) both occur in the District.

No endangered mammals are known to occur on WPAs within the District, though a report of a gray wolf, a threatened species, has been recorded. The candidate species Dakota skipper is known to occur on the District land.

Birds
Waterfowl Production Areas in the District contain a complex of habitat types that help support over 260 species of birds, 135 of which nest within the District. The non-game bird point count included 41 native prairie and 14 seeded native sites on five WPAs. A total of 76 species were found. Twenty-eight of these were neotropical migrants. No new species were found this year in this 6-year study. Bird numbers continue to be down from previous years. There were three bald eagle nesting attempts in the District. Wilson's phalarope, Minnesota lists as "threatened," and "species of concern", marbled godwit have been sited on WPA's in the District.

Waterfowl species that commonly breed in the area include blue-winged teal, mallard, pintail, wood duck, redhead, canvasback, and Canada goose. Canada geese continue to increase as breeders and snow geese as migrants. High priority waterfowl species are northern pintail (nester and migrant), American black duck (migrant), mallard (nester and migrant) and lesser scaup (migrant).

Mammals
The District contains a complex of habitat types that help support 55 species of mammals. Field observations indicate that mammal species are abundant on WPAs and range from the pygmy shrew to the white-tailed deer. Occasional moose wander through the District. The District Scent Post Surveys revealed and abundance of red fox, raccoon, and skunks, all predate grassland bird nests extensively.

Fish
There are 18 species of fish that are documented in wetlands on WPAs within the District. There are low numbers of game fish and high numbers of minnows and rough fish. Due to the shallow nature of the wetlands there is a high probability of winterkill.

Reptiles and Amphibians
There is very limited documentation of reptiles and amphibians that occur on WPAs within the District. No surveys have been conducted to determine species occurrence. Several species of turtles, snakes, salamanders, and frogs have been observed.

3.3.5 Cultural Resources

The area encompassed by Morris WMD exhibits evidence of human use and occupation for the past 6,000 years, possibly for the past 9,000 years. At least 750 prehistoric and historic period archeological sites and certain other cultural resources have been recorded; of which 100 sites are on District waterfowl production areas. With less than two per cent of the land having been surveyed for cultural resources, good potential exists for many unrecorded sites from the earliest Paleo Indian, Archaic, Woodland, Indian, and Euro-American cultures such as camps, villages, bison-kills, traditional cultural and sacred sites, subsistence procurement activities, trading posts, pioneer and other farmsteads, road and trails, and landscapes.

Cultural resources are important parts of the Nation's heritage: "those parts of the physical environment – natural and built – that have cultural value to some kind of sociocultural group ... [and] those non-material human social institutions...." King, p.9. The Service is committed to protecting valuable records of human interactions with each other and the landscape. Protection is accomplished in conjunction with the Service's mandate to protect fish, wildlife, and plant resources. (See the CCP for a complete review of cultural resource issues.)

3.3.6 Social and Economic Factors

The majority of neighbors accept the fact that the Federal government owns land for waterfowl production, and most have a general appreciation for the value of wildlife. However, these neighbors expect the land to be managed for wildlife and not ignored. Their opinions of wildlife agencies, environmental groups, and wildlife in general is greatly influenced by the way these lands are managed. If a WPA is ignored, allowing the habitat condition to decrease in quality and noxious weeds to increase in abundance, opinions quickly become negative. However, if the land is managed for the best interest of wildlife and habitat conditions are maintained, these opinions become positive for wildlife benefits both on and off Service-managed lands.

A variety of wildlife-oriented recreation activities are available to the public. Some of these include hiking, bird watching, photography, snowshoeing, mushroom hunting, cross-country skiing, hunting, and trapping in accordance with State regulations. The WPAs are open year round for these activities. Travel on WPAs is limited to foot or horseback only and overnight camping and fires are prohibited.

Local communities benefit from the money spent by people using WPAs for recreational activities. The largest beneficial impact comes from hunters because hunting is the most frequent recreational use.

3.4 Litchfield Wetland Management District

3.4.1 Introduction

The Litchfield Wetland Management District (WMD) was established in 1978 to manage tracts purchased under the Small Wetlands Acquisition Program. The District manages 146 Waterfowl Production Areas (WPAs) covering 32,528 acres of fee title lands. In addition, 415 wetland easements totaling 34,970 wetland acres, four grassland easements totaling 202 acres and 35 Farmers Home Association (FmHa) conservation easements totaling 2,458 acres are administered by the District. These tracts are scattered throughout the 10 central counties of Minnesota.

District lands include portions of the Northern Mixed Forest, Eastern Hardwood Forest, Oak Savanna, and Tallgrass Prairie Biomes. Soils, precipitation, climate, water quality, and land use vary greatly but essentially all areas have been greatly altered and degraded by development.

3.4.2 Climate

The District is located in central Minnesota. The area has a typical continental climate with wide temperature extremes from summer to winter. The moderating effect of the oceans on temperature is virtually non-existent here. Annually, temperature extremes can differ by 140 degrees or more.

Mean annual precipitation varies west to east across the District from 24 inches in the west to 29 inches in the east. The number of days that the ground is covered with 6 inches of snow averages 40 in the southwest to 70 in the northeast. Twelve inches of snow-cover averages 15 to 30 days southwest to northeast, respectively. The last frost occurs in early to mid-May and the first frost falls during the last week in September during a normal year.

3.4.3 Soils

The Litchfield Wetland Management District is broken into a series of geographic regions that were all formed from glacial activity reaching back 40-plus thousand years. Four major glacial periods resulted in a lot of earth moved by ice and water and the large-scale mixing of soils. As the glaciers melted, silts and clays were deposited in some areas and runoff deposited sands and gravels in other areas.

After the last glacier (more than 9,000 years ago) a combination of environmental factors (wind, water, topography, fire, plants, animals) determined the types of topsoil which developed over the glacial formations. These factors have provided the District with an amazing variety of soil types; everything from peat bogs to sand dunes and from rock outcrops to deep soil prairies are found. Soil pH factors range from strongly acid (pH = 4.5+) to strongly alkaline (pH = 9.0). Over 100 soils series are named within the District.

3.4.4 Natural Resources

3.4.4.1 Plants
Plant diversity in the District is very good. It is located in the transition zone between the three major continental biomes; the eastern hardwood forests, the northern coniferous forest, and the tallgrass prairie. The glacial topography of rolling hills and wetland valleys further divides the landscape into a mosaic of woodland savanna and prairie that represents nearly all gradations between wet and dry and between acid and alkaline.

The 10-county District contains 33 plant communities. A plant inventory conducted during the 1980s revealed approximately 350 plant species on WPAs. With new WPAs acquired in the eastern portion of the District, this number should increase substantially. About 1,150 species of vascular plants occur in the District.

Endangered/Threatened
The western prairie fringed orchid is a federally threatened species that may occur in the District. It is found in sedge meadows, especially in groundwater seeps at the base of ancient beach ridges. The prairie bush clover may occur in the District; it is found in dry, gravelly hill prairies, often in association with big bluestem and Indian grass.

Grassland
The District was predominantly native grassland prior to settlement. The lack of fire has allowed succession to occur and much unbroken native grassland is now brush or woodland. The Service has planted permanent grassland onto all of its acquired cropland. Of the 32,528 acres in the Litchfield District, approximately 2,320 acres is unbroken native prairie and 15,670 acres have been seeded to native and introduced

Table 7: Major Habitat Types of Waterfowl Production Areas in the Litchfield Wetland Management District

Habitat Type		Acres
Native Prairie (virgin)		2,653
Other grasslands/farmland		14,310
Forested/brushland		2,969
Wetland/riverine		13,281
	Total	33,213

grasses of various combinations of species. Wherever noxious weeds and chemical use are not a problem, natural selection and the use of native prairie harvested seed have placed many forb species into the seeded grasslands.

Wetland

Wetlands have always been a major focus in the District. Approximately 12,520 acres of wetlands occur on District WPAs. Over 3,000 acres of those are restored wetlands. Total wetland plant diversity in the District is high. Nearly all wetland types are represented from wet meadows to lakes and from hardwood swamps and tamarack bogs to calcareous fens. Not much species inventory has occurred in most wetland community types.

Forested

The District does not normally purchase forestland. Often small oak groves and/or wooded building sites are included in the prairie/cropland wetland complexes acquired. Generally woodlots are not encouraged as they often cause management problems such as tree invasion onto grasslands, prescribed fire planning problems, and the presence of avian and mammalian predator habitat. Some of the state endangered oak savanna habitat will be grazed or burned to manage this plant community.

Noxious Weeds

All of the noxious weed species listed by the State of Minnesota are found on Districts' WPAs. Control of these species is necessary to maintain good relationships with neighbors and local government units. District staff use an aggressive, integrated program of prescribed burning, interseeding, cooperative farming, and mechanical, chemical, and biological control methods in an attempt to minimize weed complaints and impacts to non-target species.

3.4.4.2 Animals

Endangered/Threatened

Piping plover (threatened Great Plains population) occur in the District. The endangered winged mapleleaf mussel may also occur in the District. Bald eagles (threatened) commonly use WPAs during migration periods and throughout the summer. To date, no eagles are known to nest on WPAs.

The District is in the peripheral range of the Eastern cougar (endangered) and the gray wolf (threatened).

Birds

About 290 species of birds are known to pass through the District during migration; 177 species are known to nest within the District.

The most frequently found nesting waterfowl in the District include mallards, blue-winged teal, and wood ducks. Other species observed during the 4-square mile counts include shoveler, green-winged teal, redhead, ruddy duck, ring-necked duck, canvasback, scaup, pintail, gadwall, widgeon, goldeneye, bufflehead, and common, hooded and red-breasted mergansers. Canada geese nest in the District and are common to the point of being a nuisance to farmers. Trumpeter swan, previously considered to be extirpated from the District, has been listed as threatened on the State's list of "special concern" species. A reintroduction program for the species is ongoing between the Service, the Minnesota DNR, Hennepin County Parks, and the Trumpeter Swan Society. Free-flying individuals continue to successfully nest on Pelican Lake WPA in Wright County.

Great blue herons, black-crowned night herons, great egrets, green-backed herons, white pelicans, American coots, double-crested cormorants, western and pied-billed grebes, and common loons were sighted during the 4-square mile counts this spring. Other water birds included the red-necked grebe, Virginia rail, and sora rail. Some State species of special concern use the District habitats including yellow and king rails, common moorhen, and American white pelican. The State-listed threatened, horned grebe also uses the District during migration.

Black terns, piping plover, common tern, Forester's terns, Franklin gulls, lesser yellowlegs, common snipe, upland sandpipers, and killdeer occur on District lands. Marbled godwits and Wilson's phalarope also use the District habitats.

Great-horned owls, red-tailed hawks, and American kestrels are common residents. Northern harriers, and Cooper's, broad-winged, and red-shouldered hawks, and short-eared, barred, long-eared, screech, and saw-whet owls are less common residents. Occasional sightings of turkey vultures, osprey, goshawks, and sharp-shinned, rough-legged, Swainson's and ferruginous hawks are reported. Rarely, golden eagles, peregrine, prairie falcons and snowy owls may be sighted. Bald eagle nesting is increasing in the District.

Mammals
Of the more than 80 species of mammals in Minnesota, 60 occur within the District. The following occur only rarely within the District: moose, mule deer, mountain lion, timber wolf, spotted skunk, river otter, black bear, prairie vole, porcupine, snowshoe hare, eastern pipistrel, and woodland jumping mouse.

Fish
There are 145 native and 14 non-native species of fishes in Minnesota waters; of these, 93 are found in the lakes, streams, and marshes of the District. Although fish are not a focus of habitat management, the District's wetland habitat is extremely important in the life cycle of many fish species.

Reptiles and Amphibians
Eight species of turtles, two species of lizards, and 12 species of snakes make their homes in the Litchfield District. In addition, 14 species of salamanders, toads, and frogs are also found within the District.

Other Animals
Untold numbers of lesser animals occur within the District. Unfortunately, science has merely scratched the surface concerning the distribution and life history of most of these very important creatures in the food web. Considering that more than 30 distinct plant communities exist within the District, diversity of these lesser creatures is high and probably numbers in the thousands if not the tens of thousands of species.

3.4.5 Cultural Resources

The area encompassed by Litchfield WMD exhibits evidence of human use and occupation for the past 6,000 years, possibly for the past 9,000 years. At least 1,100 prehistoric and historic period archeological sites and certain other cultural resources have been recorded; of which 100 sites are on District waterfowl production areas. With less than two per cent of the land having been surveyed for cultural resources, good potential exists for many unrecorded sites from the earliest Paleo Indian, Archaic, Woodland, Indian, and Euro-American cultures such as camps, villages, bison-kills, traditional cultural and sacred sites, subsistence procurement activities, trading posts, pioneer and other farmsteads, road and trails, and landscapes.

Cultural resources are important parts of the Nation's heritage: "those parts of the physical environment — natural and built — that have cultural value to some kind of sociocultural group ... [and] those non-material human social institutions...."King, p.9. The Service is committed to protecting valuable records of human interactions with each other and the landscape. Protection is accomplished in conjunction with the Service's mandate to protect fish, wildlife, and plant resources. (See the CCP for a complete review of cultural resource issues.)

3.4.6 Social and Economic Factors

Farming and associated agri-business is the most important economic activity and the largest land use in the District. The type of farming varies greatly from south to north; cash cropping dominates the more fertile prairie soils in the south and west, while dairy and beef operations and more diversified cropping dominate the north and east. A steadily increasing number of farmers derive less than half of their income from farming, especially near the larger cities in the District. Many farms near the metropolitan areas have been divided into lots and converted to residential housing for people working in the city. Also, most of the children of existing farmers are deciding to work city jobs instead of working the family farm.

Many existing farms are being sold to neighboring farmers; thus, the average farm size is increasing. Many cattle owners have moved to a feedlot operations and have plowed up or idled their pasture land. As the landowners are deriving less income from the land itself, more and more parcels are being put into conservation programs and set aside for wildlife. This change in land values has opened up nearly endless possibilities for the private lands/wetland restoration program and the fee and easement acquisition programs.

3.5 Windom Wetland Management District

3.5.1 Introduction

The Windom Wetland Managment District was established in 1990 and includes 54 Waterfowl Production Areas (WPAs) covering 10,923 acres of fee title lands. In addition, 34 wetland easements totaling 2,200 wetland acres, six grassland easements totaling 316 acres and eight Farmers Home Association (FmHA) conservation easements totaling 290 acres are managed by the District.

All WPAs and easements are located in Cottonwood, Faribault, Freeborn, Jackson, Nobles, and Watonwan counties. The District includes 12 southwestern Minnesota counties.

3.5.2 Climate

The District is located in Southwestern Minnesota. The area has a typical continental climate with wide temperature extremes from summer to winter. The moderating effect of the oceans on temperature is virtually non-existent here. Annually, temperature extremes can differ by 130 degrees or more.

Annual precipitation averages about 27 inches per year. In normal years, the last frost occurs in early to mid-May and the first frost falls during the last week in September.

3.5.3 Soils

The soils in the District were mainly formed in calcareous loamy glacial till, or in sandy to clayey lacustrine sediments. In the southwestern corner of the District, the soils were mostly formed in loess overlying glacial till and in outwash sediments .

3.5.4 Natural Resources

Intensive row crop agriculture dominates land use in the District. The topography is nearly level to gently sloping. The Missouri Coteau, which is located in South Dakota, extends into southwestern Minnesota.

3.5.4.1 Plants
Endangered/Threatened
The western prairie fringed orchid is a federally threatened species that may occur in the District. It is found in sedge meadows, especially in groundwater seeps at the base of ancient beach ridges. The federally threatened prairie bush clover may occur in the District; it is found in dry, gravelly hill prairies, often in association with big bluestem and Indian grass.

Grassland
Northern tallgrass prairie was the original pre-settlement vegetation type. Less than 1 percent of the native pre-settlement vegetation remains.

Wetland
Over 90 percnet of the wetlands in Southwest Minnesota have been drained. Undrained Type I and II wetlands are extremely rare.

Forested
Larger blocks (80-plus acres) of forest are very rare. Trees are primarily associated with riparian corridors, shelter belts and wind breaks.

Noxious Weeds
Canada thistle is the primary problem, followed by musk thistle. Noxious weed control is a political necessity in southwestern Minnesota.

3.5.4.2 Animals
Endangered/Threatened
The Topeka shiner (*Notropis topeka*) were once common to small to mid-sized prairie streams in the central United States. Now listed as endangered, These fish inhabit streams that usually run continually and that have good water quality and cool to moderate temperatures. The occurrence of the species at known collection sites has decreased by approximately 70 percent, mostly in the past 40 to 50 years. The fish has

Table 8: Major Habitat Types of Waterfowl Production Areas in the Windom Wetland Management District

Habitat Type	Acres
Native prairie (virgin)	422
Other grasslands/farmland	7,564
Forested/brushland	543
Wetland/riverine	4,140
Total	12,669

been negatively affected by habitat destruction, sedimentation, and changes in water quality. Topeka shiners now exist primarily in small, isolated populations in Iowa, Minnesota and portions of South Dakota.

The threatened Bald Eagle and candidate species Dakota skipper also occur on the District.

Birds

Waterfowl Production Areas within the District contain a complex of habitat types that help support over 200 species of birds, many of which nest within the District. Waterfowl species that commonly breed in the area include blue-winged teal, mallard, pintail, wood duck, and Canada goose.

Mammals

The District contains a complex of habitat types that help support approximately 50 species of mammals. Field observations indicate that mammal species are abundant on WPAs and range from the pygmy shrew to the white-tailed deer. Occasional moose wander through the District.

Fish

There are approximately 15 species of fish that are documented in wetlands on WPAs within the District. There are low numbers of game fish and high numbers of minnows and rough fish. Due to the shallow nature of the wetlands there is a high probability of winterkill.

Reptiles and Amphibians

There is very limited documentation of reptiles and amphibians that occur on WPAs within the District. A recent survey identified seven species of reptiles and amphibians, although this list is not considered exhaustive.

3.5.5 Cultural Resources

The area encompassed by Windom WMD exhibits evidence of human use and occupation for the past 6,000 years, possibly for the past 9,000 years. At least 1000 prehistoric and historic period archeological sites and certain other cultural resources have been recorded; of which 50 sites are on District waterfowl production areas. With less than two per cent of the land having been surveyed for cultural resources, good potential exists for many unrecorded sites from the earliest Paleo Indian, Archaic, Woodland, Indian, and Euro-American cultures such as camps, villages, bison-kills, traditional cultural and sacred sites, subsistence procurement activities, trading posts, pioneer and other farmsteads, road and trails, and landscapes.

Cultural resources are important parts of the Nation's heritage: "those parts of the physical environment – natural and built – that have cultural value to some kind of sociocultural group ... [and] those non-material human social institutions...."King, p.9. The Service is committed to protecting valuable records of human interactions with each other and the landscape. Protection is accomplished in conjunction with the Service's mandate to protect fish, wildlife, and plant resources." (See the CCP for a complete review of cultural resource issues.)

3.5.6 Social and Economic Factors

Recreational use of District WPAs is primarily hunting. Pheasant hunting is most popular, followed by waterfowl and deer. The economy is primarily dependent on agriculture and is currently depressed due to the extreme weather conditions of the last 5 years.

3.6 Big Stone Wetland Management District

3.6.1 Introduction

The Big Stone WMD was established in 1996 to acquire and manage lands under the Small Wetlands Acquisition Program within Lincoln and Lyon counties. It currently includes 11 WPAs covering 2,344 acres of fee title lands, eight habitat and/or wetland easements covering 989 acres, and three FmHA Conservation Easements covering 160 acres for a grand total of 3,493 acres of habitat.

3.6.2 Climate

The District is located in southwestern Minnesota. The area has a typical continental climate with wide temperature extremes from summer to winter. The moderating effect of the oceans on temperature is virtually non-existent here. Annually, temperature extremes can differ by 130 degrees or more.

Annual precipitation averages about 27 inches per year. In normal years, the last frost occurs in early to mid-May and the first frost falls during the last week in September.

3.6.3 Soils

The soils in the District were mainly formed in calcareous loamy glacial till, or in sandy to clayey lacustrine sediments. In the southwestern corner of the District, the soils were mostly formed in loess overlying glacial till and in outwash sediments .

3.6.4 Natural Resources

Intensive row crop agriculture dominates land use in the District. The topography is nearly level to gently sloping. The Missouri Coteau, which is located in South Dakota, extends into southwestern Minnesota.

3.6.4.1 Plants
Endangered/Threatened
The western prairie fringed orchid is a federally threatened species that may occur in the District. It is found in sedge meadows, especially in groundwater seeps at the

Table 9: Major Habitat Types of Waterfowl Production Areas in the Big Stone Wetland Management District

Habitat Type	Acres
Native prairie (virgin)	25 acres
Other grasslands/farmlands	1,445
Forested/brushland	34
Wetland/riverine	839
Total	2,343

base of ancient beach ridges. The federally threatened prairie bush clover may occur in the District; it is found in dry, gravelly hill prairies, often in association with big bluestem and Indian grass.

Grassland
Northern tallgrass prairie was the original pre-settlement vegetation type. Less than 1 percent of the native pre-settlement vegetation remains.

Wetland
Over 90 percent of the wetlands in southwest Minnesota have been drained. Undrained Type I and II wetlands are extremely rare.

Forested
Larger blocks (80-plus acres) of forest are very rare. Trees are primarily associated with riparian corridors, shelter belts and wind breaks.

Noxious Weeds
Canada thistle is the primary problem, followed by musk thistle. Noxious weed control is a political necessity in southwestern Minnesota.

3.6.4.2 Animals
Endangered/Threatened
The federally listed endangered Topeka shiner, federally listed threatened Bald Eagle and candidate species Dakota skipper are known to occur or may occur on land controlled by the District.

Birds
Waterfowl Production Areas within the District contain a complex of habitat types that help support more than 200 species of birds, many of which nest within the District.

Waterfowl species that commonly breed in the area include blue-winged teal, mallard, pintail, wood duck, and Canada goose.

Mammals
The District contains a complex of habitat types that help support approximately 50 species of mammals. Field observations indicate that mammal species are abundant on WPAs and range from the pygmy shrew to the white-tailed deer. Occasional moose wander through the District.

Fish
Approximately 15 species of fish are documented in wetlands on WPAs within the District. There are low numbers of game fish and high numbers of minnows and

rough fish. Due to the shallow nature of the wetlands there is a high probability of winterkill.

Reptiles and Amphibians

There is very limited documentation of reptiles and amphibians that occur on WPAs within the District. A recent survey identified seven species of reptiles and amphibians, although this list is not considered exhaustive.

3.6.5 Cultural Resources

The area encompassed by Big Stone WMD exhibits evidence of human use and occupation for the past 6,000 years, possibly for the past 9,000 years. At least 211 prehistoric and historic period archeological sites and certain other cultural resources have been recorded; of which 8 sites are on District waterfowl production areas. With less than two per cent of the land having been surveyed for cultural resources, good potential exists for many unrecorded sites from the earliest Paleo Indian, Archaic, Woodland, Indian, and Euro-American cultures such as camps, villages, bison-kills, traditional cultural and sacred sites, subsistence procurement activities, trading posts, pioneer and other farmsteads, road and trails, and landscapes.

Cultural resources are important parts of the Nation's heritage: "those parts of the physical environment – natural and built – that have cultural value to some kind of sociocultural group ... [and] those non-material human social institutions...."King, p.9. The Service is committed to protecting valuable records of human interactions with each other and the landscape. Protection is accomplished in conjunction with the Service's mandate to protect fish, wildlife, and plant resources. (See the CCP for a complete review of cultural resource issues.)

3.6.6 Social and Economic Factors

Recreational use of District WPAs is primarily hunting. Pheasant hunting is most popular, followed by waterfowl and deer. The economy is primarily dependent on agriculture and is currently depressed due to the extreme weather conditions of the last 5 years.

4.0 Environmental Consequences

This chapter evaluates three alternatives on the basis of environmental consequences or impacts to the environment. Alternative 1 would maintain management on current land, but no additional land would be acquired. Under Alternative 2 (No Action), land holdings would be increased to goal acres and current management practices would be maintained. Alternative 3 (Preferred Alternative) would increase land holdings to goal acres and expand management for waterfowl, other trust species and the public. Alternative represents implementation of the CCP and is the Service's preferred alternative.

Photo Copyright by Jan Eldridge

4.1 Impacts Associated with Wildlife and Habitat

4.1.1 Waterfowl Productivity

Under Alternative 1, waterfowl production would likely remain the same initially. As the maintenance backlog was reduced, more funding would be available for restoration of grasslands and wetland and watershed improvements, which could gradually increase waterfowl production.

Alternative 2 (No Action) would result in a decrease of waterfowl production and use on Service lands. Acquisition of essential upland and wetland habitats would be unfocused and would be based only on availability and opportunity, resulting in more isolated, smaller parcels of land. Management activities would be spread over a broad area making it less effective in creating habitat attractive to waterfowl. Waterfowl would continue a slow decline except in years of abundant water.

Waterfowl production would be enhanced under Alternative 3 (Preferred Alternative) because both habitat quantity and habitat quality would be improved. Waterfowl Production Areas would be expanded in areas of prime waterfowl use. Nesting success would improve in response to Districts following, where possible, HAPET recommendations for nesting platforms and predator management. In South Dakota, agricultural fields converted to permanent cover had lower nest destruction rates due to predation 10 years after initial conversion (Duebbert and Lokemoen 1976). Similar predictions have been made in other areas of the Prairie Pothole Region (Klett et al. 1988). Additional resting and feeding habitats would also disperse staging birds over a larger area and decrease the chance of catastrophic accident or disease. Additional habitat would also help ensure that migrating ducks arrive on their northern breeding grounds in better reproductive condition (Krapu 1992).

Additional waterfowl production would also be achieved through the implementation of an intensive program to increase nest success. Nest cylinders for mallards should produce 0.3 fledglings per wetland acre (Prairie Pothole Joint Venture Plan (PPJVP), 1989). Additional predator management, particularly for fox, would also enhance waterfowl production on the Districts. An electric fence study on a 359 acres of uplands associated with large wetlands in western Minnesota produced nest successes of 75 percent compared to 5 to 1.5 percent without a predator barrier. Other techniques such as constructing islands to reduce avian predation on nesting birds, and simply removing tall trees and shrubs used as perches by avian predators have been shown to be effective.

4.1.2 Other Migratory Birds

Impacts to other migratory birds would be negligible under Alternative 1. While no new grasslands would be acquired, current management would continue on existing District land. Our knowledge of WPA use by non-waterfowl migratory birds would be limited because bird counts would be done only on request.

Alternative 2 (No Action) would act to solidify conditions that have contributed to continued long-term declines for many grassland-dependent bird species that utilize the Districts. This would occur because management would be unfocused and opportunistic. The resulting land acquisition would be scattered and require more time and effort to manage.

Alternative 3 (Preferred Alternative) would benefit grassland-dependent bird species by providing additional nesting, resting, and feeding habitats. Several species whose population status is of special management concern could benefit directly. These include the American bittern, upland sandpiper, least bittern, black tern, northern harrier, dickcissel, short-eared owl, greater prairie chicken, sedge wren, loggerhead shrike, grasshopper sparrow, savannah sparrow, Henslow's sparrow, field sparrow, bobolink, and western meadowlark.

Re-establishment of wetlands, wet prairies, sedge meadows, and associated grasslands would create habitats essential for many nesting and migrating songbirds. Large wetlands, particularly wetland complexes with interspersed grassy uplands, are vital to the survival of many of these species in western Minnesota. Wet prairies and sedge meadows are particularly important as they thaw earlier in the spring and provide an important early source of insects and other invertebrates for grassland birds. These areas also tend to stay moist longer into the summer, thus prolonging insect and invertebrate availability.

4.1.3 Threatened and Endangered Species

Under Alternative 1, populations of endangered and threatened species would experience no impact or would benefit slightly. While we would continue to avoid actions that harm endangered or threatened species, under this alternative the Districts would not acquire additional habitat, nor would we improve monitoring and enhance protection. Exclusive management focus on existing land could result in habitat improvements that would benefit populations of threatened and endangered species.

Alternative 2 (No Action) would have a negative impact on threatened and endangered species that utilize the District's lands, as critical habitats would degrade at an accelerated rate due to the dilution of management activities.

Alternative 3 (Preferred Alternative) may benefit threatened and endangered species by restoring and preserving additional wetland and upland habitats and by substantially increasing monitoring and research on Districts aimed at certain species.

4.1.4 Native Species

Biodiversity of wildlife and plants generally depends on the size of habitat blocks available and their relation to each other. While we would restore native grasslands using local ecotypes of mixed native grasses and forbs, the small block size and scattered nature of existing WPAs would limit our ability to enhance native grasslands. Use of the WPAs by native wildlife species would be limited by the carrying capacity of the existing WPAs.

Since Alternatives 2 and 3 emphasize habitat preservation, restoration, and enhancement, the greatest increases in resident wildlife other than waterbirds would be noted in those species dependent on wetlands and associated grasslands, namely muskrat, raccoon, mink, weasel, reptiles, amphibians and, to some extent, white-tailed deer. In addition, as water quality improves, important fish populations would be expected to increase in proportion to the amount of quality habitat made available.

Alternative 2 (No Action) involves areas scattered over a large area and would contribute some to safeguarding or promoting biodiversity. Alternative 3 (Preferred Alternative) involves the largest amount of new habitat of the greatest-sized blocks, thus would likely lead to increased biodiversity of the area. Both Alternative 2 and Alternative 3 would enhance and protect biodiversity due to the net increase in and protection of diverse habitats. These would include seasonal wetlands, wet meadows, native prairies, and riparian associations, all of which have experienced serious declines in the area since settlement. Once restored, these areas could create a number of interconnected habitat niches for indigenous wildlife that currently do not exist on the District, thus increasing the overall diversity District land and the surrounding area. Alternative 3 would do the most for enhancing native species and biological diversity as land acquisition, restoration, and preservation would be targeted in areas that will create additional habitat and improve existing managed areas.

4.1.5 Biological Inventories and Monitoring

Under Alternative 1, there would be no change in either the volume of data collected or the kind of data collected on District lands. The Districts would continue to conduct the 4-square-mile monitoring program and the monitoring of nesting structures. Routine surveys such as the scent post survey and bird counts would continue and some non-routine surveys, such as deformed frog surveys, would be conducted when requested. Our knowledge of District lands and wildlife would increase only slowly.

Impacts to biological inventories and monitoring under Alternative 2 (No Action) would be the same as Alternative 1.

Under Alternative 3 (Preferred Alternative), our knowledge of the Districts' habitat and wildlife populations would improve greatly and management would be more firmly rooted in sound science. We would employ a scientifically defensible means to monitor and evaluate habitats and populations under this alternative. Geographic Information Systems (GIS) use would increase under this alternative, and we would inventory the hydrological systems within the Districts, invertebrate communities, and monitor contaminant levels in water flowing into District wetlands. Surveys and monitoring of threatened and endangered species, invertebrates and unique communities would increase.

4.1.6 Federal Trust Species versus Resident Wildlife

Under Alternative 1, federal trust species such as migratory birds would not gain habitat. Current management -- restoring native grasslands and improving wetlands via water control -- would benefit migratory bird species currently using WPAs. Resident wildlife would not experience immediate impacts under Alternative 1, however there is potential for these species to be negatively impacted by predation or disease if the Service does not achieve goal acre acquisition.

Alternative 2 (No Action) would have both potentially positive and potentially negative impacts for resident and trust species. Habitat quantity would be enhanced by acquiring the full goal acres agreed to by counties, however that gain would be countered by the Districts' management practices not expanding with acreage. Essentially, there would be more land but less management of that land, which could result in less than desirable habitat for some species.

Alternative 2 would potentially have some positive impact on resident wildlife that utilize the Districts due to the reduced level of habitat disturbance or management and invasion of woody plants and exotic species. Deer and pheasant, for example, may respond to increased brush and tree cover.

Alternative 2 would lead to results that are similar to Alternative 1 with a continued decline in overall species richness and abundance.

Alternative 3 (Preferred Alternative) would improve existing management practices in a variety of ways to benefit waterfowl and other trust wildlife species. Habitat would be increased through acquiring the agreed-upon goal acres, and management practices would be expanded with that increase in acres. Under this alternative, the Districts would follow the SWAP guidelines, which focus on providing the mission components for the Wetland Management District landscape. Land owned by the Service in fee-title would be complemented by greater conservation involvement of local landowners and partners, resulting in better wildlife habitat outside of the Districts' borders.

Alternative 3 (Preferred Alternative) would benefit some resident wildlife. Since this alternative emphasizes habitat preservation, restoration, and enhancement, the greatest increase in resident wildlife would be noted in those species dependent on wetlands and associated grasslands, namely greater prairie chickens, sharp-tailed grouse, ring-necked pheasant, muskrat, white-tailed deer, weasel, river otter, coyote, amphibians and reptiles. Other furbearers such as red fox, skunk, raccoon, and mink would benefit outside areas where predators are actively controlled.

Alternative 3 (Preferred Alternative) would preserve biological diversity by restoring and preserving diverse habitats, including seasonal wetlands, wet meadows, native prairies, and riparian associations, all of which have experienced serious declines since settlement. Once restored, these areas could create a number of interconnected habitat niches for indigenous and migrant wildlife that currently do not exist on the Districts, thus increasing the overall biological diversity of the Districts and the State. There is reason to believe, however, that over a long period of time, species loss will occur due to the isolated nature and small size of the habitat units and their exposure to predation and edge effects (Soule and Terborgh, 1999).

4.1.7 Invasive Species

Under all of the Alternatives, invasive species would be controlled on District lands through aggressive efforts with partners. This would include using a variety of means to control both native and non-native fauna and flora.

Under Alternative 1, Districts would continue to control invasive species through aggressive efforts with partners. Efforts include burning, chemical application and biological control.

Under Alternative 2 (No Action), Districts would continue to combat invasive species, however the increase in land with no increase in staffing would probably result in less successful control of invasive species.

Under Alternative 3 (Preferred Alternative), the Districts would continue to employ burning, chemical application and biological control. The amount of land on which invasive species control would be needed would increase under this alternative, however staffing levels would also increase.

4.1.8 Habitat Restoration and Management

Virtually all fee title acquisitions of lands for Waterfowl Production Areas involve uplands and wetlands that need to be restored to benefit waterfowl and other wildlife. Generally, these lands are in cropland when purchased and the wetlands have been drained or otherwise negatively altered. Restoration of uplands involves continued cropping for one or more years to prepare the soil for the planting of grasses and forbs. Restoration of wetlands generally involves the plugging of surface drainage ditches and/or the breaking of drainage tile lines to restore the natural water regime in the basin. Some restorations involve the installation of water control structures to provide managers with water management capability to keep wetland vegetation optimal and to provide for the seasonal water level needs of waterfowl, shorebirds, and other wetland-dependent wildlife. These restoration efforts involve short-term disturbances to wildlife, temporary soil erosion while uplands are in crops, and perhaps minor, short-term degradation of water quality. However, once restoration is complete, there is a marked increase in water quality, soil protection, and wildlife protection which lasts indefinitely.

Once restored, management practices are periodically used to keep uplands and wetlands in optimum conditions for wildlife. These practices include noxious weed control by mowing, spot herbicide application, and release of plant-specific insect pests; interseeding of native forbs; periodic haying; mowing of invading tree and shrubs; timber removal to restore native prairie; and prescribed fire. All of these tools of habitat management are used periodically depending on habitat conditions on a given WPA. There are generally short-term disturbances to wildlife and seasonal loss of habitat which may displace some wildlife. However, long-term benefits of healthy habitat include more diverse and abundant wildlife populations. Of all management practices, prescribed fire is the most carefully used due to inherent dangers of fire to both Service personnel and property beyond the WPA.

Under Alternative 1, no additional habitat would be managed as no additional land acquisition would occur under this alternative. Upland management would focus on restoring and managing native grasslands using local ecotypes of mixed native grasses and forbs. This would include converting non-native grasslands to native grasslands. There would be some increases in available upland habitat through the Service's existing Private Lands program, the State of Minnesota's Private Lands program, and various USDA programs. Existing wetlands would be enhanced by increasing water control and improving watersheds. There would be some increases in available wetland habitat through the Service's Partners for Wildlife Private Lands program, the State of Minnesota's Private Lands program, and various USDA programs.

Alternative 2 (No Action) and Alternative 3 (Preferred Alternative) have the potential to increase both the amount and quality of habitat available, although each in varying degrees. Alternative 2 would continue with the status quo of purchasing land over large geographic areas. This would result in an overall reduction of management intensity as each District approaches goal acres in fee and easement acquisition. Management would continue but the time frame would be extended. There would be increased habitat for nesting waterfowl. Alternative 3 (Preferred Alternative) would focus land acquisition over smaller areas and thereby target habitat restorations where they can contribute the most to providing high quality habitats for wildlife.

4.1.9 Contaminants

Under Alternative 1, water quality within District wetlands would remain about the same, or could possibly improve as technology, techniques, and programs evolve to address current issues associated with runoff. Sediment loads would remain fairly high as long as unprotected banks and valley slopes continue to erode and export sediment to waterways feed District wetlands. USDA soil conservation requirements currently minimize soil erosion on neighboring farms with highly erodible soil, but sediment and farm chemicals continue to enter waterways that feed District wetlands. No coordinated effort, other than the current USDA programs, are anticipated with this alternative.

Alternative 2 (No Action) and Alternative 3 (Preferred Alternative) would reduce sedimentation and improve water quality within District wetlands through an intensified and coordinated effort. Highly erodible lands would be converted to permanent cover, stream banks and waterways would be stabilized through vegetative plantings or natural development, and filter wetlands/sediment retention basins would be constructed to cleanse tile waters entering District wetlands. Re-establishment of tree canopies over certain stream edges would stabilize stream banks, reduce summer water temperatures for aquatic organisms, and provide a micro environment required by many fish and wildlife species. Alternative 3 would have the greatest effect in this regard as land acquisition, restoration, and preservation would be targeted to high priority areas.

Alternative 3 has the best potential for reducing contaminants entering wetlands on the District because it would provide benefits extending beyond District borders. Cooperating landowners within the Districts' watershed would be offered incentives and/or would be compensated through cost-sharing agreements for applying conservation and environmental farming practices on their lands.

4.1.10 Partners for Fish and Wildlife Program

Alternative 1 would increase reliance on the Partners for Fish and Wildlife Program to achieve conservation objectives because of the lack of land acquisition.

Under Alternative 2 (No Action), the Partners for Fish and Wildlife Program would remain the same in terms of size and scope.

In Alternative 3 (Preferred Alternative), the Partners for Fish and Wildlife Program would remain the same in size but would be focused within high priority areas within the Districts.

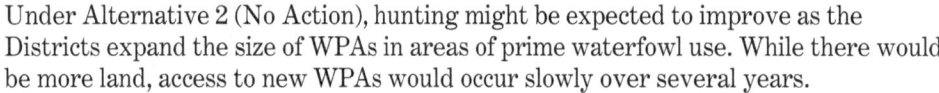

4.2 Impacts Associated with People

4.2.1 Wildlife-Dependent Recreation and Education

4.2.1.1 Hunting and Fishing

In the short-term, Alternative 1 would have no impact on hunting. The Districts would continue to maintain the recruitment rate of waterfowl, and habitat for white-tailed deer would be managed as it is currently managed. Access for hunting would be unchanged. In the long-term, the lack of focus on predator management and the small size and edge nature of WPAs could result in predation contributing to less quality hunting. There would be little to no expansion of new hunting areas available.

Under Alternative 2 (No Action), hunting might be expected to improve as the Districts expand the size of WPAs in areas of prime waterfowl use. While there would be more land, access to new WPAs would occur slowly over several years.

Alternative 3 (Preferred Alternative) provides for acquiring land up to the agreed-upon goal acres with a focus on expanding the size of WPAs in areas of prime water-fowl use. The focus on predator management (electric fencing, predator control, islands, etc.) could potentially improve the quality of waterfowl hunting on the Districts. Construction of additional parking areas would improve access for hunters as well as other visitors.

Alternative 3 (Preferred Alternative) would expand and improve public hunting opportunities on the Districts beyond Alternative 1 and Alternative 2 (No Action). The Service is required to allow public hunting on District lands within current state seasons and guidelines as long as it is compatible with the Districts's objectives.

Opportunities for fishing would be unchanged under Alternative 1. Wetlands would be restored via water control and improving watersheds, thus improving conditions for fish. Public access would be available to the extent that it is available today.

Increased land holdings and improved wetlands would result in better opportunities for fishing under Alternative 2 (No Action). Access to new WPAs would occur slowly over several years.

Alternative 3 (Preferred Alternative) would slightly increase fishing opportunities on the Districts due to better access, as well as facility safety and maintenance.

4.2.1.2 Trails

Under Alternative 1, maintenance of and access to existing trails would be unchanged to somewhat improved. Without new land to manage and as the maintenance backlog was reduced, more operating and maintenance funding would be available to enhance existing trails.

Maintenance of existing trails would be somewhat diminished under Alternative 2 (No Action) because staff would have more land to manage with the same human resources. Access to and trails on newly acquired land would occur slowly and depend on the availability of staff and funding.

Alternative 3 (Preferred Alternative) would create opportunities to expand and improve District trails. Additional parking areas would improve access to WPAs.

4.2.1.3 Signing and Interpretation

Signing and interpretation at WPAs throughout the Districts would be unchanged under Alternative 1. No new facilities would be added, but signing would be maintained on existing areas.

Land holdings would be expanded under Alternative 2 (No Action), however access to newly acquired areas would be gradual. Staffing would not increase under this alternative, so development of signs and interpretive sites would occur depending on staff availability and funding.

Opportunities for public use would be improved under Alternative 3 (Preferred Alternative) through the construction of additional parking areas and interpretive kiosks on existing and newly acquired lands. New signing would be required for any new tracts. Interpretive signing would be developed for any new trails or public observation areas constructed on newly acquired tracts.

4.2.1.4 Environmental Education

In the short-term, environmental education programming would continue as it currently exists under Alternative 1. No new lands would be acquired, so programming would focus on existing lands and habitats. In the long-term, more funding might be available as the maintenance backlog was reduced and more funding became available for environmental education programming.

Under Alternative 2 (No Action), funding and staff availability for environmental education would gradually decrease as operating and maintenance funding was spread over more land. Programming would focus on existing land because access to newly acquired land would be provided sporadically as staff and funding became available.

Alternative 3 (Preferred Alternative) would result in expanded environmental educational use of existing and new areas. Restoration of pothole type wetlands and native grasslands in the watershed would allow students to view and study the predominant habitat that early Minnesota settlers found in the area.

4.3 Impacts Associated with Operations

4.3.1 Land Acquisition

Alternative 1 would result in no additional land acquisition within the Districts. District staff would manage fee title land already in the system and would not increase the District holdings.

Under Alternatives 2 and 3, land acquisition by the Service could involve up to 164,068 acres over the next 15 years (based on a future funding). These acquisitions could involve wetland, grassland or flowage easements and fee-title purchases or a combination of all methods, depending on the site and circumstances. Lands to be acquired would be delineated according to criteria designed to benefit breeding waterfowl. All lands acquired by the Service would be administered and managed by one of the six Wetland Management Districts as part of the National Wildlife Refuge System. Tracts in which less than fee-title agreements are negotiated would remain in private ownership. All restoration and preservation would be carried out on a tract-by-tract basis as participants and fiscal resources become available over a 15-year time period. All acquisition would be on a willing-seller basis. Funding for land acquisition would be from the Migratory Bird Conservation Fund using proceeds from the sale of Federal duck stamps, based on the authority of the Migratory Bird Conservation Act - Small Wetlands Acquisition Program.

4.3.2 Staffing

Under Alternative 1, there would be no change in staffing levels or the amount of land managed by District staff. Current management practices would continue in all respects (habitat restoration, inventorying and monitoring, public use), and thus no impacts to staff are likely.

Alternative 2 (No Action) proposes acquisition of the agreed-upon goal acres for the six Districts but no change in the current level of staffing.

Alternative 3 (Preferred Alternative) would expand staffing levels along with acquiring the agreed-upon goal acres for each District.

4.3.3 Facilities and Equipment

Under Alternative 1, facilities and equipment funding would remain the same. However, the spending power would increase over time as no additional lands would be added to the Districts in the future. This assumes a continuation of historic funding levels. Under Alternative 2 (No Action) and Alternative 3 (Preferred Alternative), facilities and equipment funding would remain relatively the same. However, under Alternative 3, management efficiencies would be attained as larger blocks of habitat would reduce the per acre cost of management.

4.3.4 Management Consistency Among Districts

Efforts to achieve consistency would be minimal under Alternative 1 and Alternative 2 (No Action). Work on individual development plans for WPAs would occur as time and staffing permit. The plans would be recorded in GIS and would document ownership boundaries, habitat, facilities and history of management. Limited coordination would occur among the Minnesota Wetland Management Districts and Districts in Iowa, Wisconsin, North Dakota and South Dakota.

Management consistency would increase greatly under Alternative 3 (Preferred Alternative). Development plans for every WPA would be completed within 3 years under this alternative. The plans would be recorded in GIS and would document ownership boundaries, habitat, facilities and history of management. There would be a concerted effort to make management consistent within the Minnesota Wetland Management Districts as well as Districts in Iowa, Wisconsin and the Dakotas.

4.4 Cumulative Impact Analysis

"Cumulative impact" is the term that refers to impacts on the environment that result from the incremental impact of the proposed action when added to other past, present and reasonably foreseeable future actions, regardless of what agency (federal or non-federal) or person undertakes such other actions. Cumulative impacts can result from individually minor but collectively significant actions taking place over a period of time. In this section, the cumulative impacts of each of the three alternatives are discussed in terms of waterfowl, migratory birds, listed species, wetland and riparian habitat, and prairie restoration.

4.4.1 Waterfowl

The prairie pothole region has historically been recognized as the most important waterfowl production area in North America. Surveys have shown that although this area represents only 10 percent of the breeding habitat, it averages 50 to 75 percent of the duck recruitment each year in North America. Chapter 3 of the CCP documents several factors in waterfowl production:

- The prairie pothole region has been recognized as the most important waterfowl production area in north America.

- Waterfowl depend on wetlands during the breeding season for food and shelter.

- Massive conversion of wetlands and prairie to agricultural fields has dramatically altered the landscape, the hydrology, and the region's carrying capacity for waterfowl.

- Research has shown that ducks nesting in large blocks of grassland habitat (1,000 to 10,000 acres) reproduce more successfully than ducks nesting in smaller blocks (200 to 500 acres).

- The average block size for WPAs in Minnesota is only 210 acres.

- Although the more common species of ducks and geese in Minnesota have increased in population over the last decade, many are still below the goals of the North American Plan.

All three alternatives will focus on waterfowl. Alternative 3 will have the largest positive cumulative benefit to waterfowl by increasing habitat available for waterfowl nesting as well as intensifying management of that habitat. The cumulative effect of no acquisition under Alternative 1 is a reduced recruitment rate to the continental waerfowl population due to higher predation rates on existing small block sizes.

Under alternatives 1 and 2, management would continue to improve waterfowl habitat and productivity would likely be lower than under Alternative 3. Ultimately, alternatives 1 and 2 would contribute less to increasing duck populations than Alternative 3. Many species are experiencing population declines, and existing recruitment rates have not achieved the goal of reversing population trends. Recruitment on many WPAs is less than losses to predation due at least in part to small habitat block size.

Public ownership is an essential tool in protecting these habitats. In Minnesota, only 150,000 acres of native prairie remain out of an original 18 million. Between 1780 and 1980, approximately 78.7 percent of wetlands within the prairie pothole and parkland transition areas were lost, and we continue to lose an estimated 2.4 percent of remaining wetlands every year. Combined with the effects of the Minnesota Department of Natural Resources activities and action by non-governmental conservation organizations, the Service can make a difference in habitat quality and waterfowl numbers within the region. In the short-term, during an era of budget cuts for state agencies like the Department of Natural Resources, the Service may play a particularly important role in conserving waterfowl habitat.

Alternative 3 also proposes more aggressive efforts to reduce predation on waterfowl nests, which would contribute to increased production. A major factor depressing duck numbers is low nest success due to nest destruction by predators on small units of habitat. Predators are quick to find these remnant areas and concentrate their hunting activities on the vulnerable ground nests of waterfowl. In some habitats, predators such as red fox, raccoon, mink, and skunk are able to take virtually every duck nest and many of the attendant hens.

Management decisions on the Minnesota Wetlands Management Districts have the potential to make a difference in the quality of habitat that is available; WPAs administered by the Districts encompass more than three-quarters of all Service land in the prairie pothole region of Minnesota.

4.4.2 Migratory Birds

Minnesota Wetland Management Districts contain habitat important to bird species other than waterfowl, including songbirds, marsh and wading birds, shorebirds, raptors, and upland game birds. Some of the factors relevant to migratory bird habitat are offered in the following list; Chapter 3 of the CCP offers greater detail.

- Approximately 243 species of birds regularly use the Districts at some time during the year, with 152 nesting species.

- In the Districts, 48 birds identified as "species of concern" are rare, declining, or dependent on vulnerable habitats, including 43 that breed there.

- About 44 percent of the species of concern depend on some type of grassland habitat.

- In North America, grassland birds have exhibited steeper declines than any other avian group.

- It is important to maintain a mosaic of grassland habitats to meet the varying needs of grassland birds.

- Some of the species of concern found in the Districts are area-sensitive, which means they require large, contiguous blocks of habitat to reproduce successfully.

Each alternative would have a different effect on migratory birds. The cumulative benefit of Alternative 3 would be the most positive because the habitat base increases and is enhanced, and management is intensified.

In the long-term, Alternative 1 would have a negative impact on migratory birds. The needs of area-sensitive species that are declining, such as Greater Prairie Chicken, Northern Harrier, Upland Sandpiper, Henslow's Sparrow and Savannah Sparrow, would not be met in WPAs that average 210 acres in size. Population declines would likely continue. Habitat may improve as staff are able to concentrate on projects on existing lands rather than restoration of new lands, but the small block size would limit the WPAs' usefulness to migratory birds. If other conservation organizations were to follow the same course, negative impacts to migratory birds would be exasperated.

Increasing land holdings but maintaining current management as described in Alternative 2 (No Action) would have a neutral to slight benefit for migratory birds. The amount of habitat would increase as the Districts bought lands to the goal acres agreed to by each county within the District, but staffing levels would remain unchanged and restoration projects would be completed according to time demands. If other conservaton organizations are not actively acquiring land, this alternative would have a greater long-term benefit even if land is not restored immediately because it would mean that habitat is at least being set aside for conservation purposes. If other agencies and organizations do pursue land acquisition, and if those lands adjoing WMD lands, this alternative provides even greater benefits because it would provide some buffer.

Under Alternative 3, the combination of acquiring land up to the goal acres agreed to by each county within the Districts and expanding management would contribute to improved breeding and nesting success. Focused predator management would also contribute to nesting success. This alternative would position the Service to contribute to improved migratory bird population numbers, and benefits would be even greater if the Minnesota Department of Natural Resources and non-government conservation organizations also focused acquisition and management efforts on migratory birds. Wetland Management Districts' land acquisition and restoration efforts could be enhanced on parcels with proximity to six national wildlife refuges in central and western Minnesota. Considering the total acreage of the Wetland Management Districts in western Minnesota (257,542 acres with both fee title and easements), management activities laid out under this alternative would greatly influence habitat available to migratory birds.

4.4.3 Endangered and Threatened Species

This section describes animals that are Federally listed under the Endangered Species Act of 1973, as amended, and are listed as either endangered or threatened.

The proposed action may affect, but is not likely to adversely affect, any federally listed or proposed threatened or endangered species. This precludes the need for further action on this project as required under Section 7 of the Endangered Species Act of 1973, as amended.

Under all three alternatives, endangered and threatened species would be protected and actions that might harm them would be avoided. The primary difference among the alternatives is the land acquisition and expanded management provided in Alternative 3, which would benefit all of the listed species found on the Districts. Habitat loss is a factor in the population declines that led to these species being listed, thus the alternative that supports expanding the habitat available to them can be expected to provide the greatest benefit.

Under Alternative 1, listed species would likely experience long-term decline because habitat does not meet the needs of the species that require larger block sizes. Lack of sufficient habitat would be compounded if the Department of Natural Resources and non-government conservation organizations also stopped acquiring land.

Alternative 2 would be somewhat beneficial to listed species because over time it would provide more habitat. The quality of this habitat would not be tremendously high because management (and staffing levels) would not change, but in the long-term land would be preserved for future restoration. This alternative would have greater benefits if the State and non-governmental organizations acquired land adjoining or near existing WPAs.

Alternative 3 provides for both more habitat being conserved and expanded management for restoring land, which would have the greatest benefit for threatened and endangered species. In the case of listed species, Service efforts are particularly vital, with or without the efforts of other conservation agencies and organizations. As the primary federal agency charged with protecting threatened and endangered species, the Service has a unique responsibility to these species. If the State and non-government conservation organizations also acquire and restore habitat, benefits to listed species would be even greater.

4.4.3.1 Threatened Mammals

Gray wolf, *Canis lupus*: Experts estimate approximately 2,000 gray wolves presently occur in Minnesota. Wolf numbers and range appear to be increasing in Minnesota. Wolves are no longer exclusive residents of Minnesota's forested wilderness areas, and adult wolves from Minnesota have dispersed through central and western Minnesota to North and South Dakota. The Service recognizes the improving range and security of the species and has reclassified the wolf as threatened.

4.4.3.2 Endangered / Threatened Birds

Bald Eagle, *Haliaeetus leucocephalus*: Bald Eagles have increased in abundance and distribution across the United States, including Minnesota. In the 1990s nesting territories increased in Minnesota every year from 437 in 1990, to 618 in 1995. Increasing numbers of migrating and wintering eagles also occur across Minnesota where they find sheltered night roosts and feed on waterfowl, smaller wild mammals, and fish in open water areas. Bald Eagles became endangered because of habitat loss, but especially because of DDT use following World War II. They have since been reclassifed as threatened. Today, the DDT threat is largely gone. Now the challenge is to prevent contamination and loss of sites that eagles depend on for nesting, feeding, migration, and wintering.

Piping Plover, *Charadius melodus*: Piping Plovers are tenuously present in Minnesota; the Great Plains population is listed as threatened. They nest in Lake of the Woods, east of the Districts. Piping Plovers nest in coastal areas, but they are also prairie birds, nesting across the Great Plains of the United States and Canada, but in perilously low numbers. The loss of prairie wetland areas contributes to their decline. Like many shorebirds, Piping Plovers feed on immature and adult insects and other invertebrates at the water's edge. They winter primarily along beaches, sandflats, and algal flats on the Gulf of Mexico.

Least Tern (eastern population), *Sterna antillarum:* The federally listed endangered Least Tern nests along large rivers of the Colorado, Red, Mississippi, and Missouri River systems. This species is a potential nester in the Missouri River area. It nests on sand and gravel bars and protected beach areas of large rivers and winters in coastal Central and South America. The species is endangered because human disturbance and alteration of river systems has rendered much of its nesting habitat unusable. Pesticides may reduce food available to the tern by reducing the numbers of small fish in their feeding areas.

4.4.3.3 Endangered Fish

Topeka shiner (*Notropis topeka*) This species was once common to small to mid-sized prairie streams in the central United States. Now listed as endangered, these fish inhabit streams that usually run continually and that have good water quality and cool to moderate temperatures. The occurrence of the species at known collection sites has decreased by approximately 70 percent, mostly in the past 40 to 50 years. The fish has been negatively affected by habitat destruction, sedimentation, and changes in water quality. Topeka shiners now exist primarily in small, isolated populations in Iowa, Minnesota and portions of South Dakota.

4.4.4 Wetlands and Riparian Habitat

All alternatives will focus on wetland and riparian habitat, but the positive cumulative impact of Alternative 3 will be the greatest because of the focused wetland management, acquisition and outreach to wetland throughout the Districts.

- The prairie pothole region once included about 20 million acres of these small wetlands.

- Today, only about 5.3 million acres remain in 2.7 million basins within five states; drainage has been so extensive that in many areas the water table has been lowered and the hydrology of the entire region has been transformed.

- More than 78 percent of the remaining wetland basins are smaller than 1 acre in size.

- Nearly two out of three of the remaining wetlands in Minnesota are privately owned; consequently, they are vulnerable to continued drainage, development, and pollution.

- Saving single, isolated wetlands is much less valuable than saving several wetlands in a wetland complex.

- Freshwater wetlands like those in the prairie pothole region are among the most productive in the world.

- Wetland restoration and management are high priorities in the Districts.

Under Alternative 1, wetlands and riparian habitat would not gain increased benefit and may actually degrade as land use impacts water quality around the WMDs.

Conservation efforts by the Minnesota Department of Natural Resources and non-government conservation organizations could mitigate this impact if they acquired land adjoining the WPAs and restored wetlands. Restoration efforts on wetlands and streams adjoining the Districts' WPAs could improve water quality and wetland functions. If other agencies did not set aside additional land, the negative impact of the Service not acquiring land to the agreed upon goal acres for each county would be greater.

Alternative 2 would benefit wetlands and riparian areas somewhat on individual WPAs as land is acquired over time. Although restoration would not be immediate, land uses that impact water quality, such as growing crops and grazing cattle, would likely be discontinued. These benefits would be augmented if other conservation entities acquired and restored land, but the benefits provided under Alternative 2 would not be diminished if others did not pursue land acquisition.

With its land acquisition and expanded management components, Alternative 3 would provide the most benefits to wetland and riparian habitat. Land would be acquired to the goal acres agreed upon by each county within the Districts, and management would be expanded to allow more timely restoration of these lands. Healthier wetland and riparian complexes in bigger blocks of land would benefit all wetland-dependent species. The positive benefits would be greater if the Minnesota Department of Natural Resources and non-government conservation organizations were also acquiring and restoring habitat, however the positive impacts would not be diminished if others did not pursue the same course.

4.4.5 Prairie Restoration

All alternatives would increase the amount of prairie but the positive cumulative impacts of Alternative 3 will be greatest because of the focused and strategic land acquisition and prairie restoration with native prairie species.

- There is perhaps no ecosystem on earth that has been so completely altered.

- Prairie landscapes once covered the entire western edge of Minnesota; now, less than 1 percent of the original prairie is left.

- Prairie landscapes contain hundreds of species of plants, invertebrates, and wildlife. Some prairies contain as many as 200 plant species.

- Over the past decade, virtually all plantings of upland cover on Waterfowl Production Areas have been with native grasses. In recent years, a more diverse mixture of native forbs and warm and cool season native grasses have been used.

- Prescribed fire remains a critical tool for maintaining the diversity and vigor of existing and restored prairie plants. Prescribed burns can only be done during a small window of time in the spring, so the number of acres that can be burned each spring is limited. As a result, most WPAs can not be burned on a rotation frequent enough to suppress invading shrubs and trees. Some of the Districts use haying and grazing as additional means of maintaining grassland integrity.

- The Districts also manage grasslands through the selective application of herbicides during restoration.

Over time, Alternative 1 would benefit prairie habitat within the Districts as lands were restored. Without additional lands being acquired, staff would be able to concentrate restoration efforts and invasive species erradication on existing lands. Prairie habitat would not be expanded under Alternative 1. If the Minnesota Department of Natural Resources, national wildlife refuges and conservation organizations discontinued acquiring and restoring prairie habitat, there would be a negative impact to the species that require prairie, which is already one of the most altered landscape in the nation.

Under Alternative 2, benefits to prairie habitat and wildlife-species that depend on prairie would be greater because land would be acquired over time and restoration would occur according to staff and funding availability. Management would not be expanded under this alternative, but land would at least be set aside for future restoration. Prairie restoration on WPAs would complement prairie restoration on national wildlife refuges in western Minnesota. Benefits would be greater if the State and non-government conservation organizations continue to acquire land for prairie restoration, particularly if that land adjoins or is proximate to WPA lands.

Benefits to prairie habitat would be greatest under Alternative 3 because it allows for both acquisition of land to the goal acres agreed upon by each county in the District and for expanded management. Prairie would be restored at a faster pace than under Alternative 2. Block sizes would be greater, allowing for greater diversity of plant species. Benefits would be greater if the Minnesota Department of Natural Resources and non-government organizations continued prairie restoration efforts. Work on prairie habitats on national wildlife refuges in the area of the Wetland Management Districts would complement the benefits of prairie restoration on WPAs.

4.5 Prescribed Fire as a Management Tool

4.5.1 Social Implications

Prescribed burns will have an effect on the local public. Concern by the public is expressed every time a fire is set. A prescribed burn will effect and benefit the local community in many ways. These benefits must be explained to the public at every opportunity. The Districts' Fire Management Plans (FMP) provides additional detail beyond what is captured in this section and will be adopted through this EA.

A prescribed burn on a District will be a direct benefit to the public in creating recreational opportunities through increased wildlife populations for hunting and observation. If a wildfire is started on or near District land, the areas that were previously prescribed burned and the firebreaks intended for prescribed burning will be of extreme benefit in controlling the fire.

The aspect of the fire that will solicit the most public concern will be the smoke. Smoke from a District fire could impair visibility on roads and become a hazard. Actions to manage smoke include: use of road guards and pilot car, signing, altering ignition techniques and sequence, halting ignition, suppressing the fire, and use of local law enforcement as traffic control. Burning will be done only on days that the smoke will not be blown across the community or when the wind is sufficient as not to cause heavy concentrations.

If the State of Minnesota institutes smoke management regulations, the FMP will be amended to ensure consistency with those regulations. Combustion of fuels during prescribed fire operations may temporarily impact air quality, but the impacts are mitigated by small burn unit size, the direction of winds the burns are conducted with, and the distance from population centers. All efforts will be taken to assure that smoke does not impact smoke sensitive areas such as roads and local residences. In the event of wind direction changes, mitigative measures will be taken to assure the public safety and comfort. District staff will work with neighboring agencies and in consultation with State air quality personnel to address smoke issues that require additional mitigation.

The fire prescription portion of the Annual Prescribed Fire Plan for each WPA proposed to be burned during the burning season will have specific mitigative measures to deal with unexpected smoke management problems. This will included identified problems that unforecasted wind changes may cause and measures to be employed to protect the public.

The emotional impact of a prescribed fire on the local residents must also be considered. A great deal of public concern may arise with any kind of smoke from the District. This concern can be relieved only by a concerted effort by District personnel to carefully inform the local citizens about the prescribed burning program. Emphasis will be placed on the benefits to wildlife as well as the safety precautions in effect. Formal interpretive programs both on and off the District, explaining the prescribed burning program, will be encouraged.

4.5.2 Cultural and Archaeological Resources

There may be archaeological sites within prescribed burn units. When these units are burned, it is doubtful that the fire will have any adverse impact on the sites. The fire will be only a temporary disturbance to the vegetation in the area and in no way destroy or reduce the archaeologic value. All artifacts are buried well beneath the surface. No above ground evidence exists. No known sites will be impacted by prescribed burning operations.

4.5.3 Flora

The prescribed burning program will have a visible impact on vegetation and the land. Immediately after a fire much of the land will be blackened. There will be no grasses or ground forbs remaining and most of the higher brush such as oak sprouts and willow will be bare of leaves. Trees will be scorched up to 20 feet above the ground. This will be particularly noticeable on the light colored bark of aspen and birch. There may be large areas up to one acre in size interspersed throughout the burn that are untouched by the fire. This may be a result of wet ground conditions or a break in fuel continuity.

Within three days after the burn the grasses and forbs will begin to grow. The enriched soil will promote rapid growth such that after two or three weeks the ground will be completely covered. The willow and oak will, in many cases, re-sprout. The bases of the trees as well as the burned slash and stumps will be partially or completely covered by the new growth. Some of the less fire resistant trees will show signs of wilting and may succumb within a month or two. Generally speaking, after one seasons regrowth, any sign of the prescribed burn will be difficult to detect without close examination. After two or three years it will be virtually impossible to detect the presence of the fire.

Other more long lived signs of the burn will remain for an indefinite period of time. The firebreaks will not be allowed to grow over as their benefit could be realized in a wildfire situation as well as in future prescribed burns. Vehicle tracks through the burn are visible on the freshly burned ash and may be longer lived if the vehicle became stuck or created tire grooves in the ground. Travel across the burn area will be kept to a minimum. Vehicle travel is necessary in some instances, such as lighting the fire lines or quickly getting water to an escape break-over point. A fire plow will be used only in the event that a break-over does occur and cannot be controlled by any other method. The deep trench of the plow would leave a very long lived scar. This trench could be repaired by filling, which would eliminate it from view after five to ten years.

4.5.4 Listed Species

The potential impacts of fire on listed species is likely to be neutral to positive if there is any impact. Efforts will be made to protect any plants listed as threatened or endangered from damage by prescribed fire.

4.5.5 Soils

The disturbances to the soil by fire are similar to those caused by any other manipulative practice applied to the land. A farming, logging, or flooding operation will have no greater or lesser impact. All three are applied on the District at the present time.

The effect of fire to the soil is dependent largely on the fire intensity and duration. On areas with high fuel loads, a slow backing fire is usually required for containment and desirable results. The intense heats generated by this type fire to kill unwanted plant species or remove slash will have a greater effect on the soils than fast, cool head-fires used on farm fields and wildlife openings. The cool, moist soils of wetter areas in the burn units or areas with little fuel will be unaffected by the fire.

The severity of damage to the soil depends also to a great degree on the thickness and composition of the organic mantle. In many cases where only the top layer of the mantle is scorched or burned, no damage will result to the soil below. This is usually experienced in the forested areas of the burn units.

On open areas such as dry grassland or wet meadow sites, the blackening of the relatively thin mantle will cause greater heat absorption and retention from the sun. This will encourage earlier germination during the spring growing season.

Nutrient release occurs as a result of the normal decomposition process. Fire on the soil will greatly speed up the process. The rate and amount of nutrients released will again be dependent on the fire duration and intensity as well as the amount of humus, duff and other organic materials present in the mantle. The increase, immediately after a burn, of calcium, potash, phosphoric acid and other minerals will give the residual and emergent vegetation a short term boost. However, the rapid leaching through the sandy soils will cause rapid runoff of these nutrients and only short term benefits. The increased nutrification of the soil by the emergent vegetation and increased nutrient release result in rapid regrowth of grasses and other succulent vegetation on the sites.

There is no evidence to show that the direct heating of the soil by the burning of material above it with a fire of low intensity has any significant adverse affect. Fire on these types of soil has little total affect on the soils, and in most cases would be beneficial.

4.5.6 Escaped Fire

With any prescribed fire there always exists the possibility of its escape into the surrounding area. This can be caused by one or more factors which may be preventable or non-preventable. Inadequate firebreaks, too few personnel, unpredicted changes in weather conditions, peculiar fuel type, being in too big a hurry, and insufficient knowledge of fire behavior are a few factors which could cause loss of control. There is no doubt that an escaped fire could turn into a very serious situation. The damage that could result would be much less severe on the District than if it encroached on private land where buildings, equipment, and land improvements would be involved. Extreme care, careful planning, and adherence to the unit prescription will be exercised when prescribed burning all units with emphasis employed when burning areas that are near or adjacent to WPA boundaries.

In the event that a prescribed fire does jump a firebreak and burn into unplanned areas, there is a high probability of rapid control with minimal adverse impact. In general, prescribed burns will be small in size (average 75 to 150 acres), have light fuel loads (0.25 to 3 tons of fuel per acre), will be burned under low fuel moisture conditions, and will be burned under specific wind direction and atmosphere stability conditions. The network of firebreaks and roads will greatly assist in rapid containment. In most cases all of the District fire fighting equipment will be immediately available at the scene with all nearby water sources previously located. The applicable DNR fire suppression crews and local fire departments will always be notified of a prescribed burn. Thus, maximum numbers of experienced personnel and equipment are immediately available for wildfire suppression activities.

4.6 Impacts Common to All Alternatives

4.6.1 Climate Change

All Alternatives would positively increase carbon sequestration, but the cumulative impact of Alternative 3 would be greatest because more land would be acquired and planted with native vegetation.

In January 2001, the Department of Interior issued an order requiring its land management agencies to consider potential climate change impacts as part of long range planning endeavors.

The increase of carbon within the earth's atmosphere has been linked to the gradual rise in surface temperature commonly referred to as global warming. In relation to comprehensive conservation planning for national wildlife refuges, carbon sequestration constitutes the primary climate-related impact to be considered in planning. The U.S. Department of Energy's "Carbon Sequestration Research and Development" (U.S. DOE, 1999) defines carbon sequestration as "...the capture and secure storage of carbon that would otherwise be emitted to or remain in the atmosphere."

The land is a tremendous force in carbon sequestration. Terrestrial biomes of all sorts – grasslands, forests, wetlands, tundra, perpetual ice and desert – are effective both in preventing carbon emission and acting as a biological "scrubber" of atmospheric carbon monoxide. The Department of Energy report's conclusions noted that ecosystem protection is important to carbon sequestration and may reduce or prevent loss of carbon currently stored in the terrestrial biosphere.

Conserving habitat for wildlife is the heart of any long range plan for units of the National Wildlife Refuge System. Under all alternatives considered in this EA, land and water would be conserved and enhance carbon sequestration. This in turn contributes positively to efforts to mitigate human-induced global climate changes. The Preferred Alternative would have the most positive impact as it calls for increases in both acquisition and active management and improvement of habitat.

4.6.2 Environmental Justice

None of the proposed alternatives disproportionately place an adverse environmental, economic, social, or health impacts on minority or low-income populations.

Executive Order 12898 "Federal Actions to Address Environmental Justice in Minority Populations and Low-Income Populations" was signed by President Bill Clinton on February 11, 1994, to focus Federal attention on the environmental and human health conditions of minority and low-income populations with the goal of achieving environmental protection for all communities. The Order directed Federal agencies to develop environmental justice strategies to aid in identifying and addressing disproportionately high and adverse human health or environmental effects of their programs, policies, and activities on minority and low-income populations. The Order is also intended to promote nondiscrimination in Federal programs substantially affecting human health and the environment, and to provide minority and low-income communities access to public information and participation in matters relating to human health or the environment.

4.6.3 Unavoidable Adverse Impacts

Under all Alternatives, the potential development of access roads, trails, dikes, control structures, fences, visitor parking areas, and reclamation of former building sites could lead to local and short-term negative impacts to plants, soil, and some wildlife species. Some loss of cultural resources could occur by restoring former wetlands. Greater public use may result in increased littering, noise, and vehicle traffic.

4.6.4 Short-Term Use Versus Long-Term Productivity

The local short-term uses of the environment under Alternatives 2 and 3 include wetland restoration and enhancement, and conversions of other lands to wetlands or upland cover. Both alternatives would also include development of public use facilities. The resulting long-term effects of these alternatives include increased protection of threatened and endangered species, increased waterfowl and songbird production, and long-term recovery of a myriad of species dependent on quality wetland and grassland habitats. In addition, the public will gain long-term opportunities for wildlife-oriented recreation and education.

4.6.5 Irreversible and Irretrievable Commitments of Resources

Funding and personnel commitments by the Service or other organizations under all three alternatives would be unavailable for other programs. Fee-title acquisition of lands by the Service would make them "public lands" and preclude individual freedom to use these lands in accordance with individual desires. Traditional land uses may change since uses on Service lands must be shown to be compatible with the purposes for which the land is acquired. Any lands purchased will lose their potential for future development by the private sector as long as they remain in public ownership. Structural improvements that are purchased with any land may be declared surplus to government needs and sold or demolished on site.

4.6.6 Property Taxes and the Districts Revenue Sharing Act

The Districts Revenue Sharing Act of June 15, 1935, as amended, provides for annual payments to counties or the lowest unit of government that collects and distributes taxes based on acreage and value of District land located within the county. The monies for these payments come from two sources: (1) net receipts from the sale of products from National Wildlife Refuge System lands (oil and gas leases, timber sales, grazing fees, etc.) and (2) annual Congressional appropriations. Annual Congressional appropriations, as authorized by a 1978 amendment, were intended to make up the difference between the net receipts from the Districts Revenue Sharing Fund and the total amount due to local units of government.

Payments to the counties are calculated based on whichever of the following formulas provides the largest return: (1) $.75 per acre; (2) 25 percent of the net receipts collected from Districts lands in the county; or (3) three-quarters of 1 percent of the appraised value. In the State of Minnesota, three-quarter of 1 percent of the appraised value always brings the greatest return to the taxing bodies. Using this method, lands are re-appraised every 5 years to reflect current market values.

In addition, at the time of purchase if revenue sharing payments are anticipated to fall short, a "Trust Fund Payment" of up to 10 percent of the purchase price is made to the county. The intent of this payment is to provide a principle cash investment off of which the interest can be used to make up the difference in the revenue sharing payment and the actual taxes on the property purchased. Therefore, fee-title land acquisition by the Service should not adversely affect tax revenues if private lands are purchased by the Service and removed from the area tax base.

4.6.7 Relocation Benefits

The uniform Relocation Assistance and Real Property Acquisition Policies Act of 1970, as amended (Uniform Act), provides for certain relocation benefits to home owners, businesses, and farm operators who chose to sell land to the Service. The law provides for benefits to eligible owners and tenants in the following areas:

- Reimbursement of reasonable moving and related expenses;

- Replacement housing payments under certain conditions;

- Relocation assistance services to help locate replacement housing, farm, or business properties;

- Reimbursement of certain necessary and reasonable expenses incurred in selling real property to the government.

4.6.8 Landowner Rights Adjacent to Districts Lands

Service or other agency control of access, land use practices, water management practices, hunting, fishing, and general use next to any tracts acquired under Alternative 2 (No Action) or Alternative 3 (Preferred Alternative) is limited only to those lands in which the Service or other entities have acquired that ownership interest. Any landowners adjacent to lands acquired retain all the rights, privileges, and responsibilities of private land ownership, including the right of access, hunting, vehicle use, control of trespass, right to sell to any party, and obligation to pay taxes.

Any land acquired for the Minnesota Wetland Management Districts would be purchased from willing sellers.

4.6.9 Crop Depredation

Neighboring farmers are suffering crop losses due to grazing geese. Geese graze on soybeans and to a lesser extent on corn for several weeks in the spring. Damage by grazing geese and goslings usually occurs when adjacent farmland is within 10 miles of Service wetlands. Crop damage varies by location, with some District neighbors suffering greater losses than others.

Under all of the alternatives, Districts would continue to assist landowners suffering crop depredation when requested. Assistance in the past has been given to those landowners losing soybeans to Canada geese with goslings. For this the Districts provide technical advice on scare tape, goose-proof fences, scarecrows, and propane guns and shell crackers.

4.6.10 Cultural Resources

The consequences of each alternative in terms of cultural resources are the same. Undertakings accomplished on the District have the potential to impact cultural resources. Although the presence of cultural resources including historic properties cannot stop a federal undertaking, the undertakings are subject to Section 106 of the National Historic Preservation Act and sometimes other laws.

The District Manager will, during early planning, provide the Regional Historic Preservation Officer a description and location of all projects, activities, routine maintenance and operations that affect ground and structures, requests for permitted uses, and alternatives being considered. The RHPO will analyze these undertakings for potential to affect historic properties and enter into consultation with the public and local government officials to identify concerns about impacts by the undertaking. This notification will be at least equal to, preferably with, public notification accomplished for NEPA and compatibility.

4.7 Agricultural Production

The WPAs form a tiny fraction of the total acreage available for agricultural production within the Districts ranging from .01 to 2.2 percent of available land in the six Districts. Any change in land use brought about by acquisition or management would have minimal effect in overall agricultural production. The alternatives outlined in this section discuss the direction of these small changes.

Alternative 1 would have negligible effects on existing agricultural production. No new land would be acquired for the Districts, leaving it available for farming. On the other hand, much of the land the Service would be interested in acquiring is considered marginal farmland, and landowners would have one less potential buyer for land they want to sell.

Alternative 2 (No Action) could result in somewhat reduced agricultural production when existing cropland is converted to wetland or permanent upland cover. Approximately 3,000 acres of cropland is acquired in the six Districts annually by the Service and converted to wildlands (willing seller only). However, these lands are spread over a 43-county area, resulting in minimal impacts.

Alternative 3 (Preferred Alternative) could result in reduced agricultural production when existing croplands are converted to wetland or permanent upland cover. Approximately 45,000 acres of cropland in the Districts could be acquired by the Service and converted to wildlands (willing seller only) over the next 15 years. Certain programs, such as the Conservation Reserve Program (CRP) and other State and Federal private lands programs, offer landowners short-term contracts while keeping land in private ownership. Any conversion of agricultural land to other uses would occur gradually as acquisition and habitat restoration dollars become available over time and as landowners emerge as willing participants and/or sellers.

Table 10: Summary of Environmental Impacts

Issues and Needs	Alternative 1	Alternative 2	Alternative 3 (Preferred Alternative)
Impacts Associated with Wildlife and Habitat			
Waterfowl Productivity	Waterfowl productivity on District lands would remain the same.	Waterfowl productivity on District lands would slightly decrease over time due to acquisition of isolated, smaller parcels of land.	Waterfowl productivity would increase on District lands due to increased quantity and quality of habitat.
Other Migratory Birds	Species requiring larger block sizes would gradually decline. Other species would benefit from continued grassland restoration and wetland and watershed improvement.	Same as Alternative 1.	Would result in increased migratory bird use and productivity of District lands as additional land is acquired focusing on prime habitat and bigger block sizes. Implementation of habitat management programs would also benefit migratory birds.
Threatened and Endangered Species	Populations of listed species on District land would likely remain the same or increase slightly as grasslands are restored and wetlands and the watershed are improved.	Populations of listed species on District land would likely remain the same or decrease slightly as critical habitats degrade due to the dilution of management activities.	Populations of listed species on District land would likely increase over time as new lands are added to the Districts in a manner aimed at concentrating resources in high priority areas within the Districts.
Native Species	Populations of native species would remain the same or decline somewhat depending on their adaptability to edge habitat.	Native species would benefit from acquisition and gradual restoration of land depending on their adaptability to edge habitat.	Focus on acquiring larger block sizes and prime habitat would benefit native species. Native species would benefit from efforts to prohibit the introduction of non-natives.
Biological Inventories and Monitoring	Biological inventories and monitoring would continue at the existing level.	Same as Alternative 1.	Inventories and monitoring would be significantly expanded and techniques would be scientifically defensible. Management would be more soundly based on sound science.
Federal Trust Species vs. Resident Wildlife	Efforts to balance needs of resident wildlife and trust species would remain the same as Districts continue to work with state wildlife agencies and local organizations.	Same as Alternative 1.	Positive impact as Districts continue work with state wildlife agencies and expand these efforts to include incentives to local landowners to implement techniques for creating, maintaining and enhancing habitat.
Invasive Species	Impact would be neutral – existing efforts to control invasive species would continue.	Acquisition of additional land while maintaining current management practices and staffing would negatively impact invasive species control. There would be fewer staff to cover more acres.	Same as Alternative 1.

Table 10: Summary of Environmental Impacts

Issues and Needs	Alternative 1	Alternative 2	Alternative 3 (Preferred Alternative)
Habitat Restoration and Management	Positive impacts due to continued grassland restoration and wetland/watershed improvement on existing land. Because no new land would be acquired, funding would be available for habitat restoration.	Slightly negative impact due to acquisition based on opportunity rather than habitat quality and having fewer staff to manage more land.	Positive impact due to acquisition focused on prime habitat and larger WPA block size, and increases in staffing that allow active management of newly acquired lands.
Contaminants	Water quality would improve as grassland restoration and wetland/watershed restoration continues on existing lands.	Water quality would remain the same or improve as grassland restoration and wetland and watershed improvements were implemented. Benefits would be limited by staff and funding availability for work on newly acquired lands.	Positive impacts due to combination of more land being acquired and restored, more staff available for restoration and technical assistance, and working with cooperating landowners in the Districts on applying conservation and environmental farming practices on their lands.

Impacts Associated with Public Use

Wildlife Dependent Recreation and Education	Opportunities would remain the same and possibly improve as funding became available for augmenting programs.	Opportunities would decrease due to limits on staffing and funding. More land would be available for access and programs, however these would only be added as funding permitted.	Opportunities would be expanded on existing and newly acquired WPAs.

Impacts Associated with Operations

Land Acquisition	No additional land acquisition would occur on the Districts.	Somewhat positive impact. Districts would continue acquiring lands up to the goal acres agreed to by each county in the District (164,068 in total remaining for all districts). Acquisition would be sporadic and unfocused.	Positive impact. Districts would continue acquiring land up to the goal acres agreed upon by each county (164,068 remaining for all six districts), and acquisition would focus on prime habitat follow SWAP guidelines.
Partners for Fish and Wildlife Program	Program would increase in size as efforts previously spent on land acquisition would be shifted to this program. Area of influence (scope) would remain the same.	Program would remain the same in size and scope.	Program would remain the same in size but would be focused within high priority areas within the Districts.
Equipment	Equipment funding would remain the same. However, the spending power would increase over time as no additional lands would be added to the Districts in the future. This assumes a continuation of historic funding levels.	Equipment funding would remain the same.	Equipment funding would remain the same. Management efficiencies would be attained as larger blocks of habitat would reduce the per acre cost of management.

Table 10: Summary of Environmental Impacts

Issues and Needs	Alternative 1	Alternative 2	Alternative 3 (Preferred Alternative)
Management Consistency Among Districts	Somewhat positive impact. Individual WPA plans would be developed as staff and funding permit; no coordination among the WMDs in Minnesota and border states would be achieved.	Same as Alternative 1.	Positive impact. Development plans for WPAs would be completed within 3 years; management among the WMDs in Minnesota would be more consistent with districts in border states.
General Impacts Analysis: Habitat Restoration			
Fire Management	Positive impacts. Fire management would continue to be used as a habitat restoration tool, and all Service policies would be followed to assure the safety of neighboring property.	Same as Alternative 1.	Same as Alternative 1.
Climate Change	Positive impact in carbon sequestration.	Same as Alternative 1.	Same as Alternative 1.
Environmental Justice	No impact to minority or low income populations would occur.	Same as Alternative 1.	Same as Alternative 1.
Crop Depredation	Positive impact. Districts would continue to work with local landowners to reduce depradation..	Same as Alternative 1.	Same as Alternative 1.
Archeological and Cultural Values	Positive impact. Historic preservation would continue on existing District lands.	Positive impact. Historic preservation would continue on existing and newly acquired District lands.	Same as Alternative 2.

Chapter 5: List of Preparers

Don Hultman	*Refuge Supervisor, Great Lakes/Big Rivers Regional Office, Fort Snelling, Minnesota (former).* Contributed to writing and editing the EA.
Kevin **Brennan**	*Wetland Manager, Fergus Falls Wetland Management District, Fergus Falls, Minnesota.* Responsible for public involvement, CCP/EA preparation and review, and implementation of the CCP.
Barry Christenson	*Wetland Manager, Litchfield Wetland Management District, Litchfield Minnesota.* Responsible for public involvement, CCP/EA preparation and review.
John Dobrovolny	*Regional Historic Preservation Officer, Great Lakes/Big Rivers Regional Office, Fort Snelling, Minnesota.* Responsible for cultural resources information and NEPA compliance.
Mike Marxen	*CCP Coordinator, Region 1, U.S. Fish & Wildlife Service.* Responsible for public involvement and CCP preparation and review.
Jan Eldridge, Ph.D.	*Fish and Wildlife Biologist, Great Lakes/Big Rivers Regional Office, Fort Snelling, Minnesota.* Responsible for CCP preparation and review, environmental assessment preparation, and NEPA compliance.
Thomas Larson	Chief, Ascertainment and Planning, *Great Lakes/Big Rivers Regional Office, Fort Snelling, Minnesota.* Contributed to writing and editing the EA.
Mary Mitchell	*Wildlife Biologist/Regional GIS Coordinator, Great Lakes/Big Rivers Regional Office, Fort Snelling, Minnesota.* Responsible for GIS development.
John Schomaker, Ph.D.	*Refuge Planning Specialist/CCP Coordinator, Great Lakes/Big Rivers Regional Office, Fort Snelling, Minnesota.* Responsible for CCP preparation.
Gary Muehlenhardt	*Wildlife Biologist, Great Lakes/Big Rivers Regional Office, Ft. Snelling, Minnesota.* Contributed to writing the EA.
Tom Magnuson	*Fish and Wildlife Biologist, Great Lakes/Big Rivers Regional Office, Fort Snelling, Minnesota.* Contributed to writing the EA.
Jane Hodgins	*Technical Writer/Editor, Ascertainment and Planning, Great Lakes/Big Rivers Regional Office, Fort Snelling, Minnesota.* Responsible for CCP preparation.

Bibliography

Ball, I.J. Eng, R. L., Ball, S. K. 1995. Population density and productivity of ducks of large grassland tracts in northcentral Montana. Wildlife Society Bulletin 23:767-773.

Burger, L. D., L. W. Burger, Jr., and J. Faaborg. 1994. Conservation of nongame birds and waterfowl: conflict or complement? Trans. N. Amer. Wildl. Nat. Resour. Conf. 59:337-347.

Duebbert, H. F., and J.R. Lokemoen. 1976. Duck nesting in fields of undisturbed grass-legume cover. J. Wildl. Manage. 40:39-49.

Fitzgerald, J. A., D. N. Pashley, S. J. Lewis, and B. Pardo. 1998. Partner's in Flight Bird Conservation Plan for the Northern Tallgrass Prairie (Physiographic Area 40). Version 1.0 59pp.

Herkert. J. R. 1994. The effects of habitat fragmentation on Midwestern grassland bird communities. Ecological Applications 4: 461-471.

Herkert, J.R. 1994. Breeding bird communities of Midwestern prairie fragments: the effects of prescribed burning and habitat-area. Natural Areas Journal 14: 128-135.

Hunter, M.L. 1995. Fundamentals of conservation biology. Rand McNally, Inc. Taunton, MA 482 pp.

Johnson, D. H. and M. D. Schwarz. 1993b. The Conservation Reserve Program: habitat for grassland birds. Great Plains Research 3: 273-295.

Johnson, R.G. and S. A. Temple. 1990. Nest predation and brood parasitism of tallgrass prairie birds. J. Wildl. Mgmt. 54:106-111.

Klett, A.T., T.L. Shaffer, and D.L. Johnson. 1988. Duck nest success in the prairie pothole region. J.Wildl. Manage. 52: 431-440.

Knopf, F. L. 1994. Avian assemblages on altered grasslands. Studies in Avian Biology 15: 247-257.

Krapu G.L. and K.J. Reineke. 1992. Foraging ecology and nutrition. *In* Ecology and Management of Breeding Waterfowl, *Eds.* D. J. Batt, A.D. Afton, M.G. Anderson, C.D. Ankney, D. H. Johnson, J.A. Kadlec, and G. L. Krapu. PP 1-29.

Sample, D. W. and M. J. Mossman. 1997. Managing habitat for grassland birds: a guide for Wisconsin. Wisconsin Department of Natural Resources. 154pp.
Samson, F. B. and F. L. Knopf. 1996. Prairie conservation: preserving North America's most endangered ecosystem. Island Press, Washington D.C.

Samson, F. B. and F. L. Knopf. 1994. Prairie conservation in North America. BioScience 44: 418-421.

Soule, M. E. and J. Terborgh. 1999. Conserving nature at regional and continental scales–a scientific program for North America. BioScience 49: 809-817.

Stewart, R.E., and H.A. Kantrud. 1971. Classification of natural ponds and lakes in the glaciated prairie region. U.S. Fish and Wildlife Service Resource Publication 92. 57pp.

Tilman, D. and J. A. Downing. 1994. Biodiversity and stability in grasslands. Nature 367:363-65.

Wiens, J. A. 1995. Habitat fragmentation: Island versus landscape perspectives on bird conservation. Ibis 137: 97-104.

Table 7: Wetland Management District Issues

	Alt. 1	Alt. 2	Alt. 3	Alt. 4
Wildlife & Habitat				
1. Low waterfowl productivity	1	5	9	7
2. Strategic acquisition	1	6	8	9
3. Managing uplands	1	5	9	6
4. Managing and restoring wetlands	1	6	9	7
5. Improve biological inventories and monitoring.	5	5	10	6
6. Stem loss of prairie migrating birds.	1	6	7	5
7. Manage to preserve & enhance endangered species.	1	6	7	5
8. Reintroduce rare native species.	1	5	6	5
9. Mitigate negative external influences on WPAs.	1	6	8	5
10. Needs of federal trust species vs. resident species.	1	5	7	5
11. Reduce crop loss from Canada geese.	1	7	8	5
12. Control of invasive species.	1	7	8	5
People				
1. Conflicting views on cost vs. benefit of public land.	5	5	7	5
2. Provide adequate facilities for the public in a compatible way.	1	6	8	4
Operations				
1. Improve operations through increased staff and fund-raising.	1	5	10	7
2. Ensure all Districts apply policy and practice in a consistent manner.	1	6	10	6

Alternative 1: No management; stop all management actions.
Alternative 2: Maintain current level and program.
Alternative 3: Implement CCP (preferred)
Alternative 4: Focus management and land acquisition program.

Table 8: Objectives of the Wetland Management Districts

Objectives	Alt. 1	Alt. 2	Alt. 3	Alt.4
Objective 1: Strive to preserve and maintain the diversity and increase the abundance of waterfowl species of the Northern Tallgrass Prairie Ecosystem.	1	5	9	8
Objective 2: Within current acquisition acreage goals, identify the highest priority acres for acquisition taking into account block size and waterfowl productivity data. These priority areas should drive acquisition efforts whenever possible.	1	5	8	9
Objective 3: Restore native prairie plant communities using local ecotypes of seed and maintain the vigor of these stands through natural processes such as fire.	1	7	9	6
Objective 4: Restore functioning wetland complexes within Waterfowl Production Areas (WPAs). There should be no drained wetlands on WPAs.	1	6	9	6
Objective 5: Maintain the cyclic productivity of wetlands on WPAs by increasing the amount and quality of water level management.	1	5	9	4
Objective 6: Monitor the impact of management on target species as directed by the Monitoring Plan. Monitoring is an integral part of management decisions within the Districts.	2	4	9	6
Objective 7: Collect baseline biological data using proven scientific methods so that adequate information is available to evaluate management actions.	5	4	8	6
Objective 8: Preserve, restore, and enhance habitats to support diverse migratory bird populations.	1	6	9	8
Objective 9: Preserve, enhance, and restore rare native Northern Tallgrass Prairie flora and fauna that may become extinct.	2	6	8	8
Objective 10: Preserve, restore, and enhance rare and endangered native communities.	1	6	8	8
Objective 11: Where feasible in both ecological and social/economic terms, reintroduce native species on WPAs in cooperation with the Minnesota DNR.	1	5	8	6
Objective 12: Assess the external threats to each WPA during the preparation of individual WPA Development Plans. Develop action plans to address these threats.	1	6	8	7
Objective 13: Preserve, restore, and enhance resident wildlife populations where compatible with waterfowl production and preservation of other trust resources.	1	6	6	7
Objective 14: Work with the Minnesota DNR and the Department of Agriculture to seek sustainable solutions to the impact of Canada geese on adjacent private croplands.	1	5	7	5
Objective 15: Continue efforts for direct control of invasive species to minimize damage to aquatic and terrestrial communities.	1	5	8	6
Objective 16: Ultimately, our efforts should lead to a long-term solution to the problem of invasive species with increased emphasis on biological control.	1	5	8	6
Objective 17: Continue efforts to restore wetlands and better define the role of each District in assisting private landowners with upland and riparian restorations.	5	5	7	6

Table 8: Objectives of the Wetland Management Districts (continued)

Objectives	Alt. 1	Alt. 2	Alt. 3	Alt.4
Objective 18: Service land acquisition should have no negative impact on net revenues to local government.	10	3	6	4
Objective 19: Understand and communicate the economic effects of Federal land ownership on local communities.	1	5	8	5
Objective 20: Provide opportunities for compatible public uses that promote understanding and appreciation of the Prairie Pothole Region.	2	6	8	5
Objective 21: Promote greater understanding and awareness of the Wetland Management District programs, goals and objectives.	1	6	9	7
Objective 22: Provide opportunity for environmental education that advances public and private stewardship responsibility for the Prairie Pothole Region and brings about understanding of the multiple values of prairie wetlands and grasslands.	1	6	8	5
Objective 23: Provide necessary levels of maintenance, technician, and administrative support staff to achieve other Wetland Management District goals.	2	5	10	4
Objective 24: Provide all Districts with adequate and safe office, maintenance, and equipment storage facilities.	2	5	10	5
Objective 25: Acquire adequate equipment and vehicles to achieve other District goals. Maintain District equipment and vehicles at or above Service standards.	2	5	10	5
Objective 26: Ensure that annual capital development funds are large enough to meet necessary development of new WPA land.	2	5	9	5
Objective 27: Annually, have adequate funds available to permit completion of maintenance needs for each Wetland District's current land base of WPAs.	2	5	9	5
Objective 28: Complete Geographic Information System (GIS) based WPA Development Plans for each unit in each District.	2	6	8	5
Objective 29: Provide Districts with GIS to assist with acquisition, restoration, management, and protection of public and private lands.	2	6	8	5
Objective 30: Develop and apply consistent policies for habitat, public use, and and resource protection. Ensure frequent coordination among Districts, both in Minnesota and in neighboring states with WPAs (North Dakota, South Dakota, Iowa and Wisconsin).	2	4	8	5

Appendix N: Drainage Policy

Wetland Management District
Ditch and Tile Maintenance Policy

This policy applies to existing constructed ditches or tiles that come onto Waterfowl Production Areas (WPAs) where no reservation of a drainage easement exists in the WPA title/deed. If there is a drainage reservation in the deed, we will follow the terms of that reservation.

- No new wetland or upland drainage facility will be allowed within a WPA.

- Existing drainage cannot be improved beyond the original construction.

  - Tile may not be replaced with a larger tile.

  - Ditches may not be cleaned out beyond original depth, width or length

  - Ditches may not be replaced with tile lines except where either the tile is installed at the same or higher elevation than the original ditch bottom or in other rare exceptions to solve severe erosion.

- All materials cleaned out of the ditch will be removed from the WPA.

- All construction sites on WPAs will be seeded down to a grass mix specified by the Service.

- Cleanout activities will not be allowed during the waterfowl breeding season (April 1 through August 1).

- If silt deposition is a concern, the Service will request that a grassed waterway or silt basin be installed upstream of our property to help reduce future siltation.

- Cleanout of natural (never ditched) drainageways will not be allowed.

- Ditch and tile maintenance work on WPAs will only be done after the Wetland District Manager has approved the project and issued a special use permit. (Note: Compatibility Determinations are not necessary since the Service does not control maintenance of the system; the Service only controls the timing and scope of maintenance)

- Landowners may still be subject to Swampbuster, WCA and COE rules on maintenance and abandonment of ditches.

- Mowing or spraying of approved herbicide in a ditch after August 1 may be permitted in lieu of excavation.

- If the ditch has not been cleaned or a tile not functioned for 25-plus years and/or the watershed above the ditch has been substantially altered since the Service purchased the property (i.e significant increase in flows or degradation of water quality) a formal ROW request maybe required as determined by the Wetland Manager.

Appendix O: Disposition of Public Comments on the Draft CCP

Minnesota Districts: Summary of Public Comments Received

- Public funds should be used to purchase or improve only fee title lands, not easements.

- No buildings should be built on public lands - even for administration.

- USDA program lands should be managed for wildlife and open to the public.

- FWS acquisition in the Heron Lake Watershed should be approved by the Heron Lake Area Restoration.

- Private lands within the historic Heron Lake should be condemned and restored and managed for wildlife.

- FWS Realty process too slow - landowners have to wait too long.

- Request that WPAs be used for non-motorized bike and hike trails

- Pheasant wintering areas on WPAs

- Establishment of food plots on WPAs

- Establishment of shelter belts on WPAs

- Increased management of resident Canada Geese

- Support for continuing the private lands program

- Numerous letters of general support for acquisition and management - keep up the good work

Responses to above comments:

1. *Public funds should be used to purchase or improve only fee-title lands, not easements that do not allow public access.*

   The Small Wetlands Acquisition Program has included a perpetual easement program component since its inception in 1959. The acquisition model designed at that time was to purchase a core area in fee title that would provide a waterfowl brood marsh with surrounding permanent nesting cover. Perpetual Wetland Easements would protect satellite wetlands within one mile radius of this core area. These satellite easement wetlands could then be used by waterfowl for breeding and feeding purposes, while the same birds could utilize the fee title area (WPA) for nesting and brood rearing.

   Since 1959, land use has changed. In response to these land use changes, the Service has expanded its suite of land protection programs. Habitat easements, which protect both upland and wetland habitats, has been successfully used to protect and restore important wildlife habitat since the mid-1990s.

   Advantages to protecting wildlife habitat through perpetual easements include the initial reduced acquisition costs, reduced long-term management expenses and less public resistance to excessive fee title acquisition.

   Fee title acquisition is the most frequently used land protection method within the five Minnesota Wetland Management Districts (180,267 fee-title acres versus 70,749 perpetual easement acres), representing 71.8% of lands acquired. Based on waterfowl biology habitat needs and land-owner interests, the Service does not agree that we should eliminate the perpetual easement program. The CCP proposes to continue both the traditional wetland and the newer habitat (grasslands and wetlands) easements to protect high priority wildlife habitats in cooperation with willing landowners.

2. *No buildings such as Headquarters, Offices, or Maintenance facilities should be built on FWS managed lands.*

Personnel, equipment and materials are essential for the acquisition, restoration, protection and management of lands for the National Wildlife Refuge System. These resources require facilities, and it has been the Service's practice to place these facilities on NWRS lands in locations where there is minimal impact to wildlife or their habitats.

Visitor services facilities are also necessary to enhance the public's knowledge and understanding about issues that challenge the health of our wildlife resources. These facilities can also encourage appropriate use of NWRS lands and provide information that contributes to a quality experience by the visiting public.

Facilities within the Minnesota Wetland Districts occupy only a minute portion of fee-title acreage. For example, the Windom headquarters complex is set on three acres - 0.02% of the District's fee title acreage. Other districts are similar. As new facilities are planned in the future, the Service will continue to consider all impacts and effects of such plans on wildlife habitat and make every attempt to minimize long-term adverse impacts.

3. *Any private lands that come into federal ownership through delinquent loan payments with the USDA should become public lands, managed for wildlife and open for public use such as hunting.*

The Service agrees that certain lands with high value to wildlife which come into USDA ownership should appropriately be added to the National Wildlife Refuge System. In the 1990's, the Service worked closely with USDA to transfer Farmers Home Administration Inventory Properties in the NWRS. Many of these tracts are now actively managed for wildlife and open for public use. Other tracts are protected from habitat destruction through perpetual conservation easements enforced by the Service.

The Service will continue to look for opportunities to work in partnership with the USDA to permanently protect high value wildlife habitat.

4. *Several comments were received that addressed Service land acquisition procedures in terms of the approval process and timeliness of appraisals and offers to willing sellers.*

The U.S. Fish and Wildlife Service acquires lands in Minnesota for the Small Wetlands Acquisition Program under an agreement with the State of Minnesota. This agreement provides an opportunity for comments by locally elected officials. Prior to final acquisition approval by the State of Minnesota (through the Land Exchange Board headed by the Governor), each tract is discussed and reviewed in detail with the Commissioners of the County were the tract is located. Township boards are also informed of these proposed acquisitions and invited to attend and participate in the meeting with the County Commissioners. Interested members of the public may attend these meetings and make comments.

The Service believes the current approval process provides ample opportunity for review and comment by locally elected officials and the public and does not support the addition of another layer of approval to this process.

The U.S. Fish and Wildlife Service Small Wetlands Acquisition Program is a willing seller program. Land condemnation has not been used by the program in the past and there are no plans to use condemnation in the future. Although its use would allow critical acquisitions to go forward in some cases where landowners are not interested in selling, the long-term negatives associated with condemnation often outweigh the short-term gain. The Service is proud of its willing seller - willing buyer methodology and the CCP maintains that means of land acquisition.

The Service agrees there is a need to reduce the length of time now typically required to make an acquisition offer to a landowner. The Service can be more responsive to acquisition opportunities and more effective in protecting wildlife habitat by reducing the time required to complete the appraisal process and make an offer. The CCP addresses this issue. On page 52, Goal 3/ Objective 3.3 outlines a timetable which would reduce the time allowed to make an offer to a landowner to seven months.

Additionally, the Service Realty Branch just recently made organizational changes designed to streamline the process time line.

5.   *Several comments were received supporting increased management efforts for resident wildlife, notably, white-tailed deer and pheasants.*

As indicated in the CCP, the primary purpose of the U.S. Fish and Wildlife Service's Waterfowl Production Areas is to provide optimum habitat for breeding and nesting waterfowl. Although every management practice we implement for waterfowl may not be optimum for resident wildlife, we believe the majority of our actions are mutually beneficial. Several Districts have ongoing food plot or feeder crib programs, often in cooperation with Minnesota DNR or a local Pheasants Forever Chapter. It is the Service's intention to allow limited continued use of both food plots and feeder cribs. A draft compatibility determination to maintain food plots on critical sites has been prepared for public review and comment. That document helps managers determine where food plots or feeder cribs can be used and where they must be prohibited to ensure that our management is consistent with Service goals and national policy.

6. *One reviewer expressed a desire that Waterfowl Production Areas be used more to meet the needs of non-motorized bike and hike trail enthusiasts.*

Waterfowl Production Areas are part of the National Wildlife Refuge System (NWRS). The 1997 Refuge Improvement Act provides specific guidance to the Service concerning management of the NWRS and establishes wildlife conservation as the singular mission of this system. All uses of Refuge System lands must be compatible with the mission of the system and purpose of the specific unit involved. The Refuge Improvement Act established six priority uses of the NWRS. These priority uses all depend on the presence of or expectation of the presence of wildlife, and thus are called wildlife dependent uses. These uses include: hunting, fishing, wildlife observation, photography, environmental education, and interpretation.

Non-motorized bike and hike trails are not specifically identified as a priority public use. Each request for a bike/hike trail would need to be evaluated as a case-by-case basis. Many factors would need to be evaluated to determine the trail's potential impact on the WPA, and ultimately if the activity could be considered compatible with the purpose for which the land was acquired.

7. *Several reviewers expressed a desire that the Minnesota Wetland Districts make a commitment to increase efforts to manage resident Canada geese, specifically to minimize crop damage.*

Within the federal government, animal depredation responsibility rests primarily with the U.S. Department of Agriculture's Animal Plant Health and Inspection Service. Regardless of that mandate, the Minnesota Wetland Districts have been assisting Minnesota DNR with local goose depredation issues. In May of 2000 DNR and the Service agreed that each district would increase its cooperative efforts to assist local DNR offices with goose complaints which originate from WPAs. Each district has designated a staff person to respond to and work with their local DNR counterparts. Additionally, several districts have submitted funding requests to develop and manage a depredation program which could include an initiative to purchase small food plots in strategic locations on private land. Fencing to prevent geese from entering neighboring fields can also be effective in certain cases, but similarly is dependent on new specific funding.

8. *Numerous comments were received in support of the Service's Partners for Fish and Wildlife Program.*

The Partners for Fish and Wildlife Program has been extremely successful since its conception in 1986. Minnesota Wetland Management District staffs have been at the national forefront of wetland restoration and with the enthusiastic support of landowners throughout western Minnesota have restored thousands of wetlands previously drained for agricultural purposes. In recent years, we have also been working with landowners and private conservation groups to restore native grasslands and interest in this program is growing each year. The CCP declares our intention to continue working with interested private landowners and with a multitude of partners to accomplish conservation work on private land as well as public land as long as that work is supported by Congress.

9.   *Numerous letters were received which expressed strong support for continuing the Small Wetlands Acquisition Program.*

The U.S. Fish and Wildlife Service appreciates the support of individuals, local sportsmen groups, and larger non-profit conservation organizations and their affiliated local chapters for our ongoing efforts to improve Service lands and add new lands for waterfowl and other wildlife. This CCP will provide a roadmap for future management which should increase and improve our efforts to work with partners to meet our Congressional mandate for management of migratory birds, especially waterfowl, in Minnesota.